ON COMMON GROUND

BRIDGING THE MORMON EVANGELICAL DIVIDE

VINCENT DIGIROLAMO

ON COMMON GROUND

BRIDGING THE MORMON-EVANGELICAL DIVIDE

© Copyright 2008 Celestine Publishing

Library of Congress Control Number: 2008900084

ISBN–13: 978-0-9786815-3-1
ISBN–10: 0-9786815-3-3

First Printing, January 2008

Printed in the United States of America

Celestine Publishing, LLC
9660 Falls of Neuse Road
Suite 138, #146
Raleigh, North Carolina 27615

www.CelestinePublishing.com

Cover design by David DiGirolamo
Web Site by Jonathan (Chad) DiGirolamo

Book Cover Design

The book cover design depicts both ancient records commonly written on papyrus and stored as scrolls and other accounts written on more durable metal plates of brass, copper and sometimes gold.

The debate over the interpretation of the words accepted as authentic and comprising the biblical accounts found in the Old and New Testaments started as early as the fourth century and continues today. They have been translated and retranslated countless times since then in numerous languages even while those languages themselves have continued to evolve.

During the early nineteenth century, a young man by the name of Joseph Smith, Jr. published a book, the *Book of Mormon,* which he claimed was translated from gold plates by the gift and power of God. This new record reportedly contains the accounts of several ancient civilizations that occupied the Americas from approximately 2000 BC until 421 AD. It is a history of their dealings with God, and perhaps most notably, recounts Christ's visit to the Americas shortly after His resurrection.

From these events which occurred early in American history, a new Christian religion and church was established; The Church of Jesus Christ of Latter-day Saints. Since its establishment, these additional records, cherished by Latter-day Saints as companion scriptures to the biblical accounts, have influenced the lives of millions of people domestically and internationally.

The so called divide that exists between men of different religious persuasions, or in this case between Latter-day Saints and Evangelicals, often occurs when people compare the beliefs, faith, and knowledge of their own religious experience with those of their fellowmen.

On Common Ground is my humble attempt to bridge this divide by providing access to gospel principles in an organized way; principles that are held by Latter-day Saints and shared by the rest of the Christian world as true.

The real value of this book is found by answering a personal challenge to an experiment with the word of God to know if the principles presented here are indeed true, and by so doing, discover the common ground that exists between men of faith in Christ.

Acknowledgements

I would like to express my love and gratitude to my parents who got me off on a great start in the religion of their choice and that of my forefathers, but more especially for their ever present loving Christian example to me, not only through my formative years, but always.

To my friends and editors, Tom and Louise Franza, for giving freely of their time, support, friendship, example and love since childhood and throughout our many endeavors these days to *change the known built world.* Thank you both for your honest and objective advice on this publication.

And to the many teachers, friends, and relatives, from all faiths, who have discussed important principles of faith and religious doctrine with me; thank you. All of your good examples and wise counsel have lead me to the knowledge I have about the principles practiced by members of The Church of Jesus Christ of Latter-day Saints and the many other Christian denominations with which I have shared fellowship, thereby allowing me to make possible an attempt at this monumental task.

I especially appreciate the artistic work of our sons, David and Chad. David took my prototype cover design and created the final rendering, and Chad turned the book cover into a 3D model for the website. Both of their eager and talented activities inspired me to press on with its publication at an even greater pace. And many thanks to our son Mike McKell for his editorial advice and getting the word out - un misionero una vez, un misionero de corazón para siempre.

A special thanks to my wife Dana and daughters Aliana, Nikki and Cami for your patience and love, and for enduring yet another book. And to our son Elder Morgan Chase McKell who is currently serving in the Oregon Portland Mission - ama los a que enseñes y sirvas.

This book is dedicated to those who first seek to understand. May we all find our common ground with each other, and with it do much good in that part of the world God has placed us.

God Bless, Vinny DiGirolamo

Contents

If any of you lack wisdom,
let him ask of God,
that giveth to all men liberally,
and upbraideth not;
and it shall be given him.

James 1:5

Author's Note

I once ran the town's local youth football league with three hundred and fifty children and six hundred or so complaining parents. No matter how noble our intent to organize and provide a healthy sports program for the community, people complained continuously as though our Board of Directors had some ulterior motive governing every decision. It seemed as though someone was opposing us every step of the way.

As I discussed my dilemma with the town's Mayor one day at a fund raising event, I asked him how he was able to deal with such a disagreeable public for so many years and still maintain his good nature and desire to serve.

Smiling at my query, the Mayor patiently explained to me his formula for successful community relations. He said, *"Educate them. Educate them on the issues and the logic behind your decisions, and then watch what happens. They don't have to agree with you, and believe me they won't, but they will respect you for listening to them and letting them air their opinions. Oh,"* he added, *"and never take it personally; the noise will subside."*

I listened to his sage counsel. He said I didn't have to convince them that my decisions were right; I just had to educate them on what was considered in the process and why we selected a particular course of action. From that point forward I tried to educate every disgruntled parent I met and also took the added opportunity to invite them to volunteer and help our fledgling administration. Some sheepishly declined, never to be seen again, while others willingly volunteered. Over time the wave of negative press subsided significantly and a healthy sports program moved forward.

Likewise, *On Common Ground: Bridging The Mormon-Evangelical Divide* is a different approach from what is normally presented in the press. Like the football league, I find that people tend to focus on the differences or the negatives rather than on the common or positive truths of the matter. A biased press (and there are those that do exist) is capable of creating or widening a divide that does not even exist, at least not to the extent some would have you believe. Regrettably, the truth often doesn't make it to the headlines unscathed.

Here, instead of addressing the differences between Latter-day Saint beliefs and the rest of the Christian world, I present for your consideration the beliefs we share in common by providing scriptural verses commonly held as true principles by both Latter-day Saints and our Christian brothers in a topical index.

The scriptural verses come from both the Bible and other volumes Latter-day Saints value equally as the word of God. Principles of truth are presented in a topical index so the reader may more easily locate, compare and contrast different topics with Latter-day Saint beliefs. For example, if you wanted to research just how Latter-day Saints practice *prayer* or the principles related to *prayer,* going to the topic of *prayer* and reading all of the guidance or principles listed will provide you with new insights on shared beliefs.

If you are able to objectively consider each principle on its own merit, I believe you will find a significant number of Latter-day Saint principles in this publication that you also hold as true principles, regardless of their origin, interpretation, or how they are practiced in your own religion. These principles then become part of our common ground.

If you disagree with a statement, then you need only cross it off your list and not consider it part of the principles you hold to be true, believe in, or agree with. That is the beauty of this exercise, agree or disagree as you may, the remaining principles are the ones in which there is a shared strong belief and is common ground. Essentially, you are provided with Latter-day Saint principles in addition to the principles found in the Old and New Testaments for consideration. I believe this is where we need to start.

There are many other principles - not included here - that some Christians would have a hard time understanding because of their terminology, the setting in which they were given, or their meanings, all of which would have to be understood in the context of Latter-day Saint views on the plan of salvation and the history of its church. Therefore, I have made a sincere effort in *On Common Ground* to only include those principles we might share; truths that are easily recognized among Christians as true.

It is my hope that this principle-centered presentation will help all Christians to in some way better understand Mormon beliefs, alleviate misconceptions, dispel misinformation, and allay fears or concerns they may have about their Latter-day Saint neighbors.

Of course, the natural follow-up question will continue to be, *what are the uncommon grounds between the Latter-day Saints and the rest of Christianity?* To me, there are only two topics that I would even suggest as uncommon; they are the need for a prophet in our day and the authenticity of the *Book of Mormon: Another Testament of Jesus Christ.*

These two topics alone generally receive the majority of the negative press, and all others rest on these two alone. However, I will leave the specifics of those topics to the countless authors who have spent their energies in these areas, and prefer instead, to look at the glass as half full by providing you with more than two thousand principles to consider as our common ground; catalogued under more than fifteen hundred key words.

This does not preclude the honest seeker of truth from weighing all of the evidence presented to them. It is simply not my intent to give audience to the uncommon ground in this book, but instead shed some meaningful light on the common; focusing on shared principles of truth and experience. Nevertheless, in all cases, I would highly encourage all those who first seek to understand to go directly to the source by asking a Latter-day Saint you know or by inviting the missionaries in your area to discuss their beliefs with you; first hand.

To Latter-day Saints who are also curious to know more about the common ground we share with our Christian associates and even the people of all faiths, Christian and non-Christian alike, I would similarly suggest that you participate in religious studies with them as the occasion permits, and share your beliefs, faith, knowledge and testimonies with those who wish to know more; there is nothing new here, but always, seek first to understand.

May God bless you with His grace as you seek to understand the common ground on which we all stand in our belief in Jesus Christ, His gospel, and the true and abiding principles presented here.

*All scripture is given by
inspiration of God,
and is profitable for doctrine,
for reproof, for correction,
for instruction in righteousness:
That the man of God may be
perfect, thoroughly furnished
unto all good works.*

2 Timothy 3:16-17

On Common Ground

All Mormons, Evangelicals, Catholics, Baptists, Lutherans, Methodists, Episcopalians, Presbyterians and many other traditional and non-traditional religions who believe in Christ are Christians. Why? Because their fundamental belief in Christ and their practice of moral principles, values, and gospel tenets give them hope in the promise of salvation through Christ, a personal witness of His grace, and experience in His ways.

The common ground is the beliefs, principles, and values they share, not in the way that they are interpreted or practiced, nor their origins, but in the manifestation of the fruits they bear and the manner of men they become through living those principles.

On Common Ground: Bridging the Mormon-Evangelical Divide has its roots in the *Principles with Promise* series which catalogs principles found in the scriptural text that different religions hold to be true or holy writ from God; principles that govern our world and our relationships with God, our fellowman, ourselves, our governments, the building of God's kingdom, and the priesthood. They are God-given principles that are unchanging, universal and eternal, or in other words, they are considered true principles by those who practice them.

The first book in the *Principles with Promise* series addresses Latter-day Saint scriptures with their associated principles and supporting references. The second publication in the series addresses topics and principles found only in the Old and New Testaments; principles which Christian denominations interpret and practice in many different ways. *Principles with Promise: Old Testament, New Testament* does not distinguish between the various practices of Christian denominations; the series only lists the principles in their purest form directly from the scriptures.

Why On Common Ground?

Considering the ever increasing interest in Latter-day Saint beliefs that exists between Evangelicals and Mormons, it seemed to me a good idea to provide an easy reference for those of all Christian faiths to contrast and compare the core principles that make up their own beliefs with those of Latter-day Saint theology. *On Common Ground* seeks to provide a clearer understanding between the vast majority of all believers in Christ.

If it is not clear from the onset of this title and opening paragraphs, Latter-day Saints also believe and practice principles found in the Old and New Testaments. During the development of the recently released *Principles with Promise* series, I found that there is however, much, much more ground that is common between Mormons and Evangelical Christians, Catholics, and Protestant religions than one might know about or even expect. This book is my attempt to point out our shared principles of truth; ones that we will all agree are just that ... true.

What's in a Title?

As the title of this book was considered, it went through several iterations to best capture its intent and I believe the deliberations in determining the right title is worth reviewing. By going through the process with me, I hope you will gain a clearer understanding of some basic issues when considering anyone's beliefs. Initially, the title read *On Common Ground: Gospel Principles Latter-day Saints and the Rest of the Christian World Agree On.*

As I thought about the word *agree* in the proposed title, I realized that quite often, or more often than not, religious discussions end with the only agreement as the one to *agree to disagree*; respectfully of course. The Mormon-Evangelical divide is not the only one; there are divides that continue between many if not most Christian religions. Even individual Christian denominations interpret the same biblical verse differently and, in turn, transform it into different denominational practices and beliefs. Continued debate gives me no assurance that there will be full agreement among Christian sects any time soon.

The subtitle was then changed to *Gospel Principles Latter-day Saints and the Rest of the Christian World Believe.* The word *believe* seemed more appropriate because it does not assume *agreement.* Beliefs are personal and cherished, and who am I to tell anyone what they believe in or should believe in. It does, however, say that you and I hold similar beliefs or certain principles to be true, regardless of interpretation or practice.

As I discussed the evolving book title with a Christian colleague during our morning Bible study – yes I said Bible study – he suggested there are different meanings for the word *gospel* among Christians and that the use of the word in my book's title paints an entirely different picture for some evangelicals than what I may have intended. He explained that some Christians accept a more narrowly defined definition of *gospel* or the *'good news'* to mean what Paul stated in 1 Corinthians 15:1-4

"Moreover, brethren, I declare unto you the gospel which I preached unto you, which also ye have received, and wherein ye stand; by which also ye are saved, if ye keep in memory what I preached unto you , unless ye have believed in vain. For I delivered unto you first of all that which I also received, how that Christ died for our sins according to the scriptures; and that he was buried, and that he rose again the third day according to the scriptures." 1 Cor. 15:1-4

My friend further commented that principles outside of the stated definition above, Christ's death and resurrection, would not be considered *gospel* according to Paul's definition. You see, Latter-day Saints use the word *gospel* to include the more comprehensive list of principles practiced with Christ's atonement and resurrection at the center. The *good news* includes all of the principles we consider His *gospel*. So once again, the search continued for a title that would describe all of the principles beyond a limited definition of *gospel*.

As we discussed the difference in terminology, thinking of another widely used Latter-day Saint term I suggested the word *eternal* instead of *gospel* but was unsure how it would be understood by other Christians. To Latter-day Saints, God is Eternal; it is one of His names. For example, eternal punishment refers to God's punishment, and therefore His principles are Eternal because they are His. But my friend countered, when he thinks of *eternal,* he thinks in terms of *forever,* not God. Are you getting a better picture by now how difficult it can be to find common ground, even in terminology differences?

This dialogue alone illustrates the difficulty when people from different religious persuasions discuss important topics of faith. It is paramount that meaningful dialog start with a clear understanding of the terminology used to describe beliefs. All faiths come with a vocabulary and culture of their own; all do, no exceptions. Once again, we tried to find another word or phrase that would paint the correct picture for all who believe in true principles or principles of truth.

Ahha, we thought, perhaps if we agreed on the assumption that Christians believe all principles found in scripture to be true, regardless of how they are interpreted or treated, and that that assumption would also include the gospel principle Paul spoke of in 1 Cor. 15 as part of the mix. Perhaps the subtitle could be more rightly stated as, *Principles of Truth Latter-day Saints and the Rest of the Christian World Believe.* We were getting closer and had both learned a few things in the process.

I do not say we interpret or practice the *principles of truth* similarly, only that we hold them to be true or believe them to be true principles. I also want to bring Christians to a better understanding about the principles Latter-day Saints include from the additional volumes they hold as scripture, including the *Book of Mormon: Another Testament of Jesus Christ,* the *Doctrine and Covenants,* and the *Pearl of Great Price.* To this end, I selected a number of principles I felt most Christians would view as true principles. But, would other Christians be willing to evaluate additional Latter-day Saint principles that have a familiar ring of truth with already established biblical principles?

I can not answer that question for you, but the fact that you have this book in your hands would suggest that you are open to this approach; an approach already shared by millions of people who have sought first to understand. But I hope as one who seeks to understand that you will start with the core beliefs of any religion and work from there. Please do not be roped into believing the political rhetoric of today or the uninformed, anti-literature designed to disprove, discourage and dismay the honest in heart, the new convert, or even the devout member of any particular faith, but instead, find that common ground.

Though I considered the title, *Finding Common Ground,* I did not select the word *finding* because I truly believe we are beyond this point in our understanding of the moral principles and values practiced across the Christian world. People already notice or credit Latter-day Saints for their industry, organization, community, integrity, focus on family and for the moral principles they practice, and even greater numbers of people are acknowledging Latter-day Saint belief in Christ and the message they teach. The common ground already exists.

When I finally felt prepared to pass this title by one of my editors, he proposed yet another variation of the title, *On Common Ground: Mormon, Catholic and Protestant Principles,* but he admitted he didn't know where Evangelical Christians fit in or how to represent them in the title. Since numerous evangelical groups and denominations have emerged without claiming any allegiance to Catholic or Protestant roots, he was not sure how to include them in the title. So my quest for a title that made sense continued.

One morning I decided to do an internet search to see where the greatest amount of education might be needed (see the Author's Note regarding the Mayor's advice to educate people). Having participated in several forums of religious debate myself, I entered the key search words *Mormon* and *Evangelical*. That search indicated an even wider and more active debate between Latter-day Saint beliefs and those of evangelicals.

I read a number of articles monitoring the Presidential campaign from 2005 until today, all of which mention an increased interest in the beliefs of members of The Church of Jesus Christ of Latter-day Saints with several books on the market trying to address a *divide*. Interest in the church also ranked highest on MSN's poll for most popular topic the week the day I looked.

It seemed that the preponderance of articles focused on the *divide* between Mormon and Evangelical beliefs, and it became clear to me that by bridging that divide, in addition to Mormons and Evangelicals benefiting, all Christians would similarly benefit. I also saw an opportunity to educate not only Evangelical Christians, Catholics and Protestants alike on our shared beliefs, but an equal opportunity to educate Latter-day Saints on shared Christian beliefs.

Hence the current title was born; *On Common Ground: Bridging the Mormon-Evangelical Divide.* The title is designed to not only get your attention, but goes to the heart of the matter with those whom I have found to be most vocal about the differences. This work is my attempt to cross the divide by educating Evangelical Christians and their Christian neighbors, the Mormons, on their shared beliefs in a principle-centered approach, one where principles held as truth and practiced by each in some manner are laid out in a topical guide or concordance for your consideration.

What is the Common Ground?

On Common Ground is not meant to be a discussion about the doctrinal differences or the practices of our shared principles; it is simply to lay the groundwork for increased understanding of the principles we share in common, not the ones where I feel there will be significant or outright disagreement. This work is designed to explore more deeply the principles that Latter-day Saints believe and that Evangelicals would agree as true principles or statements of truth if they were to be used by their minister or priest in a Sunday sermon.

The common ground between Christian faiths already exists and that is what this book is about. It is my hope and belief that in the course of this experiment, an honest evaluation of both the biblical and selected Latter-day Saint principles presented here will demonstrate an even larger category of common beliefs with your neighbors than you might have otherwise realized. This is my real intent.

On Common Ground is also intended to clarify some misconceptions, but more importantly to help establish the common ground between principles practiced by Latter-day Saints and those practiced by other Christian denominations with some measure of order. Latter-day Saint principles included in this publication are only a subset of what they believe in or what I sometimes refer to as *much, much more.* Nevertheless, each Mormon principle included in this publication was carefully selected to illustrate teachings the Christian world might consider as true.

Perhaps there are subjects, like *free agency* or *free will* that will immediately give rise to conflict between your beliefs and Latter-day Saint teaching, but those conflicts are not Mormon-unique. These same conflicts in belief also exist between different Christian denominations; some believe in *free will* while others do not. If the Bible had a principle related to one of the fifteen hundred key words in this book, I included it. If additional principles found in other Latter-day Saint scripture had a high probability of acceptance by my fellow Christians, I included them. Now it is up to the reader to decide if it is a true principle or not.

If you become interested in having a more comprehensive listing of Latter-day Saint principles, scriptures and references, I would recommend you to *Principles with Promise: For members of The Church of Jesus Christ of Latter-day Saints.* For those who would like to explore a new principle-centered biblical concordance, *Principles with Promise: Old Testament, New Testament* similarly captures hundreds of principles and their supporting references that are topically cross-referenced in an organized way.

If you do not find a favorite verse of yours in *On Common Ground*, it may be included in the *Principles with Promise* series as a reference verse to a main principle. *On Common Ground* is perhaps the middle ground between these two publications without the thousands of supporting reference verses.

The Unity of the Faith

Speaking of principles, one of my favorite scriptures is found in the New Testament, Ephesians, chapter 4, verses 11 through 13.

And he gave some, apostles; and some, prophets; and some, evangelists; and some, pastors and teachers; For the perfecting of the saints, for the work of the ministry, for the edifying of the body of Christ: Till we all come in the unity of the faith, and of the knowledge of the Son of God, unto a perfect man, unto the measure of the stature of the fulness of Christ. Eph. 4:11-13

Regarding this verse, I have often asked this question of my biblical colleagues, *Are we there yet?* Undoubtedly, as the common ground will be different for each person of every religious persuasion, so will the answer to this question. *On Common Ground* illustrates that there is much to consider through understanding and comparing principles taught in the Bible and additional Latter-day Saint scripture; holy writ considered to be the sacred word of God.

The reason I refer to Ephesians 4:11-13 is to help focus a sincere study of the principles around the thought that someday we will all come together in *the unity of the faith.* What that means to me is that the common ground will eventually be what God, the Master bridge builder, declares to be true; things as they really are ... interpreted, understood, acknowledged and practiced by everyone in His prescribed way.

May I suggest there will be a day when we will all see eye to eye on most if not all the issues that we consider today to be differences, and on that day it will not matter who is right or who is wrong on any particular note, but only that *right is right.* And also, how grateful we will be that the eyes of our understanding have been opened, and that together, we will learn anew that Jesus is indeed the Christ and that not one endeavor on our part to understand or become like Him has been in vain.

An Uncommon Experiment

During a missionary discussion with two of my dear Christian friends one day, I listed forty-six principles on the subject of *Teach, Teachable,* and *Teacher* to illustrate the *much, much, more* Latter-day Saints claim to be available through the restored gospel of Jesus Christ. I stripped away all of the scriptural reference information so no one could tell from what volume or chapter of scripture the principles came, unless they were scriptorians of course.

I then created a short quiz from the list and asked my friends which principles they agreed with or recognized from the Bible and to place a star next to these. Then I asked them to identify those principles they agreed with as true principles, but were not sure if they were biblical. They only had to consider each as a true principle based on its own merit, and again they placed a star next to the principle if they felt it was true.

Finally, I asked them to identify those principles they did not believe were correct or true principles and to place an 'X' next to them. During the quiz, I asked them not to try and guess which principles were biblical and which might be from additional Latter-day Saint scriptures, but to be honest in their evaluation. I believe they did just that.

Surprisingly, when the quiz was completed, my friends agreed with forty-five out of forty-six principles. They considered them as being true principles, regardless of where they came from. The interesting point I want to make is that only eleven of the forty-six principles were quotes strictly from the Old and New Testaments, and that several others could be found in multiple volumes.

That means there were approximately thirty to thirty-five other principles my two Christian friends felt were true beyond what is found in the biblical text. These thirty plus principles are moral principles found in Latter-day Saint scripture and taught on Sundays, lived in our homes; principles believed and practiced.

While this experiment did not mean my friends agreed with the interpretations or origins of any of the principles listed (biblical or not), it was a clear indication to me that there is definitely common ground beyond the biblical text and that a deeper exploration of those principles and values will foster a greater understanding and relationships between our faiths.

As mentioned earlier, *On Common Ground* has its roots in the *Principles with Promise* series, a new series of scriptural concordances; principle centered topical guides that catalog action-based principles and their associated promises found in holy writ. Principles of all kinds have been extracted directly from the text, cataloged, and include the laws, ordinances, commandments, and doctrines regarding our personal journey here on the earth and in the life to come. The series was developed to catalog principles of truth and belief from a number of religions, but started with Latter-day Saint and Christian text.

The reason I mention this yet again is to identify that the first piece of common ground is indeed the Bible, what both Latter-day Saints and the rest of the Christian world believe to be the word of God, regardless of how it is interpreted and practiced by the various denominations or congregations. The reason I say *"the rest of the Christian world"* is so that you may know that Mormons, like their Christian neighbors, believe, teach, preach, confess, declare, accept, have faith in, strive to be like, and love Jesus Christ as the son of God, their Lord and Redeemer; the Savior of the world. While the Mormon faith is not tied to any established religion of today, the roots are Christian and deeply rooted in Christ.

In countless discussions with Christians of all persuasions, I have heard time and time again that they believe in the only true interpretation of the Bible and that the rest of the Christian world, though entitled to their opinion, is not correct. I suppose I am guilty of thinking the same way at times, but this is not what we will focus on here.

People have a right to their opinion and may indeed interpret the same scriptural verses differently. Actually, I feel it is a given that you will do just that. Even within the same church, two people may interpret the same verse differently. They have different ideas on who Christ was, what He was, and where He is now ... but He is still Christ to them.

Some agree in free agency, free will or the freedom to choose, while others believe in predestiny which is contrary to the notion of free agency. Some Christians practice baptism by immersion and others by sprinkling water. There are those who agree in personal revelation and others who feel that time has past. Many believe they are the only ones to be saved and unless you follow their prescribed rules and their interpretation of biblical principles, you cannot be saved. Some declare they have authority to act in the name of God, some earn it by academic degree, and still others say it is given freely to all. Such discussions leave you wondering; can there ever be unity in the faith?

If a person believes in free agency, baptism by immersion, personal revelation, Christ as the Savior of mankind, in salvation by grace, that God gives authority to man in some way, you might just have found some of the common ground between Latter-day Saint beliefs and your own, but not with another Christian faith. Keep in mind that *On Common Ground* is not here to dispute or interpret the practice of each principle, but instead is designed to simply provide you with the principles found in the Bible and additional Latter-day Saint scriptures that we all may accept or believe as true principles.

The question to ask yourself as you go through this exercise is simply, *Do I believe this to be a true principle or not?* I know that for some to consider principles not found in the Bible as being true may be a leap of faith. If this is the case, I don't recommend you consider them as direct biblical principles, but perhaps consider them as principles derived from other biblical principles or universal truths not found in the Bible.

There are scientific principles like gravity that are not explained in the Bible per say, but exist none the less. There are great philosophers and notable authors who proclaim undeniable truths that we cherish, but which are not found in the Bible. I am not suggesting that all truths must be contained in the Bible or contribute to the more important topic of Christ and His salvation, but some may feel this way.

I have found different Christian faiths to be open to the same experiment my friends participated in. People willing to apply their hearts and minds to an honest evaluation of the principles presented, independent of how the principle is practiced, begin to understand the message *On Common Ground* was intended to bring. During the experiment, you will either agree or disagree that each principle, biblical or not, is true or not. The experiment is simple but yields a greater understanding of all values.

What I also find interesting is that the objective comparison of verses in different versions of the Bible, including the King James Version (KJV), New American Standard, the New International Version (NIV) and others, will similarly spark discussion and controversy.

Christians familiar with one version of the Bible over the other will agree and disagree on certain points of doctrine from the same verse, their interpretation, practice, and method for implementing the principle. Some consider the KJV outdated and the NIV more relevant and closer to the original Hebrew and Greek translations, while even others prefer the New International Standard. In fact, many people are quite vocal about their positions; end of discussion.

I am, as are all Latter-day Saints, schooled in the KJV of the Bible. It is our standard, established to be so in the early days of the church and is the version used in *On Common Ground*. I have found in my studies that as I seek to learn about a particular topic, verses throughout the KJV Bible are linked to other words in different books or even within the same book, providing me with a better understanding of the principle because of that link.

My experience with the NIV is that the new English translation does not make the same ties between the same verses made in the KJV because the words have been translated differently. I am not suggesting that the NIV is inferior to the KJV, nor am I even remotely qualified to do that. All I wish to point out is that this work calls out principles from the KJV and their NIV counterpart may not exist under the selected key words, or may not even exist at all (for example, compare Isaiah 28:10). It is up to each person to decide on the truthfulness of each principle, regardless of which version of the Bible is used.

On Common Ground will actually allow you to achieve two things if you try the experiment; first, you may find the opportunity to evaluate your own belief, position, opinion, understanding, and practice of the principles extracted from the Bible alone. Secondly, having done so, you may become more open to consider the truth or error of the additional principles taught by Latter-day Saints as part of their accepted scripture; the word of God they accept from other ancient and Latter-day prophets.

On Common Ground does not represent a complete compilation of the principles taught by Latter-day Saints. They are only selected principles I feel the Christian world at large will accept as true principles regardless of their origin or practice. Again, if you heard them in a sermon or homily, would you agree with them as true principles or would you demand to see the reference your Pastor, Minister or Priest used? Only you can answer that question.

Principles with Promise

Principles are unchanging, universal, God-given laws that govern human behavior and growth, both spiritual and temporal. They are fundamental truths that characterize our relationships with God and our fellowman, the world we live in, and the heavens above. They consist of the laws, ordinances, commandments, and guidance intended by God for the welfare, happiness, perfection, and salvation of the human soul.

Principles exist as simple statements of truth or as self-evident statements of fact. They are found as directives that require action or as guidelines that follow the *cause and effect* construct, the *if-then* principle, or simply, the *principle with promise*. Many of the principles used in *On Common Ground* include these *if-then* principles. *If* you do something (the principle), *then* you will realize some benefit or consequence for your action (the promise).

We are guided by the scriptures and counseled by our leaders and teachers to live the principles more fully and is often said in summary about the topic being presented or declared as a more general, overarching guidance. At times you may have wondered, however, to which principles are they referring, and exactly what are they that we might live them more fully?

With this in mind, Dr. Steven R. Covey has said, *"When we value correct principles, we have truth - knowledge of things as they are."* Therefore, I am certain that I am not alone in listing these principles so as to know them better; seeking knowledge of things as they truly are.

Each principle was extracted from the scriptures with the greatest of care, one verse at a time, and cataloged under one or more key words using the conventions found in typical scriptural concordances or topical guides. If a particular verse appeared to be an action statement, a statement that described something we should be doing or a simple statement of fact, it was cataloged under the primary topic it addressed.

For example, if a statement was referring to *faith*, it was filed under a collection of verses that also spoke to some aspect of *faith*; what it is, how to obtain it, exercise it, experiment with it, and grow it.

Having accumulated more than four thousand principles as defined above, they were listed under more than nineteen hundred key words in the original study, with similar principles and references grouped together as seemed appropriate. Very rarely did a single verse address only one topic area or one action and therefore, more often than not, the same principle is cataloged under several of the key words.

On Common Ground is a subset of that study. Principles listed in *On Common Ground* do not include the thousands of supporting references found in scripture. This book only makes it a little easier to find a principle under a topic. Realistically speaking, short of being a well versed scriptorian, who can recite chapter and verse from memory more than one hundred or so of their favorite principles?

Navigating *On Common Ground*

On Common Ground can be used in several different ways. This book can be used like any other topical guide or concordance to research specific biblical topics for increased understanding. If you want to research a particular topic, you similarly enter this book under that topical word, like *charity*, *grace*, or *hope*, and identify the principle or set of principles you wish to understand or include in your research, whether it be for personal edification or in preparation for a talk or sermon on Sunday or other teaching assignment.

I believe that during this process you will also find yourself considering the efficacy of different biblical principles as well as whether you agree with the Latter-day Saint text; it is inevitable. For some it may be the first time they see the principle in this light. Once discovered and believed as true, the apostle John counseled us, *If ye know these things, happy are ye if ye do them.* John 13:17.

The second use for this volume is actually its primary purpose for being published, the experiment described above, to simply consider whether you believe a biblical principle and the additional Latter-day Saint principles to be true or not. If you do, then add it to your common ground, points where you can agree in principle, obtain greater understanding, and perhaps improve relationships with your neighbor and community. If you do not agree that it is a correct principle, then add it to the list of biblical principles you likewise do not believe or practice.

I would like to leave you with one more perspective before I close this section. Would you agree that God set a plan in motion long before you or I were born and He placed us in it? How He did that is not relevant to this discussion, only that He put in place laws that govern the world we live in; laws that were determined for the benefit of each of us and *happy are ye if ye do them.*

On Common Ground serves in part as a ready reference book to assist you in your understanding of the principles found in the Bible and others found in Latter-day Saint text and believed by them to be the word of God to man in these, what Mormons consider to be the latter-days.

Principles are grouped alphabetically by *key words* found in each principle. While most principles are action oriented, there are many principles included in these lists that are statements of fact or simply stated eternal truths. A Topical Index is provided at the end to help to quickly locate principles by a key word search and page numbers.

The selection of key words for each principle was based on the topic that the principle primarily addressed. You will find that many of the principles are listed under several different key words because of the rich associations with multiple topics. Cataloging principles under multiple key words was one of the greatest challenges as you could continue a project like this indefinitely if you tried to include all of the possible links. The reader is therefore encouraged to search related topic areas for a more complete picture or better understanding.

Distinguishing between biblical principles and Latter-day Saint principles could have been done by italicizing or coloring one or the other, changing the font of the text, or even coloring the background of one to set it apart from the other, but I believe that all of these options would have offered the impression that Latter-day Saints did not believe whole-heartedly in the biblical principles presented here.

With these many options available, I decided that it would be best to just cite the reference verse after the principle to designate its origin. You can check which volume they belong to by the abbreviations provided just prior to the concordance section.

Curiously, there were several times during this compilation that I almost eliminated a biblical principle thinking it was a Latter-day Saint principle the Christian world might not agree with. When I realized it was not a principle unique to additional Mormon scripture, I considered my discovery. I too am always discovering more and more truths every day and more and more common ground with my fellow Christians.

In this publication, the principle will either come from the Bible or one of the three other books used by Latter-day Saints; the *Book of Mormon: Another Testament of Jesus Christ, the Doctrine and Covenants,* and the *Pearl of Great Price.* In other words, if the principle is cited from Matt. 3:6, you will know it comes from the New Testament book of Matthew, chapter 3, verse 6. Similarly, for a principle cited from 3 Ne. 1:4, you will be able to recognize it as Latter-day Saint scripture by its reference to Third Nephi in the Book of Mormon. Again, the key of abbreviations for all of the scriptural volumes is provided on the pages preceding the Principle-Centered Topical Guide.

The Love of Christ

As you can see from the discussion above, there are many topics to consider for a more serious deliberation on the common ground that exists between religions. There are different cultures to learn about and different terminologies in the same language that need to be identified. Only when a certain level of understanding is achieved can each principle be explored on its own merit; but explore we must.

I also suggest that during any discussion on religious topics consider the two greatest commandments, to love God, and the second like unto the first, to love your neighbor as thyself.

Jesus said unto him, Thou shalt love the Lord thy God with all thy heart, and with all thy soul, and with all thy mind. This is the first and great commandment. And the second is like unto it, Thou shalt love thy neighbour as thyself. On these two commandments, hang all the law and the prophets. Matt 22:37-40

I believe that the greatest level of communication and understanding is achieved when a spirit of love is present between those participating in the discussion; no judgments, no preconceived battle lines, only love. Love is universally understood and when present, fosters an environment where the spirit may also abide in abundance.

Remember, *for where two or three are gathered together in my name, there am I in the midst of them.* Matt 18:20

May the Lord God be ever present during our endeavors to increase our understanding of that common ground between our faiths and during religious discussion, *Till we all come in the unity of the faith, and of the knowledge of the Son of God, unto a perfect man, unto the measure of the stature of the fulness of Christ.* Eph. 4:11-13

To me, Paul's reference to *all* is not just Latter-day Saints and the rest of the Christian world, but includes all mankind, past, present and future, and it is my sincere belief, the only way to get there is *to know the love of Christ which passeth knowledge, that ye might be filled with all the fullness of God.* Eph. 3:19-20

And he gave some, apostles;
and some, prophets;
and some, evangelists;
and some, pastors and teachers;
For the perfecting of the saints, for
the work of the ministry,
for the edifying of the body of
Christ: Till we all come in the unity
of the faith, and of the knowledge
of the Son of God, unto a perfect
man, unto the measure of the
stature of the fulness of Christ.

Eph. 4:11-13

Consider These Things

Consider what I say; and the Lord give thee understanding in all things.
2 Tim. 2:7

The following personal stories are provided for your consideration. They depict real situations between me and my fellowman and are intended to illustrate the common ground that exists between two people or more of different faiths. These are situations that have taught me a true principle or true principles through experience and I am sure you have your own faith filled stories to add to mine.

I think it is appropriate to illustrate several personal accounts on how principles listed in this book might be internalized and acted upon; thereby witnessing to us their truthfulness by the fruits they bear. I do not expect that you will agree with all or any of my interpretations of the following accounts, but will instead *consider* in your own life the possibility that these and other principles found in scripture are equally true.

Prayer and Service

It was the last day of my tour at the Pentagon and I felt the need to dress in jeans rather than my uniform to clean out my desk that wintry morning. Thinking to myself, perhaps I would find the opportunity to help some stranded motorist on my way to work, I dressed for that possibility. Most days during my commute I saw someone changing a tire or with their red flashers on because of a stalled vehicle.

I was always dressed in my white uniform or was rushing to a meeting and had no time to stop and help or the safety of the free world would be in jeopardy. Though that was certainly not necessarily the case, I would have liked to stop more often than I did to help the stranded motorists over the years.

But today was different and I decided to be more particularly on the look out for someone in need. You might think this a strange way to be thinking, but I was thankful for the several years of good fortune in my hourly commute back and forth without real incident, and this was my way of saying thank you to God for his tender mercies in my life.

I was a little disappointed that I did not see anyone in need on my way to Washington DC, a rare day indeed, but the weather was turning nasty. Snow and sleet were now hitting the area and my thoughts turned to getting out of DC as quickly as possible or being left stranded in the endless hours of the beltway's bumper to bumper traffic. I took care of business at the Pentagon as quickly as I could and headed out into the now blizzard-like weather.

The traffic was already heavy when I noticed a set of flashing hazard lights up ahead on the median between the main road and an off-ramp. I thought to myself, perhaps I can be of service and looked closely to determine what might be needed. If it was car problems, I was not a mechanic but could get them to one if need be. I wanted to follow through on my earlier thoughts to help someone in need despite the weather and saw the man changing his back tire, so I pulled over in front of his car and offered my assistance while an endless stream of traffic passed by.

He was an older man and was almost done changing the tire when I asked if I could help. He accepted my offer as his hands were nearly frozen. I gave him my gloves so he could warm up his hands and went to work tightening the lug nuts, replacing the hub cap and jacking down the car; it only took a few minutes.

As I was tightening the lug nuts, he asked me if he could pay me for my service. To that I relied, *no nothing, this was something I wanted to do for you.* Surprised at my response he exclaimed, *Pray to God!* To his comment I said, *that's all the thanks I need, to know that you pray to God.*

He then told me his name, happier than at first, and said to me, *I am a Deacon in the First Baptist Church in Washington DC.* I said, *well, I am an Elder in The Church of Jesus Christ of Latter-day Saints! Glad to meet you sir.* He then followed with, *I can hardly believe it, and he sent me an Elder! I prayed for help and the Lord sent me an Elder!* We shook hands, spoke a short while and blessed each others lives as we parted ways.

Even if but for a short moment, two men of faith came together in a time of need; his need for help and my need to serve. But here is the question worth asking, Why did I prepare to serve that day? Was it the whisperings of the Spirit I believed in that morning? Why did my roadside friend pray to God for assistance and why did I acknowledge his prayer as sufficient payment?

My answer is that it is all about true principles and practicing them for the promised blessings, many blessings of which include further testimonies or witnesses that they are indeed true principles. Two strangers became friends, forever friends by practicing true principles. The divide some speak of did not exist on that street in Washington, DC one wintry afternoon.

The Holy Spirit

Once I was on a deployment in the Navy with a friend and fellow Christian. We were both pilots supporting an aircraft carrier operating off Key West, Florida. One evening we were engaged in a discussion about Latter-day Saint beliefs. I knew my friend to be a virtuous man and he was single at the time. We talked well into the evening.

During our discussion, I noticed that familiar spirit we call the Holy Ghost or the Holy Spirit present in good measure and asked my friend, *do you recognize the Spirit when it is present?* He replied, *yes, I feel it right now.* This experience taught me several important lessons. We both felt and recognized the Spirit at the same time, yet we were of different faiths. I learned that evening that my Christian brethren can and do recognize the Spirit as they consider correct principles and at times like this, they can feel it as I do.

After his tour of duty in the Navy, he went his way, got married and I heard he became a minister of a church. My only regret that night we spoke is that I did not point out to him that we were specifically discussing the gospel of Jesus Christ as taught by Latter-day Saints when we both acknowledged the Spirit, and that it wasn't the voice of warning we felt, which would have said to flee, it was the Spirit of perfect mildness and peace; perhaps even *the love of Christ which passeth knowledge* (Eph. 3:19-20). That night, we stood on common ground and truth was spoken there.

Faith and Fasting

I was out one evening with a fellow Latter-day Saint visiting, or what we call Home Teaching another member of our church in Monterey, California. As we were about to leave, it is customary to offer a prayer over the family in that home. When we bowed our heads to pray, the head of the household asked if we would mention a little boy in our prayer that he knew who had a brain tumor and would be operated on that week. We included the boy in our prayer and departed.

The following week, I wanted to experiment by fasting for some worthy cause. Latter-day Saints fast once a month as a church and contribute the money we would have spent on the two meals we intentionally miss to assist with the needs of people in our area, but we are also encouraged to fast on our own on another day in the month or as we feel the need. So this was a private decision of mine to fast on my own. I thought of this little boy, and not knowing his name or anything other than his impending operation, I dedicated my fast for him.

For some unknown reason this fast was extremely difficult for me. I had a headache and felt as though I would starve before the twenty-four hour fast was over. I passed through the kitchen on a number of occasions and considered breaking my fast early but resisted the temptation. Finally, I decided that I would succumb to my hunger, break my fast early and eat; besides, I had not told anyone what I was doing, who would know?

At the very moment my hand reached for the pantry door, a still small voice whispered clear as day, *if you knew this child, you would continue your fast.* Immediately my arm dropped to my side and I left the kitchen. I continued my fast, perhaps more so on bended knee. I will never forget those words, though I never knew the outcome of the operation or even the little boy's name for whom I fasted; God will provide for his needs, I am sure of that.

I also learned several important lessons that day. God knows the intents of our hearts, noble or not, and that He can and will lead us along His paths if we but strive to live His glorious and true principles. Just as we are counseled to pray in secret, I would recommend we occasionally fast in secret, in fact, I believe that is the preferred way.

Yes, we can know for ourselves what is true by having faith in the word of God and in the true principles He has given us for the benefit of our souls and our salvation. Is there not significant common ground between you and me on these and many more points of faith, values and principles?

Family First

The ship docked in Halifax, Nova Scotia and the Officers of Christian Fellowship were sponsoring a retreat somewhere on a Canadian mountainside. This Navy training cruise was our break from the academic semester at the Academy and our opportunity to train and to become more seaworthy. As the ship docked in Halifax, a midshipman friend of mine invited me to attend the retreat during liberty; our time off from the rigors of the cruise.

He knew I had an interest in these types of activities and he was an active member in his church; I was not yet a Latter-day Saint but was interested in knowing more of my Christian friend's beliefs. Summer cruises gave us a chance to see what the real Navy was about, and since I had already been to the town of Halifax on a prior Sea Cadet cruise, I accepted his offer to join the retreat.

The bus loaded about thirty people from the ship and local residents to begin our trek to a park in the nearby mountains. Once settled at the retreat location, we began to have discussions centering on scriptural themes. The retreat included guest speakers, refreshments and a workshop. The environment was very relaxed and the people friendly, but it was the workshop I remember most.

We broke up into groups of six or eight people with a facilitator. The very first question posed to my group was, *What is the most important thing in your life today?*

Wow, what a challenging question, I thought. The first person answered positively without hesitation, *The most important thing in my life today is my study of the Bible.* Then he elaborated on how his study of the Bible made all of the difference in the world to him. I thought again to myself, *Hmmm, interesting. More power to him if he feels that his study of the Bible is the most important thing in his life today.*

I glanced around the group and determined I would be the last to report. *Whew, more time to think of what is most important to me.* But before I could think, the next person answered, *The most important thing in my life today is my study of the Bible.*

Wow, I thought, *two people with the same important thing. That's great. What a coincidence.* Well, the process continued around the circle of participants, each comment with slight variations, like *the most important thing to me and my wife is our study of the Bible.*

I began to feel a little uncomfortable by the theme this working group seemed to be following because I had not studied the Bible yet to any great degree. Had I missed something in the preceding meetings or was this whole discussion preplanned?

No, I reasoned, *these people didn't even know each other.* They seemed sincere enough, but the answer seemed very similar or a little contrived with minor variations. Now I did feel a little cornered as it was my turn to respond. I couldn't say anything about the Bible without lying and I wasn't about to start now, of all places, not in the middle of a retreat.

I took a deep breath and spoke my heart's felt answer, *the most important thing to me in my life today is my family and I just want to thank someone for them.* Of course, that someone I had in mind was God himself. Interestingly to me, there was a profound silence from the group. I even felt a tinge of concern from the participants; concerned that I had not yet experienced the joy of Bible study. *But that's okay,* I thought, I had touched the group with a sincere and honest answer.

Now more than thirty years later, my response is still the same, the *most important thing to me in my life today is my family and I just want to thank someone for them,* except today, my family and I enjoy a daily study of the scriptures together and we know a lot more about Who I am thankful to. Like my Christian friends, we have experienced the great joy associated with studying the scriptures and living the principles we accept as true, and we encourage all to do the same.

How Do You Know?

For weeks I debated whether to keep this section in or out of *On Common Ground* because it might be perceived as preaching and does describe some of the more personal experiences I have had with the principles we may or may not share. Like the preceding accounts that have been presented, where I have tried to illustrate where the application of principles yields a particular outcome, this section similarly includes my experiences with principles that may or may not necessarily be accepted by the rest of the Christian world or even considered possible today.

But I reasoned, again, it is up to you to decide for yourself if the principles themselves or the application thereof are correct or incorrect; are they truth or error? There are some that believe in miracles while others do not, but to me, one of the greatest miracles is the change of heart. And given the broad range of beliefs among Christians gives me the heart to venture with an account of the following experiences that perhaps several readers will agree or relate to them in some meaningful way. So I decided, from the words of encouragement I often hear from my brother Ed, to *Go For It.*

At times, it appears to me, that by saying something matter of factly, whether it be true or false, the words seem to carry a level of credibility. I find this to be true, especially if the comment comes from your pastor or a close friend that you trust, some renowned author or even perpetuated on the internet by complete strangers. In many cases, prejudice and bias by those outside of our religion have hindered (or blinded) their's and others people's eyes to an objective appraisal and acceptance of true principles.

The tone of the critical dialog itself in many cases is not what I would call the Lord's way, so please don't accept their words as sufficiency for truth, but instead test it out for yourselves, and as the title of this section suggests, *consider what I say; and the Lord give thee understanding in all things.* 2 Tim. 2:7.

To me, there is only one source to go to on a matter of truth; our Maker. *Trust in the LORD with all thine heart; and lean not unto thine own understanding.* Prov. 3:5   With this, I believe that the Lord is the only true source on Which we can rely, and in Whom we can trust and have faith. A young man in his early years taught me this one great principle; *we can know for ourselves.*

Jesus is the Christ

I used to jog with a fellow pilot and Christian friend I knew to be a great sciptorian. He had a goal to write a book on the Apostle James one day, someone to whom he felt he could relate. I asked him how to get started in scripture studies, and he quickly recommended that I first spend fifteen minutes a day on some book or subject that I liked. He warned me that fifteen minutes would grow into thirty minutes and then forty-five. I followed his counsel and selected a book called *Jesus the Christ* which I quickly became engrossed in.

When I finished that book, I switched to the scriptures and began reading them regularly; starting with the Old Testament and reading every morning for fifteen minutes or more. As I experienced this new adventure for myself, he was right, fifteen minutes did turn into forty-five, and at times I found myself pushing the limits of my schedule to make it into work on time.

At one point in my study of the Old Testament, it became clear to me that the prophets and the people of that time were looking forward to their deliverance by a Promised Messiah. I was not concerned about any other principle being true, but more specifically wanted to know if Jesus Christ was indeed who he said he was; the Son of God, the Promised Messiah.

Perhaps, I thought to myself, if I had sufficient faith in James 1:5, a New Testament principle Latter-day Saints revere, and other principles I believe in, I might likewise find out for myself.

If any of you lack wisdom; let him ask of God, that giveth to all men liberally, and upbraideth not; and it shall be given him. James 1:5.

On bended knee I asked God in earnest one evening, having studied it out in my own mind, *Is Jesus Christ, the Promised Messiah spoken of in the Old Testament?* That day I received my answer with all the warm feelings of my heart – *Yes, He is* – and I now knew it for myself and not from any other source.

I learned at that very moment in the privacy of my room, that Jesus was indeed the Christ, the Son of God, and no manner of argument to the contrary could ever convince me otherwise. It was a peaceful, warm, loving assurance that I will always cherish and never forget; even *the love of Christ that passeth knowledge.*

Given this experience, several of my Christian friends have expressed to me for various reasons, that they are not comfortable with trusting the feelings of the heart as an indication from God on any matter. They feel the heart is unreliable and easily deceived; a fallen and deprived member of our body. This certainly may be true or occur at times, but it is my experience that in instances related to a witness of Christ and the truths of His gospel, there is no deception. If you can not trust your heart on matters of import like this, I would ask, what can you trust?

It is sometimes difficult to explain a feeling or unique taste to someone who has not experienced it for themselves, they do not even believe it can happen in the way I described, or again, the heart is an unreliable source for judging truth. Nevertheless, I would like to try by likening my experience to the experience the two travelers had on the road to Emmaus after Christ's resurrection just prior to revealing Himself to a gathering of the apostles.

Two travelers were walking to Emmaus, approximately five miles from Jerusalem, and were discussing the events leading up to the recent crucifixion of Christ. While traveling to Emmaus, the resurrected *Jesus himself drew near, and went with them. But their eyes were holden that they should not know him.* Luke 24:15-16. They did not recognize him.

As they walk together, Jesus expounds the scriptures to them, *beginning at Moses and all the prophets, he expounded unto them in all the scriptures the things concerning himself.* Luke 24:27. Arriving in Emmaus, the travelers invite Him to eat with them and He accepts.

And it came to pass, as he sat at meat with them, he took bread, and blessed it, and brake, and gave to them. And their eyes were opened, and they knew him; and he vanished out of their sight. Luke 24:30-31.

These two men had not known that it was the resurrected Jesus who walked with them, taught them, and then broke bread with them. But at the very moment they become aware of it, He departed from their sight.

The similarity of this story with the burning confirmation I received in my heart that Jesus Christ is indeed that Promised Messiah is found in the conversation that follows their visit from Him. *And they said one to another, Did not our heart burn within us, while he talked with us by the way, and while he opened to us the scriptures?* Luke 24:32

Their hearts burned within them, testifying that they were in the presence of their Savior, and though that sure knowledge and awareness was held from them in His presence, they knew it afterwards and marveled. Again, *did not our heart burn within us* provides, in my mind, a clear example of how God does indeed communicate with us at times. We therefore come to a more certain knowledge of the truth being declared at the time we receive it.

The now astonished and excited travelers return to Jerusalem with haste. There, as they recount their story on the way to Emmaus, Christ appears to those gathered, and what a wonderful day that was. Christ did it all in His perfect way.

It is my humble belief that God reveals the truth of His words, which include His principles, in many different ways to us, regardless of our religious persuasion. My testimony of Christ was received in the way I described and I believe it is not as uncommon as you may think; it happened in times of old as it can and does happen today.

What more would anyone need than God's own testimony that Jesus is the Christ, or in other words, *What greater witness can you have than from God?* D&C 6:23

If we receive the witness of men, the witness of God is greater: for this is the witness of God which he hath testified of his Son. 1 Jn. 5:9.

This is why I named this section, *Consider These Things*. My experience is that you can know for yourself if any of the principles found in the scriptures are true, and I believe that many of my Christian friends may feel the same way, though certainly, others will not. Are you ready to try the virtue of the word of God?

A Changed Heart

I have often marveled at the *born again* phenomenon which my Christian friends experience in the various denominations with whom I have come in contact. At the Naval Academy, I had my first experiences with Midshipmen and Naval Officers who claimed this mighty change in heart. The individual experiences expressed to me by each person I know varies, as well as their definition of the term *born again*.

The common thread I have noticed is that a profound change in heart takes place that motivates that person to a heightened sense of purpose in Christ. This is often accompanied with the energy to teach their beliefs at every opportunity and a deeper commitment towards living correct and moral principles. But, have you ever asked yourself how so many people from various Christian denominations, who interpret or practice the same principles differently, can similarly claim to be *born again*?

I have often felt to be an outsider looking in when many have asked me when I had been *born again* or in other words, taken and confessed Jesus as my personal Savior and experienced this change in heart. Having been raised of goodly parents, I have always believed in Jesus Christ since the days of my early youth, and saw no need to confess in their prescribed manner.

My associates never seemed to be content with my response and I did not feel entirely comfortable trying to explain my position to them; as I was unlearned in the scriptures at that time in my life. Therefore, according to some of my friends, I had not yet been saved. At times I have felt uncomfortable with their assessment and thought, *who are you do decide if I am saved or not?*

When I studied more closely this topic of being *born again*, I came across numerous scriptures in the New Testament and also in the Book of Mormon describing it. My research concluded that this change in heart might be desirable to experience; becoming that new creature in Christ. I even prayed for it, earnestly at times, but it did not happen like I thought it would. Instead, it would actually occur many years later when I gained an understanding of the principles that might be involved in how people experience this change in heart; becoming born again and the resultant effect that change might have on their lives.

There is actually a story in the Book of Mormon that made it clearer to me than other scriptures did on how people become born again. The story is about a king who after loosing a fight he started tries to save his life by offering up only *half* his kingdom. Later that same king is taught about God and is willing to forsake his earthly kingdom and give up *all* his sins to know Him.

The following two verses provided the key that unlocked the door to becoming born again or born of God for me.

Now the king, fearing he should lose his life, said: If thou wilt spare me, I will grant unto thee whatsoever thou wilt ask, even to half of the kingdom. Alma 20:23

As you can see, the king bargains for his life, but he is only willing to give up half his kingdom to save it and would rather die otherwise. But later in the story, the king is taught the gospel of Jesus Christ and this is his response.

And it came to pass that after Aaron had expounded these things unto him, the king said: what shall I do that I may have this eternal life of which thou hast spoken? Yea, what shall I do that I may be born of God, having this wicked spirit rooted out of my breast, and receive his Spirit, that I may be filled with joy, that I may not be cast off at the last day?

Behold, said he, I will give up all that I possess, yea, I will forsake my kingdom, that I may receive this great joy... and I will give away all my sins to know thee. Alma 22:15-18

I believe from my own experience that the principles taught in these two verses are true. They helped me understand what I needed to know to affect this change in my own life. But I also believe they explain how so many people from various Christian faiths and religious backgrounds likewise come to be born of God.

They similarly follow the scriptural instructions that are found in the Bible; true principles on how to obtain a new heart. And though the instructions are easily understood, they are not necessarily easy for the natural man to do. It takes faith, a belief that Christ can bring about the change, a willingness to follow Him with *all* your heart, and perhaps most significantly, giving up not a portion of your sins, but instead, *all* of them to know God.

Christ did not say only this person or that person should be *born again*, He said, *except a man be born again, he cannot see the kingdom of God,* John 3:3. When a person's heart is right before God, one of the greatest miracles takes place and that man or woman's life is changed. Having been born of God, a man is newly formed, new perspectives are achieved, and a new appreciation for Christ and His atonement are gained. Once that occurs, how you express yourself to your fellowmen or how you live your life from that point forward continues to be a matter of choice.

Remember, *On Common Ground* was written to help Mormons and Christians alike to understand each others shared beliefs. From the many experiences I have had with my friends across the broad spectrum of Christian beliefs, I maintain that practicing true principles recorded in the scriptures will most certainly yield the promised blessings.

Like my testimony of Christ received years earlier, I arrived at a point in my life where I became weary of living with one foot in the world and one foot living the gospel. That can be a very difficult balancing act at times. It was only when I was willing to give up my hold on the world and follow Him, trusting completely; my heart was right before God. My change took place just as it is described in the New Testament.

Marvel not that I said unto thee, Ye must be born again. The wind bloweth where it listeth, and thou hearest the sound thereof, but canst not tell whence it cometh, and whiter it goeth: so is every one that is born of the Spirit. John 3:7-8

To some, the change and experience is a more profound, but mine was only slightly noticeable to me over several days and then became more obvious when I realized I was actually thinking differently about the choices I was making. The changing wind had come and though barely noticed it at first, it did indeed come, and now I looked at life through a new set of lenses.

The change gave me the additional courage to make better decisions that I previously had trouble making, and it helped me align my life more closely with the principles of truth I so cherished and believed. It was time to really live what I believed, and my new heart gave me the requisite courage to act in a manner I felt was more acceptable to God. In some ways it was also the most difficult time in my life as I resolutely began to choose the right and let the consequences for my actions be what they may.

Nevertheless, I was happier than I had ever been before and knew that God had brought this magnificent change in heart to me because I had exercised my agency and faith to follow Him; willing to give up all of my worldly aspirations and sins to know Him. I have seen these same changes occur in my Christian friends when they similarly have yielded up their hearts to God and turned from the world. Essentially they *look to God and live,* and that my friend is our common ground.

Belief, Faith, Knowledge

After a profound change in heart like this takes place, I have noticed that there is a tendency by some to think that everything else they believe in must certainly be true also. They therefore feel and are usually very vocal about it that everyone needs to see the new light of which they are now made aware of; and why not?

Christ instructed Simon Peter - *Simon, behold, Satan hath desired to have you, that he may sift you as wheat: But I have prayed for thee, that thy faith fail not: and when thou art converted, strengthen thy brethren.* Luke 22:31-32.

Unfortunately, my fellow Christians and I may quickly appear to some as being know-it-alls. As I see it, we can have a better influence on our friends and family if we temper the language we use to describe our experience without offending our listeners. Believing something is true is quite different than having faith in a true thing, and also different than knowing something is true. Not everyone is ready to know something, much less believe it, when you only recently came to a knowledge of it yourself.

Latter-day Saints teach that, *faith is not to have a perfect knowledge of things; therefore if ye have faith ye hope for things which are not seen, which are true.* Alma 32:21. The three words not included in a similar biblical verse on faith found in Hebrews 11:1, are the words *which are true.*

You may believe in anything you want to, but faith is a little different than belief. Belief is certainly one of the required ingredients for faith, but to have real faith, more than belief, requires a belief in something that is true. Let me try to explain these thoughts with a story found in the New Testament about a woman who has faith in Christ.

The women who suffered with a blood issue made her way through the pressing throng of people, reached out to touch the hem of Christ's garment with her hand, having the faith that by so doing she would be healed. This woman believed first that Christ could heal her. She applied her faith and acted on it, and thereby came to a knowledge that her faith was based on a true principle. She now knew for herself that what she believed in was true and she had successfully exercised her faith to be healed.

Christ confirmed this when he turned to find who had touched Him, noticing that virtue had left His body, and said, *Daughter, be of good comfort; thy faith hath made thee whole. And the woman was made whole from that hour.* Matt. 9:22. She had believed and exercised faith in a true principle and now knew it was indeed true; not from any other source.

However, though a true principle has yielded its faithful promise, the remainder of our beliefs is not always centered on true principles. We should choose our words carefully to distinguish the differences between belief, faith and knowledge when we discuss our shared beliefs as to not offend or appear to be a know it all; and I think you will agree that no one may be saved by believing a false principle.

With a little help from the spirit and a lot of experience, I am confident that you and I will learn how to better express the deepest convictions and feelings of our heart as to lead others to that same knowledge we possess. Perhaps you would also therefore agree that the experiment to determine the truth of all things has only just begun for both you and me.

As we experiment or *try the virtue of the word of God*, each opportunity taken by us will yield unique blessings and testimonies of the truth for that principle; our own personal heaven sent witness of the truth. You will thereby weave together a beautiful tapestry of your own experience by trying the virtue of the word of God, and you will come closer to seeing things as they truly are; God's common ground.

Me, Mine, All Mine

We were filled with excitement and anticipation as Mom went to the hospital to deliver her fifth child. I was about eight years old at the time. Unfortunately, my Dad returned home from the hospital with the sad news that our little brother, Thomas, did not make it. He had died because of a disease called German measles which did not allow his lungs to develop properly. We were all deeply disappointed and saddened by the news.

Not understanding much about life at eight, I recall crying in my bed that night thinking about the loss. I had really looked forward to the new addition to our family. While crying, I determined that God surely must exist, just like my parents had taught me, and so I began reasoning with Him. I told God that I would be willing to do anything He required of me to have another brother or sister.

This is the first prayer I ever remember saying, *"God, please send us another baby and I promise I will be the best brother ever."* Following my prayer, I remember being able to sleep because in an eight year old's mind, I had made a deal.

You can imagine my surprise when my parents announced the following year that Mom was expecting another child. I rejoiced and remembered my prayer and my promise. The news renewed my commitment to be the best brother I could be. Our little sister Eileen was born that October and Dad took all four of us to the hospital. We watched as Mom threw candy out of her hospital window to our open arms below.

From the day of Eileen's arrival home, I tried to be the best brother I could be, and I remember celebrating her birth by thanking God often; for surely He had heard my prayer. I willingly babysat her, changed her diapers, told her bedtime stories about the *ker-plunk* capers, kept her involved in my teenage activities, and made her a movie star in my Super 8mm magic film productions.

I considered Eileen to be a gift sent from God in answer to my prayer. I believed that with all my heart, so much so that I affectionately nick-named my little sister, *Me, Mine, All Mine.* I loved her as much as any brother could at that early age; and still do. And I offer this story for your consideration, thinking it might bring us both back to center stage regarding several principles that are directly related to a verse found in the New Testament that we Christians share.

Except ye be converted, and become as little children, ye shall not enter into the kingdom of heaven. Matt. 18:3.

There are so many things to consider that are important to our salvation, including this one. It amazes me sometimes just how hard we, as adults, have to work to become like the child we once were; pure, innocent, trusting, believing, and willing to do whatever it takes for the promised blessings of God. Why is it so hard to become even as we once were?

This is a story of faith, prayer, trust, and making and keeping covenants with God; yes, even a child of eight can make and keep covenants. And finally, it is a story of thanksgiving and gratitude which we believe are essential gospel principles that should be reflected in our actions; God-given principles we all must consider if we are serious about living with Him someday, don't you agree?

I believe we all face the same challenges in today's world and in life in general. Perhaps by identifying our common plights will give way to accepting and working within the common ground we share. Certainly, if a prayer can be uttered by an eight year old child who turns to God for help, we too can combine our faithful actions and prayers for the common good and the welfare of our families, friends, and our fellowman. All men share this responsibility.

Fertile Ground

On the first Sunday of the month, each Latter-day Saint has the opportunity to bear their testimony to the rest of the congregation if they feel so inclined. During the meeting, they describe their personal experiences and truths they have come to know; experiences that have increased their faith in Christ and His gospel. We call it bearing one's testimony and it is akin to confessing that Jesus is the Christ, our Lord and Savior.

We as a people are counseled to strengthen our testimony by sharing it, and perhaps it is something you likewise do in your own settings. The scriptures are rich with encouragement and guidance regarding our witness of Christ. Here are several examples.

Be not thou therefore ashamed of the testimony of our Lord. 2 Tim. 1:8.

Whosoever shall confess that Jesus is the Son of God, God dwelleth in him, and he in God. 1 Jn. 4:15

How shall we escape, if we neglect so great salvation; which at the first began to be spoken by the Lord, and was confirmed unto us by them that heard him; God also bearing them witness, both with signs and wonders, and with divers miracles, and gifts of the Holy Ghost, according to his own will? Heb. 2:3-4

Witnessing or bearing ones testimony is yet another piece of common ground to consider. Similar to my experience with my born again Christian friends who confessed Christ at every opportunity, our testimonies often include a description of what we believe is true, what principles we may be exercising our faith in, and how and why we have come to this knowledge.

Also, the account of our experiences and witnesses are not a one time event, but rather a continuum of events that strengthens our faith and secures us more firmly in the knowledge of God and His ways. While there are those significant, life altering changes of heart that do occur, more often than not the changes are incremental; known only to you and God.

Friends of mine once showed me by example, that the abundant life we seek is not achieved in an instant, but instead is experienced over a lifetime of service and devotion to God. Latter-day Saints are often accused of working their way into heaven, but from my perspective, any good work we do is simply a reflection of our gratitude for the many testimonies we have of true principles. Like our Christian brethren who experience the benefits of living gospel principles, we act on that which we believe in, exercise faith in, or know.

My friends, I know that Jesus is the Christ, the Promised Messiah of the Old Testament. How do I know? It is a knowledge received from God in His way, described in the scriptures and experienced in person. I know that He lives and loves each of us with a perfect love, and that He understands our earthly trails better than anyone can. Through living true and correct principles which are written in God's word, you may likewise receive a new heart and know these things for yourself; that is, if you don't already know.

I also have a testimony of many more principles I believe to be true beyond what is presented here, but this publication is certainly a good place to get started to find the common ground that exists between you and I. My experiences lead me to believe that adherence to the principles listed in the Topical Guide that follows this section will indeed bring the promised blessings from heaven; not only common ground, but the fertile ground we share with our Christian neighbors.

And yes, I do look forward to that time that we will all come together in *the unity of faith* as Christ reveals Himself to us, even as He is, and then we will see eye to eye things as they really are. For now, I am grateful for the good and true principles that we have in the scriptures, internalized in the hearts and minds of many, but more especially, for the good that comes from living them.

We as Latter-day Saints and fellow Christians *believe in being honest, true, chaste, benevolent, virtuous, and in doing good to all men; indeed, we may say that we follow the admonition of Paul - We believe all things, we hope all things, we have endured many things, and hope to be able to endure all things.*

If there is anything virtuous, lovely, or of good report or praiseworthy, we seek after these things. A of F–13. Together, let us seek and cultivate that common ground we share in Christ.

Consider what I say;
and the Lord give thee
understanding in all things.

2 Tim. 2:7

Bible Reference Abbreviations

The following standard scriptural abbreviation conventions apply.

THE OLD TESTAMENT

Genesis	Gen.	Ecclesiastes	Eccl.
Exodus	Ex.	The Song of Solomon	Song
Leviticus	Lev.	Isaiah	Isa.
Numbers	Num.	Jeremiah	Jer.
Deuteronomy	Deut.	Lamentations	Lam.
Joshua	Josh.	Ezekiel	Ezek.
Judges	Judg.	Daniel	Dan.
Ruth	Ruth	Hosea	Hosea
1 Samuel	1 Sam.	Joel	Joel
2 Samuel	2 Sam.	Amos	Amos
1 Kings	1 Kgs.	Obadiah	Obad.
2 Kings	2 Kgs.	Jonah	Jonah
1 Chronicles	1 Chr.	Micah	Micah
2 Chronicles	2 Chr.	Nahum	Nahum
Ezra	Ezra	Habakkuk	Hab.
Nehemiah	Neh.	Zephaniah	Zeph.
Esther	Esth.	Haggai	Hag.
Job	Job	Zechariah	Zech.
Psalms	Ps.	Malachi	Mal.
Proverbs	Prov.		

THE NEW TESTAMENT OF
OUR LORD AND SAVIOUR JESUS CHRIST

Matthew	Matt.	1 Timothy	1 Tim.
Mark	Mark	2 Timothy	2 Tim.
Luke	Luke	Titus	Titus
John	John	Philemon	Philem.
The Acts	Acts	Hebrews	Heb.
Romans	Rom.	James	James
1 Corinthians	1 Cor.	1 Peter	1 Pet.
2 Corinthians	2 Cor.	2 Peter	2 Pet.
Galatians	Gal.	1 John	1 Jn.
Ephesians	Eph.	2 John	2 Jn.
Philippians	Philip.	3 John	3 Jn.
Colossians	Col.	Jude	Jude
1 Thessalonians	1 Thes.	Revelation	Rev.
2 Thessalonians	2 Thes		

Additional Latter-day Saint Scripture

The following standard scriptural abbreviation conventions apply.

THE BOOK OF MORMON
ANOTHER TESTAMENT OF JESUS CHRIST

First Nephi	1 Ne.	Alma	Alma
Second Nephi	2 Ne.	Helaman	Hel.
Jacob	Jacob	Third Nephi	3 Ne.
Enos	Enos	Fourth Nephi	4 Ne.
Jarom	Jarom	Mormon	Morm.
Omni	Omni	Ether	Ether
Words of Mormon	W of M.	Moroni	Moro.
Mosiah	Mosiah		

THE DOCTRINE AND COVENANTS
OF THE CHURCH OF JESUS CHRIST OF LATTER–DAY SAINTS

CONTAINING REVELATIONS GIVEN TO JOSEPH SMITH, THE PROPHET WITH SOME
ADDITIONS BY HIS SUCCESSORS IN THE PRESIDENCY OF THE CHURCH

Doctrine and Covenants	D&C
Official Declaration 1	OD1
Official Declaration 2	OD2

THE PEARL OF GREAT PRICE

A SELECTION FROM THE REVELATIONS, TRANSLATIONS, AND NARRATIONS OF
JOSEPH SMITH FIRST PROPHET, SEER, AND REVELATOR TO
THE CHURCH OF JESUS CHRIST OF LATTER–DAY SAINTS

Book of Moses	Moses	Facsimile No. 3	FAC3
The Book of Abraham	Abr.	Joseph Smith – Matthew	JS–M
Facsimile No. 1	FAC1	Joseph Smith – History	JS–H
Facsimile No. 2	FAC2	The Articles of Faith	A of F

*If any of you lack wisdom,
let him ask of God,
that giveth to all men liberally,
and upbraideth not;
and it shall be given him.*

James 1:5

A Principle Centered Topical Guide

As described earlier, the remainder of this book lists both biblical and selected Latter-day Saint principles you may or may not accept as true principles depending on your core beliefs; the choice is ultimately yours whether you believe them to be true or not. There are over 2,000 principles cataloged under more than 1,500 key words which will assist you in locating a topic of interest.

The author assumes all editorial responsibilities and apologizes beforehand for any errors in spelling, text, formatting or the selection of scriptural principles; they are there. Therefore, you are encouraged to provide feedback regarding recommended corrections and changes for future discussions or editions. To do this, please send your comments to Celestine Publishing, LLC at 9660 Falls of Neuse Rd, STE 138, #146, Raleigh, NC 27615 or provide your comments at www.celestinepublishing.com.

ABASE

Whosoever shall exalt himself shall be abased; and he that shall humble himself shall be exalted. Matt. 23:23 (D&C 101:42)

ABHOR, ABHORANCE

Behold, my soul abhorreth sin, and my heart delighteth in righteousness; and I will praise the holy name of my God. 2 Ne. 9:49

ABIDE, ABODE

They that are wise and have received the truth, and have taken the Holy Spirit for their guide, and have not been deceived – verily I say unto you, they shall not be hewn down and cast into the fire, but shall abide the day. D&C 45:57

Abide ye in the liberty wherewith ye are made free; entangle not yourselves in sin, but let your hands be clean until the Lord comes. D&C 88:86

I am the vine, yea are the branches: He that abideth in me, and I in him, the same bringeth forth much fruit: for without me ye can do nothing. John 15:5

ABOMINABLE, ABOMINATION

Yea, they have chosen their own ways, and their soul delighteth in their abominations. Isa. 66:3

Wo be unto you because of your wickedness and abominations! Hel. 7:27

They provoked him to jealousy with strange gods, with abominations provoked they him to anger. Duet 32:16

God knoweth your hearts: for that which is highly esteemed among men is abomination in the sight of God. Luke 16:15

And the LORD said unto them - Go through the midst of the city, through the midst of Jerusalem, and set a mark upon the foreheads of the men that sigh and that cry for all the abominations that be done in the midst thereof. Ezek. 9:4

The thoughts of the wicked are an abomination to the LORD: but the words of the pure are pleasant words Prov. 15:26

Were they ashamed when they had committed abominations? nay, they were not at all ashamed, neither could they blush: therefore they shall fall among them that fall: at the time that I visit them they shall be cast down, saith the LORD. Jer. 6:15

Thou shalt not lie with mankind, as with womankind: it is abomination. Lev. 18:22

The children of Judah have done evil in my sight, saith the LORD: they have set their abominations in the house which is called by my name, to pollute it. Jer. 7:30

Son of man, cause Jerusalem to know her abominations. Ezek. 16:2

ABSTAIN, ABSTINENCE

Now the Spirit speaketh expressly, that in the latter times some shall depart from the faith, giving heed to seducing spirits, and doctrines of devils; Speaking lies in hypocrisy; having their conscience seared with a hot iron; Forbidding to marry, and commanding to abstain from meats, which God hath created to be received with thanksgiving of them which believe and know the truth. 1 Tim. 4:1-3

ABUNDANCE, ABUNDANT

[Serve] the Lord thy God with joyfulness, and with gladness of heart, for the abundance of all things. Deut. 28:47

Ye shall serve the LORD your God, and he shall bless thy bread, and thy water; and I will take sickness away from the midst of thee. Ex. 23:25

He which soweth sparingly shall reap also sparingly; and he which soweth bountifully shall reap also bountifully. 2 Cor. 9:6

ACCOUNT, ACCOUNTABLE, ACCOUNTABILITY

His lord said unto him: Well done, thou good and faithful servant: thou hast been faithful over a few things, I will make thee ruler over many things: enter thou into the joy of thy lord. Matt. 25:21

For it is written, As I live, saith the Lord, every knee shall bow to me, and every tongue shall confess to God. So then every one of us shall give account of himself to God. Rom. 14:12

Unto whomsoever much is given, of him shall be much required: and to whom men have committed much, of him they will ask the more. Luke 12:48

We believe that governments were instituted of God for the benefit of man; and that he holds men accountable for their acts in relation to them, both in making laws and administering them, for the good and safety of society. D&C 134:1

ACCUSATION, ACCUSE

Accuse not a servant unto his master, lest he curse thee, and thou be found guilty. Prov. 30:10

Against an elder, receive not an accusation but before two or three witnesses. 1 Tim. 5:19

A false witness shall not be unpunished, and he that speaketh lies shall not escape. Prov. 19:5

Do violence to no man, neither accuse any falsely; and be content with your wages. Luke 3:14

ACKNOWLEDGE

Hear, ye that are far off, what I have done; and, ye that are near, acknowledge my might. Isa. 33:13

Acknowledge your unworthiness before God at all times. Alma 38:14

Acknowledge to our everlasting shame that all his judgments are just. Alma 12:15

LORD, thou art our father; we are the clay, and thou our potter; and we all are the work of thy hand. Isa. 64:8

Acknowledge thine iniquity that thou hast transgressed against the LORD thy God, and hast scattered thy ways to the strangers under every green tree, and ye have not obeyed my voice, saith the LORD. Jer. 3:13

In all thy ways acknowledge him, and he shall direct thy paths. Prov. 3:6

ADD, ADDITIONAL

Ye shall not add unto the word which I command you, neither shall ye diminish ought from it, that ye may keep the commandments of the LORD your God which I command you. Deut. 4:2

Which of you by taking thought can add one cubit unto his stature? Matt. 6:27

ADMINISTER, ADMINISTRATION

Ye must visit the poor and the needy and administer to their relief, that they may be kept until all things may be done according to my law which ye have received. D&C 44:6

That ye may walk guiltless before God, I would that ye should impart of your substance to the poor, every man according to that which he hath, such as feeding the hungry, clothing the naked, visiting the sick and administering to their relief, both spiritually and temporally, according to their wants. Mosiah 4:26

ADMONISH, ADMONITION

They were admonished continually by the word of God. Omni 1:13

Ye fathers, provoke not your children to wrath: but bring them up in the nurture and admonition of the Lord. Eph. 6:4

I, Enos, knowing my father that he was a just man – for he taught me in his language, and also in the nurture and admonition of the Lord – and blessed be the name of my God for it. Enos 1:1

Those who committed sin, that were in the church, should be admonished by the church. Mosiah 26:6

Be not ashamed, neither confounded; but be admonished in all your high-mindedness and pride, for it bringeth a snare upon your souls. D&C 90:17

Let the word of Christ dwell in you richly in all wisdom; teaching and admonishing one another in psalms and hymns and spiritual songs, singing with grace in your hearts to the Lord. Col. 3:16

ADOPT, ADOPTION

For as many as are led by the Spirit of God, they are the sons of God. For ye have not received the spirit of bondage again to fear; but ye have received the Spirit of adoption, whereby we cry, Abba, Father. The Spirit itself beareth witness with our spirit, that we are the children of God: And if children, then heirs; heirs of God, and joint-heirs with Christ; if so be that we suffer with him, that we may be also glorified together. Rom 8:14-18

ADULTERY

Thou shalt not commit adultery. Ex. 20:14

Thou shalt not lie carnally with thy neighbour's wife, to defile thyself with her. Lev. 18:20-24

He that looketh upon a woman to lust after her shall deny the faith, and shall not have the Spirit; and if he repents not he shall be cast out. D&C 42:23

Behold, it is written by them of old time, that thou shalt not commit adultery; But I say unto you, that whosoever looketh on a woman, to lust after her, hath committed adultery already in his heart. Behold, I give you a commandment, that ye suffer non of these things to enter into your heart; For it is better that ye should deny yourselves of these things, wherein ye will take up your cross than that ye should be cast into hell. 3 Ne. 12:27-30 (Matt. 5:27-28)

Whosoever putteth away his wife, and marrieth another, committeth adultery: and whosoever marrieth her that is put away from her husband committeth adultery. Luke 16:18

ADVERSARY

Give none occasion to the adversary to speak reproachfully. 1 Tim. 5:14

Watch, for the adversary spreadeth his dominions, and darkness reigneth. D&C 82:5

Be sober, be vigilant; because your adversary the devil, as a roaring lion, walketh about, seeking whom he may devour: 1 Pet. 5:8

You should not have feared man more than God. Although men set at naught the counsels of God, and despise his words - yet you should have been faithful; and he would have extended his arm and supported you against all the fiery darts of the adversary; and he would have been with you in every time of trouble. D&C 3:7

Agree with thine adversary quickly, whiles thou art in the way with him; lest at any time the adversary deliver thee to the judge, and the judge deliver thee to the officer, and thou be cast into prison. Matt. 5:25

ADVERSITY

My son, peace be unto thy soul; thine adversity in thine afflictions shall be but a small moment. D&C 121:7

AFFAIRS

A good man sheweth favour, and lendeth: he will guide his affairs with discretion. Ps. 112:5

AFFECTION

Set your affection on things above, not on things on the earth. Col. 3:2

Cry unto God for all thy support; yea, let all thy doings be unto the Lord, and whithersoever thou goest let it be in the Lord; yea, let all thy thoughts be directed unto the Lord; yea, let the affections of thy heart be placed upon the Lord forever. Alma 37:36

AFFLICT, AFFLICTION

Be patient in afflictions. D&C 31:9

O LORD, my strength, and my fortress, and my refuge in the day of affliction. Jer. 16:19

To him that is afflicted, pity should be shewed from his friend. Job 6:14

Behold, I have refined thee, but not with silver; I have chosen thee in the furnace of affliction. Isa. 48:10

I will cry unto thee in all mine afflictions. Alma 33:11

If thou draw out thy soul to the hungry, and satisfy the afflicted soul; then shall thy light rise in obscurity, and thy darkness be as the noonday: And the LORD shall guide thee continually. Isa. 58:10

I would exhort you to have patience, and that ye bear with all manner of afflictions; that ye do not revile against those who do cast you out because of your exceeding poverty, lest ye become sinners like unto them. Alma 34:40

I know your manifold transgressions and your mighty sins: they afflict the just, they take a bribe, and they turn aside the poor in the gate from their right. Amos 5:12

Whosoever shall put their trust in God shall be supported in their trials, and their troubles, and their afflictions. Alma 36:3

I did look unto my God, and I did praise him all the day long; and I did not murmur against the Lord because of mine afflictions. 1 Ne. 18:16

Why should I give way to temptations, that the evil one have place in my heart to destroy my peace and afflict my soul? 2 Ne. 4:27

O then, if I have seen so great things, if the Lord in his condescension unto the children of men hath visited men in so much mercy, why should my heart weep and my soul linger in the valley of sorrow, and my flesh waste away, and my strength slacken, because of mine afflictions? 2 Ne. 4:26

Have patience, and bear with those afflictions, with a firm hope that ye shall one day rest from all your afflictions. Alma 34:41

Many are the afflictions of the righteous: but the LORD delivereth him out of them all Ps. 34:19

The poor man cried, and the LORD heard him, and saved him out of all his troubles. Ps. 34:6

AFRAID

Be ye afraid of the sword: for wrath bringeth the punishments of the sword, that ye may know there is a judgment. Job 19:29

Be strong and of a good courage; be not afraid, neither be thou dismayed; for the LORD thy God is with thee whithersoever thou goest. Josh. 1:9

Be not afraid, only believe. Mark 5:36

Be not afraid of sudden fear, neither of the desolation of the wicked, when it cometh. For the LORD shall be thy confidence, and shall keep thy foot from being taken. Prov. 3:25-26

AGAINST

They are more righteous than you, for they have not sinned against that great knowledge which ye have received. Hel. 7:24

Wo unto them that fight against God and the people of his church. 2 Ne. 25:14

Have we not all one father? hath not one God created us? why do we deal treacherously every man against his brother, by profaning the covenant of our fathers? Mal. 2:10

Preach against all lyings, and deceivings, and envyings, and strifes, and malice and revilings, and stealing, robbing, plundering, murdering, committing adultery, and all manner of lasciviousness, crying that these things ought not so to be. Alma 16:18

Magnify not thyself against the Lord. Jer. 48:26

AGENCY

We claim the privilege of worshiping Almighty God according to the dictates of our own conscience, and allow all men the same privilege, let them worship how, where, or what they may. A of F-11

There is nothing that the Lord thy God shall take in his heart to do but what he will do it. Abr. 3:17

It is given unto them to know good from evil; wherefore they are agents unto themselves. Moses 6:56

Men are free according to the flesh; and all things are given them which are expedient unto man. And they are free to choose liberty and eternal life, through the great Mediator of all men, or to choose captivity and death, according to the captivity and power of the devil; for he seeketh that all men might be miserable like unto himself. 2 Ne. 2:27

Choose for thyself, for it is given unto thee. Moses 3:17

Act for yourselves; for behold, God hath given unto you a knowledge and he hath made you free. Hel. 14:30

Men should be anxiously engaged in a good cause, and do many things of their own free will, and bring to pass much righteousness; For the power is in them, wherein they are agents unto themselves. And inasmuch as men do good they shall in nowise lose their reward. D&C 58:27-28

AGREE

Friend, I do thee no wrong: didst not thou agree with me for a penny? Take that thine is, and go thy way: I will give unto this last, even as unto thee. Matt. 20:1-14

Agree with thine adversary quickly, whiles thou art in the way with him; lest at any time the adversary deliver thee to the judge, and the judge deliver thee to the officer, and thou be cast into prison. Matt. 5:25

ALIVE

Knowing that Christ being raised from the dead dieth no more; death hath no more dominion over him. For in that he died, he died unto sin once: but in that he liveth, he liveth unto God. Likewise reckon ye also yourselves to be dead indeed unto sin, but alive unto God through Jesus Christ our Lord. Rom. 6:9-11

ALL THINGS

Be obedient in all things. 2 Cor. 2:9

Let all things be done decently and in order. 1 Cor. 14:40

How is it that ye have forgotten that the Lord is able to do all things according to his will, for the children of men, if it so be that they exercise faith in him? 1 Ne. 7:12

Evil men understand not judgment: but they that seek the LORD understand all things. Prov. 28:5

I can do all things through Christ which strengtheneth me. Philip. 4:13

I know, in the strength of the Lord thou canst do all things. Alma 20:4

Teach them all things pertaining to righteousness. Alma 21:23

Feast upon the words of Christ; for behold, the words of Christ will tell you all things what ye should do. 2 Ne. 32:3

Every man that striveth for the mastery is temperate in all things. 1 Cor. 9:25

My people must be tried in all things, that they may be prepared to receive the glory that I have for them, even the glory of Zion; and he that will not bear chastisement is not worthy of my kingdom. D&C 136:31

These things have I spoken unto you, being yet present with you. But the Comforter, which is the Holy Ghost, whom the Father will send in my name, he shall teach you all things, and bring all things to your remembrance, whatsoever I have said unto you. John 14:25-26

We believe in being honest, true, chaste, benevolent, virtuous, and in doing to all men; indeed, we may say that we follow the admonition of Paul - We believe all things, we hope all things, we have endured many things, and hope to be able to endure all things. If there is anything virtuous, lovely, or of good report or praiseworthy, we seek after these things. A of F–13

Thou shalt thank the Lord thy God in all things. D&C 59:7

Charity suffereth long, and is kind, and envieth not, and is not puffed up, seeketh not her own, is not easily provoked, thinketh no evil, and rejoiceth not in iniquity but rejoiceth in the truth, beareth all things, believeth all things, hopeth all things, endureth all things. Moro. 7:45 (1 Cor. 13:4-13)

Do all things without murmurings and disputings: That ye may be blameless and harmless, the sons of God, without rebuke, in the midst of a crooked and perverse nation, among whom ye shine as lights in the world. Philip. 2:14-15

He that overcometh shall inherit all things; and I will be his God, and he shall be my son. But the fearful, and unbelieving, and the abominable, and murderers, and whoremongers, and sorcerers, and idolaters, and all liars, shall have their part in the lake which burneth with fire and brimstone: which is the second death. Rev. 21:7

I would that ye would be diligent and temperate in all things. Alma 38:10

All things must be done in the name of Christ, whatsoever you do in the Spirit; And ye must give thanks unto God in the Spirit for whatsoever blessing ye are blessed with. D&C 46:31-32

LORD, thou hast searched me, and known me. Thou knowest my downsitting and mine uprising, thou understandest my thought afar off. Thou compassest my path and my lying down, and art acquainted with all my ways. For there is not a word in my tongue, but, lo, O LORD, thou knowest it altogether. Ps. 139:1-5

Believe in God; believe that he is, and that he created all things, both in heaven and in earth; believe that he has all wisdom, and all power, both in heaven and in earth; believe that man doth not comprehend all the things which the Lord can comprehend. Mosiah 4:9

The things which are impossible with men are possible with God. Luke 18:27

Receive the Holy Ghost, that ye may have all things made manifest. Moses 8:24

According as his divine power hath given unto us all things that pertain unto life and godliness, through the knowledge of him that hath called us to glory and virtue: Whereby we are given unto us exceeding great and precious promises: that by these ye might be partakers of the divine nature, having escaped the corruption that is in the world through lust. 2 Pet. 1:3-4

Teach ye diligently and my grace shall attend you, that you may be instructed more perfectly in theory, in principle, in doctrine, in the law of the gospel, in all things that pertain unto the kingdom of God, that are expedient for you to understand. D&C 88:78

The woman saith unto him, I know that Messias cometh, which is called Christ: when he is come, he will tell us all things. John 4:25

**ALLOT, ALLOTTED,
ALLOTMENT**

I ought to be content with the things which the Lord hath allotted unto me. Alma 29:3

ALMS, ALMSGIVING

Cornelius, a centurion of the band called the Italian band, a devout man, and one that feared God with all his house, which gave much alms to the people, and prayed to God alway. Acts 10:2

When thou doest alms let not thy left hand know what thy right hand doeth; That thine alms may be in secret; and thy Father who seeth in secret, himself shall reward thee openly. 3 Ne. 13:3-4

ALPHA

I am Alpha and Omega, the beginning and the ending, saith the Lord, which is, and which was, and which is to come, the Almighty. Rev. 1:8

ALWAYS

What I say unto one I say unto all; pray always lest that wicked one have power in you, and remove you out of your place. D&C 93:49

Pray always and I will pour out my Spirit upon, and great shall be your blessing - yea, even more than if you should obtain treasures of earth and corruptibleness to the extent thereof. D&C 19:38

Men ought always to pray, and not to faint. Luke 18:1

AMBASSADOR

A wicked messenger falleth into mischief: but a faithful ambassador is health. Prov. 13:17

AMEND

Thus saith the LORD of hosts, the God of Israel, Amend your ways and your doings, and I will cause you to dwell in this place. Jer. 7:3

ANGEL

When we cried unto the LORD, he heard our voice, and sent an angel. Num. 20:16

Be not forgetful to entertain strangers: for thereby some have entertained angels unawares. Heb. 13:2

Let no man beguile you of your reward in a voluntary humility and worshiping of angels, intruding into those things which he hath not seen, vainly puffed up by his fleshly mind. Col. 2:18

Blessed be the God of Shadrach, Meshach, and Abed-nego, who hath sent his angel, and delivered his servants that trusted in him, and have changed the king's word, and yielded their bodies, that they might not serve nor worship any god, except their own God. Dan. 3:28

I saw another sign in heaven, great and marvellous, seven angels having the seven last plagues; for in them is filled up the wrath of God. Rev. 15:1

It is by faith that miracles are wrought; and it is by faith that angels appear and minister unto men; wherefore if these things have ceased wo be unto the children of men, for it is because of unbelief, and all is vain. Moro. 7:37

ANGER, ANGRY

He that is slow to anger is better than the mighty; and he that ruleth his spirit than he that taketh a city. Prov. 16:32

Do [no] evil in the sight of the LORD, to provoke him to anger. 2 Kgs. 17:17

Wherefore, we would to God that we could persuade all men not to rebel against God, to provoke him to anger, but that all men would believe in Christ, and view his death, and suffer his cross and bear the shame of the world. Jacob 1:8

Cease from anger, and forsake wrath: fret not thyself in any wise to do evil. Ps. 37:8

Make no friendship with an angry man; and with a furious man thou shalt not go: Lest thou learn his ways, and get a snare to thy soul. Prov. 22:24-25

Whosoever is angry with his brother without a cause shall be in danger of the judgment: and whosoever shall say to his brother, Raca, shall be in danger of the council: but whosoever shall say, Thou fool, shall be in danger of hell fire. Matt. 5:22

A gift in secret pacifieth anger: and a reward in the bosom strong wrath. Prov. 21:14

Be ye angry, and sin not: let not the sun go down upon your wrath: Neither give place to the devil. Eph. 4:26

Be not hasty in thy spirit to be angry: for anger resteth in the bosom of fools. Eccl. 7:9

Behold, this is not my doctrine, to stir up the hearts of men with anger, one against another; but this is my doctrine, that such things should be done away. 3 Ne. 11:30

He wrought much wickedness in the sight of the LORD, to provoke him to anger. 2 Kgs. 21:6

ANOINT, ANOINTING

Is any sick among you? let him call for the elders of the church; and let them pray over him, anointing him with oil in the name of the Lord: And the prayer of faith shall save the sick, and the Lord shall raise him up; and if he have committed sins, they shall be forgiven him. James 5:14-15

ANSWER

A man hath joy by the answer of his mouth: and a word spoken in due season, how good is it. Prov. 15:23

Sanctify the Lord God in your heats; and be ready always to give an answer to every man that asketh you a reason of the hope that is in you with meekness and fear: Having a good conscience; that, whereas they speak evil of you, as of evildoers, they may be ashamed that falsely accuse your good conversation in Christ. 1 Pet. 3:15-16

Answer not a fool according to his folly, lest thou also be like unto him. Answer a fool according to his folly, lest he be wise in his own conceit. Prov. 26:4-5

He that answereth a matter before he heareth it, it is folly and shame unto him. Prov. 18:13

I will make there an altar unto God, who answered me in the day of my distress, and was with me in the way which I went. Gen. 35:3

A SOFT answer turneth away wrath: but grievous words stir up anger. Prov. 15:1

The heart of the righteous studieth to answer: but the mouth of the wicked poureth out evil things. Prov. 15:28

The Son of God shall come in his glory; and his glory shall be the glory of the Only Begotten of the Father, full of grace, equity, and truth, full of patience, mercy, and long-suffering, quick to hear the cries of his people and to answer their prayers. Alma 9:26

APOSTASY

Let no man deceive you by any means: for that day shall not come, except there come a falling away first, and that man of sin be revealed, the son of perdition; who opposeth and exalteth himself above all that is called God, or that is worshiped; so that he as God sitteth in the temple of God, shewing himself that he is God. 2 Thes. 2:3-4

APOSTLE

Ye are no more strangers and foreigners, but fellowcitizens with the saints, and of the household of God; And are built upon the foundation of the apostles and prophets, Jesus Christ himself being the chief corner stone. Eph. 2:19-20

And he gave some, apostles; and some, prophets; and some, evangelists; and some, pastors and teachers; For the perfecting of the saints, for the work of the ministry, for the edifying of the body of Christ: Till we all come in the unity of the faith, and of the knowledge of the Son of God, unto a perfect man, unto the measure of the stature of the fulness of Christ. Eph. 4:11-13

The arm of the Lord shall be revealed; and the day cometh that they who will not hear the voice of the Lord, neither the voice of his servants, neither give heed to the words of the prophets and apostles, shall be cut off from among the people. D&C 1:14

APPAREL

In like manner also, that women adorn themselves in modest apparel, with shamefacedness and sobriety; not with broided hair, or gold, or pearls, or costly array; but (which becometh women professing godliness) with good works. 1 Tim. 2:9-10

Ye are lifted up in the pride of your hearts, and wear stiff necks and high heads because of the costliness of your apparel, and persecute your brethren because ye suppose that ye are better than they. Jacob 2:13

APPEAR, APPEARANCE, APPEARING

Do ye look on things after the outward appearance? 2 Cor. 10:7

When the chief Shepherd shall appear, ye shall receive a crown of glory that fadeth not away. 1 Pet. 5:4

When thou fasteth, anoint thine head, and wash thy face; That thou appear not unto men to fast, but unto thy Father which is in secret; and thy Father, which seeth in secret, shall reward thee openly. Matt. 6:17-18

Judge not according to the appearance, but judge righteous judgment. John 7:24

We must all appear before the judgment seat of Christ; that every one may receive the things done in his body, according to that he hath done, whether it be good or bad. 2 Cor. 5:10

Abstain from all appearance of evil. 1 Thes. 5:22

APPETITE

When thou sittest to eat with a ruler, consider diligently what is before thee: And put a knife to thy throat, if thou be a man given to appetite. Prov. 23:1-2

APPLY

I applied mine heart to know, and to search, and to seek out wisdom, and the reason of things, and to know the wickedness of folly, even of foolishness and madness. Eccl. 7:25

Incline thine ear unto wisdom, and apply thine heart to understanding. Prov. 2:2

APPOINT, APPOINTMENT

[Appoint] just men to be their teachers. Mosiah 2:4

Exact no more than that which is appointed you. Luke 3:13

APPROACH

They seek me daily, and delight to know my ways, as a nation that did righteousness, and forsook not the ordinance of their God: they ask of me the ordinances of justice; they take delight in approaching to God. Isa. 58:2

APPROVE, APPROVED

Approve things that are excellent; that ye may be sincere and without offense till the day of Christ. Philip. 1:10

Study to shew thyself approved unto God, a workman that needeth not to be ashamed, rightly dividing the word of truth. 2 Tim. 2:15

ARISE

Arise, shine; for thy light is come, and the glory of the LORD is risen upon thee. Isa. 60:1

Arise ye, and let us go up to Zion unto the LORD our God. Jer. 31:6

ARMOR

Awake, my sons; put on the armor of righteousness. Shake off the chains with which ye are bound, and come forth out of obscurity, and arise from the dust. 2 Ne. 1:23

Gird up your loins, and take upon you my whole armor. D&C 27:15-18

Let us therefore cast off the works of darkness, and let us put on the armor of light. Rom. 13:12

AROUSE

Awake and arouse your faculties, even to an experiment upon my words. Alma 32:27

ARROGANCE, ARROGANCY, ARROGANT

I will cause the arrogancy of the proud to cease. 2 Ne. 23:11

The fear of the LORD is to hate evil: pride, and arrogancy, and the evil way, and the froward mouth, do I hate. Prov. 8:13

ASCRIBE

Ascribe ye strength unto God; his excellency is over Israel, and his strength is in the clouds. Ps. 68:34

ASHAMED

Were they ashamed when they had committed abominations? nay, they were not at all ashamed, neither could they blush: therefore they shall fall among them that fall: at the time that I visit them they shall be cast down, saith the LORD. Jer. 6:15

Be not thou therefore ashamed of the testimony of our Lord. 2 Tim. 1:8

I will speak of thy testimonies also before kings, and will not be ashamed. Ps. 119:46

O my God, I trust in thee: let me not be ashamed, let not mine enemies triumph over me. Yea, let none that wait on thee be ashamed: let them be ashamed which transgress without cause Ps. 25:2

Thou shalt know that I am the Lord; for they shall not be ashamed that wait for me. 1 Ne. 21:23

Whosoever shall be ashamed of me and of my words, of him shall the Son of man be ashamed, when he shall come in his own glory, and in his Father's, and of the holy angels. Luke 9:26

ASK

If any of you lack wisdom, let him ask of God, that giveth to all men liberally, and upbraideth not; and it shall be given him. But let him ask in faith, nothing wavering. For he that wavereth is like a wave of the sea driven with the wind and tossed. James 1:5-6

Thus saith the LORD, the Holy One of Israel, and his Maker, Ask me of things to come concerning my sons, and concerning the work of my hands command ye me. Isa. 45:11

Ye ask, and receive not, because ye ask amiss, that ye may consume it upon your lusts. James 4:3

They shall ask the way to Zion with their faces thitherward, , Come, and let us join ourselves to the LORD in a perpetual covenant that shall not be forgotten. Jer. 50:5

Ask, and it shall be given you; seek, and ye shall find; knock, and it shall be opened unto you. Luke 11:9

Draw near unto me and I will draw near unto you; seek me diligently and ye shall find me; ask, and ye shall receive; knock, and it shall be opened unto you. D&C 88:63

Thou shalt not ask that which is contrary to my will. Hel. 10:5
Whatsoever thing ye shall ask in faith, believing that ye shall receive in the name of Christ, ye shall receive it. Enos 1:15

By the power of the Holy Ghost ye may know the truth of all things. Moro. 10:4-5

ASSEMBLE, ASSEMBLIES

Come ye near unto me, hear ye this; I have not spoken in secret from the beginning; from the time that it was, there I: and now the Lord GOD, and his Spirit, hath sent me. Isa. 48:16

If two of you shall agree on earth as touching any thing that they shall ask, it shall be done for them of my Father which is in heaven. For where two or three are gathered together in my name, there am I in the midst of them. Matt. 18:19-20

ASSURANCE, ASSURE

Let us draw near with a true heart in full assurance of faith, having our hearts sprinkled from an evil conscience, and our bodies washed with pure water. Heb. 10:22

Let us cheerfully do all things that lie in our power; and then may we stand still, with the utmost assurance, to see the salvation of God, and for his arm to be revealed. D&C 123:17

Let all the house of Israel know assuredly, that God hath made that same Jesus, whom ye have crucified, both Lord and Christ. Acts 2:36

ASTRAY

Whoso causeth the righteous to go astray in an evil way, he shall fall himself into his own pit; but the upright shall have good things in possession. Prov. 28:10

ASTROLOGER, ASTROLOGY

Now the wise men, the astrologers, have been brought in before me, that they should read this writing, and make known unto me the interpretation thereof: but they could not shew the interpretation of the thing. Dan 5:15

ATONE, ATONEMENT

We believe that through the Atonement of Christ, all mankind may be saved, by obedience to the laws and ordinances of the Gospel. A of F-3

He cometh into the world that he may save all men if they will hearken unto his voice; for behold, he suffereth the pains of all men, yea, the pains of every living creature, both men, women, and children, who belong to the family of Adam. 2 Ne. 9:21

Ye shall have hope through the atonement of Christ and the power of his resurrection. Moro. 7:41

Believe in Christ and worship the Father in his name, with pure hearts and clean hands, and look not forward any more for another Messiah. 2 Ne. 25:16

Marvel not that I tell you these things; for why not speak of the atonement of Christ, and attain to a perfect knowledge of him, as to attain to a perfect knowledge of a resurrection and the world to come? Jacob 4:12

We also joy in God through our Lord Jesus Christ, by whom we have now received the atonement. Rom. 5:11

They all cried aloud with one voice, saying: O have mercy, and apply the atoning blood of Christ that we may receive forgiveness of our sins, and our hearts may be purified; for we believe in Jesus Christ, the Son of God, who created heaven and earth, and all things; who shall come down among the children of men. Mosiah 4:2

The natural man is an enemy to God, and has been from the fall of Adam, and will be, forever and ever, unless he yields to the enticings of the Holy Spirit, and putteth off the natural man and becometh a saint through the atonement of Christ the Lord, and becometh as a child, submissive, meek, humble, patient, full of love, willing to submit to all things which the Lord seeth fit to inflict upon him, even as a child doth submit to his father. Mosiah 3:19

Listen to the voice of Jesus Christ, your Redeemer, the Great I AM, whose arm of mercy hath atoned for your sins; Who will gather his people even as a hen gathereth her chickens under her wings, even as many will hearken to my voice and humble themselves before me, and call upon me in mighty prayer. D&C 29:1

Be reconciled unto him through the atonement of Christ, his Only Begotten Son, and ye may obtain a resurrection, according to the resurrection which is in Christ, and be presented as the first-fruits of Christ unto God, having faith, and obtained a good hope of glory in him before he manifesteth himself in the flesh. Jacob 4:11

Remember that there is no other way nor means whereby man can be saved, only through the atoning blood of Jesus Christ, who shall come. Hel. 5:9

Through his atonement and by obedience to the principles of the gospel, mankind might be saved. D&C 138:4

ATTEND

My son, attend to my words; incline thine ear unto my sayings. Let them not depart from thine eyes; keep them in the midst of thine heart. For they are life unto those that find them, and health to all their flesh. Prov. 4:20-22

AUTHOR

God is not the author of confusion, but of peace, as in all churches of the saints. 1 Cor. 14:33

[Look] unto Jesus the author and finisher of our faith; who for the joy that was set before him endured the cross, despising the shame, and is set down at the right hand of the throne of God. Heb. 12:2

AUTHORITY

When the righteous are in authority, the people rejoice: but when the wicked beareth rule, the people mourn. Prov. 29:2

By what authority doest thou these things? and who gave thee this authority to do these things? And Jesus answered and said unto them, I will also ask of you one question, and answer me, and I will tell you by what authority I do these things. Mark 11:28

We have learned by sad experience that it is the nature and disposition of almost all men, as soon as they get a little authority, as they suppose, they will immediately begin to exercise unrighteous dominion. D&C 121:39

He called his twelve disciples together, and gave them power and authority over all devils, and to cure diseases. And he sent them to preach the kingdom of God, and to heal the sick. Luke 9:1-2

Therefore leaving the principles of the doctrine of Christ, let us go on unto perfection; not laying again the foundation of repentance from dead works, and of faith toward God, Of the doctrine of baptisms, and of laying on of hands, and of resurrection of the dead, and of eternal judgment. Heb. 6:1-2

Paul, being grieved, turned and said to the spirit, I command thee in the name of Jesus Christ to come out of her. And he came out the same hour. Acts 16:18

AVENGE

Thou shalt not avenge, nor bear any grudge against the children of thy people, but thou shalt love thy neighbour as thyself: I the LORD. Lev. 19:18

AVOID

Avoid foolish questions, and genealogies, and contentions, and strivings about the law; for they are unprofitable and vain. Titus 3:9

Enter not into the paths of the wicked, and go not in the way of evil men. Avoid it, pass not by it, turn from it, and pass away. Prov. 4:14-15

AWAKE, AWAKEN

Awake my soul! No longer droop in sin. Rejoice, O my heart, and give place no more for the enemy of my soul. 2 Ne. 4:28

Awake and arouse your faculties, even to an experiment upon my words. Alma 32:27

Awake to a remembrance of the awful situation of those that have fallen into transgression. Mosiah 2:40

Awake, my sons; put on the armor of righteousness. Shake off the chains with which ye are bound, and come forth out of obscurity, and arise from the dust. 2 Ne. 1:23

Awake, awake, put on thy strength, O Zion; put on thy beautiful garments, O Jerusalem, the holy city: for henceforth there shall no more come into thee the uncircumcised and the unclean. Shake thyself from the dust; arise, sit down, O Jerusalem; loose thyself from the bands of thy neck, O captive daughter of Zion. 2 Ne. 8:24-25 (Isa. 52:1-2)

Awake thou that sleepest, and arise from the dead, and Christ shall give thee light. Eph. 5:14

Awake, awake; put on thy strength, O Zion; put on thy beautiful garments, O Jerusalem, the holy city. Isa. 52:1

AWFUL, AWFULNESS

Remember the awfulness in transgressing against that Holy God, and also the awfulness of yielding to the enticings of that cunning one. 2 Ne. 9:39

BABBLE, BABBLING

Keep that which is committed to thy trust, avoiding profane and vain babblings, and oppositions of science falsely called: Which some professing have erred concerning the faith. 1 Tim. 6:20

BABYLON

Go ye out from Babylon. Be ye clean that bear the vessels of the Lord. D&C 133:5

BACKBITE, BACKBITING

He that backbiteth not with his tongue, nor doeth evil to his neighbour, nor taketh up a reproach against his neighbour [shall abide in thy tabernacle]. Ps. 15:3

BAD

For it must needs be, that there is an opposition in all things. If not so, my first-born in the wilderness, righteousness could not be brought to pass, neither wickedness, neither holiness nor misery, neither good nor bad. 2 Ne. 2:11

We must all appear before the judgment seat of Christ; that every one may receive the things done in his body, according to that he hath done, whether it be good or bad. 2 Cor. 5:10

BALANCE

A false balance is abomination to the LORD: but a just weight is his delight. Prov. 11:1

BAPTISM, BAPTIZE

Enter ye in at the strait gate: for wide is the gate, and broad is the way, that leadeth to destruction, and many there be which go in thereat: Because strait is the gate, and narrow is the way, which leadeth unto life, and few there be that find it. Matt. 7:13-14

What have you against being baptized in the name of the Lord, as a witness before him that ye have entered into a covenant with him? Mosiah 18:10

Repent, all ye ends of the earth, and come unto me and be baptized in my name, that ye may be sanctified by the reception of the Holy Ghost, that ye may stand spotless before me at the last day. 3 Ne. 27:20

Repent and be baptized in the name of Jesus Christ, according to the holy commandment, for the remission of sins. D&C 49:13

Repent, and be baptized every one of you in the name of Jesus Christ for the remission of sins, and ye shall receive the gift of the Holy Ghost. Acts 2:38

BATTLE

The horse is prepared against the day of battle; but safety is of the LORD. Prov. 21:31

BE

I would that ye would be diligent and temperate in all things. Alma 38:10

Be sober. D&C 6:19

Be ye therefore wise as serpents and harmless as doves. Matt. 10:16

Be wise; what can I say more. Jacob 6:12

Be a just man before the Lord. Omni 1:25

Be men, and be determined in one mind and in one heart, united in all things. 2 Ne. 1:21

Be not among winebibbers; among riotous eaters of flesh: for the drunkard and the glutton shall come to poverty: and drowsiness shall clothe a man with rags. Prov. 23:20-21

Be ye not as the horse, or as the mule, which have no understanding: whose mouth must be held in with bit and bridle, lest they come near unto thee. Ps. 32:9

BEAR, BORE, BORNE

They bore with patience the persecution which was heaped upon them. Alma 1:25

Charity suffereth long, and is kind, and envieth not, and is not puffed up, seeketh not her own, is not easily provoked, thinketh no evil, and rejoiceth not in iniquity but rejoiceth in the truth, beareth all things, believeth all things, hopeth all things, endureth all things. Moro. 7:45 45 (1 Cor. 13:4-13)

There hath no temptation taken you but such as is common to man: but God is faithful, who will not suffer you to be tempted above that ye are able; but will with the temptation also make a way to escape, that ye may be able to bear it. 1 Cor. 10:13

Have patience, and bear with those afflictions, with a firm hope that ye shall one day rest from all your afflictions. Alma 34:41

I will bear the indignation of the LORD, because I have sinned against him, until he plead my cause, and execute judgment for me: he will bring me forth to the light, and I shall behold his righteousness. Micah 7:9-10

Bear record according to the truth which is in the Lamb of God. 1 Ne. 13:24

BEAST

A righteous man regardeth the life of his beast: but the tender mercies of the wicked are cruel. Prov. 12:10

BEAUTIFUL, BEAUTIFY, BEAUTY

How beautiful are they to the eyes of them who there came to the knowledge of their Redeemer; yea, and how blessed are they, for they shall sing to his praise forever. Mosiah 18:30

Thine heart was lifted up because of thy beauty, thou hast corrupted thy wisdom by reason of thy brightness: I will cast thee to the ground. Ezek. 28:17

How beautiful upon the mountains are the feet of him that bringeth good tidings, that publisheth peace; that bringeth good tidings of good, that publisheth salvation; that saith unto Zion, Thy God reigneth! Isa. 52:7

Give unto the LORD the glory due unto his name: bring an offering, and come before him: worship the LORD in the beauty of holiness. 1 Chron. 16:29

Beautify the house of the LORD which is in Jerusalem. Ezra 7:27

BECOME

Become friendly to one another. Mosiah 28:2

Though I speak with the tongues of men and of angels, and have not charity, I am become as sounding brass, or a tinkling cymbal. 1 Cor. 13:1

Moreover, thou son of man, take thee one stick, and write upon it, For Judah, and for the children of Israel his companions: then take another stick, and write upon it For Joseph, the stick of Ephraim, and for all the house of Israel his companions: And join them one to another into one stick; and they shall become one in thine hand. Ezek. 37:16-17

The natural man is an enemy to God, and has been from the fall of Adam, and will be, forever and ever, unless he yields to the enticings of the Holy Spirit, and putteth off the natural man and becometh a saint through the atonement of Christ the Lord, and becometh as a child, submissive, meek, humble, patient, full of love, willing to submit to all things which the Lord seeth fit to inflict upon him, even as a child doth submit to his father. Mosiah 3:19

Let your conversation be as it becometh the gospel of Christ: that whether I come and see you, or else be absent, I may hear of your affairs, that ye stand fast in one spirit, with one mind striving together for the faith of the gospel. Philip. 1:27

Except ye be converted, and become as little children, ye shall not enter into the kingdom of heaven. Matt. 18:3

BEG, BEGGAR

Succor those that stand in need of your succor; ye will administer of your substance unto him that standeth in need; and ye will not suffer that the beggar putteth up his petition to you in vain, and turn him out to perish. Mosiah 4:16

BEGAT, BEGET, BEGOTTEN

For God so loved the world, that he gave his only begotten Son, that whosoever believeth in him should not perish, but have everlasting life. John 3:16

Grace be unto you, and peace, from him which is, and which was, and which is to come; and from the seven Spirits which are before his throne; And from Jesus Christ, who is the faithful witness, and the first begotten of the dead, and the prince of the kings of the earth. Unto him that loved us, and washed us from our sins in his own blood, And hath made us kings and priests unto God and his Father; to him be glory and dominion for ever and ever. Rev. 1:4-6

BEGIN, BEGINNING

We have learned by sad experience that it is the nature and disposition of almost all men, as soon as they get a little authority, as they suppose, they will immediately begin to exercise unrighteous dominion. D&C 121:39

The fear of the LORD is the beginning of knowledge: but fools despise wisdom and instruction. Prov. 1:7

In the beginning was the Word, and the Word was with God, and the Word was God. John 1:1

BEGUILE

Let no man beguile you of your reward in a voluntary humility and worshiping of angels, intruding into those things which he hath not seen, vainly puffed up by his fleshly mind. Col. 2:18

BEHAVE, BEHAVIOR

Thou oughtest to behave thyself in the house of God, which is the church of the living God, the pillar and ground of the truth. 1 Tim. 3:15

What manner of men ought ye to be? Verily, I say unto you, even as I am. 3 Ne. 27:27

Be of good courage, and let us behave ourselves valiantly for our people, and for the cities of our God: and let the LORD do that which is good in his sight. 1 Chron. 19:13

BELIEF, BELIEVE

I have fasted and prayed many days that I might know these things of myself. Alma 5:46

God hath from the beginning chosen you to salvation through sanctification of the Spirit and belief of the truth. 2 Thes. 2:13

Be not afraid, only believe. Mark 5:36

But without faith it is impossible to please him: for he that cometh to God must believe that he is, and that he is a rewarder of them that diligently seek him. Heb. 11:6

Behold, I say unto you that whoso believeth in Christ, doubting nothing, whatsoever he shall ask the Father in the name of Christ it shall be granted him; and this promise is unto all, even unto the ends of the earth. Morm. 9:21

Believest thou the prophets? Acts 26:27

Trust in the living God, who is the Saviour of all men, specially of those that believe. 1 Tim. 4:10

Charity suffereth long, and is kind, and envieth not, and is not puffed up, seeketh not her own, is not easily provoked, thinketh no evil, and rejoiceth not in iniquity but rejoiceth in the truth, beareth all things, believeth all things, hopeth all things, endureth all things. Moro. 7:45 45 (1 Cor. 13:4-13)

When therefore he was risen from the dead, his disciples remembered that he had said this unto them; and they believed the scripture, and the word which Jesus had said. John 2:22

The gate of heaven is open unto all, even to those who will believe on the name of Jesus Christ, who is the son of God. Hel. 3:28

Teach any man the right way; for the right way is to believe in Christ and deny him not; for by denying him ye also deny the prophets and the law. 2 Ne. 25:28

He is the same yesterday, to-day, and forever; and the way is prepared for all men from the foundation of the world. 1 Ne. 10:18

Believe that salvation was, and is, and is to come, in and through the atoning blood of Christ, the Lord Omnipotent. Mosiah 3:18

Ye have not come thus far save it were by the word of Christ with unshaken faith in him, relying wholly upon the merits of him who is mighty to save. 2 Ne. 31:19

Wherefore, we would to God that we could persuade all men not to rebel against God, to provoke him to anger, but that all men would believe in Christ, and view his death, and suffer his cross and bear the shame of the world. Jacob 1:8

Many other signs truly did Jesus in the presence of his disciples, which are not written in this book: But these are written, that ye might believe that Jesus is the Christ, the Son of God; and that believing ye might have life through his name. John 20:30-31

We will not serve thy gods, nor worship the golden image which thou hast set up. Dan. 3:18

I know that thou canst do every thing, and that no thought can be withholden from thee. Job 42:2

Where be all his miracles which our fathers told us? Judg. 6:13

The simple believeth every word: but the prudent man looketh well to his going. Prov. 14:15

Let no man despise thy youth; but be thou an example of the believers, in word, in conversation, in charity, in spirit, in faith, in purity. 1 Tim. 4:12

All those who were true believers in Christ took upon them, gladly, the name of Christ. Alma 46:15

Believe in Christ and worship the Father in his name, with pure hearts and clean hands, and look not forward any more for another Messiah. 2 Ne. 25:16

O then despise not, and wonder not, but hearken unto the words of the Lord, and ask the Father in the name of Jesus for what things soever ye shall stand in need. Doubt not, but be believing, and begin as in times of old, and come unto the Lord with all your heart, and work out your own salvation with fear and trembling before him. Morm. 9:27

All those who shall believe on his name shall be saved in the kingdom of God. 2 Ne. 25:13

Believest thou in the power of Christ unto salvation? Alma 15:6

Believe in Christ and worship the Father in his name, with pure hearts and clean hands, and look not forward any more for another Messiah. 2 Ne. 25:16

Believe in God; believe that he is, and that he created all things, both in heaven and in earth; believe that he has all wisdom, and all power, both in heaven and in earth; believe that man doth not comprehend all the things which the Lord can comprehend. Mosiah 4:9

Search diligently, pray always, and be believing, and all things shall work together for your good. D&C 90:24

For what knowest thou, O wife, whether thou shalt save thy husband? or how knowest thou, O man, whether thou shalt save thy wife? 1 Cor. 7:16

These are written, that ye might believe that Jesus is the Christ, the Son of God; and that believing ye might have life through his name. John 20:31

Believeth all things. 1 Cor. 13:7

He staggered not at the promise of God through unbelief; but was strong in faith, giving glory to God; And being fully persuaded that, what he had promised, he was able also to perform. And therefore it was imputed to him for righteousness. Rom. 4:20-22

Believe in the Lord your God, so shall ye be established; believe his prophets, so shall ye prosper. 2 Chron. 20:20

If ye will not believe, surely ye shall not be established. Isa. 7:9

Say not, I am a child: for thou shalt go to all that I shall send thee, and whatsoever I command thee thou shalt speak. Be not afraid of their faces: for I am with thee to deliver thee, saith the LORD. Jer. 1:7-8

When I speak with thee, I will open thy mouth, and thou shalt say unto them, Thus saith the Lord GOD; He that heareth, let him hear; and he that forbeareth, let him forbear. Ezek. 3:27

BENEFIT

He doeth not anything save it be for the benefit of the world; for he loveth the world, even that he layeth down his own life that he may draw all men unto him. 2 Ne. 26:24

BESEECH, BESOUGHT

Beseech God that he will be gracious unto us. Mal. 1:9

BESET

Seeing we also are compassed about with so great a cloud of witnesses, let us lay aside every weight, and the sin which doth so easily beset us, and let us run with patience the race that is set before us. Heb. 12:1

Come and fear not, and lay aside every sin, which easily doth beset you, which doth bind you down to destruction. Alma 7:15

BEST

But covet earnestly the best gifts: and yet shew I unto you a more excellent way. 1 Cor. 12:31

BESTOW

Though I bestow all my goods to feed the poor, an though I give my body to be burned, and have not charity, it profiteth me nothing. 1 Cor. 13:3

BETRAY, BETRAYAL

All these are the beginning of sorrows. Then shall they deliver you up to be afflicted, and shall kill you: and ye shall be hated of all nations for my name's sake. And then shall many be offended, and shall betray one another, and shall hate one another. Matt. 24:8-10

BETTER

Thine own friend, and thy father's friend, forsake not; neither go into thy brother's house in the day of thy calamity: for better is a neighbour is near than a brother far off. Prov. 27:10

Say not thou, What is the cause that the former days were better than these? Eccl. 7:10

He that is slow to anger is better than the mighty; and he that ruleth his spirit than he that taketh a city. Prov. 16:32

It were better for him that a millstone were hanged about his neck, and he cast into the sea, than that he should offend one of these little ones. Luke 17:2

Choose the things that please me, and take hold of my covenant; Even unto them will I give in mine house and within my walls a place and a name better than of sons and of daughters. Isa. 56:4-5

It is better to dwell in the wilderness, than with a contentious and an angry woman. Prov. 21:19

It is better to hear the rebuke of the wise, than for a man to hear the song of fools. Eccl. 7:5

Wherefore if thy hand or thy foot offend thee, cut them off, and cast them from thee: it is better for thee to enter into life halt or maimed, rather than having two hands or two feet to be cast into everlasting fire. Matt. 18:8

It is better that thy soul should be lost than that thou shouldst be the means of bringing many souls down to destruction, by thy lying and by thy flattering words; therefore if thou shalt deny again, behold God shall smite thee, that thou shalt become dumb, that thou shalt never open thy mouth any more, that thou shalt not deceive this people any more. Alma 30:47

Let nothing be done through strife or vainglory; but in lowliness of mind let each esteem other better than themselves. Philip. 2:3

For wisdom is better than rubies; and all the things that may be desired are not to be compared to it. Prov. 8:11

If after they have escaped the pollutions of the world through the knowledge of the Lord and Savior Jesus Christ, they are again entangled therein, and overcome, the latter end is worse with them than the beginning. For it had been better for them not to have known the way of righteousness, than, after they have known it, to turn from the holy commandment delivered unto them. But it is happened unto them according to the true proverb, The dog is turned to his own vomit again; and the sow that was washed to her wallowing in the mire. 2 Pet. 2:20-22

BEWARE

Beware of pride. D&C 23:1

Beware of false prophets, who come to you in sheep's clothing, but inwardly they are ravening wolves. Ye shall know them by their fruits. 3 Ne. 14:15-20 (Matt. 7:15)

BIBLE

Moreover, thou son of man, take thee one stick, and write upon it, For Judah, and for the children of Israel his companions: then take another stick, and write upon it For Joseph, the stick of Ephraim, and for all the house of Israel his companions: And join them one to another into one stick; and they shall become one in thine hand. Ezek. 37:16-17

BIND, BOUND, BOUNDS

Let not mercy and truth forsake thee: bind them about thy neck: write them upon the table of thine heart; So shalt thou find favour and good understanding in the sight of God and man. Prov. 3:3-4

BISHOP, BISHOPRIC

A bishop then must be blameless, the husband of one wife, vigilant, sober, of good behaviour, given to hospitality, apt to teach. 1 Tim. 3:2

BITTER, BITTERNESS

The heart knoweth his own bitterness; and a stranger doth not intermeddle with his joy. Prov. 14:10

BLASPHEME, BLASPHEMOUS, BLASPHEMY

They profaned not; neither did they blaspheme Jarom 1:5

He that shall blaspheme against the Holy Ghost hath never forgiveness, but is in danger of eternal damnation. Mark 3:29

Do not they blaspheme that worthy name by the which ye are called? James 2:7

BLESS, BLESSED, BLESSING

Remember the Lord your God in the things with which he hath blessed you. Hel. 13:22

Blessed are they that keep judgment, and he that doeth righteousness at all times. Ps. 106:3

If thou shalt hearken diligently unto the voice of the LORD thy God, to observe and to do all his commandments which I command thee this day, that the LORD thy God will sit thee on high above all nations of the earth; And all these blessings shall come on thee, and overtake thee, if thou shalt hearken unto the voice of the LORD thy God. Deut. 28:1-2

The blessing of the LORD be upon you: we bless you in the name of the LORD. Ps. 129:8

Take upon you the name of Christ; that ye humble yourselves even to the dust, and worship God, in whatsoever place ye may be in, in spirit and in truth; and that ye live in thanksgiving daily, for the many mercies and blessings which he doth bestow upon you. Alma 34:38

Now bless the LORD your God. 1 Chron. 29:20

BLIND, BLINDNESS

He that hateth his brother is in darkness, and walketh in darkness, and knoweth not whither he goeth, because that darkness hath blinded his eyes. 1 Jn. 2:11

BLOOD, BLOODSHED

Shed not innocent blood. Jer. 7:6

And he took the cup, and gave thanks, and gave it to them, saying, Drink ye all of it; For this is my blood of the new testament, which is shed for many for the remission of sins. Matt. 26:28

Grace be unto you, and peace, from him which is, and which was, and which is to come; and from the seven Spirits which are before his throne; And from Jesus Christ, who is the faithful witness, and the first begotten of the dead, and the prince of the kings of the earth. Unto him that loved us, and washed us from our sins in his own blood, And hath made us kings and priests unto God and his Father; to him be glory and dominion for ever and ever. Rev. 1:4-6

Have ye walked, keeping yourselves blame-less before God? Could ye say, if ye were called to die at this time, within yourselves, that ye have been sufficiently humble? That your garments have been cleansed and made white through the blood of Christ, who will come to redeem his people from their sins? Behold, are ye stripped of pride? I say unto you, if ye are not ye are not prepared to meet God. Alma 5:27-31

Almost all things are by the law purged with blood; and without shedding of blood is no remission. Heb. 9:22

Therefore also said the wisdom of God, I will send them prophets and apostles, and some of them they shall slay and persecute: That the blood of all the prophets, which was shed from the foundation of the world, may be required of this generation. Luke 11:49-50

Wo be unto man that sheddeth blood or that wasteth flesh and hath no need. D&C 49:21

Commit no murder whereby to shed innocent blood. D&C 132:19

BOAST, BOASTING

In God we boast all the day long, and praise thy name for ever. Ps. 44:8

Let another man praise thee, and not thine own mouth; a stranger, and not thine own lips. Prov. 27:2

They that trust in their wealth, and boast themselves in the multitude of their riches; None of them can by any means redeem his brother. Ps. 49:6-7

See that ye do not boast in your own wisdom, nor of your much strength. Alma 38:11

Now ye rejoice in your boastings: all such rejoicing is evil. James 4:16

Whoso boasteth himself of a false gift clouds and wind without rain. Prov. 25:14

Boast not thyself of tomorrow; for thou knowest not what a day may bring forth. Prov. 27:1

With your mouth ye have boasted against me, and have multiplied your words against me: I have heard . Thus saith the Lord GOD; When the whole earth rejoiceth, I will make thee desolate. Ezek. 35:13-14

BODY

I keep under my body, and bring it into subjection: lest that by any means, when I have preached to others, I myself should be a castaway. 1 Cor. 9:27

What? Know ye not that your body is a temple of the Holy Ghost which is in you, which ye have of God, and ye are not your own? For ye are bought with a price: therefore glorify God in your body, and in your spirit, which are God's. 1 Cor. 6:20

If any man offend not in word, the same is a perfect man, and able also to bridle the whole body. James 3:2

We must all appear before the judgment seat of Christ; that every one may receive the things done in his body, according to that he hath done, whether it be good or bad. 2 Cor. 5:10

BOLD, BOLDLY, BOLDNESS

Use boldness, but not overbearance. Alma 38:12

BOND, BONDAGE

Release thyself from bondage. D&C 19:35

After that ye have known God, or rather are known of God, how turn ye again to the weak and beggarly elements, whereunto ye desire again to be in bondage? Gal. 4:9

There is neither Jew nor Greek, there is neither bond nor free, there is neither male nor female: for ye are all one in Christ Jesus. Gal. 3:28

BOOK, BOOKS

This book of the law shall not depart out of thy mouth; but thou shalt meditate therein day and night, that thou mayest observe to do according to all that is written therein: for then thou shalt make thy way prosperous, and then thou shalt have good success. Josh. 1:8

If any man shall take away from the words of the book of this prophecy, God shall take away his part out of the book of life, and out of the holy city, and from the things which are written in this book Rev. 22:19

BORN, BORN AGAIN, BORN OF GOD

Jesus answered, Verily, verily, I say unto thee, Except a man be born of water and of the Spirit, he cannot enter into the kingdom of God. John 3:5

Marvel not that I said unto thee, Ye must be born again. The wind bloweth where it listeth, and thou hearest the sound thereof, but canst not tell whence it cometh, and whither it goeth: so is every one that is born of the Spirit. John 3:7-8

BORROW

I would that ye should remember, that whosoever among you borroweth of his neighbor should return the thing that he borroweth, according as he doth agree. Mosiah 4:28

The rich ruleth over the poor, and the borrower is servant to the lender. Prov. 22:7

The wicked borroweth, and payeth not again: but the righteous sheweth mercy, and giveth. Ps. 37:21

Give to him that asketh thee, and from him that would borrow of thee turn not thou away. Matt. 5:42

BOW

Come, let us worship and bow down: let us kneel before the LORD our maker. Ps. 95:6

Bow down thine ear, and hear the words of the wise, and apply thine heart unto my knowledge. Prov. 22:17

BRASS

Though I speak with the tongues of men and of angels, and have not charity, I am become as sounding brass, or a tinkling cymbal. 1 Cor. 13:1

His head and his hairs were white like wool, as white as snow; and his eyes were as a flame of fire; And his feet like unto fine brass, as if they burned in a furnace; and his voice as the sound of many waters. Rev. 1:15

BREAD

He humbled thee, and suffered thee to hunger, and fed thee with manna, which thou knewest not, neither did thy fathers know; that he might make thee know that man doth not live by bread only, but by every word that proceedeth out of the mouth of the LORD doth man live. Deut. 8:3

Man shall not live by bread alone, but by every word that proceedeth out of the mouth of God. Matt. 4:4

Eateth not the bread of idleness. Prov. 31:27

Jesus took bread, and blessed it, and brake it, and gave it to the disciples, and said, Take, eat; this is my body. Matt 26:26

He that hath a bountiful eye shall be blessed; for he giveth of his bread to the poor. Prov. 22:9

BREAK, BROKEN

The LORD is nigh unto them that are of a broken heart; and saveth such as be of a contrite spirit. Ps. 34:18

BRETHREN, BROTHER

He stretched forth his hand toward his disciples, and said, Behold my mother and my brethren! For whosoever shall do the will of m Father which is in heaven, the same is my brother, and sister, and mother. Matt. 12:49-50

BRIBE, BRIBERY

I know your manifold transgressions and your mighty sins: they afflict the just, they take a bribe, and they turn aside the poor in the gate from their right. Amos 5:12

BRIDLE

See that ye bridle all your passions, that ye may be filled with love. Alma 38:12

If any man offend not in word, the same is a perfect man, and able also to bridle the whole body. James 3:2

BRING, BROUGHT

Hear the word, and receive it, and bring forth fruit. Mark 4:20

I know that if ye are brought up in the way ye should go ye will not depart from it. 2 Ne. 4:5

BROKENHEARTED

The LORD hath anointed me to preach good tidings unto the meek; he hath sent me to bind up the brokenhearted, to proclaim liberty to the captives, and the opening of the prison to them that are bound. Isa. 61:1

BUILD, BUILT

Wo unto all those who tremble, and are angry because of the truth of God! For behold, he that is built upon the rock receiveth it with gladness; and he that is built upon a sandy foundation trembleth lest he shall fall. 2 Ne. 28:28

BURDEN, BURDENSOME

We then that are strong ought to bear the infirmities of the weak, and not to please ourselves. Rom. 15:1

Cast thy burden upon the LORD, and he shall sustain thee: he shall never suffer the righteous to be moved. Ps. 55:22

In all things I have kept myself from being burdensome unto you, and so will I keep myself. 2 Cor. 11:9

BURN

They said one to another, Did not our heart burn within us, while he talked with us by the way, and while he opened to us the scriptures? Luke 24:32

BUSINESS

Now it is not common that the voice of the people desireth anything contrary to that which is right; but it is common for the lesser part of the people to desire that which is not right; therefore this shall ye observe and make it your law - to do business by the voice of the people. Mosiah 29:26

BUSYBODY

But let none of you suffer as a murderer, or as a thief, or as an evildoer, or as a busybody in other men's matters. 1 Pet. 4:15

BUY, BOUGHT

What? Know ye not that your body is a temple of the Holy Ghost which is in you, which ye have of God, and ye are not your own? For ye are bought with a price: therefore glorify God in your body, and in your spirit, which are God's. 1 Cor. 6:20

CALAMITIES, CALAMITY

Thine own friend, and thy father's friend, forsake not; neither go into thy brother's house in the day of thy calamity: for better is a neighbour is near than a brother far off. Prov. 27:10

Whoso mocketh the poor reproacheth his Maker: and he that is glad at calamities shall not be unpunished. Prov. 17:5

CALL, CALLED, CALLING

Be not ye called Rabbi: for one is your Master, Christ; and all ye are brethren. Matt. 23:8

Wo unto them that call evil good, and good evil, that put darkness for light, and light for darkness, that put bitter for sweet, and sweet for bitter. 2 Ne. 15:20

Call unto me, and I will answer thee, and shew thee great and mighty things, which thou knowest not. Jer. 33:3

Ye that is called in the Lord, being a servant is the Lord's freeman: likewise also he that is called, being free, is Christ's servant. Ye are bought with a price; be not ye the servants of men. 1 Cor 7:22-23

Call no man your father upon the earth: for one is your Father which is in heaven. Matt. 23:9

Let him that is ignorant learn wisdom by humbling himself and calling upon the Lord his God, that his eyes may be opened that he may see, and his ears opened that he may hear. D&C 136:32

Thus we may see that the Lord is merciful unto all who will, in the sincerity of their hearts, call upon his holy name. Hel. 3:27

Why should I desire more than to perform the work to which I have been called? Alma 29:6

Fight the good fight of faith, lay hold on eternal life, whereunto thou art also called, and hast professed a good profession before many witnesses. 1 Tim. 6:12

Jesus Christ is the name which is given of the Father, and there is none other name given whereby man can be saved. D&C 18:23

Call upon the name of the LORD, to serve him with one consent. Zeph. 3:9

Whosoever shall call on the name of the Lord shall be saved. Acts 2:21

Therefore leaving the principles of the doctrine of Christ, let us go on unto perfection; not laying again the foundation of repentance from dead works, and of faith toward God, Of the doctrine of baptisms, and of laying on of hands, and of resurrection of the dead, and of eternal judgment. Heb. 6:1-2

Walk worthy of the vocation where-with ye are called. Eph. 4:1

Neither be ye called masters: for one is your Master, Christ. Matt. 23:10

Give thanks unto the LORD, call upon his name, make known his deeds among the people. 1 Chron. 16:8

Praise the LORD, call upon his name, declare his doings among the people, make mention that his name is exalted. Isa. 12:4

Offer unto God thanksgiving; and pay thy vows unto the most High: And call upon me in the day of trouble: I will deliver thee, and thou shalt glorify me. Ps. 50:14-15

Call upon God in the name of mine Only Begotten, and worship me. Moses 1:17

Wherefore, thou shalt do all that thou doest in the name of the Son, and thou shalt repent and call upon God in the name of the Son forevermore. Moses 5:8

In the day of my trouble I will call upon thee: for thou wilt answer me. Ps. 86:7

Take heed to the ministry which thou hast received in the Lord, that thou fulfill it. Col. 4:17

Praise the Lord, call upon his name, declare his doings among the people, make mention that his name is exalted. Sing unto the Lord; for he hath done excellent things; this is known in all the earth. 2 Ne. 22:4-5

CANDLE

No man, when he hath lighted a candle, covereth it with a vessel, or putteth it under a bed; but setteth it on a candlestick, that they which enter in may see the light. Luke 8:16

Let your light so shine before men, that they may see your good works, and glorify your Father which is in heaven. Matt. 5:16

The spirit of man is the candle of the LORD, searching all the inward parts of the belly. Prov. 20:27

CANKER, CANKERED

Your gold and silver is cankered; and the rust of them shall be a witness against you, and shall eat your flesh as it were fire. Ye have heaped treasure together for the last days. James 5:3

CARE, CAREFUL, CAREFULLY

If ye nourish [faith] with much care it will get root, and grow up, and bring forth fruit. Alma 32:37

He that is unmarried careth for the things that belong to the Lord, how he may please the Lord: But he that is married careth for the things that are of the world, how he may please his wife. 1 Cor. 7:32-33

CARELESS

Hear now this, thou that art given to pleasures, that dwellest carelessly, that sayest in thine heart, I am, and none else beside me. Isa. 47:8

CAST

Is it not to deal thy bread to the hungry, and that thou bring the poor that are cast out to thy house? When thou seest the naked, that thou cover him; and that thou hide not thyself from thine own flesh? Isa. 58:7

Cast out the scorner, and contention shall go out; yea, strife and reproach shall cease. Prov. 22:10

These signs shall follow them that believe - in my name shall they cast out devils; they shall speak with new tongues; they shall take up serpents; and if they drink any deadly thing it shall not hurt them; they shall lay hands on the sick and they shall recover. Morm. 9:24 (Mark 16:17-18)

CATCH, CAUGHT

We which are alive and remain shall be caught up together with them in the clouds, to meet the Lord in the air: and so shall we ever be with the Lord. 1 Thes. 4:17

Jesus said unto Simon, Fear not; from henceforth thou shalt catch men. Luke 5:10

CAUSE

Strive not with a man without cause, if he have done thee no harm. Prov. 3:30

Men should be anxiously engaged in a good cause, and do many things of their own free will, and bring to pass much righteousness; For the power is in them, wherein they are agents unto themselves. And inasmuch as men do good they shall in nowise lose their reward. D&C 58:27-28

Let them shout for joy, and be glad, that favour my righteous cause: yea, let them say continually, Let the LORD be magnified, which hath pleasure in the prosperity of his servant. Ps. 35:27

CEASE

Cease from all your light speeches, from all laughter, from all your lustful desires, from all your pride and light-mindedness, and from all your wicked doings. D&C 88:121

Cease to sleep longer than is needful; retire to thy bed early, that ye may not be weary; arise early, that your bodies and your minds may be invigorated. D&C 88:124

CHANGE

Fear thou the LORD and the king: and meddle not with them that are given to change: For their calamity shall rise suddenly; and who knoweth the ruin of them both? Prov. 24:21

If ye have experienced a change of heart, and if ye have felt to sing the song of redeeming love, I would ask, can ye feel so now? Alma 5:26

CHARGE

In all this Job sinned not, nor charged God foolishly. Job 1:22

CHARITY

Remember to be charitable. Alma 34:29

Though I speak with the tongues of men and of angels, and have not charity, I am become as sounding brass, or a tinkling cymbal. 1 Cor. 13:1

Though I bestow all my goods to feed the poor, an though I give my body to be burned, and have not charity, it profiteth me nothing. 1 Cor. 13:3

And above all things have fervent charity among yourselves: for charity shall cover the multitude of sins. 1 Pet 4:8

Let no man despise thy youth; but be thou an example of the believers, in word, in conversation, in charity, in spirit, in faith, in purity. 1 Tim. 4:12

Charity suffereth long, and is kind; charity envieth not; charity vaunteth not itself, is not puffed up, Doth not behave itself unseemingly, seeketh not her own, is not easily provoked, thinketh no evil; Rejoiceth not in iniquity, but rejoiceth in the truth; Beareth all things, believeth all things, hopeth all things, endureth all things. 1 Cor. 13:4-7

Charity suffereth long, and is kind, and envieth not, and is not puffed up, seeketh not her own, is not easily provoked, thinketh no evil, and rejoiceth not in iniquity but rejoiceth in the truth, beareth all things, believeth all things, hopeth all things, endureth all things. Moro. 7:45 (1 Cor. 13:4-13)

Above all things, clothe yourselves with the bond of charity, as with a mantle, which is the bond of perfectness and peace. D&C 88:125

Above all things, put on charity, which is the bond of perfectness. Col. 3:14

CHASTE, CHASTITY

Be discreet, chaste, keepers at home, good, obedient to their own husbands, that the word of God be not blasphemed. Titus 2:5

I, the Lord God, delight in the chastity of Women. Jacob 2:28

CHASTEN, CHASTENING, CHASTISE

Despise not the chastening of the Lord, nor faint when thou art rebuked of him. Heb. 12:5

In trouble have they visited thee, they poured out a prayer when thy chastening was upon them. Isa. 26:16

[Be] chastened for all your sins, that you may be one, that you might not perish in wickedness. D&C 61:8

Chasten thy son while there is hope, and let not thy soul spare for his crying. Prov. 19:18

From the first day that thou didst set thine heart to understand, and to chasten thyself before thy God, thy words were heard, and I am come for thy words. Dan. 10:12

Behold, happy is the man whom God correcteth: therefore despise not thou the chastening of the Almighty: For he maketh sore, and bindeth up; he woundeth, and his hands make whole. Job 5:17-18

CHEEK

Behold, it is written, an eye for an eye, and a tooth for a tooth; But I say unto you, that ye shall not resist evil, but whosoever shall smite thee on thy right cheek, turn to him the other also. 3 Ne. 12:38-39 (Matt. 5:39)

CHEER, CHEERFUL, CHEERFULNESS

Cheer up your hearts, and remember that ye are free to act for yourselves - to choose the way of everlasting death or the way of eternal life. 2 Ne. 10:23

Be of good cheer. Mark 6:50

All the days of the afflicted are evil: but he that is of a merry heart hath a continual feast. Prov. 15:15

CHILD, CHILDREN

Blessed are the peacemakers: for they shall be called the children of God. Matt. 5:9

Teach his commandments unto the children of men, that they also might enter into his rest. Alma 13:6

And these words, which I command thee this day, shall be in thine heart: And thou shalt teach them diligently unto thy children, and shalt talk of them when thou sittest in thine house, and when thou walkest by the way and when thou liest down, and when thou risest up. And thou shalt bind them for a sign upon thine hand, and they shalt be as frontlets between thine eyes. And thou shalt write them upon the posts of thy house, and on thy gates. Deut. 6:6-9

He that spareth his rod hateth his son: but he that loveth him chasteneth him betimes. Prov. 13:24

Every man should impart to the support of the widows and their children, that they might not perish with hunger. Mosiah 21:17

Ye will not suffer your children that they go hungry, or naked; neither will ye suffer that they transgress the laws of God, and fight and quarrel one with another, and serve the devil, who is the master of sin, or who is the evil spirit which hath been spoken of by our fathers, he being an enemy to all righteousness. Mosiah 4:14

Withhold not correction from the child. Prov. 23:13

They shall also teach their children to pray, and to walk uprightly before the Lord. D&C 68:28

Jesus said, Suffer little children, and forbid them not to come unto me, for of such is the kingdom of heaven. Matt. 19:14

It were better for him that a millstone were hanged about his neck, and he cast into the sea, than that he should offend one of these little ones. Luke 17:2

Ye fathers, provoke not your children to wrath: but bring them up in the nurture and admonition of the Lord. Eph. 6:4

Children, obey your parents in all things: for this is well pleasing unto the Lord. Col. 3:20

Suffer the little children to come unto me, and forbid them not. Mark 10:14

Train up a child in the way he should go: and when he is old, he will not depart from it. Prov. 22:6

Love little children with a perfect love; and they are all alike and partakers of salvation. Moro. 8:17

Except ye be converted, and become as little children, ye shall not enter into the kingdom of heaven. Matt. 18:3

Bring up your children in light and truth. D&C 93:40

Ye will teach them to walk in the ways of truth and soberness. Mosiah 4:15

CHOICE, CHOOSE, CHOSE, CHOSEN

Cheer up your hearts, and remember that ye are free to act for yourselves- to choose the way of everlasting death or the way of eternal life. 2 Ne. 10:23

So the last shall be first, and the first last: for many be called, but few chosen. Matt 20:16

Choose ye this day, whom ye will serve. Alma 30:8

Choose ye this day, to serve the Lord God who made you. Moses 6:33

If it seem evil unto you to serve the LORD, choose you this day whom ye will serve; whether the gods which your fathers served that on the other side of the flood, or the gods of the Amorites, in whose land ye dwell: but as for me and my house, we will serve the LORD. Josh. 24:15

I exercise myself, to have always a conscience void of offense toward God, and toward men. Acts 24:16

Choose for thyself, for it is given unto thee. Moses 3:17

Choose the things that please me, and take hold of my covenant; Even unto them will I give in mine house and within my walls a place and a name better than of sons and of daughters. Isa. 56:4-5

O that they were wise, that they understood this, that they would consider their latter end! Deut. 32:29

Jesus answered and said unto her, Martha, Martha, thou art careful and troubled about many things: But one thing is needful: and Mary hath chosen that good part, which shall not be taken away from her. Luke 10:41-42

Men are free according to the flesh; and all things are given them which are expedient unto man. And they are free to choose liberty and eternal life, through the great Mediator of all men, or to choose captivity and death, according to the captivity and power of the devil; for he seeketh that all men might be miserable like unto himself. 2 Ne. 2:27

I have set before you life and death, blessing and cursing, therefore choose life, that both thou and thy seed may live, That thou mayest love the LORD thy God, and that thou mayest obey his voice, and that thou mayest cleave unto him, for he is thy life, and the length of thy days. Deut. 30:19-20

CHRIST

Declare his doings among the people. 2 Ne. 22:4

Feast upon the words of Christ; for behold, the words of Christ will tell you all things what ye should do. 2 Ne. 32:3

Teach any man the right way; for the right way is to believe in Christ and deny him not; for by denying him ye also deny the prophets and the law. 2 Ne. 25:28

If any man shall say unto you, Lo, here is Christ, or there; believe it not. For there shall arise false Christs, and false prophets, and shall shew great signs and wonders; insomuch that, if it were possible, they shall deceive the very elect. Matt. 24:23-24

CHURCH

Husbands, love your wives, even as Christ also loved the church, and gave himself for it. That he might sanctify and cleanse it with the washing of water by the word, That he might present it to himself a glorious church, not having spot, or wrinkle, or any such thing; but that it should be holy and without blemish. So ought men to love their wives as their own bodies. He that loveth his wife loveth himself. Eph. 5:25-28

Contend against no church, save it be the church of the devil. D&C 18:20

Why persecutest thou the church of God? Mosiah 27:13

CIRCUMCISE, CIRCUMCISION

Circumcise yourselves to the LORD, and take away the foreskins of your heart. Jer. 4:4

Thus saith the Lord GOD; No stranger uncircumcised in heart, nor circumcised in flesh, shall enter into my sanctuary, of any strangers that is among the children of Israel. Ezek. 44:9

Circumcision is that of the heart, in the spirit, and not in the letter; whose praise is not of men, but of God. Rom. 2:28-29

CLEAN, CLEANSED. CLEANLINESS

Believe in Christ and worship the Father in his name, with pure hearts and clean hands, and look not forward any more for another Messiah. 2 Ne. 25:16

Truly God is good to Israel, to such as are of a clean heart. Ps. 73:1

Have ye walked, keeping yourselves blameless before God? Could ye say, if ye were called to die at this time, within yourselves, that ye have been sufficiently humble? That your garments have been cleansed and made white through the blood of Christ, who will come to redeem his people from their sins? Behold, are ye stripped of pride? I say unto you, if ye are not ye are not prepared to meet God. Alma 5:27-31

Depart ye, depart ye, go ye out from thence, touch no unclean; go ye out of the midst of her; be ye clean, that bear the vessels of the LORD. Isa. 52:11

The LORD rewarded me according to my righteousness; according to the cleanness of my hands hath he recompensed me. Ps. 18:20

Teach my people the difference between the holy and profane, and cause them to discern between the unclean and the clean. Ezek. 44:23

What God hath cleansed, that call not thou common. Acts 10:15

Be purified and cleansed from all sin. D&C 50:28

Touch not that which is unclean; go ye out of the midst of her; be ye clean that bear the vessels of the Lord. 3 Ne. 20:41

CLEAR

Thou hypocrite, first cast out the beam out of thine own eye; and then shalt thou see clearly to cast out the mote out of thy brother's eye. Matt. 7:3-5

CLEAVE

I beseech of you in words of soberness that ye would repent, and come with full purpose of heart, and cleave unto God as he cleaveth unto you. Jacob 6:5

Therefore shall a man leave his father and his mother, and shall cleave unto his wife: and they shall be one flesh. Gen. 2:24

CLOSET

When thou prayest thou shalt not do as the hypocrites, for they love to pray, standing in the synagogues and in the corners of the streets, that they may be seen of men. Verily I say unto you, they have their reward. But thou, when thou prayest, enter into thy closet, and when thou hast shut thy door, pray to thy Father who is in secret; and thy Father, who seeth in secret, shall reward thee openly. 3 Ne. 13:5-6

CLOTHE, CLOTHES, CLOTHING

They did not send away any who were naked, or that were hungry. Alma 1:30

COME

Come unto me, all ye that labour and are heavy laden, and I will give you rest. Take my yoke upon you, and learn of me; for I am meek and lowly in heart: and ye shall find rest unto your souls. For my yoke is easy, and my burden is light. Matt. 11:28-30

If ye teach the law of Moses, also teach that it is a shadow of those things which are to come. Mosiah 16:14

Yea, come unto me and bring forth works of righteousness. Alma 5:35

Ye should come unto Christ, who is the Holy One of Israel, and partake of his salvation, and the power of his redemption. Yea, come unto him, and offer your whole souls as an offering unto him and continue in fasting and praying, and endure to the end. Omni 1:26

Come ye, and let us go to the mountain of the LORD to the house of the God of Jacob; and he will teach us of his ways and we will walk in his paths: for out of Zion shall go forth the law, and the word of the LORD from Jerusalem. Isa. 2:3

Repenteth and cometh unto me. D&C 10:67

Persuade them to come unto Christ, and partake of the goodness of God, that they may enter into his rest. Jacob 1:7

COMFORT

Be of good comfort. 2 Cor. 13:11

Proclaim the acceptable year of the LORD, and the day of vengeance of our God, to comfort all that mourn. Isa. 61:2

Blessed be God, even the Father of our Lord Jesus Christ, the Father of mercies, and the God of all comfort; Who comforteth us in all our tribulation, that we may be able to comfort them which are in any trouble, by the comfort wherewith we ourselves are comforted of God. For as the sufferings of Christ abound in us, so our consolation also aboundeth by Christ. 2 Cor. 1:3-5

[Be] willing to mourn with those that mourn; yea, and comfort those that stand in need of comfort. Mosiah 18:9

COMFORTER

These things have I spoken unto you, being yet present with you. But the Comforter, which is the Holy Ghost, whom the Father will send in my name, he shall teach you all things, and bring all things to your remembrance, whatsoever I have said unto you. John 14:25-26

Nevertheless I tell you the truth; It is expedient for you that I go away; for if I go not away, the Comforter will not come unto you; but if I depart, I will send him unto you. John 16:7

COMING

Ye should no more deny the coming of Christ. Alma 34:37

My soul delighteth in proving unto my people the truth of the coming of Christ. 2 Ne. 11:4

Wait for the coming of the Messiah. 2 Ne. 6:13

COMMAND, COMMANDMENT

Keep the commandments. Mosiah 12:33

Have his commandments always before our eyes. Mosiah 1:5

Thou shalt love the Lord thy God with all thy heart, and with all thy soul, and with all thy mind, and with all thy strength: this is the first commandment. Mark 12:30

Jesus said unto him, Thou shalt love the Lord thy God with all thy heart, and with all thy soul, and with all thy mind. This is the first and great command-ment. And the second is like unto it, Thou shalt love thy neighbour as thyself. On these two command-ments, hang all the law and the prophets. Matt 22:37-40

What thing soever I command you, observe to do it: thou shalt not add thereto, nor diminish from it. Deut. 12:32

If ye do not watch yourselves, and your thoughts, and your words, and your deeds, and observe the command-ments of God, and continue in the faith of what ye have heard concerning of our Lord, even unto the end of your lives, ye must perish. O man, remember, and perish not. Mosiah 4:30

If thou shalt hearken diligently unto the voice of the LORD thy God, to observe and to do all his command-ments which I command thee this day, that the LORD thy God will sit thee on high above all nations of the earth; And all these blessings shall come on thee, and overtake thee, if thou shalt hearken unto the voice of the LORD thy God. Deut. 28:1-2

Learn wisdom in thy youth; yea, learn in thy youth to keep the command-ments of God. Alma 37:35

Consider on the blessed and happy state of those that keep the command-ments of God. Mosiah 2:41

Be firm in keeping the command-ments. D&C 5:22

Obey my voice, and I will be your God, and ye shall be my people: and walk ye in all the ways that I have commanded you, that it may be well unto you. Jer. 7:23

Teach his commandments unto the children of men, that they also might enter into his rest. Alma 13:6

Remember ye the law of Moses my servant, which I commanded unto him in Horeb for all Israel, with the statutes and judgments. Mal. 4:4

I will give them one heart, and I will put a new spirit within you; and I will take the stony heart out of their flesh, and will give them an heart of flesh: That they may walk in my statutes, and keep mine ordinances, and do them: and they shall be my people, and I will be their God. Ezek. 11:19-20

If ye love me, keep my command-ments. D&C 124:87

Keep the commandments of God. Abr. 1:2

Keep the commandments of the Lord. 1 Ne. 8:38

If thou wilt enter into life, keep the commandments. Matt. 19:17

I love thy commandments above gold; yea, above fine gold. Ps. 119:127

Trust no one to be your teacher nor your minister, except he be a man of God, walking in his ways and keeping his commandments. Mosiah 23:14

If ye walk in my statutes and keep my commandments, and do them; Then I will give you rain in due season, and the land shall yield her increase, and the trees of the field shall yield her fruit. Lev. 26:3-4

COMMENCE

You have commenced in your youth to look to the Lord your God. Alma 38:2

COMMIT, COMMITMENT

Commit thy way unto the Lord; trust also in Him; and He shall bring it to pass. And he shall bring forth thy righteousness as the light, and thy judgment as the noonday. Ps. 37:5-6

COMMUNICATE, COMMUNICATION

Be rich in good works, ready to distribute, willing to communicate. 1 Tim. 6:18

COMPASSION, COMPASSIONATE

Some have compassion, making a difference. Jude 1:22

COMPEL

Whosoever shall compel thee to go a mile, go with him twain. 3 Ne. 12:41 (Matt. 5:41)

CONCEIT, CONCEITED

The rich man is wise in his own conceit; but the poor that hath understanding searcheth him out. Prov. 28:11

Answer a fool according to his folly, lest he be wise in his own conceit. Prov. 26:5

CONCEIVE

None calleth for justice, nor any pleadeth for truth: they trust in vanity, and speak lies; they conceive mischief, and bring forth iniquity. Isa. 59:4

CONCUBINE

For there shall not any man among you have save it be one wife; and concubines ye shall have none. Jacob 2:27

They shalt not commit whoredoms, like unto them of old, saith the Lord of Hosts. Jacob 2:31-33

CONDEMN, CONDEMNATION

He that justifieth the wicked, and he that condemneth the just, even they both are abomination to the LORD. Prov. 17:15

CONFESS, CONFESSION

Confess by the power of the Holy Ghost that Jesus is the Christ. Moro. 7:44

Confess your faults one to another, and pray one for another, that ye may be healed. The effectual fervent prayer of a righteous man availeth much. James 5:16

I was speaking, and praying, and confessing my sin and the sin of my people Israel, and presenting my supplication before the LORD my God for the holy mountain of my God. Dan. 9:20

For it is written, As I live, saith the Lord, every knee shall bow to me, and every tongue shall confess to God. Rom 14:11

If they shall confess their iniquity, and the iniquity of their fathers, with their trespass which they trespassed against me, and that also they have walked contrary unto me; And that I also have walked contrary unto them, and have brought them into the land of their enemies; if then their uncircumcised hearts be humbled, and they then accept of the punishment of their iniquity: Then will I remember my covenant with Jacob, and also my covenant with Isaac, and also my covenant with Abraham will I remember; and I will remember the land. Lev. 26:40-42

He that covereth his sins shall not prosper: but whoso confesseth and forsaketh them shall have mercy. Prov. 28:13

Whosoever shall confess that Jesus is the Son of God, God dwelleth in him, and he in God. 1 Jn. 4:15

I acknowledged my sin unto thee, and mine iniquity have I not hid. I said, I will confess my transgressions unto the LORD; and thou forgavest the iniquity of my sin. Ps. 32:5

CONFIDENCE

Confidence in an unfaithful man in time of trouble is like a broken tooth, and a foot out of joint. Prov. 25:19

CONFOUND

Let them all be confounded and turned back that hate Zion. Ps. 129:5

CONFUSE, CONFUSION

God is not the author of confusion, but of peace, as in all churches of the saints. 1 Cor. 14:33

For where envying and strife is, there is confusion and every evil work. James 3:16

CONSCIENCE

We claim the privilege of worshiping Almighty God according to the dictates of our own conscience, and allow all men the same privilege, let them worship how, where, or what they may. A of F-11

I exercise myself, to have always a conscience void of offense toward God, and toward men. Acts 24:16

Now the Spirit speaketh expressly, that in the latter times some shall depart from the faith, giving heed to seducing spirits, and doctrines of devils; Speaking lies in hypocrisy; having their conscience seared with a hot iron; Forbidding to marry, and commanding to abstain from meats, which God hath created to be received with thanksgiving of them which believe and know the truth. 1 Tim. 4:1-3

CONSECRATE, CONSECRATION

Ye must pray always, and not faint; that ye must not perform anything unto the Lord save in the first place ye shall pray unto the Father in the name of Christ, that he will consecrate thy performance unto thee, that thy performance may be for the welfare of thy soul. 2 Ne. 32:9

Teach the people, that thereby they might hear and know the commandments of God. Mosiah 6:3

CONSENT, CONTENTMENT

If sinners entice thee, consent thou not. Prov. 1:10

CONSIDER

Thus saith the Lord of Hosts; Consider your ways. Hag. 1:4-5

Stand still, and consider the wondrous works of God. Job 37:14

CONSPRIACY, CONSPIRE

We believe that rulers, states, and governments have a right, and are bound to enact laws for the protection of all citizens in the free exercise of their religious belief; but we do not believe that they have a right in justice to deprive citizens of this privilege, or proscribe them in their opinions, so long as a regard and reverence are shown to the laws and such religious opinions do not justify sedition nor conspiracy. D&C 134:7

CONSTITUTION

According to the laws and constitution of the people, which I have suffered to be established, and should be maintained for the rights and protection of all flesh, according to just and holy principles; That every man may act in doctrine and principle pertaining to futurity, according to the moral agency which I have given unto him, that every man may be accountable for his own sins in the day of judgment. D&C 101:77-78

May those principles, which were so honorably and nobly defended, namely, the Constitution of our land, by our fathers, be established forever. D&C 109:54

CONSUME

Ye ask, and receive not, because ye ask amiss, that ye may consume it upon your lusts. James 4:3

CONTEND, CONTENTION, CONTENTIOUS

Agree with thine adversary quickly, whiles thou art in the way with him; lest at any time the adversary deliver thee to the judge, and the judge deliver thee to the officer, and thou be cast into prison. Matt. 5:25

Cast out the scorner, and contention shall go out; yea, strife and reproach shall cease. Prov. 22:10

Every man should love his neighbor as himself, that there should be no contention among them. Mosiah 23:15

Shall he that contendeth with the Almighty instruct him? he that reproveth God, let him answer it. Job 40:2

Unto them that are contentious, and do not obey the truth, but obey unrighteousness, indignation and wrath. Rom. 2:8

Beloved, when I gave all diligence to write unto you of the common salvation, it was needful for me to write unto you, and exhort you that ye should earnestly contend for the faith which was once delivered unto the saints. Jude 1:3

If a wise man contendeth with a foolish man, whether he rage or laugh, there is no rest. Prov. 29:9

A brother offended is harder to be won than a strong city: and their contentions are like the bars of a castle. Prov. 18:19

The lot causeth contensions to cease, and parteth between the mighty. Prov. 18:18

This I do that I may establish my gospel, that there may not be so much contention; yea, Satan doth stir up the hearts of the people to contend concerning the points of my doctrine; and in these things they do err, for they do wrest the scriptures and do not understand them. D&C 10:63

Let there be no strife, I pray thee, between me and thee, and between my herdmen and thy herdmen; for we be brethren. Gen. 13:8

Grudge not one against another, brethren, lest ye be condemned: behold, the judge standeth before the door. James 5:9

Cease to contend one with another; cease to speak evil one of another. D&C 136:23

It is better to dwell in the wilderness, than with a contentious and an angry woman. Prov. 21:19

Take upon you the name of Christ; that ye humble yourselves even to the dust, and worship God, in whatsoever place ye may be in, in spirit and in truth; and that ye live in thanksgiving daily, for the many mercies and blessings which he doth bestow upon you. Alma 34:38

Behold, this is not my doctrine, to stir up the hearts of men with anger, one against another; but this is my doctrine, that such things should be done away. 3 Ne. 11:30

Beware, lest there shall arise contentions among you, and ye list to obey the evil spirit. Mosiah 2:32

CONTENT, CONTENTMENT

I ought to be content with the things which the Lord hath allotted unto me. Alma 29:3

CONTINUALLY, CONTINUE

Remember the words of your God; pray unto him continually by day, and give thanks unto his holy name by night. 2 Ne. 9:52

Be watchful unto prayer continually. Alma 34:39

That which is of God is light; and he that receiveth light, and continueth in God, receiveth more light; and that light groweth brighter and brighter until the perfect day. D&C 50:24

Continue in the faith grounded and settled, and be not moved away from the hope of the gospel, which ye have heard, and which was preached to every creature which is under heaven. Col. 1:23

CONTRIBUTE, CONTRIBUTION

It hath pleased them of Macedonia and Achaia to make a certain contribution for the poor saints which are at Jerusalem Rom. 15:26

CONTRITE

He offereth himself a sacrifice for sin, to answer the ends of the law, unto all those who have a broken heart and a contrite spirit. 2 Ne. 2:6-7

The LORD is nigh unto them that are of a broken heart; and saveth such as be of a contrite spirit. Ps. 34:18

Ye shall repent of your sins, and come unto me with a broken heart and a contrite spirit. 3 Ne. 12:19

CONVERSATION, CONVERSE

Let no man despise thy youth; but be thou an example of the believers, in word, in conversation, in charity, in spirit, in faith, in purity. 1 Tim. 4:12

Let your conversation be as it becometh the gospel of Christ: that whether I come and see you, or else be absent, I may hear of your affairs, that ye stand fast in one spirit, with one mind striving together for the faith of the gospel. Philip. 1:27

Let your conversation be without covetousness; and be content with such things as ye have. Heb. 13:5

Sanctify the Lord God in your heats; and be ready always to give an answer to every man that asketh you a reason of the hope that is in you with meekness and fear: Having a good conscience; that, whereas they speak evil of you, as of evildoers, they may be ashamed that falsely accuse your good conversation in Christ. 1 Pet. 3:15-16

Ye know that ye were not redeemed with corruptible things, as silver and gold, from your vain conversation received by tradition from your fathers. 1 Pet. 1:18

A wholesome tongue is a tree of life: but perverseness therein is a breach in the spirit. Prov. 15:4

CONVERT, CONVERSION, CONVERTED

Be converted and be healed. 2 Ne. 16:10

Make the heart of this people fat, and make their ears heavy, and shut their eyes; lest they see with their eyes, and hear with their ears, and understand with their heart, and convert, and be healed. Isa. 6:10

Except ye be converted, and become as little children, ye shall not enter into the kingdom of heaven. Matt. 18:3

When thou are converted, strengthen thy brethren. Luke 22:32

CONVINCE

Bring many to the knowledge of the truth, yea, convince them of the error of their ways. D&C 6:11

CORD

Enlarge the place of thy tent, and let them stretch forth the curtains of thine habitations; spare not, lengthen the cords, and strengthen thy stakes. Isa. 54:2-3

CORNER, CORNERSTONE

Ye are no more strangers and foreigners, but fellowcitizens with the saints, and of the household of God; And are built upon the foundation of the apostles and prophets, Jesus Christ himself being the chief corner stone. Eph. 2:19-20

Wherefore also it is contained in the scripture, Behold, I lay in Sion a chief corner stone, elect, precious: and he that believeth on him shall not be confounded. 1 Pet. 2:6

Wherefore, I am in your midst, and I am the good shepherd, and the stone of Israel. He that buildeth upon this rock shall never fall. D&C 50:44

Be it known unto you all, and to all the people of Israel, that by the name of Jesus Christ of Nazareth, whom ye crucified, whom God raised from the dead, even by him doth this man stand here before you whole. This is the stone which was set at nought of you builders, which is become the head of the corner. Neither is there salvation in any other: for there is none other name under heaven given among men, whereby we must be saved. Acts 4:10-12

Have ye not read this scripture; The stone which the builders rejected is become the head of the corner? Mark 12:10

CORRECT, CORRECTION

Withhold not correction from the child. Prov. 23:13

Correct thy son, and he shall give thee rest; yea he shall give delight unto thy soul. Prov. 29:17

Whoso loveth instruction loveth knowledge: but he that hateth reproof is brutish. Prov. 12:1

CORRUPT, CORRUPTIBLE, CORRUPTION

Ye know that ye were not redeemed with corruptible things, as silver and gold, from your vain conversation received by tradition from your fathers. 1 Pet. 1:18

Look forward with an eye of faith, and view this mortal body raised in immortality, and this corruption raised in incorruption, to stand before God to be judged according to the deeds which have been done in the mortal body? Alma 5:15

COUNSEL, COUNSELOR

Remember the former things of old: for I am God, and there is none else; I am God, and there is none like me, Declaring the end from the beginning, and from ancient times the things that are not yet done, saying, My counsel shall stand, and I will do all my pleasure: Calling a ravenous bird from the east, the man that executeth my counsel from a far county: yea, I have spoken it, I will also bring it to pass; I have purposed it, I will also do it. Isa. 46:9-11

Then went the Pharisees, and took counsel how they might entangle him in his talk. Matt. 22:15

For unto us a child is born, unto us a son is given; and the government shall be upon his shoulder; and his name shall be called, Wonderful, Counselor, The Mighty God, The Everlasting Father, The Prince of Peace. 2 Ne. 19:6 (Isa. 9:6)

Hearken now unto my voice, I will give thee counsel, and God shall be with thee. Ex. 18:19

A wise man will hear, and will increase learning; and a man of understanding shall attain unto wise counsels. Prov. 1:5

When they are learned they think they are wise, and they hearken not unto the counsel of God, for they set it aside, supposing they know of themselves, wherefore, their wisdom is foolishness and it profiteth them not. And they perish. But to be learned is good, if they hearken unto the counsels of God. 2 Ne. 9:28-29

Woe unto them that seek deep to hide their counsel from the LORD and their works are in the dark, and they say, Who seeth us? and who knoweth us? Isa. 29:15

Counsel with the Lord in all thy doings, and he will direct thee for good; yea,, when thou liest down at night lie down unto the Lord, that he may watch over you in your sleep; and when thou risest in the morning let thy heart be full of thanks unto God; and if ye do these things, ye shall be lifted up at the last day. Alma 37:37

Seek not to counsel the Lord, but to take counsel from his hand. Jacob 4:10

COUNTENANCE

Have ye received his image in your countenances? Alma 5:14

Blessed is the people that know the joyful sound: they shall walk, O LORD, in the light of thy countenance. Ps. 89:15

COURAGE, COURAGEOUS

Be of good courage, and let us behave ourselves valiantly for our people, and for the cities of our God: and let the LORD do   is good in his sight. 1 Chron. 19:13

Blessed be the God of Shadrach, Meshach, and Abed-nego, who hath sent his angel, and delivered his servants that trusted in him, and have changed the king's word, and yielded their bodies, that they might not serve nor worship any god, except their own God. Dan. 3:28

Be of good courage, and he shall strengthen your heart, all ye that hope in the LORD. Ps. 31:24

Be strong and of a good courage; be not afraid, neither be thou dismayed; for the Lord thy God is with thee whithersoever thou goest. Josh. 1:9

COVENANT

Remember his holy covenant. Luke 1:72

Choose the things that please me, and take hold of my covenant; Even unto them will I give in mine house and within my walls a place and a name better than of sons and of daughters. Isa. 56:4-5

They shall ask the way to Zion with their faces thitherward, , Come, and let us join ourselves to the LORD in a perpetual covenant that shall not be forgotten. Jer. 50:5

And God said, This is the token of the covenant which I make between me and you and every living creature that is with you, for perpetual generations: I do set my bow in the cloud, and it shall be for a token of a covenant between me and the earth. And it shall come to pass, when I bring a cloud over the earth, that the bow shall be seen in the cloud: And I will remember my covenant, which is between me and you and every living creature of all flesh; and the waters shall no more become a flood to destroy all flesh. Gen. 9:13

Be ye mindful always of his covenant; the word which he commanded to a thousand generations; Even of the covenant which he made with Abraham, and of his oath unto Isaac; And hath confirmed the same to Jacob for a law, and to Israel for an everlasting covenant. 1 Chron. 16:15-17

Obey my voice indeed, and keep my covenant. Ex. 19:5

Thou shalt keep my covenant therefore, thou, and thy seed after thee in their generations. Gen. 17:9

Rememberest thou the covenants of the Father unto the house of Israel? 1 Ne. 14:8

COVER

Is it not to deal thy bread to the hungry, and that thou bring the poor that are cast out to thy house? When thou seest the naked, that thou cover him; and that thou hide not thyself from thine own flesh? Isa. 58:7

COVET, COVETOUS, COVETOUSNESS

Keep all your pledges one with another; and covet not that which is thy brother's. D&C 136:20

But covet earnestly the best gifts: and yet shew I unto you a more excellent way. 1 Cor. 12:31

Thou shat not covet thy neighbour's house, thou shalt not covet thy neighbour's wife, nor his manservant, nor his maidservant, nor his ox, nor his ass, nor anything that is thy neighbour's. Ex. 20:17

Thou shalt not covet thine own property, but impart it freely. D&C 19:26

CREATE, CREATED, CREATION

Grow in the knowledge of the glory of him that created you, or in the knowledge of that which is just and true. Mosiah 4:12

He will come, and that he remembereth every creature of his creating, he will make himself manifest unto all. Mosiah 27:30

Ye were created of the dust of the earth; but behold, it belongeth to him who created you. Mosiah 2:25

Do you exercise faith in the redemption of him who created you? Do you look forward with an eye of faith, and view this mortal body raised in immortality, and this corruption raised in incorrupt-tion, to stand before God to be judged according to the deeds which have been done in the mortal body? Alma 5:15

I say unto you that if ye should serve him who has created you from the beginning, and is preserving you from day to day, by lending you breath, that ye may live and move and do according to your own will, and even supporting you from one moment to another - I say, if ye should serve him with all your whole souls yet ye would be unprofitable servants. Mosiah 2:21

CRIME

Men should be judged according to their crimes. Alma 30:11

CROOKED

Verily, verily, I say unto you that ye are called to lift up your voices as with the sound of a trump, to declare my gospel unto a crooked and perverse generation. D&C 33:2

I will go before thee, and make the crooked places straight: I will break in pieces the gates of brass, and cut in sunder the bars of iron. Isa. 45:2

CROSS

They who have endured the crosses of the world, and despised the shame of it, they shall inherit the kingdom of God. 2 Ne. 9:18

Behold, it is written by them of old time, that thou shalt not commit adultery; But I say unto you, that whosoever looketh on a woman, to lust after her, hath committed adultery already in his heart. 3 Ne. 12:27-28 (Matt 5:27-28)

He said unto them all, If any man will come after me, let him deny himself, and take up his cross daily, and follow me. Luke 9:23

Arise and gird up your loins, take up your cross, follow me, and feed my sheep. D&C 112:14

CROWN

Fear none of those things which thou shalt suffer: behold, the devil shall cast some of you into prison, that ye may be tried; and ye shall have tribulation ten days: be thou faithful unto death, and I will give thee a crown of life. Rev. 2:10

When the chief Shepherd shall appear, ye shall receive a crown of glory that fadeth not away. 1 Pet. 5:4

CRUEL, CRUELTY

The merciful man doeth good to his own soul: but he that is cruel troubleth his own flesh. Prov. 11:17

CRIED, CRY

I will cry unto thee in all mine afflictions. Alma 33:11

Cease not to cry unto the Lord. 1 Sam. 7:8

I cry unto my God in faith, and I know that he will hear my cry. 2 Ne. 33:3

Be merciful unto me, O Lord: for I cry unto thee daily. Rejoice the soul of thy servant: for unto thee, O Lord, do I lift up my soul. Ps. 86:3-5

And the said unto them- Go through the midst of the city, through the midst of Jerusalem, and set a mark upon the foreheads of the men that sigh and that cry for all the abominations that be done in the midst thereof. Ezek. 9:4

Behold, he hath heard my cry by day, and he hath given me knowledge by visions in the night-time. 2 Ne. 4:23

My soul hungered; and I kneeled down before my Maker, and I cried unto him in mighty prayer and supplication for mine own soul; and all the day long did I cry unto him; yea, and when the night came I did still raise my voice high that it reached the heavens. Enos 1:4

Cry aloud, spare not, lift up thy voice like a trumpet, and shew my people their transgression, and the house of Jacob their sins. Isa. 58:1

When we cried unto the LORD, he heard our voice, and sent an angel. Num. 20:16

I and my people did cry mightily to the Lord that he would deliver us out of the hands of our enemies. Mosiah 9:17

Hear my cry, O God; attend unto my prayer. From the end of the earth will I cry unto thee, when my heart is overwhelmed. Ps. 61:1-2

Cry unto God for all thy support; yea, let all thy doings be unto the Lord, and whithersoever thou goest let it be in the Lord; yea, let all thy thoughts be directed unto the Lord; yea, let the affections of thy heart be placed upon the Lord forever. Alma 37:36

When you do not cry unto the Lord, let your hearts be full, drawn out in prayer unto him continually for your welfare, and also for the welfare of those who are around you. Alma 34:27

The poor man cried, and the heard him, and saved him out of all his troubles. Ps. 34:6

CUMBERED

Seek not to be cumbered. D&C 66:10

CUNNING

O that cunning plan of the evil one! O the vainness, and the frailties, and the foolishness of men! When they are learned they think they are wise, and they hearken not unto the counsel of God, for they set it aside, supposing they know of themselves, wherefore, their wisdom is foolishness and it profiteth them not. 2 Ne. 9:28

Remember the awfulness in transgressing against that Holy God, and also the awfulness of yielding to the enticings of that cunning one. 2 Ne. 9:39

Be no more children, tossed to and fro, and carried about with every wind of doctrine, by the sleight of men, and cunning craftiness, whereby they lie in wait to deceive. Eph. 4:14

CUP

Jesus answered and said, Ye know not what ye ask. Are ye able to drink of the cup that I shall drink of, and to be baptized with the baptism that I am baptized with? They say unto him, We are able. Matt. 20:22

CURSE

Thou shalt not curse the deaf, nor put a stumblingblock before the blind, but shalt fear thy God: I am the LORD. Lev. 19:14

Love your enemies, bless them that curse you, do good to them that hate you, and pray for them which despitefully use you, and persecute you. Matt. 5:44

Curse not the king, no not in thy thought; and curse not the rich in thy bedchamber: for a bird of the air shall carry the voice, and that which hath wings shall tell the matter. Eccl. 10:20

Said his wife unto him, Dost thou still retain thine integrity? curse God, and die. Job 2:9

Whoso curseth his father or his mother, his lamp shall be put out in obscure darkness. Prov. 20:20

CUT, CUT OFF

Wherefore if thy hand or thy foot offend thee, cut them off, and cast them from thee: it is better for thee to enter into life halt or maimed, rather than having two hands or two feet to be cast into everlasting fire. Matt. 18:8

DAILY

He said unto them all, If any man will come after me, let him deny himself, and take up his cross daily, and follow me. Luke 9:23

Be merciful unto me, O Lord: for I cry unto thee daily. Rejoice the soul of thy servant: for unto thee, O Lord, do I lift up my soul. Ps. 86:3-5

They received the word with all readiness of mind, and searched the scriptures daily, whether those things were so. Acts 17:11

DANCE, DANCING

If thou art merry, praise the Lord with singing, with music, with dancing, and with a prayer of praise and thanksgiving. If thou art sorrowful, call on the Lord thy God with supplication, that your souls may be joyful. D&C 136:28-29

DANGER, DANGEROUS

Whosoever is angry with his brother without a cause shall be in danger of the judgment: and whosoever shall say to his brother, Raca, shall be in danger of the council: but whosoever shall say, Thou fool, shall be in danger of hell fire. Matt. 5:22

He that shall blaspheme against the Holy Ghost hath never forgiveness, but is in danger of eternal damnation. Mark 3:29

DARK, DARKEN, DARKNESS

Watch, for the adversary spreadeth his dominions, and darkness reigneth. D&C 82:5

Discretion shall preserve thee, understanding shall keep thee; To deliver thee from the way of the evil man, from the man that speaketh froward things; who leave the paths of righteousness, to walk in the ways of darkness. Prov. 2:11-13

The LORD hath a controversy with the inhabitants of the land, because there is no truth, nor mercy, nor knowledge of God in the land. By swearing, and lying, and killing, and stealing, and committing adultery, they break out, and blood toucheth blood. Hosea 4:1-2

When thine eye is evil, thy body also is full of darkness. Take heed therefore that the light which is in thee be not darkness. Luke 11:34-35

DAY, DAYS

After ye have been nourished by the good word of God all the day long, will ye bring forth evil fruit, that ye must be hewn down and cast into the fire? Jacob 6:7

I must work the works of him that sent me, while it is day: the night cometh, when no man can work. John. 9:4

Teach us to number our days, that we may apply our hearts unto wisdom. Ps. 90:12

I, the Lord God, have spoken it; but the hour and the day no man knoweth, neither the angels in heaven, nor shall they know until he comes. D&C 49:7

Heaven and earth shall pass away, but my words shall not pass away. But of that day and hour knoweth no man, no, not the angels of heaven, by my Father only. Matt 24:36

Blow ye the trumpet in Zion, and sound an alarm in my holy mountain: let all the inhabitants of the land tremble: for the day of the Lord cometh, for it is nigh at hand. Joel 2:1

They are strict to remember the Lord their God from day to day; yea, they do observe to keep his statutes, and his judgments, and his commandments continually. Alma 58:40

Wo unto him that has the law given, yea, that has all the commandments of God, like unto us, and that transgresseth them, and that wasteth the days of his probation, for awful is his state! 2 Ne. 9:27

As the partridge sitteth on eggs, and hatcheth them not; so he that getteth riches, and not by right, shall leave them in the midst of his days, and at his end shall be a fool. Jer. 17:11

Behold, look ye unto the revelations of God; for behold, the time cometh at that day when all these things must be fulfilled. Morm. 8:33

Hold thy peace at the presence of the LORD God: for the day of the LORD is at hand: for the LORD hath prepared a sacrifice, he hath bid his guests. Zeph. 1:7

Ye shall walk in all the ways which the LORD your God hath commanded you, that ye may live, and that ye may prolong your days in the land which ye shall posses. Deut. 5:33

This is the day which the LORD hath made; we will rejoice and be glad in it. Ps. 118:24

DEACON

Likewise must the deacons be grave, not doubletongued, not given to much wine, not greedy of filthy lucre; Holding the mystery of faith in a pure conscience. 1 Tim. 3:8

DEAD, DEADLY

There are also celestial bodies, and bodies terrestrial: but the glory of the celestial is one, and the glory of the terrestrial is another.　There is one glory of the sun, and another glory of the moon, and another glory of the stars: for one star differeth from another star in glory. So also is the resurrection of the dead. 1 Cor. 15:40-42

These signs shall follow them that believe - in my name shall they cast out devils; they shall speak with new tongues; they shall take up serpents; and if they drink any deadly thing it shall not hurt them; they shall lay hands on the sick and they shall recover. Morm. 9:24 (Mark 16:17-18)

Bear testimony of mine Only Begotten; his resurrection from the dead; yea, and also the resurrection of all men. Moses 7:62

DEAF

When Jesus saw that the people came running together, he rebuked the foul spirit, saying unto him, Thou dumb and deaf spirit, I charge thee, come out of him, and enter no more into him. Mark 9:25

[They] were beyond measure astonished, saying, He hath done all things well: he maketh both the deaf to hear, and the dumb to speak. Mark 7:37

DEAL, DEALING

Ye shall not steal, neither deal falsely, neither lie one to another. Lev. 19:11

Deal not foolishly. Ps. 75:4

Have we not all one father? hath not one God created us? why do we deal treacherously every man against his brother, by profaning the covenant of our fathers? Mal. 2:10

DEATH, DIED

For, behold, the Lord your Redeemer suffered death in the flesh; wherefore he suffered the pain of all men, that all men might repent and come unto him. D&C 18:11

I know that he shall rise again in the resurrection at the last day. Jesus said unto her, I am the resurrection, and the life: he that believeth in me, though he were dead, yet shall he live. John 11:24-25

He that overcometh shall inherit all things; and I will be his God, and he shall be my son. But the fearful, and unbelieving, and the abominable, and murderers, and whore-mongers, and sorcerers, and idolaters, and all liars, shall have their part in the lake which burneth with fire and brimstone: which is the second death. Rev. 21:7

When a righteous man turneth away from his righteousness, and committeth iniquity, and dieth in them; for his iniquity that he hath done shall he die. Ezek. 18:26

DEBATE

Debate thy cause with thy neighbour; and discover not a secret to another: lest he that heareth put thee to shame, and thine infamy turn not away. Prov. 25:9-10

DEBT, DEBTOR

Release thyself from bondage. D&C 19:35

Owe no man any thing, but to love one another: for he that loveth another hath fulfilled the law. Rom. 13:8

Be not thou one of them that strike hands, or of them that are sureties for debts. Prov. 22:26

After this manner therefore pray ye: Our Father who art in heaven, hallowed be thy name. Thy will be done on earth as it is in heaven. And forgive us our debts, as we forgive our debtors. And lead us not into temptation, but deliver us from evil. For thine is the kingdom, and the power, and the glory, forever. Amen. 3 Ne. 13:9-13 (Matt. 6:9-13)

DECEIT, DECEITFULLY, DECEIVE

Cursed be he that doeth the the work of the LORD deceitfully. Jer. 48:10

By thy sorceries were all nations deceived. Rev. 18:23

Wine is a mocker, strong drink is raging: and whosoever is deceived thereby is not wise. Prov. 20:1

Beware of false prophets, which come to you in sheep's clothing, but inwardly they are ravening wolves. Ye shall know them by their fruits. Matt. 7:15-16

A false witness shall not be unpunished, and he that speaketh lies shall not escape. Prov. 19:5

Be not deceived; God is not mocked: for whatsoever a man soweth, that shall he also reap. Galtians 6:7

Wo unto them that are deceivers and hypocrites, for, thus saith the Lord, I will bring them to judgment. D&C 50:6

Be not a witness against thy neighbour without cause; and deceive not with thy lips. Prov. 24:28

Whoso treasureth up my word, shall not be deceived. JS-M 1:37

Ye shall not steal, neither deal falsely, neither lie one to another. Lev. 19:11

Be no more children, tossed to and fro, and carried about with every wind of doctrine, by the sleight of men, and cunning craftiness, whereby they lie in wait to deceive. Eph. 4:14

If any man shall say unto you, Lo, here is Christ, or there; believe it not. For there shall arise false Christs, and false prophets, and shall shew great signs and wonders; insomuch that, if it were possible, they shall deceive the very elect. Matt. 24:23-24

DECLARE

Declare in Zion the vengeance of the LORD our God, the vengeance of His temple. Jer. 50:28

All the multitude kept silence, and gave audience to Barnabas and Paul, declaring what miracles and wonders God had wrought among the Gentiles by them. Acts 15:12

Ye shall bear record of me, even Jesus Christ, that I am the Son of the living God, that I was, that I am, and that I am to come. D&C 68:6

Let us declare in Zion the work of the LORD our God. Jer. 51:10

Praise the LORD, call upon his name, declare his doings among the people, make mention that his name is exalted. Isa. 12:4

Declare his doings among the people. 2 Ne. 22:4

Declare the things which ye have heard, and verily believe, and know to be true. D&C 80:4

DECREE, DECREED

Now, the decrees of God are unalterable; therefore, the way is prepared that whosoever will may walk therein and be saved. Alma 41:8

WOE unto them that decree unrighteous decrees, and that write grievousness which they have prescribed. Isa. 10:1

DEED, DEEDS

Watch yourselves, and your thoughts, and your words, and your deeds, and observe the commandments of God, and continue in the faith of what ye have heard concerning the coming of the Lord, even unto the end of your lives. Mosiah 4:30

Do you exercise faith in the redemption of him who created you? Do you look forward with an eye of faith, and view this mortal body raised in immortality, and this corruption raised in incorrup-tion, to stand before God to be judged according to the deeds which have been done in the mortal body? Alma 5:15

DEFER

When thou vowest a vow unto God, defer not to pay it; for he hath no pleasure in fools: pay that which thou hast vowed. Eccl. 5:4

DEFILE

That which cometh out of the man, that defileth the man. For from within, out of the heart of men, proceed evil thoughts, adulteries, fornications, murders, thefts, covetousness, wicked-ness, deceit, lascivious-ness, an evil eye, blasphemy, pride, foolish-ness: All these evil things come from within, and defile the man. Mark 7:20-23

The children of Judah have done evil in my sight, saith the LORD: they have set their abominations in the house which is called by my name, to pollute it. Jer. 7:30

There shall in no wise enter into [the temple] any thing that defileth, neither whatsoever worketh abomination, or maketh a lie: but they which are written in the Lamb's book of life. Rev. 21:27

Do not ye yet understand, that whatsoever entereth in at the mouth goeth into the belly, and is cast out into the draught? But those things which proceed out of the mouth come froth from the heart; and they defile the man. For out of the heart proceed evil thoughts, murders, adulteries, fornications, thefts, false witness, blasphemies: These are the things which defile a man: but to eat with unwashen hands defileth not a man. Matt: 17-20

Thou shalt not lie carnally with thy neighbour's wife, to defile thyself with her. Lev. 18:20-24

Neither shalt thou lie with any beast to defile thyself therewith. Lev. 18:23

Thou hast defiled thy sanctuaries by the multitude of thine iniquities, by the iniquity of thy traffick; therefore will I bring forth a fire from the midst of thee, it shall devour thee. Ezek. 28:18-19

DEFRAUD

[Let] no man go beyond and defraud his brother in any matter: because that the Lord is the avenger of all such, as we also have forewarned you and testified. 1 Thes. 4:6

Thou shalt not defraud thy neighbour, neither rob him. Lev. 19:13

DELIGHT

I delight to do thy will, O my God: yea, thy law is within my heart. Ps. 40:8

Delight thyself also in the LORD; and he shall give thee the desires of thine heart. Ps. 37:4

They seek me daily, and delight to know my ways, as a nation that did righteousness, and forsook not the ordinance of their God: they ask of me the ordinances of justice; they take delight in approaching to God. Isa. 58:2

Yea, they have chosen their own ways, and their soul delighteth in their abominations. Isa. 66:3

If thou turn away thy foot from the sabbath, from doing thy pleasure on my holy day; and call the sabbath a delight, the holy of the LORD, honorable; and shalt honor him, not doing thy own ways, nor finding thine own pleasure, nor speaking thine own words: Then shalt thou delight thyself in the LORD; and I will cause thee to ride upon the high places of the earth, and feed thee with the heritage of Jacob thy father: for the mouth of the LORD hath spoken it. Isa. 58:13-14

DELIVER, DELIVERANCE

If ye do return unto the LORD with all your hearts, then put away the strange gods and Ashtaroth from among you, and prepare your hearts unto the LORD, and serve him only: and he will deliver you out of the hand of the Philistines. 1 Sam. 7:3

Do ye suppose that the Lord will still deliver us, while we sit upon our thrones and do not make use of the means which the Lord has provided for us? Alma 60:21

Thy God whom thou servest continually, he will deliver thee. Dan. 6:16

DENY

Ye should no more deny the coming of Christ. Alma 34:37

He said unto them all, If any man will come after me, let him deny himself, and take up his cross daily, and follow me. Luke 9:23

Teach any man the right way; for the right way is to believe in Christ and deny him not; for by denying him ye also deny the prophets and the law. 2 Ne. 25:28

He that looketh upon a woman to lust after her shall deny the faith, and shall not have the Spirit; and if he repents not he shall be cast out. D&C 42:23

Who is a liar but he that denieth that Jesus is the Christ? He is antichrist, that denieth the Father and the Son. 1 Jn. 2:22-23

Yea, wo be unto him that hearkeneth unto the precepts of men, and denieth the power of God, and the gift of the Holy Ghost! 2 Ne. 28:26

If ye deny the Holy Ghost when it once has had place in you, and ye know that ye deny it, behold, this is a sin which is unpardonable. Alma 39:6

Teach any man the right way; for the right way is to believe in Christ and deny him not; for by denying him ye also deny the prophets and the law. 2 Ne. 25:28

DEPART

Train up a child in the way he should go: and when he is old, he will not depart from it. Prov. 22:6

Depart from evil, and do good; seek peace, and pursue it. Ps. 34:14

DESIRE

For wisdom is better than rubies; and all the things that may be desired are not to be compared to it. Prov. 8:11

Let us not be desirous of vain glory, provoke-ing one another, envying one another. Gal. 5:26

Contend no more against the Holy Ghost, but that ye receive it, and take upon you the name of Christ; that ye humble yourselves even to the dust, and worship God, in whatsoever place ye may be in, in spirit and in truth; and that ye live in thanksgiving daily, for the many mercies and blessings which he doth bestow upon you. Alma 34:38

Delight thyself also in the LORD; and he shall give thee the desires of thine heart. Ps. 37:4

Yea, in the way of thy judgments, O LORD, have we waited for thee; the desire of our soul is to thy name, and to the remembrance of thee. Isa. 26:8

As newborn babes, desire the sincere milk of the word, that ye may grow thereby. 1 Pet. 2:2

All things whatsoever you desire of me, which are pertaining unto things of righteousness, in faith believing in me that you shall receive. D&C 11:13-14

DESPISE

Because ye despise this word, and trust in oppression or perverseness, and stay thereon: Therefore this iniquity shall be to you as a breach ready to fall, swelling out in a high wall, whose breaking cometh suddenly at an instant. Isa. 30:12-13

Ye despisers, and wonder, and perish: for I work a work in your days, a work which ye shall in no wise believe, though a man declare it unto you. Acts 13:41

Let no man despise thy youth; but be thou an example of the believers, in word, in conversation, in charity, in spirit, in faith, in purity. 1 Tim. 4:12

Let not him that eateth despise him that eateth not; and let not him which eateth not judge him that eateth. Rom. 14:3

Behold, happy is the man whom God correcteth: therefore despise not thou the chastening of the Almighty: For he maketh sore, and bindeth up; he woundeth, and his hands make whole. Job 5:17-18

The LORD saith, Be it far from me; for them that honour me I will honour, and they that despise me shall be lightly esteemed. 1 Sam. 2:30

He that is void of wisdom despiseth his neighbour: but a man of understanding holdeth his peace. Prov. 11:12

DESTROY, DESTROYER, DESTRUCTION

O that ye would listen to the word of his commands, and let not this pride of your hearts destroy your souls! Jacob 2:16

Woe be unto the pastors that destroy and scatter the sheep of my pasture! saith the LORD. Jer. 23:1

Come and fear not, and lay aside every sin, which easily doth beset you, which doth bind you down to destruction. Alma 7:15

Concerning the works of men, by the word of thy lips I have kept me from the paths of the destroyer. Ps. 17:4

The destruction of the transgressors and of the sinners shall be together, and they that forsake the LORD shall be consumed. Isa. 1:28

Enter ye in at the strait gate; for wide is the gate, and broad is the way, which leadeth to destruction, and many there be who go in thereat; Because strait is the gate, and narrow is the way, which leadeth unto life, and few there be that find it. 3 Ne. 14:13-14 (Matt. 7:13-14)

Suffer no ravenous wolf to enter among you, that ye may not be destroyed. Alma 5:60

Thou shouldest not have looked on the day of thy brother in the day that he became a stranger; neither shouldest thou have rejoiced over the children of Judah in the day of their destruction; neither shouldest thou have spoken proudly in the day of distress. Obad. 1:12

DETERMINE, DETERMINED, DETERMINATION

Be men, and be determined in one mind and in one heart, united in all things. 2 Ne. 1:21

DEVICE

They said, There is no hope: but we will walk after our own devices, and we will every one do the imagination of his evil heart. Jer. 18:12

DEVISE

WOE to them that devise iniquity, and work evil upon their beds! Micah 2:1

Devise not evil against thy neighbour, seeing he dwelleth securely by thee. Prov. 3:29

DEVIL, DEVILISH

Can ye think of being saved when you have yielded yourselves to become subjects to the devil? Alma 5:20

These signs shall follow them that believe - in my name shall they cast out devils; they shall speak with new tongues; they shall take up serpents; and if they drink any deadly thing it shall not hurt them; they shall lay hands on the sick and they shall recover. Morm. 9:24 (Mark 16:17-18)

Ye will not suffer your children that they go hungry, or naked; neither will ye suffer that they transgress the laws of God, and fight and quarrel one with another, and serve the devil, who is the master of sin, or who is the evil spirit which hath been spoken of by our fathers, he being an enemy to all righteousness. Mosiah 4:14

It must needs be that the devil should tempt the children of men, or they could not be agents unto themselves; for if they never should have bitter they could not know the sweet. D&C 29:39

DILIGENCE, DILIGENT, DILIGENTLY

They labored, with all diligence, according to the commandments of the Lord. Jacob 5:74

Whatsoever is commanded by the God of heaven, let it be diligently done for the house of the God of heaven. Ezra 7:23

Be thou diligent to know the state of thy flocks, and look well to thy herds. For riches are not for ever: and doth the crown endure to every generation. Prov. 27:23-24

But without faith it is impossible to please him: for he that cometh to God must believe that he is, and that he is a rewarder of them that diligently seek him. Heb. 11:6

They were men of a sound understanding and they had searched the scriptures diligently, that they might know the word of God. Alma 17:2

And these words, which I command thee this day, shall be in thine heart: And thou shalt teach them diligently unto thy children, and shalt talk of them when thou sittest in thine house, and when thou walkest by the way and when thou liest down, and when thou risest up. And thou shalt bind them for a sign upon thine hand, and they shalt be as frontlets between thine eyes. And thou shalt write them upon the posts of thy house, and on thy gates. Deut. 6:6-9

Give diligence to make your calling and election sure. 2 Pet. 1:10

The soul of the sluggard desireth, and hath nothing: but the soul of the diligent shall be made fat. Prov. 13:4

Turn to the Lord with full purpose of heart, and put your trust in him, and serve him with all diligence of mind. Mosiah 7:33

DIMINISH

Ye shall not add unto the word which I command you, neither shall ye diminish ought from it, that ye may keep the commandments of the LORD your God which I command you. Deut. 4:2

What thing soever I command you, observe to do it: thou shalt not add thereto, nor diminish from it. Deut. 12:32

DIRECT

In all thy ways acknowledge him, and he shall direct thy paths. Prov. 3:6

Be directed by the Spirit. D&C 42:13

DISCERN

Discern the signs of the times. Matt. 16:3

Discern between the righteous and the wicked, between him that serveth God and him that serveth him not. 3 Ne. 24:18

DISCORD

These six things doth the LORD hate: yea, seven are an abomination unto him: A proud look, a lying tongue, and hands that shed innocent blood, An heart that deviseth wicked imaginations, feet that be swift in running to mischief, A false witness that speaketh lies, and he that soweth discord among brethren. Prov. 6:16-19

DISCRETE, DISCRETION

Be discreet, chaste, keepers at home, good, obedient to their own husbands, that the word of God be not blasphemed. Titus 2:5

Keep sound wisdom and discretion: So shall they be life unto thy soul, and grace to thy neck. Prov. 3:21-22

My son, attend unto my wisdom, and bow thine ear to my understanding: That thou mayest regard discretion and thy lips may keep knowledge. Prov. 5:2

DISHONOR

God also gave them up to uncleanness through the lusts of their own hearts, to dishonour their own bodies between them-selves. Rom. 1:24

DISMAY, DISMAYED

Be strong and of good courage, and do it: fear not, nor be dismayed: for the LORD GOD, even my GOD, will be with thee; he will not fail thee, nor forsake thee. 1 Chron. 28:20

Be strong and of a good courage; be not afraid, neither be thou dismayed; for the Lord thy God is with thee whithersoever thou goest. Josh. 1:9

DISORDERLY

We command you, brethren, in the name of our Lord Jesus Christ, that ye withdraw yourselves from every brother that walketh disorderly, and not after the tradition which he received of us. 2 Thes. 3:6

DISPUTE

Do all things without murmurings and disputings: That ye may be blameless and harmless, the sons of God, without rebuke, in the midst of a crooked and perverse nation, among whom ye shine as lights in the world. Philip. 2:14-15

Can ye dispute the power of God? Mosiah 27:15

Dispute not because ye see not, for ye receive no witness until after the trial of your faith. Ether 12:6

DISTRIBUTE, DISTRIBUTION

Now when Jesus heard these things, he said unto him, Yet lackest thou one thing: sell all that thou hast, and distribute unto the poor, and thou shalt have treasure in heaven: and come, follow me. Luke 18:22

[Distribute] to the necessity of saints; given to hospitality. Rom. 12:13

DIVINATION

There shall be no more any vain vision nor flattering divination within the house of Israel. Ezek. 12:24

DIVINE NATURE

According as his divine power hath given unto us all things that pertain unto life and godliness, through the knowledge of him that hath called us to glory and virtue: Whereby we are given unto us exceeding great and precious promises: that by these ye might be partakers of the divine nature, having escaped the corruption that is in the world through lust. 2 Pet. 1:3-4

DIVORCE, DIVORCEMENT

What therefore God hath joined together, let not man put asunder. Mark 10:9

Whosoever putteth away his wife, and marrieth another, committeth adultery: and whosoever marrieth her that is put away from her husband committeth adultery. Luke 16:18

Unto the married I command, yet not I, but the Lord, Let not the wife depart from her husband: But and if she depart, let her remain unmarried, or be reconciled to her husband: and let not the husband put away his wife. 1 Cor. 7:10-11

DO, DOINGS, DOER

For with God nothing shall be impossible. Luke 1:37

Trust in the LORD, and do good. Ps. 37:3

Do after the will of your God. Ezra 7:18

Therefore remember, O man, for all thy doings thou shalt be brought into judgment. 1 Ne. 10:20

Declare his doings among the people. 2 Ne. 22:4

Whether therefore ye eat, or drink, or whatsoever ye do, do all to the glory of God. 1 Cor. 10:31

Let us be wise and look forward to these things, and do that which will make for the peace of this people. Mosiah 29:10

I am the vine, yea are the branches: He that abideth in me, and I in him, the same bringeth forth much fruit: for without me ye can do nothing. John 15:5

I, the Lord, am bound when ye do what I say; but when ye do not what I say, ye have no promise. D&C 82:10

He did that which was right in the sight of the LORD. 2 Chron. 29:2

This one thing I do, forgetting those things which are behind, and reaching forth unto those things which are before, I press toward the mark for the prize of the high calling of God in Christ Jesus. Philip 3:13-14

Go ye therefore, and do the works of Abraham. D&C 132:32

Work the works of God. John 6:28

If I then, your Lord and Master, have ashed your feet; ye also ought to wash one another's feet. For I have given you an example, that ye should do as I have done to you. John 13:14-15

Those things, which ye have both learned, and received, and heard, and seen in me, do: and the God of peace shall be with you. Philip. 4:9

Be ye doers of the word, and not hearers only, deceiving your own selves. For if any be a hearer of the word, and not a doer, he is like unto a man beholding his natural face in a glass: For he beholdeth himself, and goeth his way, and straightway forgetteth what manner of man he was. James 1:22-24

Say not, I will do so to him as he hath done to me; I will render to the man according to his work. Prov. 24:29

O inhabitants of Jerusalem, and men of Judah, judge, I pray you, betwixt me and my vineyard. What could have been done more to my vineyard, that I have not done in it? Isa. 5:3-4

Counsel with the Lord in all thy doings, and he will direct thee for good; yea,, when thou liest down at night lie down unto the Lord, that he may watch over you in your sleep; and when thou risest in the morning let thy heart be full of thanks unto God. Alma 37:37

To him that knoweth to do good, and doeth it not, to him it is sin. James 4:17

How is it that ye have forgotten that the Lord is able to do all things according to his will, for the children of men, if it so be that they exercise faith in him? 1 Ne. 7:12

This book of the law shall not depart out of thy mouth; but thou shalt meditate therein day and night, that thou mayest observe to do according to all that is written therein: for then thou shalt make thy way prosperous, and then thou shalt have good success. Josh. 1:8

So is the will of God, that with well doing ye may put to silence the ignorance of foolish men: As free, and not using your liberty for a cloke of maliciousness, but as the servants of God. 1 Pet. 2:15-16

Therefore, strengthen your brethren in all your conversation, in all your prayers, in all your exhortations, and in all your doings. D&C 108:7

Whatsoever ye do in word or deed, do all in the name of the Lord Jesus, giving thanks to God and the Father by him. Col. 3:17

Do well on the sabbath days. Matt. 12:12

Learn to do well; seek judgment, relieve the oppressed, judge the fatherless, plead for the widow. Isa. 1:17

Believe that ye must repent of your sins and forsake them, and humble yourselves before God; and ask in sincerity of heart that he would forgive you; and now, if you believe all these things see that ye do them. Mosiah 4:10

Cry unto God for all thy support; yea, let all thy doings be unto the Lord, and whither-soever thou goest let it be in the Lord; yea, let all thy thoughts be directed unto the Lord; yea, let the affections of thy heart be placed upon the Lord forever. Alma 37:36

Thus shall ye do in the fear of the LORD, faithfully, and with a perfect heart. 2 Chron. 19:9

Therefore, all things whatsoever ye would that men should do to you, do ye even so to them, for this is the law and the prophets. 3 Ne. 14:12 (Matt. 7:12)

Whatsoever ye do, do it heartily, as to the Lord and not unto men. Col. 3:23

By what authority doest thou these things? and who gave thee this authority to do these things? And Jesus answered and said unto them, I will also ask of you one question, and answer me, and I will tell you by what authority I do these things. Mark 11:28

DOCTRINE

Speak concerning the doctrine of Christ. 2 Ne. 31:2

Be no more children, tossed to and fro, and carried about with every wind of doctrine, by the sleight of men, and cunning craftiness, whereby they lie in wait to deceive. Eph. 4:14

For the time will come when they will not endure sound doctrine; but after their own lusts shall they heap to themselves teachers, having itching ears; And they shall turn away their ears from the truth, and shall be turned unto fables. 2 Tim. 4:3-4

Be not carried about with divers and strange doctrines. For it is a good thing that the heart be established with grace; not with meats, which have not profited them that have been occupied therein. Heb. 13:9

All scripture is given by inspiration of God, and is profitable for doctrine, for reproof, for correction, for instruction in righteousness: That the man of God may be perfect, throughly furnished unto all good works. 2 Tim. 3:16-17

Speak thou the things which become sound doctrine: That the aged men be sober, grave, temperate, sound in faith, in charity, in patience. Titus 2:1-2

This people draweth nigh unto me with their mouth, and honoureth me with their lips; but their heart is far from me. But in vain they do worship me, teaching for doctrines the commandments of men. Matt. 15:8-9

DOMINION

Let not any iniquity have dominion over me. Ps. 119:133

We have learned by sad experience that it is the nature and disposition of almost all men, as soon as they get a little authority, as they suppose, they will immediately begin to exercise unrighteous dominion. D&C 121:39

Be fruitful, and multiply, and replenish the earth and subdue it, and have dominion over the fish of the sea, and over the fowl of the air, and over every living thing that moveth upon the earth. Moses 2:28

When we undertake to cover our sins, or to gratify our pride, our vain ambition, or to exercise control or dominion or compulsion upon the souls of the children of men, in any degree of unrighteousness, behold, the heavens withdraw themselves; the Spirit of the Lord is grieved. D&C 121:37

Have dominion over the fish of the sea, and over the fowl of the air, and over the cattle, and over all the earth, and over every creeping thing that creepeth upon the earth. Gen. 1:26

DOOR

I am the door: by me if any man enter in, he shall be saved, and shall go in and out, and find pasture. John 10:9

Behold, I stand at the door, and knock: if any man hear my voice, and open the door, I will come in to him, and will sup with him, and he with me. Rev. 3:20

DOUBLE, DOUBLE MINDED

A double minded man is unstable in all his ways. James 1:8

They speak vanity every one with his neighbour: with flattering lips and with a double heart. Ps. 12:2

DOUBT, DOUBTFUL

Have faith, and doubt not. Matt. 21:21

O then despise not, and wonder not, but hearken unto the words of the Lord, and ask the Father in the name of Jesus for what things soever ye shall stand in need. Doubt not, but be believing. Morm. 9:27

DRAW NEAR

Draw nigh to God, and he will draw nigh to you. James 4:8

Draw near unto me and I will draw near unto you; seek me diligently and ye shall find me; ask, and ye shall receive; knock, and it shall be opened unto you. D&C 88:63 (James 4:8)

Let us draw near with a true heart in full assurance of faith, having our hearts sprinkled from an evil conscience, and our bodies washed with pure water. Heb. 10:22

It is good for me to draw near to God: I have put my trust in the Lord GOD. Ps. 73:28

DREAM

The prophet that hath a dream, let him tell a dream. Jer. 23:28

Now the wise men, the astrologers, have been brought in before me, that they should read this writing, and make known unto me the interpretation thereof: but they could not shew the interpretation of the thing. Dan 5:15

The secret which the king hath demanded cannot the wise men, the astrologers, the magicians, the soothsayers, shew unto the king; But there is a God in heaven that revealeth secrets, and maketh known to the king Nebuchadnezzar what shall be in the latter days. Dan. 1:27-28

I will pour out my spirit upon all flesh; and your sons and your daughters shall prophesy, your old men shall dream dreams, your young men shall see visions. Joel 2:28

DRINK, DRUNK, DRUNKENNESS

Cease drunkenness. D&C 136:24

Be not drunk with wine, wherein is excess; but be filled with the Spirit. Eph. 5:18

Be not among winebibbers; among riotous eaters of flesh: for the drunkard and the glutton shall come to poverty: and drowsiness shall clothe a man with rags. Prov. 23:20-21

Wo unto them that rise up early in the morning, that they may follow strong drink, that continue until night, and wine inflame them. 2 Ne. 15:11-12

DROSS

Take away the dross from the silver, and there shall come forth a vessel for the finer. Prov. 25:4

DUE

Withhold not good from them to whom it is due, when it is in the power of thine hand to do it. Prov. 3:27

DUMB

[They] were beyond measure astonished, saying, He hath done all things well: he maketh both the deaf to hear, and the dumb to speak. Mark 7:37

When Jesus saw that the people came running together, he rebuked the foul spirit, saying unto him, Thou dumb and deaf spirit, I charge thee, come out of him, and enter no more into him. Mark 9:25

DUST

And the LORD God formed man of the dust of the ground, and breathed into his nostrils the breath of life; and man became a living soul. Gen 2:7

DWELL

Hear now this, thou that art given to pleasures, that dwellest carelessly, that sayest in thine heart, I am, and none else beside me. Isa. 47:8

How good and how pleasant it is for brethren to dwell together in unity! Ps. 133:1

Whosoever shall confess that Jesus is the Son of God, God dwelleth in him, and he in God. 1 Jn. 4:15

EAR

For the time will come when they will not endure sound doctrine; but after their own lusts shall they heap to themselves teachers, having itching ears; And they shall turn away their ears from the truth, and shall be turned unto fables. 2 Tim. 4:3-4

Give ear, O my people, to my law: incline your ears to the words of my mouth. Ps. 78:1

The eyes of them that see shall not be dim, and the ears of them that hear shall hearken. Isa. 32:3

EARLY

O GOD, thou art my God; early will I seek thee: my soul thirsteth for thee. Ps. 63:1

EARNEST, EARNESTLY

We ought to give the more earnest heed to the things which we have heard, lest at any time we should let them slip. Heb. 2:1

Beloved, when I gave all diligence to write unto you of the common salvation, it was needful for me to write unto you, and exhort you that ye should earnestly contend for the faith which was once delivered unto the saints. Jude 1:3

EARTH

It is a light thing that thou shouldest be my servant to raise up the tribes of Jacob, and to restore the preserved of Israel: I will also give thee for a light to the Gentiles, that thou mayest be my salvation unto the end of the earth. Isa. 49:6

But the LORD is in his holy temple: let all the earth keep silence before him. Hab. 2:20

EASE, EASIER, EASINESS, EASY

He sent fiery flying serpents among them; and after they were bitten he prepared a way that they might be healed; and the labor which they had to perform was to look, and because of the simpleness of the way, or the easiness of it, there were many who perished. 1 Ne. 17:41

Thus we see that the Lord began to pour out his Spirit upon the Lamanites, because of their easiness and willingness to believe in his words. Hel. 6:36

Oh my son, do not let us be slothful because of the easiness of the way; for so was it with our fathers; for so was it prepared for them, that if they would look they might live; even so it is with us. The way is prepared, and if we will look we may live forever. Alma 37:46

EAT, EATEN

Let not him that eateth despise him that eateth not; and let not him which eateth not judge him that eateth. Rom. 14:3

If thine enemy be hungry, give him bread to eat; and if he be thirsty, give him water to drink: for thou shalt heap coals of fire upon his head, and the LORD shall reward thee. Prov. 25:21-22

They, continuing daily with one accord in the temple, and breaking bread from house to house, did eat their meat with gladness and singleness of heart. Acts 2:46

For even when we were with you, this we commanded you, that if any would not work, neither should he eat. 2 Thes. 3:10

Eat thou not the bread of him that hath an evil eye, neither desire thou his dainty meats. Prov. 23:6-8

Whether therefore ye eat, or drink, or whatsoever ye do, do all to the glory of God. 1 Cor. 10:31

Eat so much as is sufficient for thee, lest thou be filled therewith, and vomit it. Prov. 25:16

By the sweat of thy face shalt thou eat bread, until thou shalt return unto the ground. Moses 4:25

EDIFICATION, EDIFIED, EDIFY

Teach no other doctrine, Neither give heed to fables and endless genealogies, which minister questions, rather than godly edifying which is in faith: so do. 1 Tim. 1:3-4

If any man among you be strong in the Spirit, let him take with him him that is weak, that he may be edified in all meekness, that he may become strong also. D&C 84:106

Follow after the things which make for peace, and things wherewith one may edify another. Rom. 14:19

Let no corrupt communication proceed out of your mouth, but that which is good to the use of edifying, that it may minister grace unto the hearers. Eph. 4:29

ELDER

Against an elder, receive not an accusation but before two or three witnesses. 1 Tim. 5:19

Is any sick among you? let him call for the elders of the church; and let them pray over him, anointing him with oil in the name of the Lord: And the prayer of faith shall save the sick, and the Lord shall raise him up; and if he have committed sins, they shall be forgiven him. James 5:14-15

Rebuke not an elder, but intreat him as a father; and the younger men as brethren; The elder women as mothers; the younger as sisters, with all purity. 1 Tim. 5 1-2

ELECT, ELECTION

False Christs and false prophets shall rise, and shall shew signs and wonders, to seduce, if it were possible, even the elect. Mark 13:22

Give diligence to make your calling and election sure. 2 Pet. 1:10

EMPATHIZE, EMPATHY

Blessed be God, even the Father of our Lord Jesus Christ, the Father of mercies, and the God of all comfort; Who comforteth us in all our tribulation, that we may be able to comfort them which are in any trouble, by the comfort wherewith we ourselves are comforted of God. For as the sufferings of Christ abound in us, so our consolation also aboundeth by Christ. 2 Cor. 1:3-5

ENCHANTMENT

Hearken not ye to your prophets, nor to your diviners, nor to your dreamers, nor to your enchantments, nor to your sorcerers, which speak unto you, saying, Ye shall not serve the king of Babylon: For they prophesy a lie unto you. Jer. 27:9-10

END

Be obedient unto the end of your lives. Mosiah 5:8

O that they were wise, that they understood this, that they would consider their latter end! Deut. 32:29

Hold fast the confidence and the rejoicing of the hope firm unto the end. Heb. 3:6

ENDURE, ENDURANCE

Endureth to the end. Matt. 10:22

We believe in being honest, true, chaste, benevolent, virtuous, and in doing good to all men; indeed, we may say that we follow the admonition of Paul - We believe all things, we hope all things, we have endured many things, and hope to be able to endure all things. If there is anything virtuous, lovely, or of good report or praiseworthy, we seek after these things. A of F-13

Charity suffereth long, and is kind, and envieth not, and is not puffed up, seeketh not her own, is not easily provoked, thinketh no evil, and rejoiceth not in iniquity but rejoiceth in the truth, beareth all things, believeth all things, hopeth all things, endureth all things. Moro. 7:45 (1 Cor. 13:4-13)

Endureth temptation. James 1:12-15

ENEMIES, ENEMY

Love your enemies, bless them that curse you, do good to them that hate you, and pray for them which despitefully use you, and persecute you. Matt. 5:44

We made our prayer unto our God, and set a watch against them day and night. Neh. 4:9

Rejoice not when thine enemy falleth, and let not thine heart be glad when he stumbleth: Lest the LORD see it, and it displease him, and he turn away his wrath from him. Prov. 24:17-18

If thine enemy be hungry, give him bread to eat; and if he be thirsty, give him water to drink: for thou shalt heap coals of fire upon his head, and the LORD shall reward thee. Prov. 25:21-22

O Israel, ye approach this day unto battle against your enemies; let not your hearts faint, fear not and do not tremble of them neither be ye terrified because of them; for the LORD your GOD is he that goeth with you, to fight for you against your enemies, to save you. Deut. 20:3-4

Love your enemies, bless them that curse you, do good to them that hate you, and pray for them who despitefully use you and persecute you; That ye may be the children of your Father who is in heaven; for he maketh his sun to rise on the evil and on the good. 3 Ne. 12:43-45 (Matt. 5:44-45)

He doth not command us that we shall subject ourselves to our enemies, but that we should put our trust in him, and he will deliver us. Alma 61:13

ENLIGHTEN, ENLIGHTENED

Thus we can plainly discern, that after a people have been once enlightened by the Spirit of God, and have had great knowledge of things pertaining to righteousness, and then have fallen away into sin and transgression, they become more hardened, and thus their state becomes worse than though they had never known these things. Alma 24:30

For it is impossible for those who were once enlightened, and have tasted of the heavenly gift, and were made partakers of the Holy Ghost, And have tasted the good word of God, and the powers of the world to come, If they shall fall away, to renew them again unto repentance; seeing they crucify to themselves the Son of God afresh, and put him to an open shame. Heb. 6:4

ENTANGLE

If after they have escaped the pollutions of the world through the knowledge of the Lord and Savior Jesus Christ, they are again entangled therein, and overcome, the latter end is worse with them than the beginning. For it had been better for them not to have known the way of righteousness, than, after they have known it, to turn from the holy commandment delivered unto them. But it is happened unto them according to the true proverb, The dog is turned to his own vomit again; and the sow that was washed to her wallowing in the mire. 2 Pet. 2:20-22

Then went the Pharisees, and took counsel how they might entangle him in his talk. Matt. 22:15

ENTER, ENTRANCE

Strive to enter in at the strait gate: for many, I say unto you, will seek to enter in, and shall not be able. Luke 13:24

Not every one that saith unto me, Lord, Lord, shall enter into the kingdom of heaven; but he that doeth the will of my Father who is in heaven. Many will say to me in that day: Lord, Lord, have we not prophesied in thy name, and in thy name have cast out devils, and in thy name done many wonderful works? And then will I profess unto them: I never knew you; depart from me, ye that work iniquity. Matt. 7:21-23

Enter not into the paths of the wicked, and go not in the way of evil men. Avoid it, pass not by it, turn from it, and pass away. Prov. 4:14-15

Open ye the gates, that the righteous nation which keepeth the truth may enter in. Isa. 26:2

Jesus answered, Verily, verily, I say unto thee, Except a man be born of water and of the Spirit, he cannot enter into the kingdom of God. John 3:5

It is easier for a camel to go through the eye of a needle, than for a rich man to enter into the kingdom of God. Matt 19:24

Eye hath not seen, nor ear heard, neither have entered into the heart of man, the things which God hath prepared for them that love him. But God hath reveled them unto us by his Spirit; for the Spirit searcheth all things, yea, the deep things of God. 1 Cor. 2:9-10

ENTICE

If sinners entice thee, consent thou not. Prov. 1:10

ENTREAT, ENTREATED

Rebuke not an elder, but intreat him as a father; and the younger men as brethren; The elder women as mothers; the younger as sisters, with all purity. 1 Tim. 5 1-2

I would that ye should be humble, and be submissive and gentle; easy to be entreated; full of patience and long-suffering; being temperate in all things; being diligent in keeping the commandments of God at all times; asking for whatsoever things ye stand in need, both spiritual and temporal; always returning thanks unto God for whatsoever things ye do receive. Alma 7:23

ENVIOUS, ENVY

Let us not be desirous of vain glory, provoking one another, envying one another. Gal. 5:26

For where envying and strife is, there is confusion and every evil work. James 3:16

Wrath killeth the foolish man, and envy slayeth the silly one. Job 5:2

Fret not thyself because of evil doers, neither be thou envious against the workers of iniquity. Ps. 37:1

Envy not the oppressor, and choose none of his ways. Prov. 3:31-32

Walk honestly, as in the day; not in rioting and drunkenness, not in chambering and wantonness, not in strife and envying. Rom. 13:13

Let not thine heart envy sinners: but be thou in the fear of the LORD all the day long. Prov. 23:17

EQUAL, EQUALITY, EQUITY

The law of truth was in his mouth, and iniquity was not found in his lips: he walked with me in peace and equity, and did turn many away from iniquity. Mal. 2:6

Think of your brethren like unto yourselves, and be familiar with all and free with your substance, that they may be rich like unto you. Jacob 2:17

How much less to him that accepteth not the persons of princes, nor regard the rich more than the poor? for they all are the work of his hands. Job 34:19

Regardest not the person of men. Matt. 22:16

There is neither Jew nor Greek, there is neither bond nor free, there is neither male nor female: for ye are all one in Christ Jesus. Gal. 3:28

I charge thee before God, and the Lord Jesus Christ, and the elect angels, that thou observe these things without preferring one before another, doing nothing by partiality. 1 Tim. 5:21

ERR, ERROR

The leaders of this people cause them to err; and they that are led of them are destroyed. Isa. 9:16

It is a people that do err in their heart, and they have not known my ways. Ps. 95:10

The vile person will speak villany, and his heart will work iniquity, to practise hypocrisy, and to utter error against the LORD, to make empty the soul of the hungry. Isa. 32:6

ESCAPE

How shall we escape, if we neglect so great salvation; which at the first began to be spoken by the Lord, and was confirmed unto us by them that heard him; God also bearing them witness, both with signs and wonders, and with divers miracles, and gifts of the Holy Ghost, according to his own will? Heb. 2:3-4

There hath no temptation taken you but such as is common to man: but God is faithful, who will not suffer you to be tempted above that ye are able; but will with the temptation also make a way to escape, that ye may be able to bear it. 1 Cor. 10:13

ESCHEW

Let him eschew evil, and do good; let him seek peace, and ensue it. 1 Pet. 3:11

ESTABLISH, ESTABLISHED

If ye will not believe, surely ye shall not be established. Isa. 7:9

Ye that make mention of the LORD, keep not silence, And give him no rest, till he establish, and till he make Jerusalem a praise in the earth. Isa. 62:6-7

He shall not be afraid of evil tidings: his heart is fixed, trusting in the LORD. His heart is established, he shall not be afraid. Ps. 112:7-8

We thought it good to be left at Athens alone; and sent Timotheus, our brother, and minister of God, and our fellowlabourer in the gospel of Christ, to establish you, and to comfort you concerning your faith. 1 Thes. 3:1-2

Ponder the path of thy feet and let all thy ways be established. Prov. 4:26

Believe in the Lord your God, so shall ye be established; believe his prophets, so shall ye prosper. 2 Chron. 20:20

Organize yourselves; prepare every needful thing; and establish a house, even a house of prayer, a house of fasting, a house of faith, a house of learning, a house of glory, a house of order, a house of God. D&C 88:119

ESTEEM

Let nothing be done through strife or vainglory; but in lowliness of mind let each esteem other better than themselves. Philip. 2:3

God knoweth your hearts: for that which is highly esteemed among men is abomination in the sight of God. Luke 16:15

Ye shall not esteem one flesh above another, or one man shall not think himself above another. Mosiah 23:7

Let every man esteem his brother as himself, and practice virtue and holiness before me. D&C 38:24

ETERNAL, ETERNAL LIFE, ETERNALLY, ETERNITY

The eternal purposes of the Lord shall roll on, until all his promises shall be fulfilled. Morm. 8:22

Search the scriptures; for in them ye think ye have eternal life: and they are they which testify of me. John 5:39

This is life eternal, that they might know thee the only true God, and Jesus Christ, whom thou hast sent. John 17:3

Fight the good fight of faith, lay hold on eternal life, whereunto thou art also called, and hast professed a good profession before many witnesses. 1 Tim. 6:12

EVERLASTING COVENANT

Be ye mindful always of his covenant; the word which he commanded to a thousand generations; Even of the covenant which he made with Abraham, and of his oath unto Isaac; And hath confirmed the same to Jacob for a law, and to Israel for an everlasting covenant. 1 Chron. 16:15-17

The earth also is defiled under the inhabitants thereof; because they have transgressed the laws, changed the ordinance, broken the everlasting covenant. Isa. 24:5

EVERLASTING FIRE

Wherefore if thy hand or thy foot offend thee, cut them off, and cast them from thee: it is better for thee to enter into life halt or maimed, rather than having two hands or two feet to be cast into everlasting fire. Matt. 18:8

EVERLASTING LIFE

Labour not for the meat which perisheth, but for that meat which endureth unto everlasting life. John 6:27

He that heareth my word, and believeth on him that sent me, hath everlasting life, and shall not come into condemnation; but is passed from death unto life. John 5:24

But whosoever drinketh of the water that I shall give him shall never thirst; but the water that I shall give him shall be in him a well of water springing up into everlasting life. John 4:14

For God so loved the world, that he gave his only begotten Son, that whosoever believeth in him should not perish, but have everlasting life. John 3:16

EVERYWHERE

Whither shall I go from thy spirit? or whither shall I flee from thy presence? Ps. 139:4-7

EVIL

Do no evil. 2 Cor. 13:7

Touch not the evil gift, nor the unclean thing. Moro. 10:30

Be not overcome of evil, but overcome evil with good. Rom. 12:21

A man being evil cannot do that which is good; neither will he give a good gift. Moro. 7:10

The love of money is the root of all evil: which while some coveted after, they have erred from the faith, and pierced themselves through with many sorrows. 1 Tim. 6:9

It is given unto them to know good from evil; wherefore they are agents unto themselves. Moses 6:56

Take therefore no thought for the morrow, for the morrow shall take thought for the things of itself. Sufficient is the day unto the evil thereof. 3 Ne. 13:34

Turn not to the right hand nor to the left: remove thy foot from evil. Prov. 4:27

Then went the Pharisees, and took counsel how they might entangle him in his talk. Matt. 22:15

That which cometh out of the man, that defileth the man. For from within, out of the heart of men, proceed evil thoughts, adulteries, fornications, murders, thefts, covetousness, wicked-ness, deceit, lasciviousness, an evil eye, blasphemy, pride, foolishness: All these evil things come from within, and defile the man. Mark 7:20-23

Though I walk through the valley of the shadow of death, I will fear no evil: for thou art with me. Ps. 23:4

Evil shall slay the wicked: and they that hate the righteous shall be desolate. Ps. 34:21

He shall not be afraid of evil tidings: his heart is fixed, trusting in the LORD. His heart is established, he shall not be afraid. Ps. 112:7-8

Rejoice [not] to do evil, and delight in the frowardness of the wicked. Prov. 2:14

The fear of the LORD is to hate evil: pride, and arrogancy, and the evil way, and the froward mouth, do I hate. Prov. 8:13

Eat thou not the bread of him that hath an evil eye, neither desire thou his dainty meats. Prov. 23:6-8

If thou hast done foolishly in lifting up thyself, or if thou has thought evil, lay thine hand upon thy mouth. Prov. 30:32

Woe unto them that call evil good, and good evil; that put darkness for light, and light for darkness; that put bitter for sweet and sweet for bitter! Isa. 5:20

Ye have wearied the LORD with your words. Yet ye say, Wherein have we wearied him? When ye say, Every one that doeth evil is good in the sight of the LORD. Mal. 2:17

Return ye now every one from his evil way, and make your ways and your doings good. Jer. 18:11

Be ye not as your fathers, unto whom the former prophets have cried, saying, Thus saith the LORD of hosts; Turn ye now from your evil ways, and from your evil doings: but they did not hear, nor hearken unto me, saith the LORD. Zech. 1:4

Ye have wearied the LORD with your words. Yet ye say, Wherein have we wearied him? When ye say, Every one that doeth evil is good in the sight of the LORD, and he delighteth in them. Mal. 2:17

It shall come to pass at that time, that I will search Jerusalem with candles, and punish the men that are settled on their lees: that say in their heart, The LORD will not do good, neither will he do evil. Zeph. 1:12

Devise not evil against thy neighbour, seeing he dwelleth securely by thee. Prov. 3:29

Do [no] evil in the sight of the LORD, to provoke him to anger. 2 Kgs. 17:17

I have not sat with vain persons, neither will I go in with dissemblers. I have hated the congregation of evil doers; and will not sit with the wicked. Ps. 26:4-5

Depart from evil, and do good; seek peace, and pursue it. Ps. 34:14

As righteousness tendeth to life: so he that pursueth evil pursueth it to his own death. Prov. 11:19

I have refrained my feet from every evil way, that I might keep thy word. Ps. 119:101

They are not valiant for the truth upon the earth, for they proceed from evil to evil, and they know not me, saith the LORD. Jer. 9:3

Turn ye again now every one from his evil way, and from the evil of your doings, and dwell in the land that the LORD hath given unto you and to your fathers for ever and ever. Jer. 25:5

Abhor that which is evil; cleave to that which is good. Rom. 12:9

When thine eye is evil, thy body also is full of darkness. Take heed therefore that the light which is in thee be not darkness. Luke 11:34-35

Thou shalt not speak evil of thy neighbor, nor do him any harm. D&C 42:27

Do men gather grapes of thorns, or figs of thistles? Even so every good tree bringeth forth good fruit; but a corrupt tree bringeth forth evil fruit. A good tree cannot bring forth evil fruit, neither can a corrupt tree bring forth good fruit. Every tree that bringeth not forth good fruit is hewn down, and cast into the fire. Wherefore by their fruits ye shall know them. Matt. 7:16-20

See that none render evil for evil unto any man; but ever follow that which is good, both among yourselves, and to all men. 1 Thes. 5:15

Ye shall forsake all evil and cleave unto all good, that ye shall live by every word which proceedeth forth out of the mouth of God. D&C 98:11

Wo unto them that call evil good, and good evil, that put darkness for light, and light for darkness, that put bitter for sweet, and sweet for bitter. 2 Ne. 15:20

Beware, lest there shall arise contentions among you, and ye list to obey the evil spirit. Mosiah 2:32

Refuse the evil and choose the good. 2 Ne. 17:15

EXACT

Exact no more than that which is appointed you. Luke 3:13

EXALT, EXALTATION

Let not the rebellious exalt themselves. Ps. 66:7

Exalt not yourselves. D&C 112:15

Exalt the LORD our God, and worship at his holy hill; for the LORD our God is holy. Ps. 99:9

EXAMINE

Whosoever shall eat this bread, and drink this cup of the Lord, unworthily, shall be guilty of the body and blood of the Lord. But let a man examine himself, and so let him eat of that bread, and drink of that cup. For he that eateth and drinketh unworthily, eateth and drinketh damnation to himself, not discerning the Lord's body. 1 Cor. 11:27-29

EXAMPLE, ENSAMPLE

Set a good example. Alma 39:1

Those things, which ye have both learned, and received, and heard, and seen in me, do: and the God of peace shall be with you. Philip. 4:9

He that saith he abideth in him ought himself also so to walk, even as he walked. 1 Jn. 2:6

If I then, your Lord and Master, have ashed your feet; ye also ought to wash one another's feet. For I have given you an example, that ye should do as I have done to you. John 13:14-15

Let no man despise thy youth; but be thou an example of the believers, in word, in conversation, in charity, in spirit, in faith, in purity. 1 Tim. 4:12

Let your light so shine before men, that they may see your good works, and glorify your Father which is in heaven. Matt. 5:16

EXCEL, EXCELLENT

Approve things that are excellent; that ye may be sincere and without offense till the day of Christ. Philip. 1:10

God hath set some in the church, first apostles, secondarily prophets, thirdly teachers, after that miracles, then gifts of healings, helps, governments, diversities of tongues. Are all apostles? are all prophets? are all teachers? are all workers of miracles? Have all the gifts of healing? do all speak with tongues? do all interpret? But covet earnestly the best gifts: and yet shew I unto you a more excellent way. 1 Cor. 12:28-31

EXCESS

Be not drunk with wine, wherein is excess; but be filled with the Spirit. Eph. 5:18

EXCUSE

Do not endeavor to excuse yourself in the least point because of your sins, by denying the justice of God; but do you let the justice of God, and his mercy, and his long suffering have full sway in your heart, and let it bring you down to the dust in humility. Alma 42:30

EXEMPT

None shall be exempted from the justice and the laws of God, that all things may be done in order and in solemnity before him, according to truth and righteousness. D&C 107:84

EXERCISE

Exercise thyself rather unto godliness. 1 Tim. 4:7

EXHORT

They that have believeing masters, let them not despise them, because they are brethren; but rather do them service, because they are faithful and beloved, partakers of the benefit. These things teach and exhort. 1 Tim 6:3

EXIST, EXISTENCE

The fool hath said in his heart, There is no God. They are corrupt, they have done abominable works, there is none that doeth good. Ps. 14:1

EXPERIENCE

If ye have experienced a change of heart, and if ye have felt to sing the song of redeeming love, I would ask, can ye feel so now? Alma 5:26

EXTORT

Know ye not that the unrighteous shall not inherit the kingdom of God? Be not deceived: neither fornicators, nor idolaters, nor adulterers, nor effeminate, nor abusers of themselves with mankind, Nor thieves, nor covetous, nor drunkards, nor revilers, nor extortioners, shall inherit the kingdom of God. 1 Cor. 6:9-10

Thou hast taken usury and increase, and thou hast greedily gained of thy neighbours by extortion, and hast forgotten me, saith the Lord GOD. Ezek. 22:12

EYE

The eyes of them that see shall not be dim, and the ears of them that hear shall hearken. Isa. 32:3

Unto thee lift I up mine eyes, O thou that dwellest in the heavens. Ps. 123:1

FABLES

For the time will come when they will not endure sound doctrine; but after their own lusts shall they heap to themselves teachers, having itching ears; And they shall turn away their ears from the truth, and shall be turned unto fables. 2 Tim. 4:3-4

Teach no other doctrine, Neither give heed to fables and endless genealogies, which minister questions, rather than godly edifying which is in faith: so do. 1 Tim. 1:3-4

FACE, FACE TO FACE

Seek the LORD, and his strength: seek his face evermore. Ps. 105:3-4

Your iniquities have separated between you and your God, and your sins have hid his face from you, that he will not hear. Isa. 59:2

I have seen God face to face, and my life is preserved. Gen. 32:24-30

FAIL

Rejoice not when thine enemy falleth, and let not thine heart be glad when he stumbleth: Lest the LORD see it, and it displease him, and he turn away his wrath from him. Prov. 24:17-18

FAINT

Fear not, neither be faint-hearted. 2 Ne. 17:4

Men ought always to pray, and not to faint. Luke 18:1

Wait on the LORD: be of good courage, and he shall strengthen thine heart: wait, I say, on the LORD. Ps. 27:14

Let not your hearts faint. D&C 103:19

FAITH, FAITHFUL, FAITHFULLY, FAITHFULNESS

Let us be faithful in keeping the commandments of the Lord. 1 Ne. 4:1

What doth it profit, my brethren, though a man say he hath faith, and have not works? can faith save him? James. 2:14

If ye have faith as a grain of mustard seed, ye shall say unto this mountain, Remove hence to yonder place; and it shall remove; and nothing shall be impossible unto you. Matt. 17:20

It is by faith that miracles are wrought; and it is by faith that angels appear and minister unto men; wherefore if these things have ceased wo be unto the children of men, for it is because of unbelief, and all is vain. Moro. 7:37

[Look] unto Jesus the author and finisher of our faith; who for the joy that was set before him endured the cross, despising the shame, and is set down at the right hand of the throne of God. Heb. 12:2

For unto us was the gospel preached, as well as unto them: but the word preached did not profit them, not being mixed with faith in them that heard it. Heb. 4:2

Whatsoever thing ye shall ask in faith, believing that ye shall receive in the name of Christ, ye shall receive it. Enos 1:15

But without faith it is impossible to please him: for he that cometh to God must believe that he is, and that he is a rewarder of them that diligently seek him. Heb. 11:6

They were perfectly honest and upright in all things; and they were firm in the faith of Christ, even unto the end. Alma 27:27

As all have not faith, seek ye diligently and teach one another words of wisdom; yea, seek ye out of the best books words of wisdom; seek learning, even by study and also by faith. D&C 88:118

So must their wives be grave, not slanderers, sober, faithful in all things. 1 Tim. 3:11

He that hath my word, let him speak my word faithfully. Jer. 23:28

And now as I said concerning faith-faith is not to have a perfect knowledge of things; therefore if ye have faith ye hope for things which are not seen, which are true. Alma 32:21

I will sing of the mercies of the LORD for ever: with my mouth will I make known thy faithfulness to all generations. Ps. 89:1

For as the body without the spirit is dead, so faith without works is dead also. James 2:26

Have faith in God. Mark 11:22

Be faithful unto the end, and lo, I am with you. D&C 31:13

Our kings and our leaders were mighty men in the faith of the Lord. Jarom 1:7

Stand fast in the faith of Christ. Alma 46:27

I cry unto my God in faith, and I know that he will hear my cry. 2 Ne. 33:3

How is it that ye have forgotten that the Lord is able to do all things according to his will, for the children of men, if it so be that they exercise faith in him? 1 Ne. 7:12

God will support, and keep, and preserve us, so long as we are faithful unto him. Alma 44:4

We are made alive in Christ because of our faith. 2 Ne. 25:25

FAITHLESS

Then saith he to Thomas, Reach hither thy finger, and behold my hands; and reach hither thy hand, and thrust it into my side: and be not faithless, but believing. John 20:27

FALL, FALLEN, FELL

Stand fast therefore in the liberty wherewith Christ hath made us free, and be not entangled again with the yoke of bondage. Gal. 5:1

After that ye have known God, or rather are known of God, how turn ye again to the weak and beggarly elements, whereunto ye desire again to be in bondage? Gal. 4:9

FALLING AWAY

Let no man deceive you by any means: for that day shall not come, except there come a falling away first, and that man of sin be revealed, the son of perdition; who opposeth and exalteth himself above all that is called God, or that is worshiped; so that he as God sitteth in the temple of God, shewing himself that he is God. 2 Thes. 2:3-4

FALSE, FALSEHOOD, FALSELY

Do violence to no man, neither accuse any falsely; and be content with your wages. Luke 3:14

Behold how false, and also the unsteadiness of the hearts of the children of men; yea, we can see that the Lord in his great infinite goodness doth bless and prosper those who put their trust in him. Hel. 12:1

When ye offer your gifts, when ye make your sons to pass through the fire, ye pollute yourselves with all your idols, even unto this day. Ezek. 20:31

There shall be false teachers among you, who privily shall bring in damnable heresies. 2 Pet. 2:1

Be not a witness against thy neighbour without cause; and deceive not with thy lips. Prov. 24:28

As for our iniquities, we know them: in transgressing and lying against the LORD, and departing away from our God, speaking oppression and revolt, conceiving and uttering from the heart words of falsehood. Isa. 59:12-13

A false witness shall not be unpunished, and he that speaketh lies shall not escape. Prov. 19:5

Hearken not unto the words of [false] prophets that prophecy unto you; they make you vain; they speak a vision of their own heart and not out of the mouth of the LORD. Jer. 23:16

We will not serve thy gods, nor worship the golden image which thou hast set up. Dan. 3:18

This is thy lot, the portion of thy measures from me, saith the LORD; because thou hast forgotten me, and trusted in falsehood. Jer. 13:25

FALSE CHRIST

If any man shall say unto you, Lo, here is Christ, or there; believe it not. For there shall arise false Christs, and false prophets, and shall shew great signs and wonders; insomuch that, if it were possible, they shall deceive the very elect. Matt. 24:23-24

False Christs and false prophets shall rise, and shall shew signs and wonders, to seduce, if it were possible, even the elect. Mark 13:22

FALSE DOCTRINE

All those who preach false doctrines, and all those who commit whoredoms, and pervert the right way of the Lord, wo, wo, wo be unto them. 2 Ne. 28:15

Be not carried about with divers and strange doctrines. For it is a good thing that the heart be established with grace; not with meats, which have not profited them that have been occupied therein. Heb. 13:9

FALSE PROPHET

If any man shall say unto you, Lo, here is Christ, or there; believe it not. For there shall arise false Christs, and false prophets, and shall shew great signs and wonders; insomuch that, if it were possible, they shall deceive the very elect. Matt. 24:23-24

Not every one that saith unto me, Lord, Lord, shall enter into the kingdom of heaven; but he that doeth the will of my Father who is in heaven. Many will say to me in that day: Lord, Lord, have we not prophesied in thy name, and in thy name have cast out devils, and in thy name done many wonderful works? And then will I profess unto them: I never knew you; depart from me, ye that work iniquity. Matt. 7:21-23

False Christs and false prophets shall rise, and shall shew signs and wonders, to seduce, if it were possible, even the elect. Mark 13:22

Beware of false prophets, who come to you in sheep's clothing, but inwardly they are ravening wolves. Ye shall know them by their fruits. 3 Ne. 14:15-20

Beware of false prophets, which come to you in sheep's clothing, but inwardly they are ravening wolves. Ye shall know them by their fruits. Matt. 7:15-16

FALSE WITNESS

Thou shalt not bear false witness against thy neighbour. Ex. 20:16

These six things doth the LORD hate: yea, seven are an abomination unto him: A proud look, a lying tongue, and hands that shed innocent blood, An heart that deviseth wicked imaginations, feet that be swift in running to mischief, A false witness that speaketh lies, and he that soweth discord among brethren. Prov. 6:16-19

FAMILIAR

When they shall say unto you, Seek unto them that have familiar spirits, and unto wizards that peep, and that mutter: should not a people seek unto their God? Isa. 8:19

Regard not them that have familiar spirits, neither seek after wizards, to be defiled by them: I am the LORD your God. Lev. 19:31

FAMILY

Ye must always pray unto the Father in my name, that your wives and children may be blessed. 3 Ne. 18:19-21

Visit the house of each member, and exhort them to pray vocally and in secret and attend to all family duties. D&C 20:47

Take especial care of your family from this time, henceforth and forever. D&C 126:3

FASHION

The fashion of this world passeth away. 1 Cor. 7:31

FAST, FASTING

Ye shall continue in prayer and fasting from this time forth. D&C 88:76

[She] served God with fasting and prayers night and day. Luke 2:37

When thou fasteth, anoint thine head, and wash thy face; That thou appear not unto men to fast, but unto thy Father which is in secret; and thy Father, which seeth in secret, shall reward thee openly. Matt. 6:17-18

When they were sick, my clothing was sackcloth: I humbled my soul with fasting; and my prayer returned into mine own bosom. I behaved myself as though he had been my friend or brother: I bowed down heavily, as one that mourneth for his mother. Ps. 35:13-14

Moreover, when ye fast be not as the hypocrites, of a sad countenance, for they disfigure their faces that they may appear unto men to fast. Verily I say unto you, they have their reward. But thou, when thou fastest, anoint thy head, and wash thy face; That thou appear not unto men to fast, but unto thy Father, who is in secret; and thy Father, who seeth in secret, shall reward thee openly. 3 Ne. 13:16-18 (Matt. 6:16-18)

Turn ye even to me with all your heart, and with fasting, and with weeping, and with mourning: And rend your heart, and not your garments, and turn unto the LORD your God: for he is gracious and merciful, slow to anger, and of great kindness, and repenteth him of the evil. Joel 2:12-13

When ye fast, be not, as the hypocrites, of a sad countenance: for they disfigure their faces, that they may appear unto men to fast. Verily I say unto you, They have their reward. Matt. 6:16

I proclaimed a fast there, at the river of Ahava, that we might afflict ourselves before our God, to seek of him a right way for us, and for our little ones, and for all our substance. Ezra 8:21-23

FATHER

Worship the Lord thy God, and honor thy father and thy mother, that thy days may be long in the land. 1 Ne. 17:55

After this manner therefore pray ye: Our Father who art in heaven, hallowed be thy name. Thy will be done on earth as it is in heaven. And forgive us our debts, as we forgive our debtors. And lead us not into temptation, but deliver us from evil. For thine is the kingdom, and the power, and the glory, forever. Amen. 3 Ne. 13:9-13 (Matt. 6:9-13)

The God of our Lord Jesus Christ, the Father of glory, may give unto you the spirit of wisdom and revelation in the knowledge of him: The eyes of your understanding being enlightened; that ye may know what is the hope of his calling, and what the riches of the glory of his inheritance in the saints. Eph. 1:17-18

He that heareth my word, and believeth on him that sent me, hath everlasting life, and shall not come into condemnation; but is passed from death unto life. John 5:24

When thou prayest thou shalt not do as the hypocrites, for they love to pray, standing in the synagogues and in the corners of the streets, that they may be seen of men. Verily I say unto you, they have their reward. But thou, when thou prayest, enter into thy closet, and when thou hast shut thy door, pray to thy Father who is in secret; and thy Father, who seeth in secret, shall reward thee openly. 3 Ne. 13:5-6

Not every one that saith unto me, Lord, Lord, shall enter into the kingdom of heaven; but he that doeth the will of my Father who is in heaven. Many will say to me in that day: Lord, Lord, have we not prophesied in thy name, and in thy name have cast out devils, and in thy name done many wonderful works? And then will I profess unto them: I never knew you; depart from me, ye that work iniquity. Matt. 7:21-23

Let your light so shine before this people, that they may see your good works and glorify your Father who is in heaven. 3 Ne. 12:16

When ye pray, use not vain repetitions, as the heathen, for they think that they shall be heard for their much speaking. Be not ye therefore like unto them, for your Father knoweth what things ye have need of before ye ask him. 3 Ne. 13:7-8

For unto us a child is born, unto us a son is given; and the government shall be upon his shoulder; and his name shall be called, Wonderful, Counselor, The Mighty God, The Everlasting Father, The Prince of Peace. 2 Ne. 19:6 (Isa. 9:6)

For as many as are led by the Spirit of God, they are the sons of God. For ye have not received the spirit of bondage again to fear; but ye have received the Spirit of adoption, whereby we cry, Abba, Father. The Spirit itself beareth witness with our spirit, that we are the children of God: And if children, then heirs; heirs of God, and joint-heirs with Christ; if so be that we suffer with him, that we may be also glorified together. For I reckon that the sufferings of this present time are not worthy to be compared with the glory which shall be revealed in us. Rom 8:14-18

Call no man your father upon the earth: for one is your Father, which is in heaven. Matt. 23:9

Be ye therefore perfect, even as your Father in heaven is perfect. Matt. 5:48

Whoso curseth his father or his mother, his lamp shall be put out in obscure darkness. Prov. 20:20

Come out from among them, and be ye separate, saith the Lord, and touch not the unclean thing; and I will receive you, And will be a Father unto you, and ye shall be my sons and daughters. 2 Cor. 6:17

These things have I spoken unto you in proverbs: but the time cometh, when I shall no more speak unto you in proverbs, but I shall shew you plainly of the Father. John 16:25

Honour thy father and thy mother, as the LORD thy God hath commanded thee; that thy days may be prolonged, and that it may go well with thee, in the land which the LORD thy God giveth thee. Deut. 5:16

We believe in God, the Eternal Father, and in His Son, Jesus Christ, and in the Holy Ghost. A of F-1

FATHERLESS

Pure religion and undefiled before God and the Father is this, To visit the fatherless and widows in their affliction, and to keep himself unspotted from the world. James 1:27

Oppress not the widow, nor the fatherless, the stranger, nor the poor; and let none of you imagine evil against his brother in your heart. Zech. 7:10

FAVOR, FAVORED

Whoso findeth a wife findeth a good thing, and obtaineth favour of the LORD. Prov. 18:22

Jesus increased in wisdom and stature, and in favour with God and man. Luke 2:52

FEAR, FEARFUL, FEARFULNESS

Fear God. 1 Pet. 2:17

Teach me thy way, O LORD; I will walk in thy truth: unite my heart to fear thy name. Ps. 86:11

Stir them up in remembrance of the Lord their God, and perhaps they will repent and turn unto thee. Hel. 11:4

If ye are prepared, ye shall not fear. D&C 38:30

Those who are built up to to become popular in the eyes of the world [are] they who need fear, and tremble, and quake. 1 Ne. 22:23

Come and fear not, and lay aside every sin, which easily doth beset you, which doth bind you down to destruction. Alma 7:15

Fear none of those things which thou shalt suffer: behold, the devil shall cast some of you into prison, that ye may be tried; and ye shall have tribulation ten days: be thou faithful unto death, and I will give thee a crown of life. Rev. 2:10

Many of the brethren in the Lord, waxing confident by my bonds, are much more bold to speak the word without fear. Philip. 1:14

Let not thine heart envy sinners: but be thou in the fear of the LORD all the day long. Prov. 23:17

Be not wise in thine own eyes: fear the LORD and depart from evil. It shall be health to thy navel, and marrow to thy bones. Prov. 3:7-8

Fear God and give glory to him. D&C 133:38

Let no man be afraid to lay down his life for my sake; for whoso layeth down his life for my sake shall find it again. D&C 103:27

Though I walk through the valley of the shadow of death, I will fear no evil: for thou art with me. Ps. 23:4

Let not thine heart envy sinners: but be thou in the fear of the LORD all the day long. Prov. 23:17

Fear not them which kill the body, but are not able to kill the soul: but rather fear him which is able to destroy both soul and body in hell. Matt. 10:28

Let not your hearts be troubled, neither let it be afraid. John 14:27

Fear ye not the reproach of men, neither be ye afraid of their revilings. Isa. 51:7

Fear not, neither be faint-hearted. 2 Ne. 17:4

Fear not to do good. D&C 6:33

The fear of the LORD is to hate evil: pride, and arrogancy, and the evil way, and the froward mouth, do I hate. Prov. 8:13

Be strong and of good courage, and do it: fear not, nor be dismayed: for the LORD GOD, even my GOD, will be with thee; he will not fail thee, nor forsake thee. 1 Chron. 28:20

Thou shalt fear the LORD thy GOD; him shalt thou serve, and to him shalt thou cleave, and swear by his name. Deut. 10:20

In God I will praise his word, in God I have put my trust; I will not fear what flesh can do unto me. Ps. 56:4

FEAST

Feast upon that which perisheth not, neither can be corrupted, and let your soul delight in fatness. 2 Ne. 9:51

Keep thy solemn feasts, perform thy vows. Nahum 1:15

FEEBLE

Strengthen ye the weak hands, and confirm the feeble knees. Say to them that are of a fearful heart, Be strong, fear not: behold, your God will come with vengeance, even God with a recompense; he will come and save you. Isa. 35:3-4

FEED, FED

Feed thy people with thy rod, the flock of thine heritage, which dwell solitarily in the wood. Micah 7:14

Feed the flock of God which is among you, taking the oversight thereof, not by constraint, but willingly; not for filthy lucre, but of a ready mind. 1 Pet. 5:2

FEET

If I then, your Lord and Master, have ashed your feet; ye also ought to wash one another's feet. For I have given you an example, that ye should do as I have done to you. John 13:14-15

Ponder the path of thy feet and let all thy ways be established. Prov. 4:26

[She] stood at his feet behind him weeping, and began to wash his feet with tears, and did wipe them with the hairs of her head, and kissed his feet, and anointed them with the ointment. Luke 7:38

FEIGN, FEIGNED, FEIGNEDLY

O LORD, attend unto my cry, give ear unto my prayer, that goeth not out of feigned lips. Ps. 17:1

FELLOWSHIP, FELLOWSHIPPING

Fellowship one with another. Hel. 6:3

Be ye not unequally yoked together with unbelievers: for what fellowship hath righteousness with unrighteousness? and what communion hath light with darkness. 2 Cor. 6:14

FEMALE

There is neither Jew nor Greek, there is neither bond nor free, there is neither male nor female: for ye are all one in Christ Jesus. Gal. 3:28

FEW

So the last shall be first, and the first last: for many be called, but few chosen. Matt 20:16

FIELD

Lift up your eyes, and look on the fields; for they are white already to harvest. John 4:35

FIGHT, FOUGHT

Be not ye afraid of them: remember the Lord, which is great and terrible, and fight for your brethren, your sons, and your daughters, your wives, and your houses. Neh. 4:14

It shall even be as when an hungry man dreameth, and, behold, he eateth; but he awaketh, and his soul is empty: or as when a thirsty man dreameth, and, behold, he drinketh; but he awaketh, and, behold, he is faint, and his soul hath appetite: so shall the multitude of all the nations be, that fight against mount Zion. Isa. 29:8

O Israel, ye approach this day unto battle against your enemies; let not your hearts faint, fear not and do not tremble of them neither be ye terrified because of them; for the LORD your GOD is he that goeth with you, to fight for you against your enemies, to save you. Deut. 20:3-4

Fight ye not against the Lord God of your fathers; for ye shall not prosper. 2 Chron. 13:12

FILL

I am the LORD thy God, which brought thee out of the land of Egypt: open thy mouth wide, and I will fill it. Ps. 81:10

FILTH, FILTHINESS, FILTHY

The children of Israel, which were come again out of captivity, and all such as had separated themselves unto them from the filthiness of the heathen of the land, to seek the LORD God of Israel, did eat. Ezra 6:21

There is a generation that are pure in their own eyes, an yet is not washed from their filthiness. Prov. 30:12

FIND, FOUND

Ask, and it shall be given you; seek, and ye shall find; knock, and it shall be opened unto you. Luke 11:9

If thou shalt find that which thy neighbor has lost, thou shalt make diligent search till thou shalt deliver it to him again. D&C 136:26

Thou shalt seek the LORD thy God, thou shalt find him, if thou seek him with all thy heart and with all thy soul. Deut. 4:29

Come unto me, all ye that labour and are heavy laden, and I will give you rest. Take my yoke upon you, and learn of me; for I am meek and lowly in heart: and ye shall find rest unto your souls. Matt. 11:28-29

FINISHER

[Look] unto Jesus the author and finisher of our faith; who for the joy that was set before him endured the cross, despising the shame, and is set down at the right hand of the throne of God. Heb. 12:2

FLATTER, FLATTERY

Neither at any time used we flattering words, as ye know, nor a cloke of covetousness; God is witness. 1 Thes. 2:5

He that speaketh flattery to his friends, even the eyes of his children shall fail. Job 17:5

FLEE, FLED

Whither shall I go from thy spirit? or whither shall I flee from thy presence? Ps. 139:4-7

Flee fornication. 1 Cor. 6:18

Flee also youthful lusts: but follow righteous-ness, faith, charity, peace, with them that call on the Lord out of a pure heart. 2 Tim. 2:22

FLESH

He that soweth to his flesh shall of the flesh reap corruption; but he that soweth to the Spirit shall of the Spirit reap life everlasting. Gal. 6:8

They that are after the flesh do mind the things of the flesh; but they that are after the Spirit the things of the Spirit. For to be carnally minded is death; but to be spiritually minded is life and peace. Rom. 8:5-6

Vain is the help of man. Ps. 60:11

Cursed be the man that trusteth in man, and maketh flesh his arm, and whose heart departeth from the LORD. Jer. 17:5

I keep under my body, and bring it into subjection: lest that by any means, when I have preached to others, I myself should be a castaway. 1 Cor. 9:27

Have ye not read, that he which made them at the beginning made them male and female, And said, For this cause shall a man leave father and mother, and shall cleave to his wife: and they twain shall be one flesh? Wherefore they are no more twain, but one flesh. What therefore God hath joined together, let not man put asunder. Matt. 19:4-6

Though we walk in the flesh, we do not war after the flesh: Casting down imaginations, and every high thing that exalteth itself against the knowledge of God, and bringing into captivity every thought to the obedience of Christ. 2 Cor. 10:3,5

Walk not after the flesh, but after the Spirit. Rom. 8:4

Put ye on the Lord Jesus Christ, and make not provision for the flesh, to fulfil the lusts thereof. Rom. 13:14

FLOCK

Be thou diligent to know the state of thy flocks, and look well to thy herds. Prov. 27:23-27

FOLLOW, FOLLOWER, FOLLOWING

Be a greater follower of righteousness. Abr. 1:2

Follow after righteousness. 2 Ne. 8:1

Then Jesus beholding him loved him, and said unto him, One thing thou lackest: go thy way, sell whatsoever thou hast, and give to the poor, and thou shalt have treasure in heaven: and come, take up the cross, and follow me. Mark 10:21

He that tilleth his land shall be satisfied with bread: but he that followeth vain persons is void of understanding. Prov. 12:11

He that followeth after righteousness and mercy, findeth life, righteousness, and honour. Prov. 21:21

If thou wilt be perfect, go and sell that thou hast, and give to the poor, and thou shalt have treasure in heaven: and come and follow me. Matt. 19:21-22

He said unto them all, If any man will come after me, let him deny himself, and take up his cross daily, and follow me. Luke 9:23

Turn not aside from following the LORD, but serve the LORD with all your heart. 1 Sam 12:20

Come, follow me. Luke 18:22

FOLLY

Hear what God the LORD will speak: for he will speak peace unto his people, and to his saints: but let them not turn again to folly. Ps. 85:8

FOOD

He causeth the grass to grow for the cattle, and herb for the service of man; that he may bring forth food out of the earth. Ps. 104:14

Every creature of God is good, and nothing to be refused, if it be received with thanksgiving: For it is sanctified by the word of God and prayer. 1 Tim. 4:4-5

Now the Spirit speaketh expressly, that in the latter times some shall depart from the faith, giving heed to seducing spirits, and doctrines of devils; Speaking lies in hypocrisy; having their conscience seared with a hot iron; Forbidding to marry, and commanding to abstain from meats, which God hath created to be received with thanksgiving of them which believe and know the truth. 1 Tim. 4:1-3

FOOL, FOOLISH, FOOLISHLY, FOOLISHNESS

The fool hath said in his heart, There is no God. They are corrupt, they have done abominable works, there is none that doeth good. Ps. 14:1

He that walketh with wise men shall be wise: but a companion of fools shall be destroyed. Prov. 13:20

Go from the presence of a foolish man, when thou preceivest not in him the lips of knowledge. Prov. 14:7

Surely these are poor; they are foolish: for they know not the way of the LORD, nor the judgment of their God. Jer. 5:4

Avoid foolish questions, and genealogies, and contentions, and strivings about the law; for they are unprofitable and vain. Titus 3:9

Answer not a fool according to his folly, lest thou also be like unto him. Answer a fool according to his folly, lest he be wise in his own conceit. Prov. 26:4-5

The natural man receiveth not the things of the Spirit of God: for they are foolishness unto him: neither can he know them, because they are spiritually discerned. 1 Cor. 2:14

Be not over much wicked, neither be thou foolish: why shouldest thou die before thy time? Eccl. 7:17

Speak not in the ears of a fool: for he will despise the wisdom of thy words. Prov. 23:9

Deal not foolishly. Ps. 75:4

Suffer not yourself to be led away by any vain or foolish thing. Alma 39:11

Forsake the foolish, and live; and go in the way of understanding. Prov. 9:6

FOOT

Turn not to the right hand nor to the left: remove thy foot from evil. Prov. 4:27

FORCE

The merciful man doeth good to his own soul: but he that is cruel troubleth his own flesh. Prov. 11:17

Surely the churning of milk bringeth forth butter, and the wringing of the nose bringeth forth blood: so the forcing of wrath bringeth forth strife. Prov. 30:33

FORGAT, FORGET, FORGOT, FORGOTTEN

Zion said, the LORD hath forsaken me, and my LORD hath forgotten me. Can a woman forget her sucking child, that she should not have compassion on the son of her womb? yea, they may forget, yet will I not forget thee. Isa. 49:14-15

Only take heed to thyself, and keep thy soul diligently, lest thou forget the things which thine eyes have seen, and lest they depart from thine heart all the days of thy life: but teach them thy sons, and thy sons sons. Deut. 4:9

The wicked shall be turned into hell, and all the nations that forget God. Ps. 9:17

FORGIVE, FORGIVENESS

Then came Peter to him, and said, Lord, how oft shall my brother sin against me, and I forgive him? till seven times? Jesus saith unto him, I say not unto thee, Until seven times: but, until seventy times seven. Matt. 18:21-22

Ye shall also forgive one another your trespasses. Mosiah 26:31

If thy brother shall trespass against thee, go and tell him his faults between thee and him alone. Matt. 18:15

Be ye kind one to another, tender-hearted, forgiving one another, even as God for Christ's sake hath forgiven you. Eph. 4:32

Forgive if ye have ought against any. Mark 11:25

Believe that ye must repent of your sins and forsake them, and humble yourselves before God; and ask in sincerity of heart that he would forgive you; and now, if you believe all these things see that ye do them. Mosiah 4:10

I, the Lord, will forgive whom I will forgive, but of you it is required to forgive all men. D&C 64:10

FORMER DAYS

Say not thou, What is the cause that the former days were better than these? Eccl. 7:10

FORNICATION

Flee fornication. 1 Cor. 6:18

FORSAKE, FORSAKEN, FORSOOK

He that covereth his sins shall not prosper: but whoso confesseth and forsaketh them shall have mercy. Prov. 28:13

The destruction of the transgressors and of the sinners shall be together, and they that forsake the LORD shall be consumed. Isa. 1:28

Thine own friend, and thy father's friend, forsake not; neither go into thy brother's house in the day of thy calamity: for better is a neighbour is near than a brother far off. Prov. 27:10

Zion said, the LORD hath forsaken me, and my LORD hath forgotten me. Can a woman forget her sucking child, that she should not have compassion on the son of her womb? yea, they may forget, yet will I not forget thee. Isa. 49:14-15

Let the wicked forsake his way, and the unrighteous man his thoughts: and let him return unto the LORD, and he will have mercy upon him; and to our God, for he will abundantly pardon. Isa. 55:7

FREE, FREEDOM, FREELY

Stand fast in the liberty where with ye have been made free. Mosiah 23:13

We believe that no government can exist in peace, except such laws are framed and held inviolate as will secure to each individual the free exercise of conscience, the right and control of property, and the protection of life. D&C 134:2

Think of your brethren like unto yourselves, and be familiar with all and free with your substance, that they may be rich like unto you. Jacob 2:17

FREE AGENCY

I exercise myself, to have always a conscience void of offense toward God, and toward men. Acts 24:16

FRIEND, FRIENDSHIP

Become friendly to one another. Mosiah 28:2

A man that hath friends must shew himself friendly: and there is a friend that sticketh closer than a brother. Prov. 18:24

FROWARD

Thorns and snares are in the way of the froward: he that doth keep his soul shall be far from them. Prov. 22:5

He that hath a froward heart findeth no good: and he that hath a perverse tongue falleth into mischief. Prov 17:20

Put away from thee a froward mouth, and perverse lips put far from thee. Prov. 4:24

FRUIT, FRUITFUL

If ye walk in my statutes and keep my commandments, and do them; Then I will give you rain in due season, and the land shall yield her increase, and the trees of the field shall yield her fruit. Lev. 26:3-4

I am the vine, yea are the branches: He that abideth in me, and I in him, the same bringeth forth much fruit: for without me ye can do nothing. John 15:5

Hear the word, and receive it, and bring forth fruit. Mark 4:20

Honour the Lord with thy substance, and with the first fruits of all thine increase. Prov. 3:9-10

Ye should humble yourselves before God, and bring forth fruit meet for repentance. Alma 13:13

FURNACE

Behold, I have refined thee, but not with silver; I have chosen thee in the furnace of affliction. Isa. 48:10

GAIN

For what is a man profited, if he shall gain the whole world, and lose his own soul? or what shall a man give in exchange for his soul? Matt.16:26

Whosoever will save his life shall lose it; but whosoever shall lose his life for my sake and the gospel's, the same shall save it. For what shall it profit a man, if he shall gain the whole world, and lose his own soul? Mark 8:36

What is the hope of the hypocrite, though he hath gained, when God taketh away his soul? Will God hear his cry when trouble cometh upon him? Job 27:8-9

He that walketh righteously, and speaketh uprightly; he that despiseth the gain of oppressions, that shaketh his hands from holding of bribes, that stoppeth his ears from hearing of blood, and shutteth his eyes from seeing evil; He shall dwell on high: his defence shall be the munitions of rocks: bread shall be given him; his waters shall be sure. Isa. 33:15-16

GARMENTS

The woman shall not wear that which pertaineth unto a man, neither shall a man put on a women's garment: for all that do so are abomination unto the LORD thy God. Deut. 22:5

I will greatly rejoice in the LORD, my soul shall be joyful in my God; for he hath clothed me with the garments of salvation, he hath covered me with the robe of righteousness. Isa. 61:10

GATE

Open ye the gates, that the righteous nation which keepeth the truth may enter in. Isa. 26:2

Strive to enter in at the strait gate: for many, I say unto you, will seek to enter in, and shall not be able. Luke 13:24

Yea, thus we see that the gate of heaven is open unto all, even to those who will believe on the name of Jesus Christ, who is the Son of God. Hel 3:28

GATHER, GATHERING

And before him shall be gathered all nations: and he shall separate them one from another, as a shepherd divideth his sheep from the goats. Matt. 25:32

If two of you shall agree on earth as touching any thing that they shall ask, it shall be done for them of my Father which is in heaven. For where two or three are gathered together in my name, there am I in the midst of them. Matt. 18:19-20

GENEALOGY

My God put into mine heart to gather together the nobles, and the rulers, and the people, that they might be reckoned by genealogy. Neh. 7:5

GENERATION

Save yourselves from this untoward generation. Acts 2:40

GENTILE

It is a light thing that thou shouldest be my servant to raise up the tribes of Jacob, and to restore the preserved of Israel: I will also give thee for a light to the Gentiles, that thou mayest be my salvation unto the end of the earth. Isa. 49:6

GENTLE, GENTLENESS

I would that ye should be humble, and be submissive and gentle; easy to be entreated; full of patience and long-suffering; being temperate in all things; being diligent in keeping the commandments of God at all times; asking for whatsoever things ye stand in need, both spiritual and temporal; always returning thanks unto God for whatsoever things ye do receive. Alma 7:23

The servant of the Lord must not strive; but be gentle unto all men, apt to teach, patient. 2 Tim. 2:24

GIFT

Every man should eat and drink, and enjoy the good of all his labor, it is the gift of God. Eccl. 3:13

But covet earnestly the best gifts: and yet shew I unto you a more excellent way. 1 Cor. 12:31

I would that ye all spake with tongues, but rather that ye prophesied: for greater is he that prophesieth than he that speaketh with tongues, except he interpret, that the church may receive edifying. 1 Cor. 14:5

A gift in secret pacifieth anger: and a reward in the bosom strong wrath. Prov. 21:14

If thou bring thy gift to the altar, and there rememberest that thy brother hath ought against thee; Leave there thy gift before the altar, and go thy way; first be reconciled to thy brother, and then come and offer thy gift. Matt. 5:23-24

Having then gifts differing according to the grace that is given to us, whether prophecy, let us prophesy according to the proportion of faith. Rom. 12:6

Whoso boasteth himself of a false gift is like clouds and wind without rain. Prov. 25:14

Neglect not the gift that is in thee. 1 Tim. 4:14

God hath set some in the church, first apostles, secondarily prophets, thirdly teachers, after that miracles, then gifts of healings, helps, governments, diversities of tongues. Are all apostles? are all prophets? are all teachers? are all workers of miracles? Have all the gifts of healing? do all speak with tongues? do all interpret? But covet earnestly the best gifts: and yet shew I unto you a more excellent way. 1 Cor. 12:28-31

A gift is as a precious stone in the eyes of him that hath it: whithersoever it turneth, it prospereth. Prov. 17:8

A man being evil cannot do that which is good; neither will he give a good gift. Moro. 7:10

Remember that every good gift cometh of Christ. Moro. 10:18

Come unto Christ, and lay hold upon every good gift, and touch not the evil gift, nor the unclean thing. Moro. 10:30

GIRD UP

Thou therefore gird up thy loins, and arise, and speak unto them all that I command thee: be not dismayed at their faces, lest I confound thee before them. Jer. 1:17

Gird up now thy loins like a man; for I will demand of thee, and answer thou me. Job 38:3

GAVE, GIVE, GIVEN

He coveteth greedily all the day long: but the righteous giveth and spareth not. Prov. 21:26

Meditate upon these things; give thyself wholly to them; that thy profiting may appear to all. 1 Tim. 4:15

Give to him that asketh thee, and from him that would borrow of thee turn not thou away. Matt. 5:42 9

GLORIFY, GLORIOUS, GLORY

Give unto the LORD the glory due unto his name; worship the LORD in the beauty of holiness. Ps. 29:2

There are also celestial bodies, and bodies terrestrial: but the glory of the celestial is one, and the glory of the terrestrial is another.   There is one glory of the sun, and another glory of the moon, and another glory of the stars: for one star differeth from another star in glory. So also is the resurrection of the dead. 1 Cor. 15:40-42

Give unto the LORD the glory due unto his name: bring an offering, and come before him: worship the LORD in the beauty of holiness. 1 Chron. 16:29

Ascribe ye strength unto God; his excellency is over Israel, and his strength is in the clouds. Ps. 68:34

Grace be unto you, and peace, from him which is, and which was, and which is to come; and from the seven Spirits which are before his throne; And from Jesus Christ, who is the faithful witness, and the first begotten of the dead, and the prince of the kings of the earth. Unto him that loved us, and washed us from our sins in his own blood, And hath made us kings and priests unto God and his Father; to him be glory and dominion for ever and ever. Amen. Rev. 1:4-6

We will glory in the Lord; yea, we will rejoice, for our joy is full; yea, we will praise our God forever. Alma 26:16

It is not good to eat much honey: so for men to search their own glory is not glory Prov. 25:27

Grow in the knowledge of the glory of him that created you, or in the knowledge of that which is just and true. Mosiah 4:12

My people have changed their glory for that which doth not profit. Jer. 2:8

Glorify God. JS-H 1:46

Who is this King of glory? The LORD of hosts, he is the King of glory. Ps. 24:8

Thus saith the LORD, Let not the wise man glory in his wisdom, neither let the mighty man glory in his might, let not the rich man glory in his riches: But let him that glorieth glory in this, that he understandeth and knoweth me Jer. 9:23-24

I seek not for honor of the world, but for the glory of my God. Alma 60:36

After this manner therefore pray ye: Our Father who art in heaven, hallowed be thy name. Thy will be done on earth as it is in heaven. And forgive us our debts, as we forgive our debtors.   And lead us not into temptation, but deliver us from evil. For thine is the kingdom, and the power, and the glory, forever. Amen. 3 Ne. 13:9-13 (Matt. 6:9-13)

Declare his glory among the heathen; his marvelous works among all nations. 1 Chron. 16:24

Give unto the LORD, ye kindreds of the people, give unto the LORD glory and strength. Give unto the LORD the glory due unto his name. 1 Chron. 16:28-29

Let no man glory in man, but rather let him glory in God. D&C 76:61

Learn and glorify the name of your God. 2 Ne. 6:4

Whether therefore ye eat, or drink, or whatsoever ye do, do all to the glory of God. 1 Cor. 10:31

How can ye believe, which receive honour one of another, and seek not the honour that cometh from God only? John 5:44

GO, GOING

Come ye, and let us go to the mountain of the LORD to the house of the God of Jacob; and he will teach us of his ways and we will walk in his paths: for out of Zion shall go forth the law, and the word of the LORD from Jerusalem. Isa. 2:3

Enter ye in at the strait gate: for wide is the gate, and broad is the way, that leadeth to destruction, and many there be which go in thereat: Because strait is the gate, and narrow is the way, which leadeth unto life, and few there be that find it. Matt. 7:13-14

Let us go into the house of the LORD. Ps. 122:1

Go ye out from among the wicked. D&C 38:42

Go in the strength of the Lord GOD: I will make mention of thy righteousness, even of thine only. Ps. 71:16

I will go before thee, and make the crooked places straight: I will break in pieces the gates of brass, and cut in sunder the bars of iron. Isa. 45:2

Ye shut up the kingdom of heaven against men: for ye neither go in yourselves, neither suffer ye them that are entering to go in. Matt. 23:13

Thou shalt do that which is right and good in the sight of the LORD: that it may be well with thee, and that thou mayest go in and possess the good land which the LORD sware unto thy fathers, To cast out all thine enemies from before thee, as the LORD hath spoken. Deut. 6:18-19

Honour thy father and thy mother, as the LORD thy God hath commanded thee; that thy days may be prolonged, and that it may go well with thee, in the land which the LORD thy God giveth thee. Deut. 5:16

Be ye angry, and sin not: let not the sun go down upon your wrath: Neither give place to the devil. Eph. 4:26

Therefore leaving the principles of the doctrine of Christ, let us go on unto perfection; not laying again the foundation of repentance from dead works, and of faith toward God, Of the doctrine of baptisms, and of laying on of hands, and of resurrection of the dead, and of eternal judgment. Heb. 6:1-2

GOD, GODHEAD

In the beginning was the Word, and the Word was with God, and the Word was God. John 1:1

Thou shalt have no other God before me. Mosiah 12:35

What greater witness can you have than from God? D&C 6:23

The LORD is the true God, he is the living God, and an everlasting king: at his wrath the earth shall tremble, and the nations shall not be able to abide his indignation. Jer. 10:10

Worship God in spirit and in truth, the true and the living God. Alma 43:10

Work the works of God. John 6:28

I am the LORD thy God from the land of Egypt, and thou shalt know no god but me: for there is no saviour beside me. Hosea 13:4

Thou shalt have no other gods before me. Ex. 20:3

GODLINESS

Lead a quiet and peaceable life in all godliness and honesty. 1 Tim. 2:2

Exercise thyself rather unto godliness. 1 Tim. 4:7

Without controversy great is the mystery of godliness: God was manifest in the flesh, justified in the Spirit, seen of angels, preached unto the Gentiles, believed on in the world, received up to glory. 1 Tim. 3:16

GOLD

I love thy commandments above gold; yea, above fine gold. Ps. 119:127

GOLDEN RULE

Therefore, all things whatsoever ye would that men should do to you, do ye even so to them, for this is the law and the prophets. 3 Ne. 14:12 (Matt. 7:12)

GOOD, GOODNESS

Rejoice in goodness. 2 Chron. 6:41

We believe in being honest, true, chaste, benevolent, virtuous, and in doing good to all men; indeed, we may say that we follow the admonition of Paul - We believe all things, we hope all things, we have endured many things, and hope to be able to endure all things. If there is anything virtuous, lovely, or of good report or praiseworthy, we seek after these things. A of F-13

Wo unto them that call evil good, and good evil, that put darkness for light, and light for darkness, that put bitter for sweet, and sweet for bitter. 2 Ne. 15:20

Trust in the LORD, and do good. Ps. 37:3

Wo unto them that turn aside the just for a thing of naught and revile against that which is good, and say that it is of no worth! 2 Ne. 28:16

Ye have wearied the LORD with your words. Yet ye say, Wherein have we wearied him? When ye say, Every one that doeth evil is good in the sight of the LORD. Mal. 2:17

Refuse the evil and choose the good. 2 Ne. 17:15

In all things shewing thyself a pattern of good works: in doctrine shewing uncorruptness, gravity, sincerity, Sound speech, that cannot be condemned; that he that is of the contrary part may be ashamed, having no evil thing to say of you. Titus 2:7-8

Believe in these words, for they are the words of Christ, and he hath given them unto me; and they teach all men that they should do good. 2 Ne. 33:10

See that you are merciful unto your brethren; deal justly, judge righteously, and do good continually. Alma 41:14

To him that knoweth to do good, and doeth it not, to him it is sin. James 4:17

Men should be anxiously engaged in a good cause, and do many things of their own free will, and bring to pass much righteousness. D&C 58:27

Fear not to do good. D&C 6:33

Be of good cheer. Mark 6:50

The LORD is good to all: and his tender mercies are over all his works. Ps. 145:9

Jesus answered and said unto her, Martha, Martha, thou art careful and troubled about many things: But one thing is needful: and Mary hath chosen that good part, which shall not be taken away from her. Luke 10:41-42

Do men gather grapes of thorns, or figs of thistles? Even so every good tree bringeth forth good fruit; but a corrupt tree bringeth forth evil fruit. A good tree cannot bring forth evil fruit, neither can a corrupt tree bring forth good fruit. Every tree that bringeth not forth good fruit is hewn down, and cast into the fire. Wherefore by their fruits ye shall know them. Matt. 7:16

Abhor that which is evil; cleave to that which is good. Rom. 12:9

Depart from evil, and do good; seek peace, and pursue it. Ps. 34:14

Because of the house of the LORD our God I will seek thy good. Ps. 122:9

Walk in the ways of good men, and keep the paths of the righteous. Prov. 2:20

Heaviness in the heart of man maketh it stoop: but a good word maketh it glad. Prov. 12:25

Woe unto them that call evil good, and good evil; that put darkness for light, and light for darkness; that put bitter for sweet and sweet for bitter! Isa. 5:20

Return ye now every one from his evil way, and make your ways and your doings good. Jer. 18:11

Ye have wearied the LORD with your words. Yet ye say, Wherein have we wearied him? When ye say, Every one that doeth evil is good in the sight of the LORD, and he delighteth in them. Mal. 2:17

Most men will proclaim every one his own goodness: but a faithful man who can find? Prov. 20:6

It shall come to pass at that time, that I will search Jerusalem with candles, and punish the men that are settled on their lees: that say in their heart, The LORD will not do good, neither will he do evil. Zeph. 1:12

Persuadeth men to do good. Ether 4:11

Withhold not good from them to whom it is due, when it is in the power of thine hand to do it. Prov. 3:27

How beautiful upon the mountains are the feet of him that bringeth good tidings, that publisheth peace; that bringeth good tidings of good, that publisheth salvation; that saith unto Zion, Thy God reigneth! Isa. 52:7

We believe in being honest, true, chaste, benevolent, virtuous, and in doing to all men; indeed, we may say that we follow the admonition of Paul - We believe all things, we hope all things, we have endured many things, and hope to be able to endure all things. If there is anything virtuous, lovely, or of good report or praiseworthy, we seek after these things. A of F–13

Thou shalt do that which is right and good in the sight of the LORD: that it may be well with thee, and that thou mayest go in and possess the good land which the LORD swear unto thy fathers, To cast out all thine enemies from before thee, as the LORD hath spoken. Deut. 6:18-19

Prove all things; hold fast that which is good. 1 Thes. 5:21

As we have therefore opportunity, let us do good unto all men, especially unto them who are of the household of faith. Gal. 6:10

Put your trust in that Spirit which leadeth to do good–yea, to do justly, to walk humbly, to judge righteously; and this is my Spirit. D&C 11:12

I would that ye should be steadfast and immovable, always abounding in good works. Mosiah 5:15

GOSPEL

Take heed unto thyself, and unto the doctrine; continue in them: for in doing this thou shalt both save thyself, and them that hear thee. 1 Tim. 4:16

I declare unto youthe gospel which I preached unto you, which also ye have reveived, and wherein ye satnd; By which also ye are saved, if ye keep in memory what I preached unto you, unless ye have believed in vain. For I deliverd unto you first of all that which I also reveived, how that Cchrist died for our sins accodging to the scriptures; And theat he was buried, and that he rose again the third day according to the scriptures. 1 Cor. 15:1-4

To you who are troubled rest with us, when the Lord Jesus shall be revealed from heaven with his mighty angels, In flaming fire taking vengeance on them that know not God, and that obey not the gospel of our Lord Jesus Christ. 2 Thes. 1:7-8

Let your conversation be as it becometh the gospel of Christ: that whether I come and see you, or else be absent, I may hear of your affairs, that ye stand fast in one spirit, with one mind striving together for the faith of the gospel. Philip. 1:27

Learn to impart one to another as the gospel requires. D&C 88:123

I marvel that ye are so soon removed from him that called you into the grace of Christ unto another gospel. Gal. 1:6

The time is fulfilled, and the kingdom of God is at hand: repent ye, and believe the gospel. Mark 1:15

Go ye into all the world, and preach the gospel to every creature. Mark 16:15

Believe the gospel of Jesus Christ, which ye shall have among you. Morm. 3:21

GOSSIP

Thou shalt not go up and down as a talebearer among thy people. Lev. 19:16

Debate thy cause with thy neighbour; and discover not a secret to another: lest he that heareth put thee to shame, and thine infamy turn not away. Prov. 25:9-10

They learn to be idle, wandering about from house to house; and not only idle, but tattlers also and busybodies, speaking things which they ought not. 1 Tim. 5:13

Speak evil of no man, to be no brawlers, but gentle, shewing all meekness unto all men. Titus 3:2

GOVERN, GOVERNMENT

For unto us a child is born, unto us a son is given; and the government shall be upon his shoulder; and his name shall be called, Wonderful, Counselor, The Mighty God, The Everlasting Father, The Prince of Peace. 2 Ne. 19:6 (Isa. 9:6)

After the wisdom of thy God, that is in thine hand, set magistrates and judges, which may judge all the people that are beyond the river, all such as know the laws of thy God; and teach ye them that know them not. Ezra 7:25

God hath set some in the church, first apostles, secondarily prophets, thirdly teachers, after that miracles, then gifts of healings, helps, governments, diversities of tongues. Are all apostles? are all prophets? are all teachers? are all workers of miracles? Have all the gifts of healing? do all speak with tongues? do all interpret? But covet earnestly the best gifts: and yet shew I unto you a more excellent way. 1 Cor. 12:28-31

We believe that all governments necessarily require civil officers and magistrates to enforce the laws of the same; and that such as will administer the law in equity and justice should be sought for and upheld by the voice of the people if a republic, or the will of the sovereign. D&C 134:3

We believe that religion is instituted of God; and that men are amenable to him, and to him only, for the exercise of it, unless their religious opinions prompt them to infringe upon the rights and liberties of others; but we do not believe that human law has a right to interfere in prescribing rules of worship to bind the consciences of men, nor dictate forms for public or private devotion; that the civil magistrate should restrain crime, but never control conscience; should punish guilt, but never suppress the freedom of the soul. D&C 134:4

We believe that no government can exist in peace, except such laws are framed and held inviolate as will secure to each individual the free exercise of conscience, the right and control of property, and the protection of life. D&C 134:2

We believe that every man should be honored in his station, rulers and magistrates as such, being placed for the protection of the innocent and the punishment of the guilty; and that to the laws all men show respect and deference, as without them peace and harmony would be supplanted by anarchy and terror; human laws being instituted for the express purpose of regulating our interests as individuals and nations, between man and man; and divine laws given of heaven, prescribing rules on spiritual concerns, for faith and worship, both to be answered by man to his Maker. D&C 134:6

We believe that rulers, states, and governments have a right, and are bound to enact laws for the protection of all citizens in the free exercise of their religious belief; but we do not believe that they have a right in justice to deprive citizens of this privilege, or proscribe them in their opinions, so long as a regard and reverence are shown to the laws and such religious opinions do not justify sedition nor conspiracy. D&C 134:7

We believe that the commission of crime should be punished according to the nature of the offense; that murder; treason, robbery, theft, and the breach of the general peace, in all respects, should be punished according to their criminality and their tendency to evil among men, by the laws of that government in which the offense is committed; and for the public peace and tranquility all men should step forward and use their ability in bringing offenders against good laws to punishment. D&C 134:8

We do not believe it just to mingle religious influence with civil government, whereby one religious society is fostered and another proscribed in its spiritual privileges, and the individual rights of its members, as citizens, denied. D&C 134:9

We believe that all men are bound to sustain and uphold the respective government in which they reside, while protected in their inherent and inalienable rights by the laws of such governments; and that sedition and rebellion are unbecoming every citizen thus protected, and should be punished accordingly; and that all governments have a right to enact such laws as in their own judgments are best calculated to secure the public interest; at the same time, however, holding sacred the freedom of conscience. D&C 134:5

According to the laws and constitution of the people, which I have suffered to be established, and should be maintained for the rights and protection of all flesh, according to just and holy principles; That every man may act in doctrine and principle pertaining to futurity, according to the moral agency which I have given unto him, that every man may be accountable for his own sins in the day of judgment. Therefore, it is not right that any man should be in bondage one to another. And for this purpose have I established the Constitution of this land, by the hands of wise men whom I raised up unto this very purpose. D&C 101:77-80

We believe that men should appeal to the civil law for redress of all wrongs and grievances, where personal abuse is inflicted or the right of property or character infringed, where such laws exist as will protect the same; but we believe that all men are justified in defending themselves, their friends, and property, and the government, from the unlawful assaults and encroachments of all persons in times of exigency, where immediate appeal cannot be made to the laws, and relief afforded. D&C 134:11

GRACE

God resisteth the proud, but giveth grace unto the humble. James 4:6

I have come having great hopes and much desire that I should find that ye had humbled yourselves before God, and that ye had continued in the supplicating of his grace. Alma 7:3

Likewise, ye younger, submit yourselves unto the elder. Yea, all of you be subject one to another, and be clothed with humility: for God resisteth the proud, and giveth grace to the humble. 1 Pet. 5:5

Let the word of Christ dwell in you richly in all wisdom; teaching and admonishing one another in psalms and hymns and spiritual songs, singing with grace in your hearts to the Lord. Col. 3:16

Let no corrupt communication proceed out of your mouth, but that which is good to the use of edifying, that it may minister grace unto the hearers. Eph. 4:29

Gird up the loins of your mind, be sober, and hope to the end for the grace that is to be brought unto you at the revelation of Jesus Christ. 1 Pet. 1:13

Let your speech be alway with grace, seasoned with salt, that ye may know how ye ought to answer every man. Col. 4:6

We believe that through the grace of the Lord Jesus Christ we shall be saved, even as they. Acts 15:11

Behold, ye are little children and ye cannot bear all things now; ye must grow in grace and in the knowledge of the truth. D&C 50:40

GRACIOUS, GRATEFUL, GRATEFULNESS

A gracious woman retaineth honour. Prov. 11:16

Beseech God that he will be gracious unto us. Mal. 1:9

GRAIN

If ye have faith as a grain of mustard seed, ye shall say unto this mountain, Remove hence to yonder place; and it shall remove; and nothing shall be impossible unto you. Matt. 17:20

Another parable put he forth unto them, saying, The kingdom of heaven is like to a grain of mustard seed, which a man took, and sowed in his field. Matt. 13:31

GRAVEN IMAGE

They provoked him to anger with their high places, and moved him to jealousy with their graven images. Ps. 78:58

Thy graven images also will I cut off, and thy standing images out of the midst of thee; and thou shalt no more worship the work of thine hands. Micah 5:13

Thou shalt not make unto thee any graven image, or any likeness of any thing that is in heaven above, or that is in the earth beneath, or that is in the water under the earth. Thou shalt not bow down thyself to them, nor serve them: For I the LORD thy God am a jealous God, visiting the iniquity of the fathers upon the children unto the third and fourth generation of them that hate me; And shewing mercy unto thousands of them that love me, and keep my commandments. Ex. 20:4-6

GREAT, GREATER, GREATNESS

As ye have come to the knowledge of the glory of God, or if ye have known of his goodness and have tasted of his love, and have received a remission of your sins, which causeth such exceeding joy in your souls, even so I would that ye should remember, and always retain in remembrance, the greatness of God and your own nothingness, and his goodness and long-suffering towards you, unworthy creatures, and humble yourselves even in the depths of humility, calling on the name of the Lord daily, and standing steadfastly in the faith of that which is to come, which was spoken by the mouth of an angel. Mosiah 4:11

What greater witness can you have than from God? D&C 6:23

By small and simple things are great things brought to pass; and small means in many instances doth confound the wise. Alma 37:6-7

I will publish the name of the LORD: ascribe ye greatness unto our God. Deut. 32:3

GREED, GREEDINESS, GREEDY

He coveteth greedily all the day long: but the righteous giveth and spareth not. Prov. 21:26

Thou hast taken usury and increase, and thou hast greedily gained of thy neighbours by extortion, and hast forgotten me, saith the Lord GOD. Ezek. 22:12

Likewise must the deacons be grave, not doubletongued, not given to much wine, not greedy of filthy lucre; Holding the mystery of faith in a pure conscience. 1 Tim. 3:8

He that is greedy of gain troubleth his own house; but he that hateth gifts shall live. Prov. 15:27

GREET

Greet ye one another with an holy kiss. 1 Cor. 16:20

GRIEF, GRIEVE

Grieve not the holy Spirit of God, whereby ye are sealed unto the day of redemption. Eph. 4:30

Let the lying lips be put to silence; which speak grievous things proudly and contemptuously against the righteous. Ps. 31:18

GROW

Grow in the knowledge of the glory of him that created you, or in the knowledge of that which is just and true. Mosiah 4:12

Behold, ye are little children and ye cannot bear all things now; ye must grow in grace and in the knowledge of the truth. D&C 50:40

GRUDGE

Thou shalt not avenge, nor bear any grudge against the children of thy people, but thou shalt love thy neighbour as thyself: I the LORD. Lev. 19:18

Use hospitality one to another without grudging. 1 Pet. 4:9

GUARD

Be thou prepared, and prepare for thyself, thou, and all thy company that are assembled unto thee, and be thou a guard unto them. Ezek. 38:7

GUIDANCE, GUIDE

Hear thou, my son, and be wise, and guide thine heart in the way. Prov. 23:19

Woe unto you, ye blind guides, which say, Whosoever shall swear by the temple, it is nothing; but whosoever shall swear by the gold of the temple, he is a debtor! Matt. 23:16

GUILE

Be without guile. D&C 124:97

Blessed is the man unto whom the LORD imputeth not iniquity, and in whose spirit there is no guile. Ps. 32:2

Keep thy tongue from evil, and thy lips from speaking guile. Ps. 34:13

For he that will love life, and see good days, let him refrain his tongue from evil, and his lips that they speak no guile: Let him eschew evil, and do good; let him seek peace, and ensue it. 1 Pet. 3:10-11

HALLOW, HALLOWED

Hallow the sabbath day, to do no work therein. Jer. 17:24

HAND

The LORD rewarded me according to my righteousness; according to the cleanness of my hands hath he recompensed me. Ps. 18:20

For the poor shall never cease out of the land: therefore I command thee, saying, thou shalt open thine hand wide unto thy brother, to thy poor, and to thy needy, in the land. Deut. 15:11

I stretch forth my hands unto thee: my soul thirsteth after thee, and a thirsty land. Shela. Ps. 143:6

They regard not the work of the LORD, neither consider the operation of his hands. Isa. 5:12

Whatever thy hand findeth to do, do it with thy might; for there is no work, nor device, nor knowledge, nor wisdom, in the grave, whither thou goest. Eccl. 9:10

Thy graven images also will I cut off, and thy standing images out of the midst of thee; and thou shalt no more worship the work of thine hands. Micah 5:13

In that day it shall be said to Jerusalem, Fear thou not: and to Zion, Let not thine hands be slack. Zeph. 3:16

HANG

Jesus said unto him, Thou shalt love the Lord thy God with all thy heart, and with all thy soul, and with all thy mind. This is the first and great command-ment. And the second is like unto it, Thou shalt love thy neighbour as thyself. On these two command-ments, hang all the law and the prophets. Matt 22:37-40

HAPPINESS, HAPPY

Happy is that people, that is in such a case: yea, happy is that people, whose God is the LORD. Ps. 144:15

If ye know these things, happy are ye if ye do them. John 13:17

Consider on the blessed and happy state of those that keep the commandments of God. Mosiah 2:41

HARD, HARDEN, HARDHEARTED, HARNESS

Is any thing too hard for the LORD? Gen. 18:14

Harden not your heart, as in the provocation, and as in the day of temptation in the wilderness:When your fathers tempted me, proved me, and saw my work. Ps. 95:9

While his arm of mercy is extended towards you in the light of the day, harden not your hearts. Jacob 6:5-6

HARLOT

Whoso loveth wisdom rejoiceth his father: but he that keepeth company with harlots spendeth his substance. Prov. 29:3

HARM

Thou shalt not speak evil of thy neighbor, nor do him any harm. D&C 42:27

Strive not with a man without cause, if he have done thee no harm. Prov. 3:30

HARMLESS

Be ye therefore wise as serpents and harmless as doves. Matt. 10:16

HARVEST

Lift up your eyes, and look on the fields; for they are white already to harvest. John 4:35

HASTE, HASTEN, HASTY

An inheritance may be gotten hastily at the beginning; but the end thereof shall not be blessed. Prov. 20:21

Seest thou a man that is hasty in his words? there is more hope of a fool than of him. Prov. 29:20

Be not rash with thy mouth, and let not thine heart be hasty to utter any thing before God: for God is in heaven, and thou upon earth: therefore let thy words be few. Eccl. 5:2-3

Go not hastily to strive, lest thou know not what to do in the end thereof, when thy neighbour hath put thee to shame. Prov. 25:8

A faithful man shall abound with blessings: but he that maketh haste to be rich shall not be innocent. Prov. 28:20

He that hasteth to be rich hath an evil eye, and considereth not that poverty shall come upon him. Prov. 28:22

He that is slow to wrath is of great understanding: but he that is hasty of spirit exalteth folly. Prov. 14:29

HATE, HATED, HATRED

He that sinneth against me wrongeth his own soul: all they that hate me love death. Prov. 8:36

No man can serve two masters: for either he will hate the one, and love the other; or else he will hold to the one, and despise the other. Ye cannot serve God and mammon. Matt. 6:24

The fear of the LORD is to hate evil: pride, and arrogancy, and the evil way, and the froward mouth, do I hate. Prov. 8:13

Better is a dinner of herbs where love is, than a stalled ox and hatred therewith. Prov. 15:17

Love your enemies, bless them that curse you, do good to them that hate you, and pray for them who despitefully use you and persecute you; That ye may be the children of your Father who is in heaven; for he maketh his sun to rise on the evil and on the good. 3 Ne. 12:43-45

Evil shall slay the wicked: and they that hate the righteous shall be desolate. Ps. 34:21

Through thy precepts I get understanding: therefore I hate every false way. Ps. 119:104

Do not I hate them, O LORD, that hate thee? Ps. 139:21

Thou shalt not hate thy brother in thine heart: thou shalt in any wise rebuke thy neighbour and not suffer sin upon him. Lev. 19:17

He that hateth his brother is in darkness, and walketh in darkness, and knoweth not whither he goeth, because that darkness hath blinded his eyes. 1 Jn. 2:11

He that hideth hatred with lying lips, and he that uttereth a slander, is a fool. Prov. 10:18

HAUGHTINESS, HAUGHTY

Pride goeth before destruction, and an haughty spirit before a fall. Prov. 16:18

The lofty looks of man shall be humbled, and the haughtiness of men shall be bowed down, and the Lord alone shall be exalted in that day. 2 Ne. 12:11

HEAD

His mischief shall return upon his own head, and his violent dealing shall come down upon his own pate. Ps. 7:16

HEAL, HEALING

Wilt thou be made whole? John. 5:6

We believe in the gift of tongues, prophecy, revelation, visions, healing, interpretation of tongues, and so forth. A of F-7

Make the heart of this people fat, and make their ears heavy, and shut their eyes; lest they see with their eyes, and hear with their ears, and understand with their heart, and convert, and be healed. Isa. 6:10

Is any sick among you? let him call for the elders of the church; and let them pray over him, anointing him with oil in the name of the Lord: And the prayer of faith shall save the sick, and the Lord shall raise him up; and if he have committed sins, they shall be forgiven him. James 5:14-15

All they that had any sick with divers diseases brought them unto him; and he laid his hands on every one of them, and healed them. Luke 4:40

Confess your faults one to another, and ray one for another, that ye may be healed. The effectual fervent prayer of a righteous man availeth much. James 5:16

HEAR, HEARD

Cease, my son, to hear the instruction that causeth to err from the words of knowledge. Prov. 19:27

Hear thou, my son, and be wise, and guide thine heart in the way. Prov. 23:19

I would that ye should understand that the word of God was liberal unto all, that none were deprived of the privilege of assembling themselves together to hear the word of God. Alma 6:5

Let every man be swift to hear, slow to speak, slow to wrath. James 1:19

Hear ye, and give ear; be not proud: for the LORD hath spoken. Jer. 13:15

All ye inhabitants of the world, and dwellers on the earth, see ye, when he lifted up an ensign on the mountains; and when he bloweth a trumpet, hear ye. Isa. 18:3

Be ye not as your fathers, unto whom the former prophets have cried, saying, Thus saith the LORD of hosts; Turn ye now from your evil ways, and from your evil doings: but they did not hear, nor hearken unto me, saith the LORD. Zech. 1:4

O earth, earth, earth, hear the word of the LORD. Jer. 22:29

This is a rebellious people, lying children, children that will not hear the law of the LORD. Isa. 30:9

Rise up, ye women that are at ease; hear my voice, ye careless daughters; give ear unto my speech. Many days and years shall ye be troubled, ye careless women: for the vintage shall fail, the gathering shall not come. Isa. 32:9-10

Keep thy foot when thou goest to the house of God, and be more ready to hear than to give the sacrifice of fools: for they consider not that they do evil. Eccl. 5:1

Should ye not hear the words which the LORD hath cried by the former prophets, when Jerusalem was inhabited and in prosperity, and the cities thereof round about her, when men inhabited the south and the plain? Zech. 7:7

Come ye near unto me, hear ye this; I have not spoken in secret from the beginning; from the time that it was, there am I: and now the Lord GOD, and his Spirit, hath sent me. Isa. 48:16
Be ye doers of the word, and not hearers only, deceiving your own selves. For if any be a hearer of the word, and not a doer, he is like unto a man beholding his natural face in a glass: For he beholdeth himself, and goeth his way, and straightway forgetteth what manner of man he was. James 1:22-24

He that walketh righteously, and speaketh uprightly; he that despiseth the gain of oppressions, that shaketh his hands from holding of bribes, that stoppeth his ears from hearing of blood, and shutteth his eyes from seeing evil; He shall dwell on high: his defence shall be the munitions of rocks: bread shall be given him; his waters shall be sure. Isa. 33:15-16

Hear ye the word of the LORD, O house of Jacob, and all the families of the house of Israel. Jer. 2:4

My mother and my brethren are these which hear the word of God, and do it. Luke 8:21

Whoso heareth these sayings of mine and doeth them, I will liken him unto a wise man, who built his house upon a rock - And the rain descended, and the floods came, and the winds blew, and beat upon that house; and it fell not, for it was founded upon a rock. 3 Ne. 14:24-25

He that received seed into the good ground is he that heareth the word, and understandeth it; which also beareth fruit, and bringeth forth, some an hundredfold, some sixty, some thirty. Matt. 13:23

They have come up hither to hear the pleasing word of God, yea, the word which healeth the wounded soul. Jacob 2:8

HEARKEN

If ye would hearken unto the Spirit which teacheth a man to pray, ye would know that ye must pray; for the evil spirit teacheth not a man to pray, but teacheth him that he must not pray. 2 Ne. 32:8

Thou hast avouched the LORD this day to be thy God, and to walk in his ways, and to keep his statutes, and his commandments, and his judgments, and to hearken unto his voice. Deut. 26:17

Believe in the LORD your God, so shall ye be established; believe his prophets, so shall ye prosper. 2 Chron. 20:20

If thou shalt hearken diligently unto the voice of the LORD thy God, to observe and to do all his commandments which I command thee this day, that the LORD thy God will sit thee on high above all nations of the earth; And all these blessings shall come on thee, and overtake thee, if thou shalt hearken unto the voice of the LORD thy God. Deut. 28:1-2

Hearken now unto my voice, I will give thee counsel, and God shall be with thee. Ex. 18:19

Hearken unto me, ye stouthearted, that are far from righteousness. Isa. 46:12

Hearken to the words of my servants the prophets, whom I sent unto you, both rising up early, and sending , but ye have not hearkened. Jer. 26:5

If a ruler hearken to lies, all his servants are wicked. Prov. 29:12

HEART

When you do not cry unto the Lord, let your hearts be full, drawn out in prayer unto him continually for your welfare, and also for the welfare of those who are around you. Alma 34:27

While his arm of mercy is extended towards you in the light of the day, harden not your hearts. Jacob 6:5-6

Trust not in oppression, and become not vain in robbery: if riches increase, set not your heart upon them. Ps. 62:10

Ye shall repent of your sins, and come unto me with a broken heart and a contrite spirit. 3 Ne. 12:19

Let us draw near with a true heart in full assurance of faith, having our hearts sprinkled from an evil conscience, and our bodies washed with pure water. Heb. 10:22

I trust that ye are not lifted up in the pride of your hearts; yea, I trust that ye have not set your hearts upon riches and the vain things of the world. Alma 7:6

Do not ye yet understand, that whatsoever entereth in at the mouth goeth into the belly, and is cast out into the draught? But those things which proceed out of the mouth come froth from the heart; and they defile the man. For out of the heart proceed evil thoughts, murders, adulteries, fornica-tions, thefts, false witness, blasphemies: These are the things which defile a man: but to eat with unwashen hands defileth not a man. Matt: 17-20

He commanded them that they should not cease to pray in their hearts. 3 Ne. 20:1

It is a people that do err in their heart, and they have not known my ways. Ps. 95:10

Heaviness in the heart of man maketh it stoop: but a good word maketh it glad. Prov. 12:25

I suppose that ye ponder somewhat in your hearts concerning that which ye should do after ye have entered in by the way. 2 Ne. 32:1

Examine me, O LORD, and prove me; try my reins and my heart. Ps. 26:2

When a man speaketh by the power of the Holy Ghost, the power of the Holy Ghost carrieth it unto the hearts of the children of men. 2 Ne. 33:1

O that ye would listen to the word of his commands, and let not this pride of your hearts destroy your souls! Jacob 2:16

My soul delighteth in the song of the heart; yea, the song of the righteous is a prayer unto me, and it shall be answered with a blessing upon their heads. D&C 25:11-12

I beseech of you in words of soberness that ye would repent, and come with full purpose of heart, and cleave unto God as he cleaveth unto you. Jacob 6:5

If we have hardened our hearts against the word, insomuch that it has not been found in us, then will our state be awful. Alma 12:13

Seek not after riches nor the vain things of this world; for behold, you cannot carry them with you. Alma 39:14

They did fast and pray oft, and did wax stronger and stronger in their humility, and firmer and firmer in the faith of Christ, unto the filling their souls with joy and consolation, yea, even to the purifying and the sanctification of their hearts, which sanctification cometh because of their yielding their hearts unto God. Hel. 3:35

If ye have experienced a change of heart, and if ye have felt to sing the song of redeeming love, I would ask, can ye feel so now? Alma 5:26

All you who deny the beggar, because ye have not; I would that ye say in your hearts that: I give not because I have not, but if I had I would give. Mosiah 4:24

Behold, this is not my doctrine, to stir up the hearts of men with anger, one against another; but this is my doctrine, that such things should be done away. 3 Ne. 11:30

Circumcision is that of the heart, in the spirit, and not in the letter; whose praise is not of men, but of God. Rom. 2:28-29

Let not mercy and truth forsake thee: bind them about thy neck: write them upon the table of thine heart; So shalt thou find favour and good understanding in the sight of God and man. Prov. 3:3-4

Therefore shall ye lay up these my words in your heart and in your soul, and bind them for a sign upon your hand, that they may be as frontlets between your eyes. Deut. 11:18

Lay not up for yourselves treasures upon earth, where moth and rust doth corrupt, and where thieves break through and steal: But lay up for yourselves treasures in heaven, where neither moth nor rust doth corrupt, and where thieves do not break through nor steal: For where your treasure is, there will your heart be also. Matt. 6:19-21

I will give them an heart to know me, that I am the LORD: and they shall be my people, and I will be their God: for they shall return unto me with their whole heart. Jer. 24:7

He scorneth the scorners: but he giveth grace unto the lowly. Prov. 3:34

Blessed are they that keep his testimonies, and that seek him with the whole heart. Ps. 119:2

They speak vanity every one with his neighbour: with flattering lips and with a double heart. Ps. 12:2

Who can say, I have made my heart clean, I am pure from my sin? Prov. 20:9

Truly God is good to Israel, to such as are of a clean heart. Ps. 73:1

He that hath a froward heart findeth no good: and he that hath a perverse tongue falleth into mischief. Prov 17:20

Be ye of an understanding heart. Prov. 8:5

The wise in heart will receive command-ments: but a prating fool shall fall. Prov. 10:8

The heart knoweth his own bitterness; and a stranger doth not intermeddle with his joy. Prov. 14:10

The heart of the righteous studieth to answer: but the mouth of the wicked poureth out evil things. Prov. 15:28

Hear thou, my son, and be wise, and guide thine heart in the way. Prov. 23:19

He that trusteth in his own heart is a fool: but whoso walketh wisely, he shall be delivered. Prov. 28:26

As for our iniquities, we know them: in transgressing and lying against the LORD, and departing away from our God, speaking oppression and revolt, conceiving and uttering from the heart words of falsehood. Isa. 59:12-13

Cursed be the man that trusteth in man, and maketh flesh his arm, and whose heart departeth from the LORD. Jer. 17:5

Set thee up waymarks, make thee high heaps: set thine heart toward the highway, even the way which thou wentest: turn again. Jer. 31:21

The eyes of the LORD run to and fro throughout the whole earth, to shew himself strong in the behalf of them whose heart is perfect toward him. 2 Chron. 16:9

He shall turn the heart of the fathers to the children, and the heart of the children to their fathers, lest I come and smite the earth with a curse. Mal. 4:6

I will walk within my house with a perfect heart. Ps. 101:2

Oppress not the widow, nor the fatherless, the stranger, nor the poor; and let none of you imagine evil against his brother in your heart Zech. 7:10

Trust in the LORD with all thine heart; and lean not unto thine own under-standing. Prov. 3:5

Keep thy heart with all diligence; for out of it are the issues of life. Prov. 4:23

The LORD is nigh unto them that are of a broken heart; and saveth such as be of a contrite spirit. Ps. 34:18

Lift up your heart, and be glad. Moses 7:44

I applied mine heart to know, and to search, and to seek out wisdom, and the reason of things, and to know the wickedness of folly, even of foolishness and madness. Eccl. 7:25

Hear now this, thou that art given to pleasures, that dwellest carelessly, that sayest in thine heart, I am, and none else beside me. Isa. 47:8

Neither shall they walk any more after the imagination of their evil heart. Jer. 3:17
Circumcise yourselves to the LORD, and take away the foreskins of your heart. Jer. 4:4

As for them whose heart walketh after the heart of their detestable things and their abominations, I will recompense their way upon their own heads, saith the Lord GOD. Ezek. 11:21

Cast away from you all your transgressions, whereby ye have transgressed; and make you a new heart and a new spirit; for why will ye die, O house of Israel? Ezek. 18:31

There is nothing that the Lord thy God shall take in his heart to do but what he will do it. Abr. 3:17

I will give them one heart, and I will put a new spirit within you; and I will take the stony heart out of their flesh, and will give them an heart of flesh: That they may walk in my statutes, and keep mine ordinances, and do them: and they shall be my people, and I will be their God. Ezek. 11:19-20

Consider it in thine heart, that the LORD he is God in heaven above, and upon the earth beneath: there is none else. Deut. 4:39

Come unto me, all ye that labour and are heavy laden, and I will give you rest. Take my yoke upon you, and learn of me; for I am meek and lowly in heart: and ye shall find rest unto your souls. Matt. 11:28-29

Blessed are the pure in heart: for they shall see God. Matt. 5:8

Harden not your hearts, as in the provocation, in the day of temptation in the wilderness: When your fathers tempted me, proved me, and saw my works forty years. Heb. 3:8

All ye that are pure in heart, lift up your heads and receive the pleasing word of God, and feast upon his love. Jacob 3:1

Wo unto the rich, who are rich as to the things of the world. For because they are rich they despise the poor, and they persecute the meek, and their hearts are upon their treasures; where-fore, their treasure is their god. And behold, their treasure shall perish with them also. 2 Ne. 9:30

Turn to the Lord with full purpose of heart, and put your trust in him, and serve him with all diligence of mind. Mosiah 7:33

Thou shalt offer a sacrifice unto the Lord thy God in righteousness, even that of a broken heart and a contrite spirit. D&C 59:8

Continue your journey and let your heart rejoice; for behold, and lo, I am with you even unto the end. D&C 100:12

Know that there is none else save God that knowest thy thoughts and the intents of thy heart. D&C 6:16

Put away, said he, the strange gods which are among you, and incline your heart unto the LORD God of Israel. Josh. 24:23

If there be among you a poor man of one of thy brethren within any of thy gates in thy land which the LORD thy God giveth thee, thou shalt not harden thine heart, nor shut thine hand from thy poor brother. Deut. 15:7

Walk before me, as David thy father walked, in integrity of heart, and in uprightness, to do according to all that I have commanded thee, and wilt keep my statutes and my judgments. 1 Kgs. 9:4

Sow to yourselves in righteousness, reap in mercy; break up your fallow ground: for it is time to seek the LORD, till he come and rain righteousness upon you. Hosea 10:12

Turn ye even to me with all your heart, and with fasting, and with weeping, and with mourning: And rend your heart, and not your garments, and turn unto the LORD your God: for he is gracious and merciful, slow to anger, and of great kindness, and repenteth him of the evil. Joel 2:12-13

HEATHEN

Thus saith the Lord, learn not the way of the heathen, and be not dismayed at the signs of heaven; for the heathen are dismayed at them. Jer. 10:2

When ye pray, use not vain repetitions, as the heathen, for they think that they shall be heard for their much speaking. Be not ye therefore like unto them, for your Father knoweth what things ye have need of before ye ask him. 3 Ne. 13:7-8

HEAVEN

Lay not up for yourselves treasures upon earth, where moth and rust doth corrupt, and where thieves break through and steal: But lay up for yourselves treasures in heaven, where neither moth nor rust doth corrupt, and where thieves do not break through nor steal: For where your treasure is, there will your heart be also. Matt. 6:19-21

Thus saith the Lord, learn not the way of the heathen, and be not dismayed at the signs of heaven; for the heathen are dismayed at them. Jer. 10:2

HEAVY

A stone is heavy, and the sand weighty; but a fool's wrath is heavier than them both. Prov. 27:3

Come unto me, all ye that labour and are heavy laden, and I will give you rest. Take my yoke upon you, and learn of me; for I am meek and lowly in heart: and ye shall find rest unto your souls. Matt. 11:28-29

HEED

We ought to give the more earnest heed to the things which we have heard, lest at any time we should let them slip. Heb. 2:1

HELL

If thy hand offend thee, cut it off: it is better for thee to enter into life maimed, than having two hands to go into hell, into the fire that never shall be quenched. Mark 9:43

HERB

He causeth the grass to grow for the cattle, and herb for the service of man; that he may bring forth food out of the earth. Ps. 104:14

All wholesome herbs God hath ordained for the constitution, nature, and use of man - Every herb in the season thereof, and every fruit in the season thereof; all these to be used with prudence and thanksgiving. D&C 89:10

HID, HIDDEN, HIDE

Woe unto them that seek deep to hide their counsel from the LORD and their works are in the dark, and they say, Who seeth us? and who knoweth us? Isa. 29:15

HIGHMINDED

Be not highminded. Rom. 11:20

Charge them that are rich in this world, that they be not highminded, nor trust in uncertain riches, but in the living God, who giveth us richly all things to enjoy. 1 Tim. 6:17

Be not highminded, nor trust in uncertain riches, but in the living God, who giveth us richly all things to enjoy. 1 Tim. 6:17-19

HIGH PRIEST

That by two immutable things, in which it was impossible for God to lie, we might have a strong consolation, who have fled for refuge to lay hold upon the hope set before us: Which hope we have as an anchor of the soul, both sure and stedfast, and which entereth into that within the veil; Whither the forerunner is for us entered, even Jesus, made an high priest for ever after the order of Melchisedec. Heb. 6:18-19

HINDER

Woe unto you, lawyers! for ye have taken away the key of knowledge: ye entered not in yourselves, and them that were entering in ye hindered. Luke 11:52

HOLD, HOLD FAST

Hold fast the form of sound words, which thou hast heard of me, in faith and love which is in Christ Jesus. 2 Tim. 1:13

HOLINESS, HOLIER, HOLY

Observe the Sabbath day to keep it holy. D&C 68:29 (Ex. 20:8)

Let every man esteem his brother as himself, and practice virtue and holiness before me. D&C 38:24

Teach my people the difference between the holy and profane, and cause them to discern between the unclean and the clean. Ezek. 44:23

Be silent, O all flesh, before the LORD: for he is raised up out of his holy habitation. Zech. 2:13

Thou hast despised mine holy things, and hast profaned my sabbaths. Ezek. 22:8

An abomination is committed in Israel and in Jerusalem; for Judah hath profaned the holiness of the LORD which he loved, and hath married the daughter of a strange god. Mal. 2:11

Exalt the LORD our God, and worship at his holy hill; for the LORD our God is holy. Ps. 99:9

Ye shall be holy: for I the LORD God holy. Lev. 19:2

The place of my throne, and the place of the soles of my feet, where I will dwell in the midst of the children of Israel for ever, and my holy name, shall the house of Israel no more defile. Ezek. 43:7

Follow peace with all men, and holiness, without which no man shall see the Lord. Heb. 12:14

Become holy, without spot. Moro. 10:33

Remember the sabbath day, to keep it holy. Mosiah 13:16

Give not that which is holy unto the dogs, neither cast ye your pearls before swine, lest they trample them under their feet, and turn again and rend you. Matt. 7:6

Practice virtue and holiness before me continually. D&C 46:33

HOLY GHOST

For the prophecy came not in old time by the will of man: but holy men of God spake as they were moved by the Holy Ghost. 2 Pet. 1:21

For it is impossible for those who were once enlightened, and have tasted of the heavenly gift, and were made partakers of the Holy Ghost, And have tasted the good word of God, and the powers of the world to come, If they shall fall away, to renew them again unto repent-ance; seeing they crucify to themselves the Son of God afresh, and put him to an open shame. Heb. 6:4

These things have I spoken unto you, being yet present with you. But the Comforter, which is the Holy Ghost, whom the Father will send in my name, he shall teach you all things, and bring all things to your remembrance, whatsoever I have said unto you. John 14:25-26

When a man speaketh by the power of the Holy Ghost, the power of the Holy Ghost carrieth it unto the hearts of the children of men. 2 Ne. 33:1

He that shall blaspheme against the Holy Ghost hath never forgiveness, but is in danger of eternal damnation. Mark 3:29

[Peter and John] then laid they their hands on them, and they received the Holy Ghost. Acts 8:17

Whosoever speaketh a word against the Son of man, it shall be forgiven him: but whosoever speaketh against the Holy Ghost, it shall not be forgiven him, neither in this world, neither in the world to come. Matt. 12:32

HOLY SPIRIT

Grieve not the holy Spirit of God, whereby ye are sealed unto the day of redemption. Eph. 4:30

I now send upon you another Comforter, even upon you my friends, that it may abide in your hearts, even the Holy Spirit of promise, which other Comforter is the same that I promised unto my disciples, as is recorded in the testimony of John. D&C 88:3

Marvel not that I said unto thee, Ye must be born again. The wind bloweth where it listeth, and thou hearest the sound thereof, but canst not tell whence it cometh, and whither it goeth: so is every one that is born of the Spirit. John 3:7-8

As many as are led by the Spirit of God, they are the sons of God. Rom. 8:14

HONEST, HONESTLY, HONESTY

Lead a quiet and peaceable life in all godliness and honesty. 1 Tim. 2:2

Let us walk honestly, as in the day; not in rioting and drunkenness, not in chambering and wantonness, not in strife and envying. Rom. 13:13

HONOR, HONORABLE

Worship the Lord thy God, and honor thy father and thy mother, that thy days may be long in the land. 1 Ne. 17:55

Honour all men. Love the brotherhood. Fear God. Honour the king. 1 Pet. 2:17

How can ye believe, which receive honour one of another, and seek not the honour that cometh from God only? John 5:44

If thou turn away thy foot from the sabbath, from doing thy pleasure on my holy day; and call the sabbath a delight, the holy of the LORD, honorable; and shalt honor him, not doing thy own ways, nor finding thine own pleasure, nor speaking thine own words: Then shalt thou delight thyself in the LORD; and I will cause thee to ride upon the high places of the earth, and feed thee with the heritage of Jacob thy father: for the mouth of the LORD hath spoken it. Isa. 58:13-14

The LORD saith, Be it far from me; for them that honour me I will honour, and they that despise me shall be lightly esteemed. 1 Sam. 2:30

Honour thy father and thy mother. Matt. 19:19

All men should honour the Son, even as they honour the Father. John 5:23

Honoureth them that fear the Lord. Ps. 15:4

Honour thy father and thy mother, as the LORD thy God hath commanded thee; that thy days may be prolonged, and that it may go well with thee, in the land which the LORD thy God giveth thee. Deut. 5:16

Honour the LORD with thy substance, and with the firstfruits of all thine increase. Prov. 3:9

Wives shall give to their husbands honour, both to great and small. Esth. 1:20

HOPE

Have hope. Rom. 15:4

Hope thou in God. Ps. 42:5

My soul fainteth for thy salvation: but I hope in thy word. Ps. 119:81

Hold fast the confidence and the rejoicing of the hope firm unto the end. Heb. 3:6

Hope deferred maketh the heart sick. Prov. 13:12

Continue in the faith grounded and settled, and be not moved away from the hope of the gospel, which ye have heard, and which was preached to every creature which is under heaven. Col. 1:23

Charity suffereth long, and is kind, and envieth not, and is not puffed up, seeketh not her own, is not easily provoked, thinketh no evil, and rejoiceth not in iniquity but rejoiceth in the truth, beareth all things, believeth all things, hopeth all things, endureth all things. Moro. 7:45 (1 Cor. 13:4-7)

The God of our Lord Jesus Christ, the Father of glory, may give unto you the spirit of wisdom and revelation in the knowledge of him: The eyes of your understanding being enlightened; that ye may know what is the hope of his calling, and what the riches of the glory of his inheritance in the saints. Eph. 1:17-18

Gird up the loins of your mind, be sober, and hope to the end for the grace that is to be brought unto you at the revelation of Jesus Christ. 1 Pet. 1:13

If ye have no hope ye must needs be in despair; and despair cometh because of iniquity. Moro. 10:22

Be of good courage, and he shall strengthen your heart, all ye that hope in the LORD. Ps. 31:24

Sanctify the Lord God in your heats; and be ready always to give an answer to every man that asketh you a reason of the hope that is in you with meekness and fear: Having a good conscience; that, whereas they speak evil of you, as of evildoers, they may be ashamed that falsely accuse your good conversation in Christ. 1 Pet. 3:15-16

That by two immutable things, in which it was impossible for God to lie, we might have a strong consolation, who have fled for refuge to lay hold upon the hope set before us: Which hope we have as an anchor of the soul, both sure and stedfast, and which entereth into that within the veil; Whither the forerunner is for us entered, even Jesus, made an high priest for ever after the order of Melchisedec. Heb. 6:18-19

We believe in being honest, true, chaste, benevolent, virtuous, and in doing good to all men; indeed, we may say that we follow the admonition of Paul - We believe all things, we hope all things, we have endured many things, and hope to be able to endure all things. If there is anything virtuous, lovely, or of good report or praiseworthy, we seek after these things. A of F-13

Ye must press forward with a steadfastness in Christ having a perfect brightness of hope, and a love of God and of all men. 2 Ne. 31:20

And now as I said concerning faith-faith is not to have a perfect knowledge of things; therefore if ye have faith ye hope for things which are not seen, which are true. Alma 32:21

Ye shall have hope through the atonement of Christ and the power of his resurrection. Moro. 7:41

HOSPITALITY

[Distribute] to the necessity of saints; given to hospitality. Rom. 12:13

Use hospitality one to another without grudging. 1 Pet. 4:9

HOUR

Watch therefore: for ye know not what hour your Lord doth come. Matt. 24:42

Take no thought how or what ye shall speak: for it shall be given you in that same hour what ye shall speak. For it is not ye that speak, but the Spirit of your Father which speaketh in you. Matt. 10:19-20

Heaven and earth shall pass away, but my words shall not pass away. But of that day and hour knoweth no man, no, not the angels of heaven, by my Father only. Matt 24:36

Paul, being grieved, turned and said to the spirit, I command thee in the name of Jesus Christ to come out of her. And he came out the same hour. Acts 16:18

HOUSE, HOUSEHOLD

Because of the house of the LORD our God I will seek thy good. Ps. 122:9

Blessed be he that cometh in the name of the LORD: we have blessed you out of the house of the LORD. Ps. 118:26

Through wisdom is an house builded; and by understanding it is established: And by knowledge shall the chambers be filled with all precious and pleasant riches. Prov. 24:3-4

Thou oughtest to behave thyself in the house of God, which is the church of the living God, the pillar and ground of the truth. 1 Tim. 3:15

Peace be within thy walls, and prosperity within thy palaces. For my bretheren and companions' sakes, I will now say, Peace be within thee. Ps. 122:7-8

Whoso rewardeth evil for good, evil shall not depart from his house. Prov. 17:13

Keep thy foot when thou goest to the house of God, and be more ready to hear than to give the sacrifice of fools: for they consider not that they do evil. Eccl. 5:1

Beautify the house of the LORD which is in Jerusalem. Ezra 7:27

Stand in the gate of the LORD's house, and proclaim there this word, and say, Hear the word of the LORD. Jer. 7:2

Bring an offering in a clean vessel into the house of the LORD. Isa. 66:20

Woe unto him that buildeth his house in unrighteousness, and his chambers by wrong; that useth his neighbour's service without wages, and giveth him not for his work. Jer. 22:13

The children of Judah have done evil in my sight, saith the LORD: they have set their abominations in the house which is called by my name, to pollute it. Jer. 7:30

We are confounded, because we have heard reproach: shame hath covered our faces: for strangers are come into the sanctuaries of the LORD's house. Jer. 51:51

Let us go into the house of the LORD. Ps. 122:1

I had rather be a doorkeeper in the house of my God, than to dwell in the tents of wickedness. Ps. 84:10

Come, and let us go up to the mountain of the LORD, and to the house of the God of Jacob; and he will teach us of his ways, and we will walk in his paths; for the law shall go forth of Zion, and the word of the LORD from Jerusalem. Micah 4:2

Solomon determined to build an house for the name of the LORD, and an house for his kingdom. 2 Chron. 2:1

He set the porters at the gates of the house of the LORD, that none which was unclean in any thing should enter in. 2 Chron. 23:19

Gather of all Israel money to repair the house of your God from year to year. 2 Chron. 24:4-5

Whatsoever is commanded by the God of heaven, let it be diligently done for the house of the God of heaven. Ezra 7:23

Set in order thy houses; keep slothfulness and uncleanness far from you. D&C 90:18

HUMBLE, HUMILITY

Likewise, ye younger, submit yourselves unto the elder. Yea, all of you be subject one to another, and be clothed with humility: for God resisteth the proud, and giveth grace to the humble. 1 Pet. 5:5

The mean man shall be brought down, and the mighty man shall be humbled, and the eyes of the lofty shall be humbled. Isa. 5:15

When they were sick, my clothing was sackcloth: I humbled my soul with fasting; and my prayer returned into mine own bosom. I behaved myself as though he had been my friend or brother: I bowed down heavily, as one that mourneth for his mother. Ps. 35:13-14

O man, what is good; and what doth the LORD require of thee, but to do justly, and to love mercy, and to walk humbly with thy God? Micah 6:8

God resisteth the proud, but giveth grace unto the humble. James 4:6

Humble yourselves therefore under the mighty hand of God, that he may exalt you in due time. 1 Pet. 5:5-6

They did humble themselves before the Lord, and did give thanks unto him. 1 Ne. 16:32

HUNGER, HUNGRY

If thou draw out thy soul to the hungry, and satisfy the afflicted soul; then shall thy light rise in obscurity, and thy darkness be as the noonday: And the LORD shall guide thee continually. Isa. 58:10

Blessed are they which do hunger and thirst after righteousness: for they shall be filled. Matt. 5:6

Every man should impart to the support of the widows and their children, that they might not perish with hunger. Mosiah 21:17

HUSBAND

Husbands, love your wives, even as Christ also loved the church, and gave himself for it. That he might sanctify and cleanse it with the washing of water by the word, That he might present it to himself a glorious church, not having spot, or wrinkle, or any such thing; but that it should be holy and without blemish. So ought men to love their wives as their own bodies. He that loveth his wife loveth himself. Eph. 5:25-28

Their husbands love their wives, and their wives love their husbands; and their husbands and their wives love their children. Jacob 3:7

Let the husband render unto the render unto the wife due benevolence: and likewise also the wife unto the husband. 1 Cor. 7:3-5

HYMN

Let the word of Christ dwell in you richly in all wisdom; teaching and admonishing one another in psalms and hymns and spiritual songs, singing with grace in your hearts to the Lord. Col. 3:16

HYPOCRISY, HYPOCRITE

Thou hypocrite, first cast out the beam out of thine own eye; and then shalt thou see clearly to cast out the mote out of thy brother's eye. Matt. 7:3-5

Moreover, when ye fast be not as the hypocrites, of a sad countenance, for they disfigure their faces that they may appear unto men to fast. Verily I say unto you, they have their reward. But thou, when thou fastest, anoint thy head, and wash thy face; That thou appear not unto men to fast, but unto thy Father, who is in secret; and thy Father, who seeth in secret, shall reward thee openly. 3 Ne. 13:16-18 (Matt. 6:16-18)

Woe unto you, scribes and Pharisees, hypocrites! for ye pay tithe of mint and anise and cummin, and have omitted the weightier matters of the law, judgment, mercy, and faith: these ought ye to have done, and not to leave the other undone. Matt. 23:23

When thou prayest thou shalt not do as the hypocrites, for they love to pray, standing in the synagogues and in the corners of the streets, that they may be seen of men. Verily I say unto you, they have their reward. But thou, when thou prayest, enter into thy closet, and when thou hast shut thy door, pray to thy Father who is in secret; and thy Father, who seeth in secret, shall reward thee openly. 3 Ne. 13:5-6

What is the hope of the hypocrite, though he hath gained, when God taketh away his soul? Will God hear his cry when trouble cometh upon him? Job 27:8-9

Ye hypocrites, well did Esaias prophesy of you, saying, This people draweth nigh unto me with their mouth, and honoureth me with their lips; but their heart is far from me. Matt. 15:7-8

IDLE, IDLENESS, IDLER

They did become an idle people, full of mischief and subtlety. 2 Ne. 5:24

Cast away your idle thoughts and your excess laughter far from you. D&C 88:69

Thou shalt not idle away thy time, neither shalt thou bury thy talent that it may not be known. D&C 60:13

Eateth not the bread of idleness. Prov. 31:27

They learn to be idle, wandering about from house to house; and not only idle, but tattlers also and busybodies, speaking things which they ought not. 1 Tim. 5:13

See that ye refrain from idleness. Alma 38:12

IDOL, IDOLATER, IDOLATRY

Thou shalt have no other gods before me. Ex. 20:3

For rebellion is as the sin of witchcraft, and stubbornness is as iniquity and idolatry. Because thou hast rejected the word of the LORD, he hath also rejected thee from being king. 1 Sam 15:23

Their land also is full of idols; they worship the work of their own hands, that which their own fingers have made own fingers have made. Isa. 2:8

Blessed be the God of Shadrach, Meshach, and Abed-nego, who hath sent his angel, and delivered his servants that trusted in him, and have changed the king's word, and yielded their bodies, that they might not serve nor worship any god, except their own God. Dan. 3:28

Shall I not, as I have done unto Samaria and her idols, so do to Jerusalem and her idols? Isa. 10:11

Thou shalt not make unto thee any graven image, or any likeness of any thing that is in heaven above, or that is in the earth beneath, or that is in the water under the earth. Thou shalt not bow down thyself to them, nor serve them: For I the LORD thy God am a jealous God, visiting the iniquity of the fathers upon the children unto the third and fourth generation of them that hate me; And shewing mercy unto thousands of them that love me, and keep my commandments. Ex. 20:4-6

Repent, and turn yourselves from your idols. Ezek. 14:6

Worship God, for him only shalt thou serve. Moses 1:15

Know that an idol is nothing in the world, and that there is none other God but one. 1 Cor. 8:4

IMAGE

As we have borne the image of the earthly, we shall also bear the image of the heavenly. 1 Cor. 15:49

Have ye received his image in your countenances? Alma 5:14

He shall not look to the altars, the work of his hands, neither shall respect that which his fingers have made, either the groves, or the images. Isa. 17:8

IMAGINE, IMAGINATION

Suffer not yourself to be led away by any vain or foolish thing. Alma 39:11

GOD saw that the wickedness of man was great in the earth, and that every imagination of the thoughts of his heart was only evil continually. Gen. 6:5

Let none of you imagine evil in your hearts against his neighbour; and love no false oath: for all these are things that I hate, saith the LORD. Zech. 8:17

Oppress not the widow, nor the fatherless, the stranger, nor the poor; and let none of you imagine evil against his brother in your heart Zech. 7:10

Though we walk in the flesh, we do not war after the flesh: Casting down imaginations, and every high thing that exalteth itself against the knowledge of God, and bringing into captivity every thought to the obedience of Christ. 2 Cor. 10:3,5

These six things doth the LORD hate: yea, seven are an abomination unto him: A proud look, a lying tongue, and hands that shed innocent blood, An heart that deviseth wicked imaginations, feet that be swift in running to mischief, A false witness that speaketh lies, and he that soweth discord among brethren. Prov. 6:16-19

Know thou the God of thy father, and serve him with a perfect heart and with a willing mind: for the LORD searcheth all hearts, and understandeth all the imaginations of the thoughts. 1 Chron. 28:9

They said, There is no hope: but we will walk after our own devices, and we will every one do the imagination of his evil heart. Jer. 18:12

Neither shall they walk any more after the imagination of their evil heart. Jer. 3:17

IMPART

Impart the word of God, one with another, without money and without price. Alma 1:20

Learn to impart one to another as the gospel requires. D&C 88:123

IMPOSSIBLE

For with God nothing shall be impossible. Luke 1:37

If ye have faith as a grain of mustard seed, ye shall say unto this mountain, Remove hence to yonder place; and it shall remove; and nothing shall be impossible unto you. Matt. 17:20

For it is impossible for those who were once enlightened, and have tasted of the heavenly gift, and were made partakers of the Holy Ghost, And have tasted the good word of God, and the powers of the world to come, If they shall fall away, to renew them again unto repentance; seeing they crucify to themselves the Son of God afresh, and put him to an open shame. Heb. 6:4

But without faith it is impossible to please him: for he that cometh to God must believe that he is, and that he is a rewarder of them that diligently seek him. Heb. 11:6

That by two immutable things, in which it was impossible for God to lie, we might have a strong consolation, who have fled for refuge to lay hold upon the hope set before us: Which hope we have as an anchor of the soul, both sure and stedfast, and which entereth into that within the veil; Whither the forerunner is for us entered, even Jesus, made an high priest for ever after the order of Melchisedec. Heb. 6:18-19

INCENSE

Burn no incense unto other gods. Jer. 44:5

INCLINE

Put away, said he, the strange gods which are among you, and incline your heart unto the LORD God of Israel. Josh. 24:23

Incline not my heart to any evil thing, to practice wicked works with men that work iniquity. Ps. 141:4

My son, attend to my words; incline thine ear unto my sayings. Let them not depart from thine eyes; keep them in the midst of thine heart. For they are life unto those that find them, and health to all their flesh. Prov. 4:20-22

INCREASE

Jesus increased in wisdom and stature, and in favour with God and man. Luke 2:52

Trust not in oppression, and become not vain in robbery: if riches increase, set not your heart upon them. Ps. 62:10

INDIGNATION

I will bear the indignation of the LORD, because I have sinned against him, until he plead my cause, and execute judgment for me: he will bring me forth to the light, and I shall behold his righteousness. Micah 7:9-10

INFINITE

Believe in Christ and worship the Father in his name, with pure hearts and clean hands, and look not forward any more for another Messiah. 2 Ne. 25:16

INFLUENCE

We do not believe it just to mingle religious influence with civil government, whereby one religious society is fostered and another proscribed in its spiritual privileges, and the individual rights of its members, as citizens, denied. D&C 134:9

INFRINGE

We believe that religion is instituted of God; and that men are amenable to him, and to him only, for the exercise of it, unless their religious opinions prompt them to infringe upon the rights and liberties of others; but we do not believe that human law has a right to interfere in prescribing rules of worship to bind the consciences of men, nor dictate forms for public or private devotion; that the civil magistrate should restrain crime, but never control conscience; should punish guilt, but never suppress the freedom of the soul. D&C 134:4

INHERIT, INHERITANCE

Blessed are the meek: for they shall inherit the earth. Matt. 5:5

Know ye not that the unrighteous shall not inherit the kingdom of God? Be not deceived: neither fornicators, nor idolaters, nor adulterers, nor effeminate, nor abusers of themselves with mankind, Nor thieves, nor covetous, nor drunkards, nor revilers, nor extortioners, shall inherit the kingdom of God. 1Cor. 6:9-10

An inheritance may be gotten hastily at the beginning; but the end thereof shall not be blessed. Prov. 20:21

He that overcometh shall inherit all things; and I will be his God, and he shall be my son. But the fearful, and unbelieving, and the abominable, and murderers, and whore-mongers, and sorcerers, and idolaters, and all liars, shall have their part in the lake which burneth with fire and brimstone: which is the second death. Rev. 21:7

INIQUITY

Your iniquities have separated between you and your God, and your sins have hid his face from you, that he will not hear. Isa. 59:2

Not every one that saith unto me, Lord, Lord, shall enter into the kingdom of heaven; but he that doeth the will of my Father who is in heaven. Many will say to me in that day: Lord, Lord, have we not prophesied in thy name, and in thy name have cast out devils, and in thy name done many wonderful works? And then will I profess unto them: I never knew you; depart from me, ye that work iniquity. Matt. 7:21-23

Woe unto them that draw iniquity with cords of vanity, and sin as it were with a cart rope. Isa. 5:18

When a righteous man turneth away from his righteousness, and committeth iniquity, and dieth in them; for his iniquity that he hath done shall he die. Ezek. 18:26

Because iniquity shall abound, the love of many shall wax cold. Matt. 24:12

Ye are swift to do iniquity but slow to remember the Lord your God. 1 Ne. 17:45

Do no iniquity. Ps. 119:3

WOE to them that devise iniquity, and work evil upon their beds! Micah 2:1

I will declare mine iniquity; I will be sorry for my sin. Ps. 38:18

Acknowledge thine iniquity that thou hast transgressed against the LORD thy God, and hast scattered thy ways to the strangers under every green tree, and ye have not obeyed my voice, saith the LORD. Jer. 3:13

If ye have no hope ye must needs be in despair; and despair cometh because of iniquity. Moro. 10:22

Thou hast defiled thy sanctuaries by the multitude of thine iniquities, by the iniquity of thy traffick; therefore will I bring forth a fire from the midst of thee, it shall devour thee. Ezek. 28:18-19

Fret not thyself because of evil doers, neither be thou envious against the workers of iniquity. Ps. 37:1

If I regard iniquity in my heart, the Lord will not hear me. Ps. 66:18

Let not any iniquity have dominion over me. Ps. 119:133

All this evil is come upon us: yet made we not our prayer before the LORD our God, that we might turn from our iniquities and understand thy truth. Dan. 9:13

He that soweth iniquity shall reap vanity: and the rod of his anger shall fail. Prov. 22:8

If they shall confess their iniquity, and the iniquity of their fathers, with their trespass which they trespassed against me, and that also they have walked contrary unto me; And that I also have walked contrary unto them, and have brought them into the land of their enemies; if then their uncircumcised hearts be humbled, and they then accept of the punishment of their iniquity: Then will I remember my covenant with Jacob, and also my covenant with Isaac, and also my covenant with Abraham will I remember; and I will remember the land. Lev. 26:40-42

I will get me unto the great men, and will speak unto them; for they have known the way of the LORD, and the judgment of their God: but these have altogether broken the yoke, and burst the bonds. Jer. 5:5

Incline not my heart to any evil thing, to practice wicked works with men that work iniquity. Ps. 141:4

Flee out of the midst of Babylon, and deliver every man his soul; be not cut off in her iniquity; for this is the time of the LORD's vengence; he will render unto her a recompense. Jer. 51:6

Keep thy tongue from evil, and thy lips from speaking guile. Ps. 34:13

Be ashamed and confounded for your own ways, O house of Israel. Ezek. 36:32

The rebellious shall be pierced with much sorrow; for their iniquities shall be spoken upon the housetops, and their secret acts shall be revealed. D&C 1:3

If ye will sin until ye are fully ripe ye shall be cut off from the presence of the Lord. Ether 2:15

INJURE, INJURY

Ye will not have a mind to injure one another, but to live peaceably, and to render to every man according to that which is his due. Mosiah 4:13

INNOCENCE, INNOCENT

Shed not innocent blood. Jer. 7:6

These six things doth the LORD hate: yea, seven are an abomination unto him: A proud look, a lying tongue, and hands that shed innocent blood, An heart that deviseth wicked imaginations, feet that be swift in running to mischief, A false witness that speaketh lies, and he that soweth discord among brethren. Prov. 6:16-19

INQUIRE

They returned and enquired early after God. Ps. 78:34

One thing have I desired of the LORD, that will I seek after; that I may dwell in the house of the LORD all the days of my life, to behold the beauty of the LORD, and to enquire in his temple. Ps. 27:4

Have ye inquired of the Lord? 1 Ne. 15:8

Is there not here a prophet of the LORD, that we may inquire of the LORD by him? 2 Kgs. 3:11

Inquire of the Lord. Gen. 25:22

INSPIRATION, INSPIRE

All scripture is given by inspiration of God, and is profitable for doctrine, for reproof, for correction, for instruction in righteousness: That the man of God may be perfect, throughly furnished unto all good works. 2 Tim. 3:16-17

INSTRUCT, INSTRUCTION

Hear instruction, and be wise, and refuse it not. Prov. 8:33

Whoso loveth instruction loveth knowledge: but he that hateth reproof is brutish. Prov. 12:1

Poverty and shame shall be to him that refuseth instruction: but he that regardeth reproof shall be honoured. Prov. 13:18

Cease, my son, to hear the instruction that causeth to err from the words of knowledge. Prov. 19:27

He is in the way of life that keepeth instruction: but he that refuseth reproof erreth. Prov. 10:17

Buy the truth, and sell it not; also wisdom, and instruction, and understanding. Prov. 23:23

The fear of the LORD is the beginning of knowledge: but fools despise wisdom and instruction. Prov. 1:7

Take fast hold of instruction; let her not go: keep her; for she is thy life. Prov. 4:13

Hear the instruction of thy father, and forsake not the law of thy mother. Prov. 1:8

INSTRUMENT

Neither yield ye your members as instruments of unrighteousness unto sin: but yield yourselves unto God, as those that are alive from the dead, and your members as instruments of righteousness unto God. Rom. 6:13

INTEGRITY

Walk before me, as David thy father walked, in integrity of heart, and in uprightness, to do according to all that I have commanded thee, and wilt keep my statutes and my judgments. 1 Kgs. 9:4

The just man walketh in his integrity: his children are blessed after him. Prov. 20:7

INTERPRET, INTERPRETATION

Now the wise men, the astrologers, have been brought in before me, that they should read this writing, and make known unto me the interpretation thereof: but they could not shew the interpretation of the thing. Dan 5:15

I would that ye all spake with tongues, but rather that ye prophesied: for greater is he that prophesieth than he that speaketh with tongues, except he interpret, that the church may receive edifying. 1 Cor. 14:5

The secret which the king hath demanded cannot the wise men, the astrologers, the magicians, the soothsayers, shew unto the king; But there is a God in heaven that revealeth secrets, and maketh known to the king Nebuchadnezzar what shall be in the latter days. Dan. 1:27-28

Come unto God, the Holy One of Israel, and believe in prophesying, and in revelations, and in the ministering of angels, and in the gift of speaking with tongues, and in the gift of interpreting languages, and in all things which are good; for there is nothing which is good save it come from the Lord: and that which is evil cometh from the devil. Omni 1:25

God hath set some in the church, first apostles, secondarily prophets, thirdly teachers, after that miracles, then gifts of healings, helps, governments, diversities of tongues. Are all apostles? are all prophets? are all teachers? are all workers of miracles? Have all the gifts of healing? do all speak with tongues? do all interpret? But covet earnestly the best gifts: and yet shew I unto you a more excellent way. 1 Cor. 12:28-31

ISRAEL

It is a light thing that thou shouldest be my servant to raise up the tribes of Jacob, and to restore the preserved of Israel: I will also give thee for a light to the Gentiles, that thou mayest be my salvation unto the end of the earth. Isa. 49:6

Be it known unto you all, and to all the people of Israel, that by the name of Jesus Christ of Nazareth, whom ye crucified, whom God raised from the dead, even by him doth this man stand here before you whole. This is the stone which was set at nought of you builders, which is become the head of the corner. Neither is there salvation in any other: for there is none other name under heaven given among men, whereby we must be saved. Acts 4:10-12

There shall be no more any vain vision nor flattering divination within the house of Israel. Ezek. 12:24

JEALOUS, JEALOUSY

They provoked him to jealousy with strange gods, with abominations provoked they him to anger. Duet 32:16

They provoked him to anger with their high places, and moved him to jealousy with their graven images. Ps. 78:58

Do we provoke the Lord to jealousy? are we stronger than he? 1 Cor. 10:22

JEHOVAH

Let them be confounded and troubled for ever; yea, let them be put to shame, and perish: That men may know that thou, whose name alone is JEHOVAH, art the most high over all the earth. Ps. 83:18

JERUSALEM

Pray for the peace of Jerusalem: they shall prosper that love thee. Ps. 122:6

Ye that make mention of the LORD, keep not silence, And give him no rest, till he establish, and till he make Jerusalem a praise in the earth. Isa. 62:6-7

Ye are come unto mount Sion, and unto the city of the living God, the heavenly Jerusalem, and to an innumerable company of angels. Heb. 12:22

Son of man, cause Jerusalem to know her abominations. Ezek. 16:2

Shake thyself from the dust; arise, and sit down, O Jerusalem: loose thyself from the bands of thy neck, O captive daughter of Zion. Isa. 52:2

O Jerusalem, wash thine heart from wickedness, that thou mayest be saved. Jer. 4:14

Come, and let us go up to the mountain of the LORD, and to the house of the God of Jacob; and he will teach us of his ways, and we will walk in his paths; for the law shall go forth of Zion, and the word of the LORD from Jerusalem. Micah 4:2

JESUS CHRIST

His head and his hairs were white like wool, as white as snow; and his eyes were as a flame of fire; And his feet like unto fine brass, as if they burned in a furnace; and his voice as the sound of many waters. Rev. 1:15

This is life eternal, that they might know thee the only true God, and Jesus Christ, whom thou hast sent. John 17:3

Put ye on the Lord Jesus Christ, and make not provision for the flesh, to fulfil the lusts thereof. Rom. 13:14

I have told you this that ye may learn wisdom, that ye may learn of me that there is no other way or means whereby man can be saved, only in and through Christ. Alma 38:9

I know that he shall rise again in the resurrection at the last day. Jesus said unto her, I am the resurrection, and the life: he that believeth in me, though he were dead, yet shall he live. John 11:24-25

Gird up the loins of your mind, be sober, and hope to the end for the grace that is to be brought unto you at the revelation of Jesus Christ. 1 Pet. 1:13

Let all the house of Israel know assuredly, that God hath made that same Jesus, whom ye have crucified, both Lord and Christ. Acts 2:36

Happy is that people, that is in such a case: yea, happy is that people, whose God is the LORD. Ps. 144:15

Knowing that Christ being raised from the dead dieth no more; death hath no more dominion over him. For in that he died, he died unto sin once: but in that he liveth, he liveth unto God. Likewise reckon ye also yourselves to be dead indeed unto sin, but alive unto God through Jesus Christ our Lord. Romans 6:9-11

Grace be unto you, and peace, from him which is, and which was, and which is to come; and from the seven Spirits which are before his throne; And from Jesus Christ, who is the faithful witness, and the first begotten of the dead, and the prince of the kings of the earth. Unto him that loved us, and washed us from our sins in his own blood, And hath made us kings and priests unto God and his Father; to him be glory and dominion for ever and ever. Rev. 1:4-6

Wherefore also it is contained in the scripture, Behold, I lay in Sion a chief corner stone, elect, precious: and he that believeth on him shall not be confounded. 1 Pet. 2:6

Jesus increased in wisdom and stature, and in favour with God and man. Luke 2:52

[Look] unto Jesus the author and finisher of our faith; who for the joy that was set before him endured the cross, despising the shame, and is set down at the right hand of the throne of God. Heb. 12:2

Be it known unto you all, and to all the people of Israel, that by the name of Jesus Christ of Nazareth, whom ye crucified, whom God raised from the dead, even by him doth this man stand here before you whole. This is the stone which was set at nought of you builders, which is become the head of the corner. Neither is there salvation in any other: for there is none other name under heaven given among men, whereby we must be saved. Acts 4:10-12

There is neither Jew nor Greek, there is neither bond nor free, there is neither male nor female: for ye are all one in Christ Jesus. Gal. 3:28

Teach any man the right way; for the right way is to believe in Christ and deny him not; for by denying him ye also deny the prophets and the law. 2 Ne. 25:28

Be likeminded one toward another according to Christ Jesus: That ye may with one mind and one mouth glorify God, even the Father of our Lord Jesus Christ. Rom. 15:5-6

I would that ye should be perfect even as I, or your Father who is in heaven is perfect. 3 Ne. 12:48 (Matt. 5:48)

They shall mock him, and shall scourge him, and shall spit upon him, and shall kill him: and the third day he shall rise again. Mark 10:34

Thou shalt love the Lord thy God with all thy heart, with all thy might, mind and strength; and in the name of Jesus Christ thou shalt serve him. D&C 59:5

To you who are troubled rest with us, when the Lord Jesus shall be revealed from heaven with his mighty angels, In flaming fire taking vengeance on them that know not God, and that obey not the gospel of our Lord Jesus Christ. 2 Thes. 1:7-8

Repent, and be baptized every one of you in the name of Jesus Christ for the remission of sins, and ye shall receive the gift of the Holy Ghost. Acts 2:38

Remember that there is no other way nor means whereby man can be saved, only through the atoning blood of Jesus Christ, who shall come. Hel. 5:9

Wherefore, we would to God that we could persuade all men not to rebel against God, to provoke him to anger, but that all men would believe in Christ, and view his death, and suffer his cross and bear the shame of the world. Jacob 1:8

Teach them to withstand every temptation of the devil, with their faith on the Lord Jesus Christ. Alma 37:33

Believest thou in the power of Christ unto salvation? Alma 15:6

These are written, that ye might believe that Jesus is the Christ, the Son of God; and that believing ye might have life through his name. John 20:31

We command you, brethren, in the name of our Lord Jesus Christ, that ye withdraw yourselves from every brother that walketh disorderly, and not after the tradition which he received of us. 2 Thes 3:6

These are written, that ye might believe that Jesus is the Christ, the Son of God; and that believing ye might have life through his name. John 20:31

Be not ye called Rabbi: for one is your Master, Christ; and all ye are brethren. Matt. 23:8

Ye also, as lively stones, are built up a spiritual house, an holy priesthood, to offer up spiritual sacrifices, acceptable to God by Jesus Christ. 1 Pet. 2:5

We also joy in God through our Lord Jesus Christ, by whom we have now received the atonement. Rom. 5:11

There shall be no other name given nor any other way nor means whereby salvation can come unto the children of men, only in and through the name of Christ, the Lord Omnipotent. Mosiah 3:17

Ye are no more strangers and foreigners, but fellowcitizens with the saints, and of the household of God; And are built upon the foundation of the apostles and prophets, Jesus Christ himself being the chief corner stone. Eph. 2:19-20

There shall also arise false Christs, and false prophets, and shall show great signs and wonders, insomuch, that, if possible, they shall deceive the very elect, who are the elect according to the covenant. JS-M 1:22

Paul, being grieved, turned and said to the spirit, I command thee in the name of Jesus Christ to come out of her. And he came out the same hour. Acts 16:18

JOIN, JOINED

Have ye not read, that he which made them at the beginning made them male and female, And said, For this cause shall a man leave father and mother, and shall cleave to his wife: and they twain shall be one flesh? Wherefore they are no more twain, but one flesh. What therefore God hath joined together, let not man put asunder. Matt. 19:4-6

JOURNEY, JOURNEYING

Continue your journey and let your heart rejoice; for behold, and lo, I am with you even unto the end. D&C 100:12

JOY, JOYFUL, JOYFULLY

Blessed is the people that know the joyful sound: they shall walk, O LORD, in the light of thy countenance. Ps. 89:15

I will greatly rejoice in the LORD, my soul shall be joyful in my God; for he hath clothed me with the garments of salvation, he hath covered me with the robe of righteousness. Isa. 61:10

Live joyfully with the wife whom thou lovest all the days of the life of thy vanity, which he hath given thee under the sun, all the days of thy vanity: for that is thy portion in this life, and in thy labour which thou takest under the sun. Eccl. 9:9

Receive the word with joy. Alma 16:17

In the day of prosperity be joyful. Eccl. 7:14

JUDGE, JUDGMENT

Men should be judged according to their crimes. Alma 30:11

See that you are merciful unto your brethren; deal justly, judge righteously, and do good continually. Alma 41:14

Let us not therefore judge one another any more: but judge this rather, that no man put a stumbling block or an occasion to fall in his brother's way. Rom. 14:13

We must all appear before the judgment seat of Christ; that every one may receive the things done in his body, according to that he hath done, whether it be good or bad. 2 Cor. 5:10

Succor those that stand in need of your succor; ye will administer of your substance unto him that standeth in need; and ye will not suffer that the beggar putteth up his petition to you in vain, and turn him out to perish. Mosiah 4:16

Therefore remember, O man, for all thy doings thou shalt be brought into judgment. 1 Ne. 10:20

After the wisdom of thy God, that is in thine hand, set magistrates and judges, which may judge all the people that are beyond the river, all such as know the laws of thy God; and teach ye them that know them not. Ezra 7:25

Ye shall do no unrighteousness in judgment: thou shalt not respect the person of the poor, nor honor the person of the mighty: but in righteousness shalt thou judge thy neighbour. Lev. 19:15

Learn to do well; seek judgment, relieve the oppressed, judge the fatherless, plead for the widow. Isa. 1:17

O inhabitants of Jerusalem, and men of Judah, judge, I pray you, betwixt me and my vineyard. What could have been done more to my vineyard, that I have not done in it? Isa. 5:3-4

It is not good to accept the person of the wicked, to overthrow the righteous in judgment. Prov. 18:5

It is not good to have respect of persons in judgment. Prov. 24:23

Execute ye judgment and righteousness. Jer. 22:3-5

The house of Israel rebelled against me in the wilderness: they walked not in my statutes, and they despised my judgments, which if a man do, he shall even live in them; and my sabbaths they greatly polluted. Ezek. 20:13

Judge not according to the appearance, but judge righteous judgment. John 7:24

JUST, JUSTICE, JUSTLY,
JUSTIFICATION, JUSTIFY,

Be just. 2 Sam. 23:3

Justify [not] the wicked for reward 2 N.e 15:23

See that you are merciful unto your brethren; deal justly, judge righteously, and do good continually. Alma 41:14

Be a just man before the Lord. Omni 1:25

Masters, give unto your servants that which is just and equal; knowing that ye also have a Master in heaven. Col. 4:1

A false balance is abomination to the LORD: but a just weight is his delight. Prov. 11:1

I know your manifold transgressions and your mighty sins: they afflict the just, they take a bribe, and they turn aside the poor in the gate from their right. Amos 5:12

O man, what is good; and what doth the LORD require of thee, but to do justly, and to love mercy, and to walk humbly with thy God? Micah 6:8

The terrible one is brought to nought, and the scorner is consummed, and all that watch for iniquity are cut off: That make a man an offender for a word, and lay a snare for him that reproveth in the gate, and turn aside the just thing for a thing of nought. Isa. 29:20-21

Wo unto them that turn aside the just for a thing of naught and revile against that which is good, and say that it is of no worth! 2 Ne. 28:16

He that justifieth the wicked, and he that condemneth the just, even they both are abomination to the LORD. Prov. 17:15

Ye are witnesses, and God also, how holily and just and unblameably we behaved ourselves among you that believe. 1 Thes. 2:10

Put your trust in that Spirit which leadeth to do good–yea, to do justly, to walk humbly, to judge righteously. D&C 11:12

KEEP

Keep the commandments. Mosiah 12:33

Keep the commandments of the Lord. 1 Ne. 8:38

Keep the commandments of God. Abr. 1:2

If thou wilt enter into life, keep the commandments. Matt. 19:17

Be firm in keeping the commandments. D&C 5:22

Keep the way of the Lord. Gen. 18:19

Wait on the LORD, and keep his way and he shall exalt thee to inherit the land. Ps. 37:34

Thou hast commanded us to keep thy precepts diligently. Ps. 119:4

I have refrained my feet from every evil way, that I might keep thy word. Ps. 119:101

Keep the law. Prov. 28:4

Keep thy solemn feasts, perform thy vows. Nahum 1:15

The time shall come when it shall no more be expedient to keep the law of Moses. Mosiah 13:27

Only take heed to thyself, and keep thy soul diligently, lest thou forget the things which thine eyes have seen, and lest they depart from thine heart all the days of thy life: but teach them thy sons, and thy sons sons. Deut. 4:9

Ye have not kept my ways, but have been partial in the law. Mal. 2:9

Thou hast avouched the LORD this day to be thy God, and to walk in his ways, and to keep his statutes, and his commandments, and his judgments, and to hearken unto his voice. Deut. 26:17

KEY, KEYS

Woe unto you, lawyers! for ye have taken away the key of knowledge: ye entered not in yourselves, and them that were entering in ye hindered. Luke 11:52

KILL

Thou shalt not kill. Ex. 20:13

KIND, KINDNESS

She openeth her mouth with wisdom; and in her tongue is the law of kindness Prov. 31:26

Be ye kind one to another, tenderhearted, forgiving one another, even as God for Christ's sake hath forgiven you. Eph. 4:32

KING

The LORD is the true God, he is the living God, and an everlasting king: at his wrath the earth shall tremble, and the nations shall not be able to abide his indignation. Jer. 10:10

Let the children of Zion be joyful in their King. Ps. 149:2

Let Israel rejoice in him that made him: let the children of Zion be joyful in their King. Let them praise his name in the dance: let them sing praises unto him with the timbrel and harp. Ps. 149:2-3

KINGDOM

Blessed are the poor in spirit: for theirs is the kingdom of heaven. Matt 5:3

Blessed are they which are persecuted for righteousness' sake: for theirs is the kingdom of heaven. Matt. 5:10

Except ye be converted, and become as little children, ye shall not enter into the kingdom of heaven. Matt. 18:3

Another parable put he forth unto them, saying, The kingdom of heaven is like to a grain of mustard seed, which a man took, and sowed in his field. Matt. 13:31

Speak of the glory of thy kingdom, and talk of thy power; To make known to the sons of men his mighty acts, and the glorious majesty of his kingdom Ps. 145:11-12

Ye shut up the kingdom of heaven against men: for ye neither go in yourselves, neither suffer ye them that are entering to go in. Matt. 23:13

Solomon determined to build an house for the name of the LORD, and an house for his kingdom. 2 Chron. 2:1

Seek ye first the kingdom of God, and his righteousness; and all these things shall be added unto you. Matt. 6:33-34

KISS

[She] stood at his feet behind him weeping, and began to wash his feet with tears, and did wipe them with the hairs of her head, and kissed his feet, and anointed them with the ointment. Luke 7:38

KNEE, KNEEL

I have sworn by myself, the word is gone out of my mouth in righteousness, and shall not return, That unto me every knee shall bow, every tongue shall swear. Isa 45:23

For it is written, As I live, saith the Lord, every knee shall bow to me, and every tongue shall confess to God. Rom 14:11

Come, let us worship and bow down: let us kneel before the LORD our maker. Ps. 95:6

KNOCK

Ask, and it shall be given you; seek, and ye shall find; knock, and it shall be opened unto you. Luke 11:9

KNOW, KNOWLEDGE, KNOWN

They were men of a sound understanding and they had searched the scriptures diligently, that they might know the word of God. Alma 17:2

Know the LORD: for they shall all know me, from the least of them unto the greatest of them, saith the LORD; for I will forgive their iniquity, and I will remember their sin no more. Jer. 31:34

LORD, thou hast searched me, and known me. Thou knowest my downsitting and mine uprising, thou understandest my thought afar off. Thou compassest my path and my lying down, and art acquainted with all my ways. For there is not a word in my tongue, but, lo, O LORD, thou knowest it altogether. Ps. 139:1-5

Whoso loveth instruction loveth knowledge: but he that hateth reproof is brutish. Prov. 12:1

Cease, my son, to hear the instruction that causeth to err from the words of knowledge. Prov. 19:27

There shall be no other name given nor any other way nor means whereby salvation can come unto the children of men, only in and through the name of Christ, the Lord Omnipotent. Mosiah 3:17

They had waxed strong in the knowledge of the truth; for they were men of a sound understanding and they had searched the scriptures diligently, that they might know the word of God. Alma 17:2

We speak the wisdom of God in a mystery, even the hidden wisdom, which God ordained before the world unto our glory. 1 Cor. 2:7

Know ye that the LORD he is God. Ps. 100:3

According as his divine power hath given unto us all things that pertain unto life and godliness, through the knowledge of him that hath called us to glory and virtue: Whereby we are given unto us exceeding great and precious promises: that by these ye might be partakers of the divine nature, having escaped the corruption that is in the world through lust. 2 Pet. 1:3-4

Bow down thine ear, and hear the words of the wise, and apply thine heart unto my knowledge. Prov. 22:17

Know the righteousness of the LORD. Micah 6:5

I applied mine heart to know, and to search, and to seek out wisdom, and the reason of things, and to know the wickedness of folly, even of foolishness and madness. Eccl. 7:25

The priests lips should keep knowledge, and they should seek the law at his mouth: for he is the messenger of the LORD of hosts. Mal. 2:7

Go from the presence of a foolish man, when thou preceivest not in him the lips of knowledge. Prov. 14:7

Be it according to thy word: that thou mayest know that there is none like unto the LORD our God. Ex. 8:10

Be still, and know that I am God. Ps. 46:10

Walk worthy of the Lord unto all pleasing, being fruitful in every good work, and increasing in the knowledge of God. Col. 1:10

For precept must be upon precept, precept upon precept; line upon line, line upon line; here a little, and there a little: For with stammering lips and another tongue will he speak to this people. Isa. 28:10

I will behold thy face in righteousness: I shall be satisfied, when I awake, with thy likeness. Ps. 17:15

I have filled him with the spirit of God, in wisdom, in understanding, and in knowledge, and in all manner of workmanship. Ex. 31:3

Who is this that darkeneth counsel by words without knowledge? Job 38:2

If ye know these things, happy are ye if ye do them. John 13:17

Grow in the knowledge of the glory of him that created you, or in the knowledge of that which is just and true. Mosiah 4:12

Incline thine ear unto wisdom, and apply thine heart to understanding. Prov. 2:2

LABOR, LABORED, LABORING

He that tilleth his land shall have plenty of bread: but he that followeth after vain persons shall have poverty enough. Prov. 28:19

Labour not to be rich: cease from thin own wisdom. Prov. 23:4

Do not spend money for that which is of no worth, nor your labor for that which can not satisfy. 2 Ne. 9:51

What profit hath he that hath laboured for the wind? Eccl. 5:16-20

Remember the sabbath day, to keep it holy. Six days shalt thou labour, and do all thy work: But the seventh day is the sabbath of the LORD thy God: in it thou shalt not do any work, thou, nor thy son, nor thy daughter, thy man-servant, nor thy maidservant, nor thy cattle, nor thy stranger that is within thy gates: For in six days the LORD made heaven and earth, the sea, and all that in them is, and rested the seventh day: wherefore the LORD blessed the sabbath day, and hallowed it. Ex. 20:8-11

Do not run faster or labor more than you have strength and means. D&C 10:4

The labour of the righteous tendeth to life: the fruit of the wicked to sin. Prov. 10:16

Every man should eat and drink, and enjoy the good of all his labor, it is the gift of God. Eccl. 3:13

I have laboured in vain, I have spent my strength for nought, and in vain: yet surely my judgment is with the LORD, and my work with my God. Isa. 49:4

Labour not for the meat which perisheth, but for that meat which endureth unto everlasting life. John 6:27

LACK

Then Jesus beholding him loved him, and said unto him, One thing thou lackest: go thy way, sell whatsoever thou hast, and give to the poor, and thou shalt have treasure in heaven: and come, take up the cross, and follow me. Mark 10:21

If any of you lack wisdom, let him ask of God, that giveth to all men liberally, and upbraideth not; and it shall be given him. But let him ask in faith, nothing wavering. For he that wavereth is like a wave of the sea driven with the wind and tossed. James 1:5-6

LASCIVIOUS, LASCIVIOUSNESS

Who being past feeling have given themselves over unto lasciviousness, to work all uncleanness with greediness? Eph. 4:19

That which cometh out of the man, that defileth the man. For from within, out of the heart of men, proceed evil thoughts, adulteries, fornications, murders, thefts, covetousness, wickedness, deceit, lascivious-ness, an evil eye, blasphemy, pride, foolish-ness: All these evil things come from within, and defile the man. Mark 7:20-23

Preach against all lyings, and deceivings, and envyings, and strifes, and malice, and revilings, and stealing, robbing, plundering, murdering, committing adultery, and all manner of lasciviousness, crying that these things ought not so to be. Alma 16:18

LAND

Worship the Lord thy God, and honor thy father and thy mother, that thy days may be long in the land. 1 Ne. 17:55

LANDMARK

Remove not the ancient landmark, which thy fathers have set. Prov. 22:28

LATTER-DAY, LAST DAYS

Now the Spirit speaketh expressly, that in the latter times some shall depart from the faith, giving heed to seducing spirits, and doctrines of devils; Speaking lies in hypocrisy; having their conscience seared with a hot iron; Forbidding to marry, and commanding to abstain from meats, which God hath created to be received with thanksgiving of them which believe and know the truth. 1 Tim. 4:1-3

This know also, that in the last days perilous times shall come. 2 Tim. 3:1

LAUGH, LAUGHTER

Cast away your idle thoughts and your excess laughter far from you. D&C 88:69

LAW, LAWFUL, LAWFULLY

Whoso keepeth the law is a wise son: but he that is a companion of riotous men shameth his father. Prov. 28:7

But we know that the law is good, if a man use it lawfully. 1 Tim 1:8

Where there is no vision, the people perish: but he that keepeth the law, happy is he. Prov. 29:18

We believe in being subject to kings, presidents, rulers, and magistrates, in obeying, honoring, and sustaining the law. A of F-12

Understand the words of the law. Neh. 8:13

If ye teach the law of Moses, also teach that it is a shadow of those things which are to come. Mosiah 16:14

Come, and let us go up to the mountain of the LORD, and to the house of the God of Jacob; and he will teach us of his ways, and we will walk in his paths; for the law shall go forth of Zion, and the word of the LORD from Jerusalem. Micah 4:2

We know that the law is good, if a man use it lawfully. 1 Tim. 1:8

Put them in mind to be subject to principalities and powers, to obey magistrates, to be ready to every good work. Titus 3:1

His delight is in the law of the LORD; and in his law doth he mediate day and night. Ps. 1:2

Hear the instruction of thy father, and forsake not the law of thy mother. Prov. 1:8

Bind up the testimony, seal the law among my disciples. Isa. 8:16

Keep the law. Prov. 28:4

He that turneth away his ear from hearing the law, even his prayer shall be abomination. Prov. 28:9

Ye have not kept my ways, but have been partial in the law. Mal. 2:9

Woe unto you, scribes and Pharisees, hypocrites! for ye pay tithe of mint and anise and cummin, and have omitted the weightier matters of the law, judgment, mercy, and faith: these ought ye to have done, and not to leave the other undone. Matt. 23:23

Ye shall have one manner of law, as well for the stranger, as for one of your own country: for I am the LORD your God. Lev. 24:22

As the fire devoureth the stubble, and the flame consumeth the chaff, so their root shall be as rottenness, and their blossom shall go up as dust: because they have cast away the law of the LORD of hosts, and despised the word of the Holy One of Israel. Isa. 5:24

We believe that rulers, states, and governments have a right, and are bound to enact laws for the protection of all citizens in the free exercise of their religious belief; but we do not believe that they have a right in justice to deprive citizens of this privilege, or proscribe them in their opinions, so long as a regard and reverence are shown to the laws and such religious opinions do not justify sedition nor conspiracy. D&C 134:7

I delight to do thy will, O my God: yea, thy law is within my heart. Ps. 40:8

Give me understanding, and I shall keep thy law; yea, I shall observe it with my whole heart. Ps. 119:34

Give ear unto the law of our God. Isa. 1:10

He hath done that which is lawful and right; he shall surely live. Ezek. 33:16

[Obey] the voice of the LORD our God, to walk in his laws, which he set before us by his servants the prophets. Dan. 9:10

Let no man break the laws of the land, for he that keepeth the laws of God hath no need to break the laws of the land. D&C 58:21

Look forward unto that life which is in Christ, and know for what end the law was given. 2 Ne. 25:27

Bring the wicked to justice according to their crime. Alma 50:39

LAY ASIDE

Seeing we also are compassed about with so great a cloud of witnesses, let us lay aside every weight, and the sin which doth so easily beset us, and let us run with patience the race that is set before us. Heb. 12:1

LAYING ON OF HANDS

[Peter and John] then laid they their hands on them, and they received the Holy Ghost. Acts 8:17

Therefore leaving the principles of the doctrine of Christ, let us go on unto perfection; not laying again the foundation of repentance from dead works, and of faith toward God, Of the doctrine of baptisms, and of laying on of hands, and of resurrection of the dead, and of eternal judgment. Heb. 6:1-2

All they that had any sick with divers diseases brought them unto him; and he laid his hands on every one of them, and healed them. Luke 4:40

LAY UP

Lay not up for yourselves treasures upon earth, where moth and rust doth corrupt, and where thieves break through and steal: But lay up for yourselves treasures in heaven, where neither moth nor rust doth corrupt, and where thieves do not break through nor steal: For where your treasure is, there will your heart be also. Matt. 6:19-21

LEAD, LEADER, LEADERSHIP, LED

Our kings and our leaders were mighty men in the faith of the Lord. Jarom 1:7

As many as are led by the Spirit of God, they are the sons of God. Rom. 8:14

The leaders of this people cause them to err; and they that are led of them are destroyed. Isa. 9:16

Pacumeni was appointed according to the voice of the people, to be a chief judge and a governor over the people. Hel. 1:13

Wherefore, honest men and wise men should be sought for diligently, and good and wise men ye should observe to uphold; otherwise whatsoever is less than these cometh of evil. D&C 98:10

LEARN, LEARNED, LEARNING

Learn to do well; seek judgment, relieve the oppressed, judge the fatherless, plead for the widow. Isa. 1:17

When thou dost lend thy brother any thing, thou shalt not go into his house to fetch his pledge. Deut. 24:10

For precept must be upon precept, precept upon precept; line upon line, line upon line; here a little, and there a little: For with stammering lips and another tongue will he speak to this people. Isa. 28:10

With my soul have I desired thee in the night; yea, with my spirit within me will I seek thee early: for when thy judgments are in the earth, the inhabitants of the world will learn righteousness. Isa. 26:9

When they are learned they think they are wise, and they hearken not unto the counsel of God, for they set it aside, supposing they know of themselves, wherefore, their wisdom is foolishness and it profiteth them not. And they perish. But to be learned is good, if they hearken unto the counsels of God. 2 Ne. 9:28-29

I have yet many things to say unto you, but ye cannot bear them now. John 16:12

I have told you this that ye may learn wisdom, that ye may learn of me that there is no other way or means whereby man can be saved, only in and through Christ. Alma 38:9

Come unto me, all ye that labour and are heavy laden, and I will give you rest. Take my yoke upon you, and learn of me; for I am meek and lowly in heart: and ye shall find rest unto your souls. Matt. 11:28-29

Learn wisdom in thy youth; yea, learn in thy youth to keep the commandments of God. Alma 37:35

LEAVE, LEFT

Discretion shall preserve thee, understanding shall keep thee; To deliver thee from the way of the evil man, from the man that speaketh froward things; who leave the paths of righteousness, to walk in the ways of darkness. Prov. 2:11-13

LEND, LENT

I say unto you that if ye should serve him who has created you from the beginning, and is preserving you from day to day, by lending you breath, that ye may live and move and do according to your own will, and even supporting you from one moment to another - I say, if ye should serve him with all your whole souls yet ye would be unprofitable servants. Mosiah 2:21

LEWD, LEWDNESS

Cause lewdness to cease out of the land. Ezek. 23:48

LIAR, LIE, LYING

The getting of treasures by a lying tongue is a vanity tossed to and fro of them that seek death. Prov. 21:6

There shall in no wise enter into [the temple] any thing that defileth, neither whatsoever worketh abomination, or maketh a lie: but they which are written in the Lamb's book of life. Rev. 21:27

If a ruler hearken to lies, all his servants are wicked. Prov. 29:12

God shall send them strong delusion, that they should believe a lie: That they all might be damned who believed not the truth, but had pleasure in unrighteousness. 2 Thes. 2:11-12

Let the lying lips be put to silence; which speak grievous things proudly and contemptuously against the righteous. Ps. 31:18

He that hideth hatred with lying lips, and he that uttereth a slander, is a fool. Prov. 10:18

Thou shalt not lie. D&C 42:21

Let the lying lips be put to silence; which speak grievous things proudly and contemptuously against the righteous. Ps. 31:18

As for our iniquities, we know them: in transgressing and lying against the LORD, and departing away from our God, speaking oppression and revolt, conceiving and uttering from the heart words of falsehood. Isa. 59:12-13

Trust ye not in lying words. Jer. 7:4

Thou shalt not live; for thou speakest lies in the name of the LORD. Zech. 13:3

The mouth of them that speak lies shall be stopped. Ps. 63:11

Who is a liar but he that denieth that Jesus is the Christ? He is antichrist, that denieth the Father and the Son. 1 Jn. 2:22-23

Lie not one to another, seeing that ye have put off the old man with his deeds. Col. 3:9

A false witness shall not be unpunished, and he that speaketh lies shall not escape. Prov. 19:5

The Lord God hath commanded that men should not murder; that they should not lie. 2 Ne. 26:32

These six things doth the LORD hate: yea, seven are an abomination unto him: A proud look, a lying tongue, and hands that shed innocent blood, An heart that deviseth wicked imaginations, feet that be swift in running to mischief, A false witness that speaketh lies, and he that soweth discord among brethren. Prov. 6:16-19

LIBERTY

Stand fast therefore in the liberty wherewith Christ hath made us free, and be not entangled again with the yoke of bondage. Gal. 5:1

Men are free according to the flesh; and all things are given them which are expedient unto man. And they are free to choose liberty and eternal life, through the great Mediator of all men, or to choose captivity and death, according to the captivity and power of the devil; for he seeketh that all men might be miserable like unto himself. 2 Ne. 2:27

So is the will of God, that with well doing ye may put to silence the ignorance of foolish men: As free, and not using your liberty for a cloke of maliciousness, but as the servants of God. 1 Pet. 2:15-16

Proclaim liberty to the captives, and the opening of the prison to them that are bound. Isa. 61:1

Ye have not hearkened unto me, in proclaiming liberty, every one to his brother, and every man to his neighbour: behold, I proclaim a liberty for you, saith the LORD, to the sword, to the pestilence, and to the famine; and I will make you to be removed into all the kingdoms of the earth. Jer. 34:17

Ye have not hearkened unto me, in proclaiming liberty, every one to his brother, and every man to his neighbour: behold, I proclaim a liberty for you, saith the LORD. Jer. 34:15-17

The Spirit of the Lord is upon me, because he hath anointed me to preach the gospel to the poor; he hath sent me to heal the brokenhearted, to preach deliverance to the captives, and recovering of sight to the blind, to set at liberty them that are bruised, To preach the acceptable year of the Lord. Luke 4:18-19

We believe that religion is instituted of God; and that men are amenable to him, and to him only, for the exercise of it, unless their religious opinions prompt them to infringe upon the rights and liberties of others; but we do not believe that human law has a right to interfere in prescribing rules of worship to bind the consciences of men, nor dictate forms for public or private devotion; that the civil magistrate should restrain crime, but never control conscience; should punish guilt, but never suppress the freedom of the soul. D&C 134:4

LIFE, LIVES

Lead a quiet and peaceable life in all godliness and honesty. 1 Tim. 2:2

He that followeth after righteousness and mercy, findeth life, righteousness, and honour. Prov. 21:21

Whosoever will save his life shall lose it; but whosoever shall lose his life for my sake and the gospel's, the same shall save it. For what shall it profit a man, if he shall gain the whole world, and lose his own soul? Mark 8:36

Enter ye in at the strait gate; for wide is the gate, and broad is the way, which leadeth to destruction, and many there be who go in thereat; Because strait is the gate, and narrow is the way, which leadeth unto life, and few there be that find it. 3 Ne. 14:13-14 (Matt. 7:13-14)

LIFT

Lift up your heads, and rejoice, and put your trust in God, in that God who was the God of Abraham, and Isaac, and Jacob. Mosiah 7:19

Thine heart was lifted up because of thy beauty, thou hast corrupted thy wisdom by reason of thy brightness: I will cast thee to the ground. Ezek. 28:17

Lift up a standard for the people. Isa. 62:10

LIGHT

Bring up your children in light and truth. D&C 93:40

Commit thy way unto the Lord; trust also in Him; and He shall bring it to pass. And he shall bring forth thy righteousness as the light, and thy judgment as the noonday. Ps. 37:5-6

Let us therefore cast off the works of darkness, and let us put on the armor of light. Rom. 13:12

It is a light thing that thou shouldest be my servant to raise up the tribes of Jacob, and to restore the preserved of Israel: I will also give thee for a light to the Gentiles, that thou mayest be my salvation unto the end of the earth. Isa. 49:6

Arise, shine; for thy light is come, and the glory of the LORD is risen upon thee. Isa. 60:1

Ye were sometimes darkness, but now are ye light in the Lord: walk as children of light. Eph. 5:8

Come ye, and let us walk in the light of the LORD. Isa. 2:5

Let your light so shine before men, that they may see your good works, and glorify your Father which is in heaven. Matt. 5:16

Come ye and let us walk in the light of the Lord. 2 Ne. 12:5

LIKEMINDED

Be likeminded one toward another according to Christ Jesus: That ye may with one mind and one mouth glorify God, even the Father of our Lord Jesus Christ. Rom. 15:5-6

LIKENESS

I will behold thy face in righteousness: I shall be satisfied, when I awake, with thy likeness. Ps. 17:15

LIMIT

They turned back and tempted God, and limited the Holy One of Israel. Ps. 78:41

LIPS

Put away from thee a froward mouth, and perverse lips put far from thee. Prov. 4:24

My son, attend unto my wisdom, and bow thine ear to my understanding: That thou mayest regard discretion and thy lips may keep knowledge. Prov. 5:2

My lips shall not speak wickedness, nor my tongue utter deceit. Job 27:4

LIST, LISTED, LISTETH

But I say unto you, That Elias is come already, and they knew him not, but have done unto him whatsoever they listed. Likewise shall also the Son of man suffer of them. Then the disciples understood that he spake unto them of John the Baptist. Matt. 17:12-13

LIVE, LIVING

Consider on the blessed and happy state of those that keep the commandments of God. Mosiah 2:41

Ye shall forsake all evil and cleave unto all good, that ye shall live by every word which proceedeth forth out of the mouth of God. D&C 98:11

Man shall not live by bread alone, but by every word that proceedeth out of the mouth of God. Matt. 4:4

Live joyfully with the wife whom thou lovest all the days of the life of thy vanity, which he hath given thee under the sun, all the days of thy vanity: for that is thy portion in this life, and in thy labour which thou takest under the sun. Eccl. 9:9

The LORD liveth; and blessed be my rock; and let the God of my salvation be exalted. Ps. 18:46

You shall live by every word that proceedeth forth from the mouth of God. D&C 84:44

Thou shalt live together in love. D&C 42:45

LOATHE, LOATHSOME

A righteous man hateth lying: but a wicked man is loathsome, and cometh to shame. Prov. 13:5

LOFTINESS, LOFTY

The mean man shall be brought down, and the mighty man shall be humbled, and the eyes of the lofty shall be humbled. Isa. 5:15

LONGSUFFERING

LORD, thou knowest: remember me, and visit me, and revenge me of my persecutors; take me not away in thy longsuffering: know that for thy sake I have suffered rebuke. Jer. 15:15

LOOK

Oh my son, do not let us be slothful because of the easiness of the way; for so was it with our fathers; for so was it prepared for them, that if they would look they might live; even so it is with us. The way is prepared, and if we will look we may live forever. Alma 37:46

Look on every one that is proud, and bring him low; and tread down the wicked in their place. Job 40:12

Behold, it is written by them of old time, that thou shalt not commit adultery; But I say unto you, that whosoever looketh on a woman, to lust after her, hath committed adultery already in his heart. Behold, I give you a commandment, that ye suffer non of these things to enter into your heart; For it is better that ye should deny yourselves of these things, wherein ye will take up your cross than that ye should be cast into hell. 3 Ne. 12:27-30 (Matt. 5:27-28)

Look unto me, and be ye saved, all the ends of the earth: for I am God, and there is none else. Isa. 45:22

Look forward with steadfastness unto Christ, until the law shall be fulfilled. 2 Ne. 25:24

Look to God and live. Alma 37:47

He shall not look to the altars, the work of his hands, neither shall respect that which his fingers have made, either the groves, or the images. Isa. 17:8

LOOSE

Shake thyself from the dust; arise, and sit down, O Jerusalem: loose thyself from the bands of thy neck, O captive daughter of Zion. Isa. 52:2

LORD

I will bear the indignation of the LORD, because I have sinned against him, until he plead my cause, and execute judgment for me: he will bring me forth to the light, and I shall behold his righteousness. Micah 7:9-10

Know ye that the LORD he is God. Ps. 100:3

LOT

The lot causeth contensions to cease, and parteth between the mighty. Prov. 18:18

LOVE, LOVINGKINDNESS

By love, serve one another. Gal. 5:13

Love me and keep my commandments. Mosiah 13:14

Pray for the peace of Jerusalem: they shall prosper that love thee. Ps. 122:6

Love one another with a pure heart. 1 Pet. 1:22

Jesus said unto him, Thou shalt love the Lord thy God with all thy heart, and with all thy soul, and with all thy mind. This is the first and great command-ment. And the second is like unto it, Thou shalt love thy neighbour as thyself. On these two command-ments, hang all the law and the prophets. Matt 22:37-40

I will worship toward thy holy temple, and praise thy name for thy loving-kindness and for thy truth: for thou hast magnified thy word above all thy name. Ps. 138:2

If ye love me, keep my command-ments. D&C 124:87 (John 14:15)

Who shall separate us from the love of Christ? shall tribulation, or distress, or persecution, or famine, or nakedness, or peril, or sword? Rom. 8:35

I know that the words of truth are hard against all uncleanness; but the righteous fear them not, for they love the truth and are not shaken. 2 Ne. 9:40

He that loveth pleasure shall be a poor man: he that loveth wine and oil shall not be rich. Prov. 21:17

Ye must press forward with a stead-fastness in Christ having a perfect brightness of hope, and a love of God and of all men. 2 Ne. 31:20

Better is a dinner of herbs where love is, than a stalled ox and hatred therewith. Prov. 15:17

Their husbands love their wives, and their wives love their husbands; and their husbands and their wives love their children. Jacob 3:7

Love not the world, neither the things that are in the world. 1 Jn. 2:15

Love your enemies, bless them that curse you, do good to them that hate you, and pray for them which despitefully use you, and persecute you. Matt. 5:44

Love your enemies, bless them that curse you, do good to them that hate you, and pray for them who despitefully use you and persecute you; That ye may be the children of your Father who is in heaven; for he maketh his sun to rise on the evil and on the good. 3 Ne. 12:43-45 (Matt. 5:44)

Love little children with a perfect love. Moro. 8:17

He that loveth silver shall not be satisfied with silver; nor he that loveth abundance with increase: this is also vanity. Eccl. 5:10

Thou shalt live together in love. D&C 42:45

Husbands, love your wives, even as Christ also loved the church, and gave himself for it. That he might sanctify and cleanse it with the washing of water by the word, That he might present it to himself a glorious church, not having spot, or wrinkle, or any such thing; but that it should be holy and without blemish. So ought men to love their wives as their own bodies. He that loveth his wife loveth himself. Eph. 5:25-28

Let none of you imagine evil in your hearts against his neighbour; and love no false oath: for all these are things that I hate, saith the LORD. Zech. 8:17

Owe no man any thing, but to love one another: for he that loveth another hath fulfilled the law. Rom. 13:8

Thou shalt love the Lord thy God with all thy heart, and with all thy soul, and with all thy mind. Matt. 22:37

Thou shalt not avenge, nor bear any grudge against the children of thy people, but thou shalt love thy neighbour as thyself: I the LORD. Lev. 19:18

Love one another. Moses 7:33

Love the name of the LORD. Isa. 56:6

Mention the lovingkindness of the LORD, and the praises of the LORD, according to all that the LORD, hath bestowed on us, and the great goodness toward the house of Israel, which he hath bestowed on them according to his mercies, and according to the multitude of his lovingkindness. Isa. 63:7

Thou shalt love the LORD thy God with all thine heart, and with all thy soul, and with all thy might. Deut. 6:5

How excellent is thy lovingkindness, O God! therefore the children of men put their trust under the shadow of thy wings. Ps. 36:7

Thou shalt love thy neighbor as thyself. Matt. 22:39

Thou shalt love thy wife with all thy heart, and shalt cleave unto her and none else. D&C 42:22

Greater love hath no man than this, that a many lay down his life for his friends. John 15:13

Thou shalt love the Lord thy God with all thy heart, with all thy might, mind and strength; and in the name of Jesus Christ thou shalt serve him. D&C 59:5

Thou shalt love thy neighbor as thyself. D&C 59:6

Every man should love his neighbor as himself, that there should be no contention among them. Mosiah 23:15

If ye have experienced a change of heart, and if ye have felt to sing the song of redeeming love, I would ask, can ye feel so now? Alma 5:26

Thou shalt love the Lord thy God with all thy heart, and with all thy soul, and with all thy mind, and with all thy strength: this is the first commandment. Mark 12:30

LOW, LOWLINESS, LOWLY

Come unto me, all ye that labour and are heavy laden, and I will give you rest. Take my yoke upon you, and learn of me; for I am meek and lowly in heart: and ye shall find rest unto your souls. Matt. 11:28-29

Let nothing be done through strife or vainglory; but in lowliness of mind let each esteem other better than themselves. Philip. 2:3

He scorneth the scorners: but he giveth grace unto the lowly. Prov. 3:34

Teach them to never be weary of good works, but to be meek and lowly in heart. Alma 37:34

LOYAL, LOYALTY

As the LORD liveth, and as my lord the king liveth, surely in what place my lord the king shall be, whether in death or life, even there also will thy servant be. 2 Sam 15:21

LUST

They tempted God in their heart by asking meat for their lust. Ps. 78:18

Flee also youthful lusts: but follow righteousness, faith, charity, peace, with them that call on the Lord out of a pure heart. 2 Tim. 2:22

Ye ask, and receive not, because ye ask amiss, that ye may consume it upon your lusts. James 4:3

According as his divine power hath given unto us all things that pertain unto life and godliness, through the knowledge of him that hath called us to glory and virtue: Whereby we are given unto us exceeding great and precious promises: that by these ye might be partakers of the divine nature, having escaped the corruption that is in the world through lust. 2 Pet. 1:3-4

Behold, it is written by them of old time, that thou shalt not commit adultery; But I say unto you, that whosoever looketh on a woman, to lust after her, hath committed adultery already in his heart. Behold, I give you a commandment, that ye suffer non of these things to enter into your heart; For it is better that ye should deny yourselves of these things, wherein ye will take up your cross than that ye should be cast into hell. 3 Ne. 12:27-30 (Matt. 5:27-28)

He that looketh on a woman to lust after her, or if any shall commit adultery in their hearts, they shall not have the Spirit, but shall deny the faith and shall fear. D&C 63:16-18

God also gave them up to uncleanness through the lusts of their own hearts, to dishonour their own bodies between themselves. Rom. 1:24

Likewise also the men, leaving the natural use of the woman, burned in their lust one toward another; men with men working that which is unseemly, and receiving in themselves that recompence of their error which was meet. Rom. 1:27

Cease from all your light speeches, from all laughter, from all your lustful desires, from all your pride and light-mindedness, and from all your wicked doings. D&C 88:121

Put ye on the Lord Jesus Christ, and make not provision for the flesh, to fulfil the lusts thereof. Rom. 13:14

MAGIC, MAGICIAN

Now the wise men, the astrologers, have been brought in before me, that they should read this writing, and make known unto me the interpretation thereof: but they could not shew the interpretation of the thing. Dan 5:15

MAGNIFY

Magnify not thyself against the Lord. Jer. 48:26

MAKE KNOWN

Give thanks unto the LORD, call upon his name, make known his deeds among the people. 1 Chron. 16:8

MALE

There is neither Jew nor Greek, there is neither bond nor free, there is neither male nor female: for ye are all one in Christ Jesus. Gal. 3:28

MALICE

Preach against all lyings, and deceivings, and envyings, and strifes, and malice, and revilings, and stealing, robbing, plundering, murdering, committing adultery, and all manner of lasciviousness, crying that these things ought not so to be. Alma 16:18

MAN

And the LORD God formed man of the dust of the ground, and breathed into his nostrils the breath of life; and man became a living soul. Gen 2:7

MANNER

After this manner therefore pray ye: Our Father who art in heaven, hallowed be thy name. Thy will be done on earth as it is in heaven. And forgive us our debts, as we forgive our debtors. And lead us not into temptation, but deliver us from evil. For thine is the kingdom, and the power, and the glory, forever. Amen. 3 Ne. 13:9-13 (Matt. 6:9-13)

MANSION

In my Father's house are many mansions: if it were not so, I would have told you. I go to prepare a place for you. John 14:2

MARK

This one thing I do, forgetting those things which are behind, and reaching forth unto those things which are before, I press toward the mark for the prize of the high calling of God in Christ Jesus. Philip 3:13-14

And the LORD said unto them - Go through the midst of the city, through the midst of Jerusalem, and set a mark upon the foreheads of the men that sigh and that cry for all the abominations that be done in the midst thereof. Ezek. 9:4

MARRIAGE

Marriage is honourable in all, and the bed undefiled: but whoremongers and adulterers God will judge. Heb. 13:4

Now the Spirit speaketh expressly, that in the latter times some shall depart from the faith, giving heed to seducing spirits, and doctrines of devils; Speaking lies in hypocrisy; having their conscience seared with a hot iron; Forbidding to marry, and commanding to abstain from meats, which God hath created to be received with thanksgiving of them which believe and know the truth. 1 Tim. 4:1-3

Have ye not read, that he which made them at the beginning made them male and female, And said, For this cause shall a man leave father and mother, and shall cleave to his wife: and they twain shall be one flesh? Wherefore they are no more twain, but one flesh. What therefore God hath joined together, let not man put asunder. Matt. 19:4-6

MASTER

Neither be ye called masters: for one is your Master, Christ. Matt. 23:10

No man can serve two masters: for either he will hate the one, and love the other; or else he will hold to the one, and despise the other. Ye cannot serve God and mammon. Matt. 6:24

MATTER

He that handleth a matter wisely shall find good: and whoso trusteth in the LORD, happy is he. Prov. 16:20

But let none of you suffer as a murderer, or as a thief, or as an evildoer, or as a busybody in other men's matters. 1 Pet. 4:15

He that answereth a matter before he heareth it, it is folly and shame unto him. Prov. 18:13

MEAN

The mean man shall be brought down, and the mighty man shall be humbled, and the eyes of the lofty shall be humbled. Isa. 5:15

MEANS

Do ye suppose that the Lord will still deliver us, while we sit upon our thrones and do not make use of the means which the Lord has provided for us? Alma 60:21

MEAT

For when for the time ye ought to be teachers, ye have need that one teach you again which be the first principles of the oracles of God; and are become such as have need of milk, and not of strong meat. Heb 5:12

Now the Spirit speaketh expressly, that in the latter times some shall depart from the faith, giving heed to seducing spirits, and doctrines of devils; Speaking lies in hypocrisy; having their conscience seared with a hot iron; Forbidding to marry, and commanding to abstain from meats, which God hath created to be received with thanksgiving of them which believe and know the truth. 1 Tim. 4:1-3

MEDDLE

Fear thou the LORD and the king: and meddle not with them that are given to change: For their calamity shall rise suddenly; and who knoweth the ruin of them both? Prov. 24:21

MEDITATE

Meditate upon these things; give thyself wholly to them; that thy profiting may appear to all. 1 Tim. 4:15

I will meditate in thy precepts, and have respect unto thy ways. Ps. 119:15

This book of the law shall not depart out of thy mouth; but thou shalt meditate therein day and night, that thou mayest observe to do according to all that is written therein: for then thou shalt make thy way prosperous, and then thou shalt have good success. Josh. 1:8

His delight is in the law of the LORD; and in his law doth he mediate day and night. Ps. 1:2

MEEK, MEEKNESS

Blessed are the meek: for they shall inherit the earth. Matt. 5:5

Teach them to never be weary of good works, but to be meek and lowly in heart; for such shall find rest to their souls. Alma 37:34

Speak evil of no man, to be no brawlers, but gentle, shewing all meekness unto all men. Titus 3:2

The Spirit of the Lord GOD is upon me; because the hath anointed me to preach good tidings unto the meek. Isa. 61:1

Seek ye the LORD, all ye meek of the earth, which have wrought his judgment; seek righteousness, seek meekness: it may be ye shall be hid in the day of the LORD's anger. Zeph. 2:3

Come unto me, all ye that labour and are heavy laden, and I will give you rest. Take my yoke upon you, and learn of me; for I am meek and lowly in heart: and ye shall find rest unto your souls. Matt. 11:28-29

MEET, MEETING

Prepare to meet God. Alma 12:24

Prepare to meet thy God, O Israel. Amos 4:12

Are ye stripped of pride? I say unto you, if ye are not ye are not prepared to meet God. Alma 5:28

MELCHISEDEC

That by two immutable things, in which it was impossible for God to lie, we might have a strong consolation, who have fled for refuge to lay hold upon the hope set before us: Which hope we have as an anchor of the soul, both sure and stedfast, and which entereth into that within the veil; Whither the forerunner is for us entered, even Jesus, made an high priest for ever after the order of Melchisedec. Heb. 6:18-19

MEN

Likewise also the men, leaving the natural use of the woman, burned in their lust one toward another; men with men working that which is unseemly, and receiving in themselves that recompence of their error which was meet. Rom. 1:27

MENTION

Ye that make mention of the LORD, keep not silence, And give him no rest, till he establish, and till he make Jerusalem a praise in the earth. Isa. 62:6-7

Mention the lovingkindness of the LORD, and the praises of the LORD, according to all that the LORD, hath bestowed on us, and the great goodness toward the house of Israel, which he hath bestowed on them according to his mercies, and according to the multitude of his lovingkindness. Isa. 63:7

MERCIFUL, MERCY

Blessed are the merciful: for they shall obtain mercy. Matt. 5:7

Let them now that fear the LORD say, that his mercy endureth forever. Ps. 118:4

The LORD is good to all: and his tender mercies are over all his works. Ps. 145:9

He that covereth his sins shall not prosper: but whoso confesseth and forsaketh them shall have mercy. Prov. 28:13

Let thy mercies come also unto me, O LORD, even thy salvation, according to thy word. So shall I have wherewith to answer him that reproacheth me: for I trust in thy word. Ps. 119:41-42

Let not mercy and truth forsake thee: bind them about thy neck: write them upon the table of thine heart; So shalt thou find favour and good understanding in the sight of God and man. Prov. 3:3-4

He that followeth after righteousness and mercy, findeth life, righteousness, and honour. Prov. 21:21

The merciful man doeth good to his own soul: but he that is cruel troubleth his own flesh. Prov. 11:17

O man, what is good; and what doth the LORD require of thee, but to do justly, and to love mercy, and to walk humbly with thy God? Micah 6:8

Also unto thee, O Lord, belongeth mercy: for thou renderest to every man according to his work. Ps. 62:12

See that you are merciful unto your brethren; deal justly, judge righteously, and do good continually. Alma 41:14

The wicked borroweth, and payeth not again: but the righteous sheweth mercy, and giveth. Ps. 37:21

Be ye therefore merciful, as your Father also is merciful. Luke 6:36

I am like a green olive tree in the house of God: I trust in the mercy of God for ever and ever. Ps. 52:8

MERRY

Is any merry? Let him sing psalms. James 5:13

A merry heart doeth good a medicine: but a broken spirit drieth the bones. Prov. 17:22

MESSENGER

The priests lips should keep knowledge, and they should seek the law at his mouth: for he is the messenger of the of hosts. Mal. 2:7

They mocked the messengers of God, and despised his words, and misused his prophets, until the wrath of the arose against his people, till there was no remedy. 2 Chron. 36:16

MESSIAH

The woman saith unto him, I know that Messias cometh, which is called Christ: when he is come, he will tell us all things. John 4:25

MIGHT, MIGHTILY, MIGHTY

Our kings and our leaders were mighty men in the faith of the Lord. Jarom 1:7

Whatever thy hand findeth to do, do it with thy might; for there is no work, nor device, nor knowledge, nor wisdom, in the grave, whither thou goest. Eccl. 9:10

MILE

Whosoever shall compel thee to go a mile, go with him twain. 3 Ne. 12:41 (Matt. 5:41)

MILK

For when for the time ye ought to be teachers, ye have need that one teach you again which be the first principles of the oracles of God; and are become such as have need of milk, and not of strong meat. Heb 5:12

MIND, MINDED, MINDFUL

They received the word with all readiness of mind, and searched the scriptures daily, whether those things were so. Acts 17:11

Ye will not have a mind to injure one another, but to live peaceably, and to render to every man according to that which is his due. Mosiah 4:13

Young men likewise exhort to be sober minded. Titus 2:6

Be spiritually minded. Rom. 8:6

Be of one mind. 2 Cor. 13:11

Gird up the loins of your mind, be sober, and hope to the end for the grace that is to be brought unto you at the revelation of Jesus Christ. 1 Pet. 1:13

A double minded man is unstable in all his ways. James 1:8

He is proud, knowing nothing, but doting about questions and strifes of words, whereof cometh envy, strife, railings, evil surmisings, Perverse disputings of men of corrupt minds, and destitute of the truth, supposing that gain is godliness: from such withdraw thyself. 1 Tim. 6:4-5

They that are after the flesh do mind the things of the flesh; but they that are after the Spirit the things of the Spirit. For to be carnally minded is death; but to be spiritually minded is life and peace. Rom. 8:5-6

Be ye transformed by the renewing of your mind, that ye may prove what is that good, and acceptable, and perfect, will of God. Rom. 12:2

MINISTER, MINISTERING, MINISTRY

Even as the Son of man came not to be ministered unto, but to minister, and to give his life a ransom for many. Matt. 20:28

If thou put the brethren in remembrance of these things, thou shalt be a good minister of Jesus Christ, nourished up in the words of faith and of good doctrine, whereunto thou hast attained. 1 Tim. 4:6

Trust no one to be your teacher nor your minister, except he be a man of God, walking in his ways and keeping his commandments. Mosiah 23:14

Take heed to the ministry which thou hast received in the Lord, that thou fulfill it. Col. 4:17

Minister unto the saints. Rom. 15:25

MIRACLE, MIRACULOUS

Peter said unto him, Aeneas, Jesus Christ maketh thee whole: arise, and make thy bed. And he arose immediately. Acts 9:34

How shall we escape, if we neglect so great salvation; which at the first began to be spoken by the Lord, and was confirmed unto us by them that heard him; God also bearing them witness, both with signs and wonders, and with divers miracles, and gifts of the Holy Ghost, according to his own will? Heb. 2:3-4

[They] were beyond measure astonished, saying, He hath done all things well: he maketh both the deaf to hear, and the dumb to speak. Mark 7:37

Where be all his miracles which our fathers told us? Judg. 6:13

All the multitude kept silence, and gave audience to Barnabas and Paul, declaring what miracles and wonders God had wrought among the Gentiles by them. Acts 15:12

MISCHIEF

His mischief shall return upon his own head, and his violent dealing shall come down upon his own pate. Ps. 7:16

O full of all subtilty and all mischief, thou child of the devil, thou enemy of all righteousness, wilt thou not cease to pervert the right ways of the Lord. Acts 13:10

These six things doth the LORD hate: yea, seven are an abomination unto him: A proud look, a lying tongue, and hands that shed innocent blood, An heart that deviseth wicked imaginations, feet that be swift in running to mischief, A false witness that speaketh lies, and he that soweth discord among brethren. Prov. 6:16-19

Oppress not the widow, nor the fatherless, the stranger, nor the poor; and let none of you imagine evil against his brother in your heart Zech. 7:10

He that diligently seeketh good procureth favour: but he that seeketh mischief, it shall come unto him. Prov. 11:27

None calleth for justice, nor any pleadeth for truth: they trust in vanity, and speak lies; they conceive mischief, and bring forth iniquity. Isa. 59:4

MISSIONARY WORK

The Lord appointed other seventy also, and sent them two by two before his face into every city and place, whither he himself would come. Luke 10:1

MOCK, MOCKING, MOCERY

They mocked the messengers of God, and despised his words, and misused his prophets, until the wrath of the LORD arose against his people, till there was no remedy. 2 Chron. 36:16

They shall mock him, and shall scourge him, and shall spit upon him, and shall kill him: and the third day he shall rise again. Mark 10:34

MODEST, MODESTY

In like manner also, that women adorn themselves in modest apparel, with shamefacedness and sobriety; not with broided hair, or gold, or pearls, or costly array; but (which becometh women professing godliness) with good works. 1 Tim. 2:9-10

MONEY

Do not spend money for that which is of no worth, nor your labor for that which can not satisfy. 2 Ne. 9:51

The love of money is the root of all evil: which while some coveted after, they have erred from the faith, and pierced themselves through with many sorrows. 1 Tim. 6:9

MOSES, LAW OF MOSES

Look forward unto that life which is in Christ, and know for what end the law was given. 2 Ne. 25:27

If ye teach the law of Moses, also teach that it is a shadow of those things which are to come. Mosiah 16:14

MOTHER

Worship the Lord thy God, and honor thy father and thy mother, that thy days may be long in the land. 1 Ne. 17:55

Honour thy father and thy mother, as the LORD thy God hath commanded thee; that thy days may be prolonged, and that it may go well with thee, in the land which the LORD thy God giveth thee. Deut. 5:16

Whoso curseth his father or his mother, his lamp shall be put out in obscure darkness. Prov. 20:20

MOUNTAIN

How beautiful upon the mountains are the feet of him that bringeth good tidings, that publisheth peace; that bringeth good tidings of good, that publisheth salvation; that saith unto Zion, Thy God reigneth! Isa. 52:7

Come, and let us go up to the mountain of the LORD, and to the house of the God of Jacob; and he will teach us of his ways, and we will walk in his paths; for the law shall go forth of Zion, and the word of the LORD from Jerusalem. Micah 4:2

MOURN, MOURNING

Blessed are they that mourn; for they shall be comforted. Matt. 5:4

Proclaim the acceptable year of the Lord, and the day of vengeance of our God; to comfort all that mourn. Isa. 61:2

When the righteous are in authority, the people rejoice: but when the wicked beareth rule, the people mourn. Prov. 29:2

[Be] willing to mourn with those that mourn; yea, and comfort those that stand in need of comfort. Mosiah 18:9

MOUTH

My son, attend unto my wisdom, and bow thine ear to my understanding: That thou mayest regard discretion and thy lips may keep knowledge. Prov. 5:2

Out of the same mouth proceedeth blessing and cursing. My brethren, these things ought not so to be. James 3:10

Do not ye yet understand, that whatsoever entereth in at the mouth goeth into the belly, and is cast out into the draught? But those things which proceed out of the mouth come froth from the heart; and they defile the man. For out of the heart proceed evil thoughts, murders, adulteries, fornications, thefts, false witness, blasphemies: These are the things which defile a man: but to eat with unwashen hands defileth not a man. Matt: 17-20

Take heed to speak that which the Lord hath put in thy mouth. Num. 23:12

He spake by the mouth of his holy prophets, which have been since the world began. Luke 1:70

The mouth of them that speak lies shall be stopped. Ps. 63:11

Ye hypocrites, well did Esaias prophesy of you, saying, This people draweth nigh unto me with their mouth, and honoureth me with their lips; but their heart is far from me. Matt. 15:7-8

Be not rash with thy mouth, and let not thine heart be hasty to utter any thing before God: for God is in heaven, and thou upon earth: therefore let thy words be few. Eccl. 5:2-3

Suffer not thy mouth to cause thy flesh to sin; neither say thou before the angel, that it was an error. Eccl. 5:6

MOVE, MOVED

For the prophecy came not in old time by the will of man: but holy men of God spake as they were moved by the Holy Ghost. 2 Pet. 1:21

Cast thy burden upon the LORD, and he shall sustain thee: he shall never suffer the righteous to be moved. Ps. 55:22

MULTIPLY

Be fruitful, and multiply, and replenish the earth, and subdue it. Gen. 1:28

Be fruitful, and multiply, and replenish the earth and subdue it, and have dominion over the fish of the sea, and over the fowl of the air, and over every living thing that moveth upon the earth. Moses 2:28 (Gen. 1:28)

MULTITUDE

And above all things have fervent charity among yourselves: for charity shall cover the multitude of sins. 1 Pet 4:8

MURDER

The Lord God hath commanded that men should not murder; that they should not lie. 2 Ne. 26:32

Commit no murder whereby to shed innocent blood. D&C 132:19

MURMUR, MURMURING

I did look unto my God, and I did praise him all the day long; and I did not murmur against the Lord because of mine afflictions. 1 Ne. 18:16

Do all things without murmurings and disputings: That ye may be blameless and harmless, the sons of God, without rebuke, in the midst of a crooked and perverse nation, among whom ye shine as lights in the world. Philip. 2:14-15

The LORD heareth your murmurings which ye murmur against him: and what are we? your murmurings are not against us, but against the LORD. Ex. 16:8

MYSTERIES, MYSTERY

I have yet many things to say unto you, but ye cannot bear them now. John 16:12

Eye hath not seen, nor ear heard, neither have entered into the heart of man, the things which God hath prepared for them that love him. But God hath reveled them unto us by his Spirit; for the Spirit searcheth all things, yea, the deep things of God. 1 Cor. 2:9-10

And he said unto them, Unto you it is given to know the mystery of the kingdom of God: but unto them that are without, all these things are done in parables. Mark 4:11

Without controversy great is the mystery of godliness: God was manifest in the flesh, justified in the Spirit, seen of angels, preached unto the Gentiles, believed on in the world, received up to glory. 1 Tim. 3:16

We speak the wisdom of God in a mystery, even the hidden wisdom, which God ordained before the world unto our glory. 1 Cor. 2:7

Call unto me, and I will answer thee, and shew thee great and mighty things, which thou knowest not. Jer. 33:3

NAKED, NAKEDNESS

Is it not to deal thy bread to the hungry, and that thou bring the poor that are cast out to thy house? when thou seest the naked, that thou cover him; and that thou hide not thyself from thine own flesh? Isa. 58:7

Ye will not suffer your children that they go hungry, or naked; neither will ye suffer that they transgress the laws of God, and fight and quarrel one with another, and serve the devil, who is the master of sin, or who is the evil spirit which hath been spoken of by our fathers, he being an enemy to all righteousness. Mosiah 4:14

NAME

Learn and glorify the name of your God. 2 Ne. 6:4

Love the name of the LORD. Isa. 56:6

Thou shalt not live; for thou speakest lies in the name of the LORD. Zech. 13:3

All those who were true believers in Christ took upon them, gladly, the name of Christ. Alma 46:15

Whatsoever ye do in word or deed, do all in the name of the Lord Jesus, giving thanks to God and the Father by him. Col. 3:17

These are written, that ye might believe that Jesus is the Christ, the Son of God; and that believing ye might have life through his name. John 20:31

Be it known unto you all, and to all the people of Israel, that by the name of Jesus Christ of Nazareth, whom ye crucified, whom God raised from the dead, even by him doth this man stand here before you whole. This is the stone which was set at nought of you builders, which is become the head of the corner. Neither is there salvation in any other: for there is none other name under heaven given among men, whereby we must be saved. Acts 4:10-12

Praise ye the name of the LORD. Ps. 135:1

Solomon determined to build an house for the name of the LORD, and an house for his kingdom. 2 Chron. 2:1

Let them be confounded and troubled for ever; yea, let them be put to shame, and perish: That men may know that thou, whose name alone is JEHOVAH, art the most high over all the earth. Ps. 83:18

The place of my throne, and the place of the soles of my feet, where I will dwell in the midst of the children of Israel for ever, and my holy name, shall the house of Israel no more defile. Ezek. 43:7

Yea, in the way of thy judgments, O LORD, have we waited for thee; the desire of our soul is to thy name, and to the remembrance of thee. Isa. 26:8

A good name is rather to be chosen than great riches, and loving favour rather than silver and gold. Prov. 22:1

The name of the LORD is a strong tower: the righteous runneth into it, and is safe. Prov. 18:10

When he seeth his children, the work of mine hands, in the midst of him, they shall sanctify my name, and sanctify the Holy One of Jacob, and shall fear the God of Israel. Isa. 29:23

Thou shalt not take the name of the Lord thy God in vain. Mosiah 13:15

Walk in the name of the LORD our God for ever and ever. Micah 4:5

Thou shalt not take the name of the LORD thy God in vain; for the LORD will not hold him guiltless that taketh his name in vain. Ex. 20:7

Remember the name of the LORD our God. Ps. 20:7

NARROW

Enter ye in at the strait gate; for strait is the gate, and narrow is the way that leads to life, and few there be that find it; but wide is the gate, and broad the way which leads to death, and many there be that travel therein, until the night cometh, wherein no man can work. 3 Ne. 27:33

NATION

Let the heavens be glad, and the earth rejoice: and let men say among the nations, the LORD reigneth. 1 Chron. 16:31

And before him shall be gathered all nations: and he shall separate them one from another, as a shepherd divideth his sheep from the goats. Matt. 25:32

Open ye the gates, that the righteous nation which keepeth the truth may enter in. Isa. 26:2

NATURAL

Likewise also the men, leaving the natural use of the woman, burned in their lust one toward another; men with men working that which is unseemly, and receiving in themselves that recompence of their error which was meet. Rom. 1:27

NATURAL MAN

The natural man receiveth not the things of the Spirit of God: for they are foolishness unto him: neither can he know them, because they are spiritually discerned. 1 Cor. 2:14

NECK

He, that being often reproved hardeneth his neck, shall suddenly be destroyed, and that without remedy. Prov. 29:1

They dealt proudly, and hearkened not unto thy commandments, but sinned against thy judgments, (which if a man do, he shall live in them;) and withdrew the shoulder, and hardened their neck Neh. 9:29

NEED, NEEDFUL, NEEDY

When ye pray, use not vain repetitions, as the heathen, for they think that they shall be heard for their much speaking. Be not ye therefore like unto them, for your Father knoweth what things ye have need of before ye ask him. 3 Ne. 13:7-8

For the poor shall never cease out of the land: therefore I command thee, saying, thou shalt open thine hand wide unto thy brother, to thy poor, and to thy needy, in the land. Deut. 15:11

NEGLECT, NEGLIGENT

Neglect not the gift that is in thee. 1 Tim. 4:14

Be not now negligent: for the LORD hath chosen you to stand before him, to serve him, and that ye should minister unto him. 2 Chron. 29:11

NEIGHBOR

Thou shalt not bear false witness against thy neighbour. Ex. 20:16

Thou shalt not avenge, nor bear any grudge against the children of thy people, but thou shalt love thy neighbour as thyself: I the LORD. Lev. 19:18

I would that ye should remember, that whosoever among you borroweth of his neighbor should return the thing that he borroweth, according as he doth agree, or else thou shalt commit sin, and perhaps thou shalt cause thy neighbor to commit sin also. Mosiah 4:28

Withdraw thy foot from thy neighbour's house; lest he be weary of thee, and so hate thee. Prov. 25:17

NEW COVENANT, EVERLASTING COVENANT

Moreover I will make a covenant of peace with them; it shall be an everlasting covenant with them: and I will place them, and multiply them, and will set my sanctuary in the midst of them for evermore. Ezek. 37:26

Behold, the days come, saith the LORD, that I will make a new covenant with the house of Israel, and with the house of Judah. Jer. 31:31

NIGHT

I must work the works of him that sent me, while it is day: the night cometh, when no man can work. John. 9:4

NOTHING, NOTHINGNESS

For with God nothing shall be impossible. Luke 1:37

I am the vine, yea are the branches: He that abideth in me, and I in him, the same bringeth forth much fruit: for without me ye can do nothing. John 15:5

If ye have faith as a grain of mustard seed, ye shall say unto this mountain, Remove hence to yonder place; and it shall remove; and nothing shall be impossible unto you. Matt. 17:20

NOURISH, NOURISHMENT

If thou put the brethren in remembrance of these things, thou shalt be a good minister of Jesus Christ, nourished up in the words of faith and of good doctrine, whereunto thou hast attained. 1 Tim. 4:6

NURTURE

Ye fathers, provoke not your children to wrath: but bring them up in the nurture and admonition of the Lord. Eph. 6:4

OATH

Let none of you imagine evil in your hearts against his neighbour; and love no false oath: for all these are things that I hate, saith the LORD. Zech. 8:17

Swear not, neither by heaven, neither by the earth, neither by any other oath: but let your yea be yea; and your nay, nay; lest ye fall into condemnation. James 5:12

OBEDIENCE, OBEDIENT, OBEY

We believe in being subject to kings, presidents, rulers, and magistrates, in obeying, honoring, and sustaining the law. A of F-12

Put them in mind to be subject to principalities and powers, to obey magistrates, to be ready to every good work. Titus 3:1

He was obedient unto the word of the Lord. 1 Ne. 2:3

Obey, I beseech thee, the voice of the LORD, which I speak unto thee: so it shall be well unto thee, and thy soul shall live. Jer. 38:20

Children, obey your parents in all things: for this is well pleasing unto the Lord. Col. 3:20

Unto them that are contentious, and do not obey the truth, but obey unrighteousness, indignation and wrath. Rom. 2:8

If ye be willing and obedient, ye shall eat the good of the land: But if ye refuse and rebel, ye shall be devoured with the sword. Isa. 1:19-20

Who is among you that feareth the LORD, that obeyeth the voice of his servant, that walketh in darkness, and hath no light? let him trust in the name of the LORD, and stay upon his God. Isa. 50:10

Teach the young women to be sober, to love their husbands, to love their children, To be discreet, chaste, keepers at home, good, obedient to their own husbands, that the word of God be not blasphemed. Titus 2:4-5

Obey my voice indeed, and keep my covenant. Ex. 19:5

Obey my voice, and I will be your God, and ye shall be my people: and walk ye in all the ways that I have commanded you, that it may be well unto you. Jer. 7:23

Be obedient in all things. 2 Cor. 2:9

Beware, lest there shall arise contentions among you, and ye list to obey the evil spirit. Mosiah 2:32

Be obedient unto the end of your lives. Mosiah 5:8

Testify that a man must be obedient to the commandments of God. 1 Ne. 22:30

Servants, be obedient to them that are your masters according to the flesh, with fear and trembling, in singleness of your heart, as unto Christ. Eph. 6:5

Take heed unto thyself, and unto the doctrine; continue in them: for in doing this thou shalt both save thyself, and them that hear thee. 1 Tim. 4:16

Though we walk in the flesh, we do not war after the flesh: Casting down imaginations, and every high thing that exalteth itself against the knowledge of God, and bringing into captivity every thought to the obedience of Christ. 2 Cor. 10:3,5

Remember to keep and do these sayings, walking in obedience to the commandments. D&C 89:18

OBSERVE, OBSERVATION

Only be thou strong and very courageous, that thou mayest observe to do according to all the law. Josh. 1:7

OBSTINATE

Thou art obstinate, and thy neck is an iron sinew, and thy brow brass. Isa. 48:4

OFFEND, OFFENDER, OFFENSE

Whosoever shall be ashamed of me and of my words, of him shall the Son of man be ashamed, when he shall come in his own glory, and in his Father's, and of the holy angels. Luke 9:26

Approve things that are excellent; that ye may be sincere and without offense till the day of Christ. Philip. 1:10

I exercise myself, to have always a conscience void of offense toward God, and toward men. Acts 24:16

A brother offended is harder to be won than a strong city: and their contentions are like the bars of a castle. Prov. 18:19

Wherefore if thy hand or thy foot offend thee, cut them off, and cast them from thee: it is better for thee to enter into life halt or maimed, rather than having two hands or two feet to be cast into everlasting fire. Matt. 18:8

The terrible one is brought to nought, and the scorner is consummed, and all that watch for iniquity are cut off: That make a man an offender for a word, and lay a snare for him that reproveth in the gate, and turn aside the just thing for a thing of nought. Isa. 29:20-21

If thy hand offend thee, cut it off: it is better for thee to enter into life maimed, than having two hands to go into hell, into the fire that never shall be quenched. Mark 9:43

Give none offense, neither to the Jews, nor to the Gentiles, nor to the church of God. 1 Cor. 10:32

If thy brother or sister offend thee, thou shalt take him or her between him or her and thee alone; and if he or she confess thou shalt be reconciled. D&C 42:88

Blessed is he, whosoever shall not be offended in me. Matt. 11:6

If any man offend not in word, the same is a perfect man, and able also to bridle the whole body. James 3:2-8

OFFER, OFFERING

Ye also, as lively stones, are built up a spiritual house, an holy priesthood, to offer up spiritual sacrifices, acceptable to God by Jesus Christ. 1 Pet. 2:5

Ye should come unto Christ, who is the Holy One of Israel, and partake of his salvation, and the power of his redemption. Yea, come unto him, and offer your whole souls as an offering unto him and continue in fasting and praying, and endure to the end. Omni 1:26

If thou bring thy gift to the altar, and there rememberest that thy brother hath ought against thee; Leave there thy gift before the altar, and go thy way; first be reconciled to thy brother, and then come and offer thy gift. Matt. 5:23-24

Offer sacrifices of righteousness. Deut. 33:19

Bring an offering in a clean vessel into the house of the LORD. Isa. 66:20

Offer unto the Lord an offering in righteousness. 3 Ne. 24:3

Give unto the LORD the glory due unto his name: bring an offering, and come before him: worship the LORD in the beauty of holiness. 1 Chron. 16:29

OIL

Is any sick among you? let him call for the elders of the church; and let them pray over him, anointing him with oil in the name of the Lord: And the prayer of faith shall save the sick, and the Lord shall raise him up; and if he have committed sins, they shall be forgiven him. James 5:14-15

OMEGA

I am Alpha and Omega, the beginning and the ending, saith the Lord, which is, and which was, and which is to come, the Almighty. Rev. 1:8

ONE

Let your conversation be as it becometh the gospel of Christ: that whether I come and see you, or else be absent, I may hear of your affairs, that ye stand fast in one spirit, with one mind striving together for the faith of the gospel. Philip. 1:27

Consider it in thine heart, that the LORD he is God in heaven above, and upon the earth beneath: there is none else. Deut. 4:39

Be men, and be determined in one mind and in one heart, united in all things. 2 Ne. 1:21

There is neither Jew nor Greek, there is neither bond nor free, there is neither male nor female: for ye are all one in Christ Jesus. Gal. 3:28

I will give them one heart, and I will put a new spirit within you; and I will take the stony heart out of their flesh, and will give them an heart of flesh: That they may walk in my statutes, and keep mine ordinances, and do them: and they shall be my people, and I will be their God. Ezek. 11:19-20

The Lord called his people ZION, because they were of one heart and one mind, and dwelt in righteousness; and there was no poor among them. Moses 7:18

Be likeminded one toward another according to Christ Jesus: That ye may with one mind and one mouth glorify God, even the Father of our Lord Jesus Christ. Rom. 15:5-6

Who is this King of glory? The LORD of hosts, he is the King of glory. Ps. 24:8

Be of one mind. 2 Cor. 13:11

Let every man deal honestly, and be alike among this people, and receive alike, that ye may be one, even as I have commanded you. D&C 51:9

They all cried with one voice, saying: Yea, we believe all the words which thou hast spoken unto us; and also, we know of their surety and truth, because of the Spirit of the Lord Omnipotent, which has wrought a mighty change in us or in our hearts, that we have no more disposition to do evil, but to do good continually. Mosiah 5:2

OPEN, OPENED

They said one to another, Did not our heart burn within us, while he talked with us by the way, and while he opened to us the scriptures? Luke 24:32

Whoso knocketh, to him will he open; and the wise, and the learned, and they that are rich, who are puffed up because of their learning, and their wisdom, and their riches - yea, they are they whom he despiseth; and save they shall cast these things away, and consider themselves fools before God, and come down in the depths of humility, he will not open unto them. 2 Ne. 9:42

Behold, I stand at the door, and knock: if any man hear my voice, and open the door, I will come in to him, and will sup with him, and he with me. Rev. 3:20

OPENLY

When thou doest alms let not thy left hand know what thy right hand doeth; That thine alms may be in secret; and thy Father who seeth in secret, himself shall reward thee openly. 3 Ne. 13:3-4

OPERATION

They regard not the work of the Lord, neither consider the operation of his hands. 2 Ne. 15:12

Because they regard not the works of the LORD, nor the operation of his hands, he shall destroy them, and not build them up. Ps. 28:5

OPINION

We believe that religion is instituted of God; and that men are amenable to him, and to him only, for the exercise of it, unless their religious opinions prompt them to infringe upon the rights and liberties of others; but we do not believe that human law has a right to interfere in prescribing rules of worship to bind the consciences of men, nor dictate forms for public or private devotion; that the civil magistrate should restrain crime, but never control conscience; should punish guilt, but never suppress the freedom of the soul. D&C 134:4

Elijah came unto all the people, and said, How long halt ye between two opinions? if the LORD be God, follow him: but if Baal, then follow him. And the people answered him not a word. 1 Kgs. 18:21

We believe that rulers, states, and governments have a right, and are bound to enact laws for the protection of all citizens in the free exercise of their religious belief; but we do not believe that they have a right in justice to deprive citizens of this privilege, or proscribe them in their opinions, so long as a regard and reverence are shown to the laws and such religious opinions do not justify sedition nor conspiracy. D&C 134:7

OPPOSE, OPPOSITE, OPPOSITION

For it must needs be, that there is an opposition in all things. If not so, my first-born in the wilderness, righteousness could not be brought to pass, neither wickedness, neither holiness nor misery, neither good nor bad. 2 Ne. 2:11

OPPRESS, OPPRESSED, OPPRESSION

Because ye despise this word, and trust in oppression or perverseness, and stay thereon: Therefore this iniquity shall be to you as a breach ready to fall, swelling out in a high wall, whose breaking cometh suddenly at an instant. Isa. 30:12-13

Oppress not the widow, nor the fatherless, the stranger, nor the poor; and let none of you imagine evil against his brother in your heart. Zech. 7:10

Trust not in oppression, and become not vain in robbery: if riches increase, set not your heart upon them. Ps. 62:10

As for our iniquities, we know them: in transgressing and lying against the LORD, and departing away from our God, speaking oppression and revolt, conceiving and uttering from the heart words of falsehood. Isa. 59:12-13

He that walketh righteously, and speaketh uprightly; he that despiseth the gain of oppressions, that shaketh his hands from holding of bribes, that stoppeth his ears from hearing of blood, and shutteth his eyes from seeing evil; He shall dwell on high: his defence shall be the munitions of rocks: bread shall be given him; his waters shall be sure. Isa. 33:15-16

He that oppresseth the poor to increase his riches, and he that giveth to the rich, shall surely come to want. Prov. 22:16

Ye shall not therefore oppress one another; but thou shalt fear thy God: for I am the LORD your God. Lev. 25:17

ORDAIN

Whoso forbiddeth to marry is not ordained of God, for marriage is ordained of God unto man. D&C 49:15 (1 Tim. 4:3)

ORDER

Set in order thy houses; keep slothfulness and uncleanness far from you. D&C 90:18

Let all things be done decently and in order. 1 Cor. 14:40

None shall be exempted from the justice and the laws of God, that all things may be done in order and in solemnity before him, according to truth and righteousness. D&C 107:84

God is not the author of confusion, but of peace, as in all churches of the saints. 1 Cor. 14:33

If a man know not how to rule his own house, how shall he take care of the church of God? 1 Tim. 3:4-5

Set in order the things that are wanting, and ordain elders in every city, as I had appointed thee. Titus 1:5

ORDINANCE

Walk in all the ordinances of the Lord. D&C 136:4

The earth also is defiled under the inhabitants thereof; because they have transgressed the laws, changed the ordinance, broken the everlasting covenant. Isa. 24:5

They seek me daily, and delight to know my ways, as a nation that did righteousness, and forsook not the ordinance of their God: they ask of me the ordinances of justice; they take delight in approaching to God. Isa. 58:2

Submit yourselves to every ordinance of man for the Lord's sake: whether it be to the king, as supreme. 1 Pet. 2:13

ORGANIZE, ORGANIZATION

Organize yourselves; prepare every needful thing; and establish a house, even a house of prayer, a house of fasting, a house of faith, a house of learning, a house of glory, a house of order, a house of God; That your incomings may be in the name of the Lord; that your outgoings may be in the name of the Lord; that all your salutations may be in the name of the Lord, with uplifted hands unto the Most High. D&C 88:119-120

ORPHAN

We are orphans and fatherless, our mothers are as widows. Lam. 5:3

OUTCAST

Hide the outcasts; bewray not him that wandereth. Isa. 16:3-5

OVERCAME, OVERCOME

Be not overcome of evil, but overcome evil with good. Rom. 12:21

If after they have escaped the pollutions of the world through the knowledge of the Lord and Savior Jesus Christ, they are again entangled therein, and overcome, the latter end is worse with them than the beginning. For it had been better for them not to have known the way of righteousness, than, after they have known it, to turn from the holy commandment delivered unto them. But it is happened unto them according to the true proverb, The dog is turned to his own vomit again; and the sow that was washed to her wallowing in the mire. 2 Pet. 2:20-22

He that overcometh shall inherit all things; and I will be his God, and he shall be my son. But the fearful, and unbelieving, and the abominable, and murderers, and whore-mongers, and sorcerers, and idolaters, and all liars, shall have their part in the lake which burneth with fire and brimstone: which is the second death. Rev. 21:7

OVERTAKE, OVERTAKEN

Again I say, hearken unto my voice, lest death shall overtake you; in an hour when ye think not the summer shall be past, and the harvest ended, and your souls not saved. D&C 45:2

OWE

Owe no man any thing, but to love one another: for he that loveth another hath fulfilled the law. Rom. 13:8

OWN

Let no man seek his own, but every man another's wealth. 1 Cor. 10:24

Charity suffereth long, and is kind, and envieth not, and is not puffed up, seeketh not her own, is not easily provoked, thinketh no evil, and rejoiceth not in iniquity but rejoiceth in the truth, beareth all things, believeth all things, hopeth all things, endureth all things. Moro. 7:45 (1 Cor. 13:4-7)

PARABLE

And he said unto them, Unto you it is given to know the mystery of the kingdom of God: but unto them that are without, all these things are done in parables. Mark 4:11

PARDON

Let the wicked forsake his way, and the unrighteous man his thoughts: and let him return unto the LORD, and he will have mercy upon him; and to our God, for he will abundantly pardon. Isa. 55:7

PART

If any man shall take away from the words of the book of this prophecy, God shall take away his part out of the book of life, and out of the holy city, and from the things which are written in this book Rev. 22:19

PARTAKE

Ye should come unto Christ, who is the Holy One of Israel, and partake of his salvation, and the power of his redemption. Yea, come unto him, and offer your whole souls as an offering unto him and continue in fasting and praying, and endure to the end. Omni 1:26

PARTIAL, PARTIALITY

I charge thee before God, and the Lord Jesus Christ, and the elect angels, that thou observe these things without preferring one before another, doing nothing by partiality. 1 Tim. 5:21

PASSION

See that ye bridle all your passions, that ye may be filled with love. Alma 38:12

PATH

Walk in the paths of righteousness. 1 Ne. 16:5

Come ye, and let us go to the mountain of the LORD to the house of the God of Jacob; and he will teach us of his ways and we will walk in his paths: for out of Zion shall go forth the law, and the word of the LORD from Jerusalem. Isa. 2:3

Enter not into the paths of the wicked, and go not in the way of evil men. Avoid it, pass not by it, turn from it, and pass away. Prov. 4:14-15

Come unto the Lord, the Holy One. Remember that his paths are righteous. 2 Ne. 9:41

PATIENCE, PATIENT, PATIENTLY

Be patient therefore, brethren, unto the coming of the Lord. James 5:7

Have patience, and bear with those afflictions, with a firm hope that ye shall one day rest from all your afflictions. Alma 34:41

If men will smite you, or your families, once, and ye bear it patiently and revile not against them, neither seek revenge, ye shall be rewarded. D&C 98:23

I would exhort you to have patience, and that ye bear with all manner of afflictions; that ye do not revile against those who do cast you out because of your exceeding poverty, lest ye become sinners like unto them. Alma 34:40

Be patient in afflictions. D&C 31:9

Submit cheerfully and with patience to all the will of the Lord. Mosiah 24:15

Many are the afflictions of the righteous: but the LORD delivereth him out of them all Ps. 34:19

Warn them that are unruly, comfort the feebleminded, support the weak, be patient toward all men. 1 Thes. 5:14

He that is slow to wrath is of great understanding: but he that is hasty of spirit exalteth folly. Prov. 14:29

Better is the end of a thing than the beginning thereof: and the patient in spirit is better than the proud in spirit. Eccl. 7:8

Seeing we also are compassed about with so great a cloud of witnesses, let us lay aside every weight, and the sin which doth so easily beset us, and let us run with patience the race that is set before us. Heb. 12:1

Be patient; be sober; be temperate; have patience, faith, hope and charity. D&C 6:19

PATTERN

In all things shewing thyself a pattern of good works: in doctrine shewing uncorrupt-ness, gravity, sincerity, Sound speech, that cannot be condemned; that he that is of the contrary part may be ashamed, having no evil thing to say of you. Titus 2:7-8

PAID, PAY, PAYMENT

When thou vowest a vow unto God, defer not to pay it; for he hath no pleasure in fools: pay that which thou hast vowed. Eccl. 5:4

When thou shalt vow a vow unto the LORD thy God, thou shalt not slack to pay it: for the LORD thy God will surely require it of thee; and it would be sin in thee. Deut. 23:21

PEACE, PEACABLE

God is not the author of confusion, but of peace, as in all churches of the saints. 1 Cor. 14:33

Blessed are the peacemakers: for they shall be called the children of God. Matt. 5:9

Ye will not have a mind to injure one another, but to live peaceably, and to render to every man according to that which is his due. Mosiah 4:13

Let him eschew evil, and do good; let him seek peace, and ensue it. 1 Pet. 3:11

Whoso shall publish peace, yea, tidings of great joy, how beautiful upon the mountains shall they be. 1 Ne. 13:37

For he that will love life, and see good days, let him refrain his tongue from evil, and his lips that they speak no guile: Let him eschew evil, and do good; let him seek peace, and ensue it. 1 Pet. 3:10-11

We believe that no government can exist in peace, except such laws are framed and held inviolate as will secure to each individual the free exercise of conscience, the right and control of property, and the protection of life. D&C 134:2

For unto us a child is born, unto us a son is given; and the government shall be upon his shoulder; and his name shall be called, Wonderful, Counselor, The Mighty God, The Everlasting Father, The Prince of Peace. 2 Ne. 19:6 (Isa. 9:6)

There is no peace, saith my God, to the wicked. Isa. 57:21

Lift up an ensign of peace, and make a proclamation of peace unto the ends of the earth; And make proposals for peace unto those who have smitten you, according to the voice of the Spirit which is in you, and all things shall work together for your good. D&C 105:39

Let the peace of God rule in your hearts, to the which also ye are called in one body; and be ye thankful. Col. 3:15

If it be possible, as much as lieth in you, live peaceably with all men. Rom. 12:18

Pray for the peace of Jerusalem: they shall prosper that love thee. Ps. 122:6

Peace be within thy walls, and prosperity within thy palaces. For my bretheren and companions' sakes, I will now say, Peace be within thee. Ps. 122:7-8

How beautiful upon the mountains are the feet of him that bringeth good tidings, that publisheth peace; that bringeth good tidings of good, that publisheth salvation; that saith unto Zion, Thy God reigneth! Isa. 52:7

Hold thy peace at the presence of the LORD God: for the day of the LORD is at hand: for the LORD hath prepared a sacrifice, he hath bid his guests. Zeph. 1:7

Love the truth and peace. Zech. 8:19

The law of truth was in his mouth, and iniquity was not found in his lips: he walked with me in peace and equity, and did turn many away from iniquity. Mal. 2:6

Flee also youthful lusts: but follow righteousness, faith, charity, peace, with them that call on the Lord out of a pure heart. 2 Tim. 2:22

Seek peace, and pursue it. Ps. 34:14

A man of understanding holdeth his peace. Prov. 11:12

Lead a quiet and peaceable life in all godliness and honesty. 1 Tim. 2:2

Follow peace with all men, and holiness, without which no man shall see the Lord. Heb. 12:14

Let the peace of God rule in your hearts. Col. 3:15
Follow after the things which make for peace, and things wherewith one may edify another. Rom. 14:19

PEARL

Give not that which is holy unto the dogs, neither cast ye your pearls before swine, lest they trample them under their feet, and turn again and rend you. Matt. 7:6

PEOPLE

Now it is not common that the voice of the people desireth anything contrary to that which is right; but it is common for the lesser part of the people to desire that which is not right; therefore this shall ye observe and make it your law - to do business by the voice of the people. Mosiah 29:26

PERIL, PERILOUS

This know also, that in the last days perilous times shall come. 2 Tim. 3:1

PERFECT, PERFECTION, PERFECTLY

The eyes of the LORD run to and fro throughout the whole earth, to shew himself strong in the behalf of them whose heart is perfect toward him. 2 Chron. 16:9

I will walk within my house with a perfect heart. Ps. 101:2

All scripture is given by inspiration of God, and is profitable for doctrine, for reproof, for correction, for instruction in righteousness: That the man of God may be perfect, throughly furnished unto all good works. 2 Tim. 3:16-17

And he gave some, apostles; and some, prophets; and some, evangelists; and some, pastors and teachers; For the perfecting of the saints, for the work of the ministry, for the edifying of the body of Christ: Till we all come in the unity of the faith, and of the knowledge of the Son of God, unto a perfect man, unto the measure of the stature of the fulness of Christ. Eph. 4:11-13

If thou wilt be perfect, go and sell that thou hast, and give to the poor, and thou shalt have treasure in heaven: and come and follow me. Matt. 19:21-22

Above all things, put on charity, which is the bond of perfectness. Col. 3:14

Above all things, clothe yourselves with the bond of charity, as with a mantle, which is the bond of perfectness and peace. D&C 88:125

If any man offend not in word, the same is a perfect man, and able also to bridle the whole body. James 3:2-8

Be ye therefore perfect, even as your Father in heaven is perfect. Matt. 5:48 (3 Ne. 12:48)

Know thou the God of thy father, and serve him with a perfect heart and with a willing mind: for the LORD searcheth all hearts, and understandeth all the imaginations of the thoughts. 1 Chron. 28:9

I am the Almighty God; walk before me, and be thou perfect. Gen. 17:1

PERFORM, PERFORMANCE

I have inclined mine heart to perform thy statutes always, even unto the end. Ps. 119:112

PERISH

Where there is no vision, the people perish: but he that keepeth the law, happy is he. Prov. 29:18

PERSECUTE, PERSECUTION

Blessed are they which are persecuted for righteousness' sake: for theirs is the kingdom of heaven. Matt. 5:10

Blessed are ye, when men shall revile you, and persecute you, and shall say all manner of evil against you falsely, for my sake. Rejoice, and be exceeding glad: for great is your reward in heaven: for so persecuted they the prophets which were before you. Matt 5:11-12

Wo unto the rich, who are rich as to the things of the world. For because they are rich they despise the poor, and they persecute the meek, and their hearts are upon their treasures; wherefore, their treasure is their god. And behold, their treasure shall perish with them also. 2 Ne. 9:30

I gave my back to the smiters and my cheeks to them that plucked off the hair: I hid not my face from shame and spitting. For the Lord GOD will help me; therefore shall I not be confounded. Isa. 50:6-7

Some were lifted up in pride, and others were exceedingly humble; some did return railing for railing, while others would receive railing and persecution and all manner of afflictions, and would not turn and revile again, but were humble and penitent before God. 3 Ne. 6:13

They mocked the messengers of God, and despised his words, and misused his prophets, until the wrath of the LORD arose against his people, till there was no remedy. 2 Chron. 36:16

There should be no persecutions among them, that there should be an equality among all men. Mosiah 27:3

If any man will sue thee at the law and take away thy coat, let him have thy cloak also. 3 Ne. 12:40

Behold, it is written, an eye for an eye, and a tooth for a tooth; But I say unto you, that ye shall not resist evil, but whosoever shall smite thee on thy right cheek, turn to him the other also. 3 Ne. 12:38-39 (Matt. 5:39)

Woe be unto the pastors that destroy and scatter the sheep of my pasture! saith the LORD. Jer. 23:1

Yea, will ye persist in supposing that ye are better one than another; yea, will ye persist in the persecution of your brethren? Alma 5:54

They bore with patience the persecution which was heaped upon them. Alma 1:25

Love your enemies, bless them that curse you, do good to them that hate you, and pray for them which despitefully use you, and persecute you. Matt. 5:44

Be sober, be vigilant; because your adversary the devil, as a roaring lion, walketh about, seeking whom he may devour; Whom resist stedfast in the faith, knowing that the same afflictions are accomplished in your brethren that are in the world. But the God of all grace, who hath called us unto his eternal glory by Christ Jesus, after that ye have suffered a while, make you perfect, stablish, strengthen, settle you. 1 Pet. 5:8-10

Therefore also said the wisdom of God, I will send them prophets and apostles, and some of them they shall slay and persecute: That the blood of all the prophets, which was shed from the foundation of the world, may be required of this generation. Luke 11:49-50

PERSUADE

He hath commanded his people that they should persuade all men to repentance. 2 Ne. 26:27

Persuadeth men to do good. Ether 4:11

Perhaps I might persuade them that they would remember the Lord their Redeemer. 1 Ne. 19:18

Do I now persuade men, or God? or do I seek to please men? for if I yet pleased men, I should not be the servant of Christ. Gal. 1:10

Wherefore, we would to God that we could persuade all men not to rebel against God, to provoke him to anger, but that all men would believe in Christ, and view his death, and suffer his cross and bear the shame of the world. Jacob 1:8

Yield to the persuasions of men no more. D&C 5:21

After this manner of language did I persuade my brethren, that they might be faithful in keeping the commandments of God. 1 Ne. 3:21

He reasoned in the synagogue every sabbath, and persuaded the Jews and the Greeks. Acts 18:4

The fulness of mine intent is that I may persuade men to come unto the God of Abraham, and the God of Isaac, and the God of Jacob, and be saved. 1 Ne. 6:4

Persuade all ye ends of the earth to repent and prepare to stand before the judgment-seat of Christ. Morm. 3:22

PERVERSE

Put away from thee a froward mouth, and perverse lips put far from thee. Prov. 4:24

Because ye despise this word, and trust in oppression or perverseness, and stay thereon: Therefore this iniquity shall be to you as a breach ready to fall, swelling out in a high wall, whose breaking cometh suddenly at an instant. Isa. 30:12-13

A wholesome tongue is a tree of life: but perverseness therein is a breach in the spirit. Prov. 15:4

PERVERT

The burden of the LORD shall ye mention no more: for every man's word shall be his burden; for ye have perverted the words of the living God. Jer. 23:36

Thou hast trusted in thy wickedness: thou hast said, None seeth me. Thy wisdom and thy knowledge, it hath perverted thee; and thou hast said in thine heart, I am, and none else beside me. Isa. 47:10

O full of all subtilty and all mischief, thou child of the devil, thou enemy of all righteousness, wilt thou not cease to pervert the right ways of the Lord. Acts 13:10

PITIFUL, PITY

To him that is afflicted, pity should be shewed from his friend. Job 6:14

PLACE

Awake my soul! No longer droop in sin. Rejoice, O my heart, and give place no more for the enemy of my soul. 2 Ne. 4:28

Contend no more against the Holy Ghost, but that ye receive it, and take upon you the name of Christ; that ye humble yourselves even to the dust, and worship God, in whatsoever place ye may be in, in spirit and in truth; and that ye live in thanksgiving daily, for the many mercies and blessings which he doth bestow upon you. Alma 34:38

PLAGUE

I saw another sign in heaven, great and marvellous, seven angels having the seven last plagues; for in them is filled up the wrath of God. Rev. 15:1

PLAIN, PLAINLY, PLAINNESS

Speaketh harshly against sin, according to the plainness of the truth. 2 Ne. 33:5

I must tell you the truth according to the plainness of the word of God. Jacob 2:11

For my soul delighteth in plainness; for after this manner doth the Lord God work among the children of men. For the Lord God giveth light unto the understanding; for he speaketh unto men according to their language, unto their understanding. 2 Ne. 31:3

These things have I spoken unto you in proverbs: but the time cometh, when I shall no more speak unto you in proverbs, but I shall shew you plainly of the Father. John 16:25

PLEAD

Learn to do well; seek judgment, relieve the oppressed, judge the fatherless, plead for the widow. Isa. 1:17

PLEASANT, PLEASE, PLEASURE

He that loveth pleasure shall be a poor man: he that loveth wine and oil shall not be rich. Prov. 21:17

Hear now this, thou that art given to pleasures, that dwellest carelessly, that sayest in thine heart, I am, and none else beside me. Isa. 47:8

But without faith it is impossible to please him: for he that cometh to God must believe that he is, and that he is a rewarder of them that diligently seek him. Heb. 11:6

God shall send them strong delusion, that they should believe a lie: That they all might be damned who believed not the truth, but had pleasure in unrighteousness. 2 Thes. 2:11-12

Yea, all things which come of the earth, in the season thereof, are made for the benefit and the use of man, both to please the eye and to gladden the heart. D&C 59:18

Do I now persuade men, or God? or do I seek to please men? for if I yet pleased men, I should not be the servant of Christ. Gal. 1:10

PLEDGE

Keep all your pledges one with another; and covet not that which is thy brother's. D&C 136:20

When thou dost lend thy brother any thing, thou shalt not go into his house to fetch his pledge. Deut. 24:10

PLUNDER

Preach against all lyings, and deceivings, and envyings, and strife, and malice and revilings, and stealing, robbing, plundering, murdering, committing adultery, and all manner of lasciviousness, crying that these things ought not so to be. Alma 16:18

POLLUTE, POLLUTION

The children of Judah have done evil in my sight, saith the LORD: they have set their abominations in the house which is called by my name, to pollute it. Jer. 7:30

PONDER

Meditate upon these things; give thyself wholly to them; that thy profiting may appear to all. 1 Tim. 4:15

Mary kept all these things, and pondered them in her heart. Luke 2:19

I suppose that ye ponder somewhat in your hearts concerning that which ye should do after ye have entered in by the way. 2 Ne. 32:1

POOR

Blessed are the poor in spirit: for theirs is the kingdom of heaven. Matt 5:3

Wo unto the rich, who are rich as to the things of the world. For because they are rich they despise the poor, and they persecute the meek, and their hearts are upon their treasures; wherefore, their treasure is their god. And behold, their treasure shall perish with them also. 2 Ne. 9:30

Succor those that stand in need of your succor; ye will administer of your substance unto him that standeth in need; and ye will not suffer that the beggar putteth up his petition to you in vain, and turn him out to perish. Mosiah 4:16

If there be among you a poor man of one of thy brethren within any of thy gates in thy land which the LORD thy God giveth thee, thou shalt not harden thine heart, nor shut thine hand from thy poor brother. Deut. 15:7

I would exhort you to have patience, and that ye bear with all manner of afflictions; that ye do not revile against those who do cast you out because of your exceeding poverty, lest ye become sinners like unto them. Alma 34:40

Wo unto him that shall say at that day, to get gain, that there can be no miracle wrought by Jesus Christ. 3 Ne. 29:7

We then that are strong ought to bear the infirmities of the weak, and not to please ourselves. Rom. 15:1

The righteous considereth the cause of the poor: but the wicked regardeth not to know it. Prov. 29:7

Ye must visit the poor and the needy and administer to their relief, that they may be kept until all things may be done according to my law which ye have received. D&C 44:6

He that oppresseth the poor to increase his riches, and he that giveth to the rich, shall surely come to want. Prov. 22:16

Rob not the poor, because he is poor. Prov. 22:22

For the poor shall never cease out of the land: therefore I command thee, saying, thou shalt open thine hand wide unto thy brother, to thy poor, and to thy needy, in the land. Deut. 15:11

POPULAR

Those who are built up to to become popular in the eyes of the world [are] they who need fear, and tremble, and quake. 1 Ne. 22:23

POSSIBLE

The things which are impossible with men are possible with God. Luke 18:27

If it be possible, as much as lieth in you, live peaceably with all men. Rom. 12:18

Trust in him at all times; ye people, pour out your heart before him: God is a refuge for us. Ps. 62:8

POWER, POWEFUL

Can ye dispute the power of God? Mosiah 27:15

It is mockery before God, denying the mercies of Christ, and the power of his Holy Spirit, and putting trust in dead works. Moro. 8:23

Yea, wo be unto him that hearkeneth unto the precepts of men, and denieth the power of God, and the gift of the Holy Ghost! 2 Ne. 28:26

Believest thou in the power of Christ unto salvation? Alma 15:6

Deny not the power of God; for he worketh by power, according to the faith of the children of men Moro. 10:7

PRAISE

How can ye believe, which receive honour one of another, and seek not the honour that cometh from God only? John 5:44

Praise the LORD, call upon his name, declare his doings among the people, make mention that his name is exalted. Isa. 12:4

Sing praise to the name of the LORD most high. Ps. 7:17

In God we boast all the day long, and praise thy name for ever. Ps. 44:8

Blessed be the name of our God; let us sing to his praise, yea, let us give thanks to his holy name, for he doth work righteousness forever. Alma 26:8

Render all the thanks and praise which your whole soul has power to possess, to that God who has created you, and has kept and preserved you, and has caused that ye should rejoice, and has granted that ye should live in peace one with another. Mosiah 2:20

Let another man praise thee, and not thine own mouth; a stranger, and not thine own lips. Prov. 27:2

We will glory in the Lord; yea, we will rejoice, for our joy is full; yea, we will praise our God forever. Alma 26:16

Praise ye the name of the LORD. Ps. 135:1

If thou art merry, praise the Lord with singing, with music, with dancing, and with a prayer of praise and thanksgiving. If thou art sorrowful, call on the Lord thy God with supplication, that your souls may be joyful. D&C 136:28-29

Thank and praise the LORD God of Israel. 1 Chron. 16:4

PRAY, PRAYER

Nevertheless, the children of God were commanded that they should gather themselves together oft, and join in fasting and mighty prayer in behalf of the welfare of the souls of those who knew not God. Alma 6:6

[She] served God with fasting and prayers night and day. Luke 2:37

What I say unto one I say unto all; pray always lest that wicked one have power in you, and remove you out of your place. D&C 93:49

Humble yourselves before the Lord, and call on his holy name, and watch and pray continually, that ye may not be tempted above that which ye can bear, and thus be led by the Holy Spirit, becoming humble, meek, submissive, patient full of love and all long suffering; Having faith on the Lord; having a hope that ye shall receive eternal life; having the love of God always in your heats, that ye may be lifted up at the last day and enter into his rest. Alma 13:28-29

We did pour out our souls in prayer to God, that he would strengthen us and deliver us out of the hands of our enemies, yea, and also give us strength that we might retain our cities, and our lands, and our possessions, for the support of our people. Alma 58:10

I have fasted and prayed many days that I might know these things of myself. Alma 5:46

Visit the house of each member, and exhort them to pray vocally and in secret and attend to all family duties. D&C 20:47

Ye should come unto Christ, who is the Holy One of Israel, and partake of his salvation, and the power of his redemption. Yea, come unto him, and offer your whole souls as an offering unto him and continue in fasting and praying, and endure to the end. Omni 1:26

The Son of God shall come in his glory; and his glory shall be the glory of the Only Begotten of the Father, full of grace, equity, and truth, full of patience, mercy, and long-suffering, quick to hear the cries of his people and to answer their prayers. Alma 9:26

Search diligently, pray always, and be believing, and all things shall work together for your good. D&C 90:24

They shall also teach their children to pray, and to walk uprightly before the Lord. D&C 68:28

When ye fast, be not, as the hypocrites, of a sad countenance: for they disfigure their faces, that they may appear unto men to fast. Verily I say unto you, They have their reward. Matt. 6:16

Therefore, strengthen your brethren in all your conversation, in all your prayers, in all your exhortations, and in all your doings. D&C 108:7

I command thee that thou shalt pray vocally as well as in thy heart; yea, before the world as well as in secret, in public as well as in private. D&C 19:28

Confess your faults one to another, and ray one for another, that ye may be healed. The effectual fervent prayer of a righteous man availeth much. James 5:16

O LORD, attend unto my cry, give ear unto my prayer, that goeth not out of feigned lips. Ps. 17:1

He that turneth away his ear from hearing the law, even his prayer shall be abomination. Prov. 28:9

In trouble have they visited thee, they poured out a prayer when thy chastening was upon them. Isa. 26:16

All this evil is come upon us: yet made we not our prayer before the LORD our God, that we might turn from our iniquities and understand thy truth. Dan. 9:13

The LORD turned the captivity of Job, when he prayed for his friends. Job 42:10

Be watchful unto prayer continually. Alma 34:39

Be merciful unto me, O Lord: for I cry unto thee daily. Rejoice the soul of thy servant: for unto thee, O Lord, do I lift up my soul. Ps. 86:3-5

Men ought always to pray, and not to faint. Luke 18:1

When thou prayest thou shalt not do as the hypocrites, for they love to pray, standing in the synagogues and in the corners of the streets, that they may be seen of men. Verily I say unto you, they have their reward. But thou, when thou prayest, enter into thy closet, and when thou hast shut thy door, pray to thy Father who is in secret; and thy Father, who seeth in secret, shall reward thee openly. 3 Ne. 13:5-6

When ye pray, use not vain repetitions, as the heathen, for they think that they shall be heard for their much speaking. Be not ye therefore like unto them, for your Father knoweth what things ye have need of before ye ask him. 3 Ne. 13:7-8

Ye are commanded in all things to ask of God, who giveth liberally; and that which the Spirit testifies unto you even so I would that ye should do in all holiness of heart, walking uprightly before me, considering the end of your salvation, doing all things with prayer and thanksgiving. D&C 46:7

After this manner therefore pray ye: Our Father who art in heaven, hallowed be thy name. Thy will be done on earth as it is in heaven. And forgive us our debts, as we forgive our debtors. And lead us not into temptation, but deliver us from evil. For thine is the kingdom, and the power, and the glory, forever. Amen. 3 Ne. 13:9-13 (Matt. 6:9-13)

Ye must always pray unto the Father in my name, that your wives and children may be blessed. 3 Ne. 18:19-21

He commanded them that they should not cease to pray in their hearts. 3 Ne. 20:1

Remember the words of your God; pray unto him continually by day, and give thanks unto his holy name by night. 2 Ne. 9:52

If ye would hearken unto the Spirit which teacheth a man to pray, ye would know that ye must pray; for the evil spirit teacheth not a man to pray, but teacheth him that he must not pray. 2 Ne. 32:8

When you do not cry unto the Lord, let your hearts be full, drawn out in prayer unto him continually for your welfare, and also for the welfare of those who are around you. Alma 34:27

Ye must pray always, and not faint; that ye must not perform anything unto the Lord save in the first place ye shall pray unto the Father in the name of Christ, that he will consecrate thy performance unto thee, that thy performance may be for the welfare of thy soul. 2 Ne. 32:9

PREACH

Preach against all lyings, and deceivings, and envyings, and strifes, and malice, and revilings, and stealing, robbing, plundering, murdering, committing adultery, and all manner of lasciviousness, crying that these things ought not so to be. Alma 16:18

I have preached righteousness in the great congregation: lo, I have not refrained my lips, O LORD, thou knowest. Ps. 40:9

Preach the word of God unto them, to stir them up in remembrance of their duty. Alma 4:19

The Spirit of the Lord is upon me, because he hath anointed me to preach the gospel to the poor; he hath sent me to heal the brokenhearted, to preach deliverance to the captives, and recovering of sight to the blind, to set at liberty them that are bruised, To preach the acceptable year of the Lord. Luke 4:18-19

THE Spirit of the Lord GOD is upon me; because the hath anointed me to preach good tidings unto the meek. Isa. 61:1

Go ye into all the world, and preach the gospel to every creature. Mark 16:15

He called his twelve disciples together, and gave them power and authority over all devils, and to cure diseases. And he sent them to preach the kingdom of God, and to heal the sick. Luke 9:1-2

Let your preaching be the warning voice, every man to his neighbor, in mildness and in meekness. D&C 38:41

Preach nothing save it were repentance and faith on the Lord, who had redeemed his people. Mosiah 18:20

PRECEPT

For precept must be upon precept, precept upon precept; line upon line, line upon line; here a little, and there a little: For with stammering lips and another tongue will he speak to this people. Isa. 28:10

I will meditate in thy precepts, and have respect unto thy ways. Ps. 119:15

I esteem all thy precepts concerning all things to be right; and I hate every false way. Ps. 119:128

Thou hast commanded us to keep thy precepts diligently. Ps. 119:4

Yea, wo be unto him that hearkeneth unto the precepts of men, and denieth the power of God, and the gift of the Holy Ghost! 2 Ne. 28:26

PREPARE, PREPARED, PREPARATION

If a man therefore purge himself from these, he shall be a vessel unto honour, sanctified, and meet for the master's use, and prepared unto every good work. 2 Tim. 2:21

Persuade all ye ends of the earth to repent and prepare to stand before the judgment-seat of Christ. Morm. 3:22

Be thou prepared, and prepare for thyself, thou, and all thy company that are assembled unto thee, and be thou a guard unto them. Ezek. 38:7

Prepare to meet thy God, O Israel. Amos 4:12

When he prepared the heavens, I was there. Prov. 8:27

The horse is prepared against the day of battle; but safety is of the LORD. Prov. 21:31

Prepare ye the way of the Lord, make straight in the desert a highway for our God. Isa. 40:3

Prepare ye the way of the Lord, make his paths straight. Luke 3:4

Prepare to meet God. Alma 12:24

Prepare ye the way of the Lord, and make his paths straight. 1 Ne. 10:8

PRESENCE

Hold thy peace at the presence of the LORD God: for the day of the LORD is at hand: for the LORD hath prepared a sacrifice, he hath bid his guests. Zeph. 1:7

PRESS

Ye must press forward with a steadfastness in Christ having a perfect brightness of hope, and a love of God and of all men. 2 Ne. 31:20

PRICE

Impart the word of God, one with another, without money and without price. Alma 1:20

Ye that is called in the Lord, being a servant is the Lord's freeman: likewise also he that is called, being free, is Christ's servant. Ye are bought with a price; be not ye the servants of men. 1 Cor 7:22-23

PRIDE, PROUD

O that ye would listen to the word of his commands, and let not this pride of your hearts destroy your souls! Jacob 2:16

Beware of pride. D&C 23:1

These six things doth the LORD hate: yea, seven are an abomination unto him: A proud look, a lying tongue, and hands that shed innocent blood, An heart that deviseth wicked imaginations, feet that be swift in running to mischief, A false witness that speaketh lies, and he that soweth discord among brethren. Prov. 6:16-19

They dealt proudly, and hearkened not unto thy commandments, but sinned against thy judgments, (which if a man do, he shall live in them;) and withdrew the shoulder, and hardened their neck Neh. 9:29

Better is the end of a thing than the beginning thereof: and the patient in spirit is better than the proud in spirit. Eccl. 7:8

The wicked, through the pride of his countenance, will not seek after God: God is not in all his thoughts. Ps. 10:4

He is proud, knowing nothing, but doting about questions and strifes of words, whereof cometh envy, strife, railings, evil surmisings, Perverse disputings of men of corrupt minds, and destitute of the truth, supposing that gain is godliness: from such withdraw thyself. 1 Tim. 6:4-5

Be not ashamed, neither confounded; but be admonished in all your high-mindedness and pride, for it bringeth a snare upon your souls. D&C 90:17

Thou shouldest not have looked on the day of thy brother in the day that he became a stranger; neither shouldest thou have rejoiced over the children of Judah in the day of their destruction; neither shouldest thou have spoken proudly in the day of distress. Obad. 1:12

God resisteth the proud, but giveth grace unto the humble. James 4:6
Cease from all your light speeches, from all laughter, from all your lustful desires, from all your pride and light-mindedness, and from all your wicked doings D&C 88:121

See that ye are not lifted up unto pride. Alma 38:11

I trust that ye are not lifted up in the pride of your hearts; yea, I trust that ye have not set your hearts upon riches and the vain things of the world. Alma 7:6

Are ye stripped of pride? I say unto you, if ye are not ye are not prepared to meet God. Alma 5:28

Pride goeth before destruction, and an haughty spirit before a fall. Prov. 16:18

Hear ye, and give ear; be not proud: for the LORD hath spoken. Jer. 13:15

PRIEST

Let thy priests be clothed with righteousness. Ps. 132:9

The priests lips should keep knowledge, and they should seek the law at his mouth: for he is the messenger of the LORD of hosts. Mal. 2:7

PRIESTCRAFT

Not every one that saith unto me, Lord, Lord, shall enter into the kingdom of heaven; but he that doeth the will of my Father who is in heaven. Many will say to me in that day: Lord, Lord, have we not prophesied in thy name, and in thy name have cast out devils, and in thy name done many wonderful works? And then will I profess unto them: I never knew you; depart from me, ye that work iniquity. Matt. 7:21-23

PRIESTHOOD

Seek ye the priesthood also. Num. 16:10
Ye also, as lively stones, are built up a spiritual house, an holy priesthood, to offer up spiritual sacrifices, acceptable to God by Jesus Christ. 1 Pet. 2:

PRINCIPLE

May those principles, which were so honorably and nobly defended, namely, the Constitution of our land, by our fathers, be established forever. D&C 109:54

Therefore leaving the principles of the doctrine of Christ, let us go on unto perfection; not laying again the foundation of repentance from dead works, and of faith toward God, Of the doctrine of baptisms, and of laying on of hands, and of resurrection of the dead, and of eternal judgment. Heb. 6:1-2

PRISON, PRISONER

Proclaim liberty to the captives, and the opening of the prison to them that are bound. Isa. 61:1

PRIVILEGE

We claim the privilege of worshiping Almighty God according to the dictates of our own conscience, and allow all men the same privilege, let them worship how, where, or what they may. A of F-11

PRIZE

This one thing I do, forgetting those things which are behind, and reaching forth unto those things which are before, I press toward the mark for the prize of the high calling of God in Christ Jesus. Philip 3:13-14

PROCEED

He humbled thee, and suffered thee to hunger, and fed thee with manna, which thou knewest not, neither did thy fathers know; that he might make thee know that man doth not live by bread only, but by every word that proceedeth out of the mouth of the LORD doth man live. Deut. 8:3

Man shall not live by bread alone, but by every word that proceedeth out of the mouth of God. Matt. 4:4

You shall live by every word that proceedeth forth from the mouth of God. D&C 84:44

Do not ye yet understand, that whatsoever entereth in at the mouth goeth into the belly, and is cast out into the draught? But those things which proceed out of the mouth come froth from the heart; and they defile the man. For out of the heart proceed evil thoughts, murders, adulteries, forn-ications, thefts, false witness, blas-phemies: These are the things which defile a man: but to eat with unwashen hands defileth not a man. Matt: 17-20

Out of the same mouth proceedeth blessing and cursing. My brethren, these things ought not so to be. James 3:10

PROCLAIM

Proclaim the everlasting gospel, by the Spirit of the living God, from people to people, and from land to land, in the congregations of the wicked, in their synagogues, reasoning with and expounding all scriptures unto them. D&C 68:1

Most men will proclaim every one his own goodness: but a faithful man who can find? Prov. 20:6

Ye have not hearkened unto me, in proclaiming liberty, every one to his brother, and every man to his neighbour: behold, I proclaim a liberty for you, saith the LORD. Jer. 34:15-17

Ye have not hearkened unto me, in proclaiming liberty, every one to his brother, and every man to his neighbour: behold, I proclaim a liberty for you, saith the LORD, to the sword, to the pestilence, and to the famine; and I will make you to be removed into all the kingdoms of the earth. Jer. 34:17

Proclaim liberty to the captives, and the opening of the prison to them that are bound. Isa. 61:1

Proclaim the acceptable year of the Lord, and the day of vengeance of our God, to comfort all that mourn. Isa. 61:2

Stand in the gate of the LORD's house, and proclaim there this word, and say, Hear the word of the LORD. Jer. 7:2

PROCRASTINATE, PROCRASTINATION

Do not procrastinate the day of your repentance until the end. Alma 34:33

PROFANE, PROFANITY

An abomination is committed in Israel and in Jerusalem; for Judah hath profaned the holiness of the LORD which he loved, and hath married the daughter of a strange god. Mal. 2:11

Neither shalt thou profane the name of God; I am Lev. 18:21

PROFESS, PROFESSION

Let us hold fast the profession of our faith without wavering; (for he is faithful that promised). Heb. 10:23

PROFIT

My people have changed their glory for that which doth not profit. Jer. 2:8

Treasures of wickedness profit nothing; but righteousness delivereth from death. Prov. 10:2

What doth it profit, my brethren, though a man say he hath faith, and have not works? can faith save him? James. 2:14

For unto us was the gospel preached, as well as unto them: but the word preached did not profit them, not being mixed with faith in them that heard it. Heb. 4:2

Of these things put them in remembrance, charging them before the Lord that they strive not about words to no profit, but to the subverting of the hearers. 2 Tim. 2:14

For what is a man profited, if he shall gain the whole world, and lose his own soul? or what shall a man give in exchange for his soul? Matt.16:26

PROLONG

Ye shall walk in all the ways which the LORD your God hath commanded you, that ye may live, and that ye may prolong your days in the land which ye shall posses. Deut. 5:33

PROMISE

The eternal purposes of the Lord shall roll on, until all his promises shall be fulfilled. Morm. 8:22

I, the Lord, am bound when ye do what I say; but when ye do not what I say, ye have no promise. D&C 82:10

Be not slothful, but followers of them who through faith and patience inherit the promises. Heb. 6:12

According as his divine power hath given unto us all things that pertain unto life and godliness, through the knowledge of him that hath called us to glory and virtue: Whereby we are given unto us exceeding great and precious promises: that by these ye might be partakers of the divine nature, having escaped the corruption that is in the world through lust. 2 Pet. 1:3-4

He staggered not at the promise of God through unbelief; but was strong in faith, giving glory to God; And being fully persuaded that, what he had promised, he was able also to perform. And therefore it was imputed to him for righteousness. Rom. 4:20-22

That which is gone out of thy lips thou shalt keep and perform; even a freewill offering, according as thou has vowed unto the LORD thy God, which thou hast promised with thy mouth. Deut. 23:23

PROPERTY

Thou shalt not covet thine own property, but impart it freely. D&C 19:26

We believe that men should appeal to the civil law for redress of all wrongs and grievances, where personal abuse is inflicted or the right of property or character infringed, where such laws exist as will protect the same; but we believe that all men are justified in defending themselves, their friends, and property, and the government, from the unlawful assaults and encroachments of all persons in times of exigency, where immediate appeal cannot be made to the laws, and relief afforded. D&C 134:11

PROPHECY, PROPHESY

Deny not the spirit of revelation, nor the spirit of prophesy. D&C 11:25

For the prophecy came not in old time by the will of man: but holy men of God spake as they were moved by the Holy Ghost. 2 Pet. 1:21

I am thy fellowservant, and of thy brethren that have the testimony of Jesus: worship God: for the testimony of Jesus is the spirit of prophecy. Rev. 19:10

I would that ye all spake with tongues, but rather that ye prophesied: for greater is he that prophesieth than he that speaketh with tongues, except he interpret, that the church may receive edifying. 1 Cor. 14:5

We believe in the gift of tongues, prophecy, revelation, visions, healing, interpretation of tongues, and so forth. A of F-7

Having then gifts differing according to the grace that is given to us, whether prophecy, let us prophesy according to the proportion of faith. Rom. 12:6

The Spirit of God came upon him, and he prophecied among them. 1 Sam. 10:10

PROPHET

Believest thou the prophets? Acts 26:27

Blessed are ye, when men shall revile you, and persecute you, and shall say all manner of evil against you falsely, for my sake. Rejoice, and be exceeding glad: for great is your reward in heaven: for so persecuted they the prophets which were before you. Matt 5:11-12

Therefore also said the wisdom of God, I will send them prophets and apostles, and some of them they shall slay and persecute: That the blood of all the prophets, which was shed from the foundation of the world, may be required of this generation. Luke 11:49-50

God hath set some in the church, first apostles, secondarily prophets, thirdly teachers, after that miracles, then gifts of healings, helps, governments, diversities of tongues. Are all apostles? are all prophets? are all teachers? are all workers of miracles? Have all the gifts of healing? do all speak with tongues? do all interpret? But covet earnestly the best gifts: and yet shew I unto you a more excellent way. 1 Cor. 12:28-31

He spake by the mouth of his holy prophets, which have been since the world began. Luke 1:70

Who is among you that feareth the LORD, that obeyeth the voice of his servant, that walketh in darkness, and hath no light? let him trust in the name of the LORD, and stay upon his God. Isa. 50:10

He that receiveth you receiveth me, and he that receiveth me receiveth him that sent me. He that receiveth a prophet in the name of a prophet shall receive a prophet's reward; and he that receiveth a righteous man in the name of a righteous man shall receive a righteous man's reward. Matt. 10:40-41

Ye are no more strangers and foreigners, but fellowcitizens with the saints, and of the household of God; And are built upon the foundation of the apostles and prophets, Jesus Christ himself being the chief corner stone. Eph. 2:19-20

The prophet that hath a dream, let him tell a dream. Jer. 23:28

They mocked the messengers of God, and despised his words, and misused his prophets, until the wrath of the LORD arose against his people, till there was no remedy. 2 Chron. 36:16

[Obey] the voice of the Lord our God, to walk in his laws, which he set before us by his servants the prophets. Dan. 9:10

Is there not here a prophet of the LORD, that we may inquire of the LORD by him? 2 Kgs. 3:11

Should ye not hear the words which the LORD hath cried by the former prophets, when Jerusalem was inhabited and in prosperity, and the cities thereof round about her, when men inhabited the south and the plain? Zech. 7:7

Hearken to the words of my servants the prophets, whom I sent unto you, both rising up early, and sending them, but ye have not hearkened. Jer. 26:5

And he gave some, apostles; and some, prophets; and some, evangelists; and some, pastors and teachers; For the perfecting of the saints, for the work of the ministry, for the edifying of the body of Christ: Till we all come in the unity of the faith, and of the knowledge of the Son of God, unto a perfect man, unto the measure of the stature of the fulness of Christ. Eph. 4:11-13

Believe in the LORD your God, so shall ye be established; believe his prophets, so shall ye prosper. 2 Chron. 20:20

Touch not mine anointed, and do my prophets no harm. 1 Chron. 16:22

Hearken not unto the words of [false] prophets that prophecy unto you; they make you vain; they speak a vision of their own heart and not out of the mouth of the LORD. Jer. 23:16

PROSPER, PROSPERITY, PROSPEROUS

Fight ye not against the Lord God of your fathers; for ye shall not prosper. 2 Chron. 13:12

In the day of prosperity be joyful. Eccl. 7:14

This book of the law shall not depart out of thy mouth; but thou shalt meditate therein day and night, that thou mayest observe to do according to all that is written therein: for then thou shalt make thy way prosperous, and then thou shalt have good success. Josh. 1:8

Believe in the Lord your God, so shall ye be established; believe his prophets, so shall ye prosper. 2 Chron. 20:20

PROSTITUTE

Do not prostitute thy daughters, to cause her to be a whore; lest the land fall into whoredom, and the land become full of wickedness. Lev. 19:29

PROVE

My soul delighteth in proving unto my people the truth of the coming of Christ. 2 Ne. 11:4

Prove all things; hold fast that which is good. 1 Thes. 5:21

Bring ye all the tithes into the storehouse, that there may be meat in mine house, and prove me now herewith, saith the LORD of hosts, if I will not open you the windows of heaven, and pour you out a blessing. Mal. 3:8-12

Be ye transformed by the renewing of your mind, that ye may prove what is that good, and acceptable, and perfect, will of God. Rom. 12:2

Harden not your heart, as in the provocation, and as in the day of temptation in the wilderness:When your fathers tempted me, proved me, and saw my work. Ps. 95:9

Examine me, O LORD, and prove me; try my reins and my heart. Ps. 26:2

PROVOKE

They made Israel to sin, in provoking the LORD God of Israel to anger with their vanities. 1 Kgs. 16:13

PRUDENT

The simple believeth every word: but the prudent man looketh well to his going. Prov. 14:15

Woe unto them that are wise in their own eyes, and prudent in their own sight! Isa. 5:21

The wisdom of the prudent is to understand his way: but the folly of fools is deceit. Prov. 14:8

PSALMS

Let us come before his presence with thanksgiving and take a joyful noise unto him with psalms. Ps. 95:2

Let the word of Christ dwell in you richly in all wisdom; teaching and admonishing one another in psalms and hymns and spiritual songs, singing with grace in your hearts to the Lord. Col. 3:16

PUBLIC

Thou shalt pray vocally as well as in thy heart; yea, before the world as well as in secret, in public as well as in private. D&C 19:28

PUBLISH

The word of the Lord was published throughout all the region. Acts 13:49

I will publish the name of the LORD: ascribe ye greatness unto our God. Deut. 32:3

Whoso shall publish peace, yea, tidings of great joy, how beautiful upon the mountains shall they be. 1 Ne. 13:37

PUNISH, PUNISHMENT

Bring the wicked to justice according to their crime. Alma 50:39

We believe that the commission of crime should be punished according to the nature of the offense; that murder; treason, robbery, theft, and the breach of the general peace, in all respects, should be punished according to their criminality and their tendency to evil among men, by the laws of that government in which the offense is committed; and for the public peace and tranquility all men should step forward and use their ability in bringing offenders against good laws to punishment. D&C 134:8

We believe that religion is instituted of God; and that men are amenable to him, and to him only, for the exercise of it, unless their religious opinions prompt them to infringe upon the rights and liberties of others; but we do not believe that human law has a right to interfere in prescribing rules of worship to bind the consciences of men, nor dictate forms for public or private devotion; that the civil magistrate should restrain crime, but never control conscience; should punish guilt, but never suppress the freedom of the soul. D&C 134:4

[Let not] the guilty and the wicked go unpunished because of their money. Hel. 7:5

PURE, PURIFIED, PURIFY

All ye that are pure in heart, lift up your heads and receive the pleasing word of God, and feast upon his love. Jacob 3:1

Love pureness of heart. Prov. 22:11

Flee also youthful lusts: but follow righteous-ness, faith, charity, peace, with them that call on the Lord out of a pure heart. 2 Tim. 2:22

Be purified and cleansed from all sin. D&C 50:28

Blessed are the pure in heart: for they shall see God. Matt. 5:8

Let no man despise thy youth; but be thou an example of the believers, in word, in conversation, in charity, in spirit, in faith, in purity. 1 Tim. 4:12

There is a generation that are pure in their own eyes, an yet is not washed from their filthiness. Prov. 30:12

Who can say, I have made my heart clean, I am pure from my sin? Prov. 20:9

Keep thyself pure. 1 Tim. 5:22

PURPOSE

The eternal purposes of the Lord shall roll on, until all his promises shall be fulfilled. Morm. 8:22

To every thing there is a season, and a time to every purpose under heaven; A time to be born, and a time to die; a time to plant, and a time to pluck up that which is planted; A time to kill, and a time to heal; a time to break down, and a time to build up; A time to weep, and a time to laugh; a time to mourn, and a time to dance; A time to cast away stones, and a time to father stones together; a time to embrace, and a time to refrain from embracing; A time to get, and a time to lose; a time to keep, and a time to cast away; A time to rend, and a time to sew; a time to keep silence, and a time to speak; A time to love, and a time to hate; a time of war, and a time of peace. Eccl. 3:1-8

QUARREL

Ye will not suffer your children that they go hungry, or naked; neither will ye suffer that they transgress the laws of God, and fight and quarrel one with another, and serve the devil, who is the master of sin, or who is the evil spirit which hath been spoken of by our fathers, he being an enemy to all righteousness. Mosiah 4:14

QUENCH

Quench not the Spirit. 1 Thes. 5:19

QUESTION

He is proud, knowing nothing, but doting about questions and strifes of words, whereof cometh envy, strife, railings, evil surmisings, Perverse disputings of men of corrupt minds, and destitute of the truth, supposing that gain is godliness: from such withdraw thyself. 1 Tim. 6:4-5

QUICK, QUICKLY

Thus we see how quick the children of men do forget the Lord their God, yea, how quick to do iniquity, and to be led away by the evil one. Alma 46:8

How quick to be lifted up in pride; yea, how quick to boast, and do all manner of that which is iniquity; and how slow are they to remember the Lord their God, and to give ear unto his counsels, yea, how slow to walk in wisdoms paths. Hel. 12:5

QUIET

Study to be quiet, and to do your own business, and to work with your own hands, as we commanded you; 1 Thes 4:11

Let it be the hidden man of the heart, in that which is not corruptible, even the ornament of a meek and quiet spirit, which is in the sight of God of great price. 1 Pet. 3:4

RABBI

Be not ye called Rabbi: for one is your Master, Christ; and all ye are brethren. Matt. 23:8

RACE

Seeing we also are compassed about with so great a cloud of witnesses, let us lay aside every weight, and the sin which doth so easily beset us, and let us run with patience the race that is set before us. Heb. 12:1

RAINBOW

And God said, This is the token of the covenant which I make between me and you and every living creature that is with you, for perpetual generations: I do set my bow in the cloud, and it shall be for a token of a covenant between me and the earth. And it shall come to pass, when I bring a cloud over the earth, that the bow shall be seen in the cloud: And I will remember my covenant, which is between me and you and every living creature of all flesh; and the waters shall no more become a flood to destroy all flesh. Gen. 9:13

RANSOM

Even as the Son of man came not to be ministered unto, but to minister, and to give his life a ransom for many. Matt. 20:28

REACH

This one thing I do, forgetting those things which are behind, and reaching forth unto those things which are before, I press toward the mark for the prize of the high calling of God in Christ Jesus. Philip 3:13-14

READINESS, READY

Sanctify the Lord God in your heats; and be ready always to give an answer to every man that asketh you a reason of the hope that is in you with meekness and fear: Having a good conscience; that, whereas they speak evil of you, as of evildoers, they may be ashamed that falsely accuse your good conversation in Christ. 1 Pet. 3:15-16

They received the word with all readiness of mind, and searched the scriptures daily, whether those things were so. Acts 17:11

REAP

Be not deceived; God is not mocked: for whatsoever a man soweth, that shall he also reap. Galtians 6:7

He which soweth sparingly shall reap also sparingly; and he which soweth bountifully shall reap also bountifully. 2 Cor. 9:6

Sow to yourselves in righteousness, reap in mercy; break up your fallow ground: for it is time to seek the LORD, till he come and rain righteousness upon you. Hosea 10:12

He that soweth to his flesh shall of the flesh reap corruption; but he that soweth to the Spirit shall of the Spirit reap life everlasting. Gal. 6:8

REASON

Paul, as his manner was, went in unto them, and three sabbath days reasoned with them out of the scriptures. Acts 17:2

Sanctify the Lord God in your heats; and be ready always to give an answer to every man that asketh you a reason of the hope that is in you with meekness and fear: Having a good conscience; that, whereas they speak evil of you, as of evildoers, they may be ashamed that falsely accuse your good conversation in Christ. 1 Pet. 3:15-16

I applied mine heart to know, and to search, and to seek out wisdom, and the reason of things, and to know the wickedness of folly, even of foolishness and madness. Eccl. 7:25

REBEL, REBELLION, REBELLIOUS

Let not the rebellious exalt themselves. Ps. 66:7

For rebellion is as the sin of witchcraft, and stubbornness is as iniquity and idolatry. Because thou hast rejected the word of the LORD, he hath also rejected thee from being king. 1 Sam 15:23

The house of Israel rebelled against me in the wilderness: they walked not in my statutes, and they despised my judgments, which if a man do, he shall even live in them; and my sabbaths they greatly polluted. Ezek. 20:13

If ye be willing and obedient, ye shall eat the good of the land: But if ye refuse and rebel, ye shall be devoured with the sword. Isa. 1:19-20

An evil man seeketh only rebellion: therefore a cruel messenger shall be sent against him. Prov. 17:11

I will cast thee from off the face of the earth: this year thou shalt die, because thou hast taught rebellion against the LORD. Jer. 28:16

God forbid that we should rebel against the LORD, and turn this day from following the LORD. Josh 22:29

Rebel not ye against the LORD. Num. 14:9

Wherefore, we would to God that we could persuade all men not to rebel against God, to provoke him to anger, but that all men would believe in Christ, and view his death, and suffer his cross and bear the shame of the world. Jacob 1:8

REBUKE

Rebuke not an elder, but intreat him as a father; and the younger men as brethren; The elder women as mothers; the younger as sisters, with all purity. 1 Tim. 5 1-2

When Jesus saw that the people came running together, he rebuked the foul spirit, saying unto him, Thou dumb and deaf spirit, I charge thee, come out of him, and enter no more into him. Mark 9:25

This witness is true. Wherefore rebuke them sharply, that they may be sound in the faith. Titus 1:13

It is better to hear the rebuke of the wise, than for a man to hear the song of fools. Eccl. 7:5

Them that sin rebuke before all, that others also may fear. 1 Tim. 5:20

LORD, thou knowest: remember me, and visit me, and revenge me of my persecutors; take me not away in thy longsuffering: know that for thy sake I have suffered rebuke. Jer. 15:15

RECEIVE

Have ye received his image in your countenances? Alma 5:14

Receive the word with joy. Alma 16:17

They received the word with all readiness of mind, and searched the scriptures daily, whether those things were so. Acts 17:11 That which is of God is light; and he that receiveth light, and continueth in God, receiveth more light; and that light groweth brighter and brighter until the perfect day. D&C 50:24

He that receiveth you receiveth me, and he that receiveth me receiveth him that sent me. He that receiveth a prophet in the name of a prophet shall receive a prophet's reward; and he that receiveth a righteous man in the name of a righteous man shall receive a righteous man's reward. Matt. 10:40-41

All ye that are pure in heart, lift up your heads and receive the pleasing word of God, and feast upon his love. Jacob 3:2

Receive all things with thankfulness. D&C 78:19

RECKON

My God put into mine heart to gather together the nobles, and the rulers, and the people, that they might be reckoned by genealogy. Neh. 7:5

Knowing that Christ being raised from the dead dieth no more; death hath no more dominion over him. For in that he died, he died unto sin once: but in that he liveth, he liveth unto God. Likewise reckon ye also yourselves to be dead indeed unto sin, but alive unto God through Jesus Christ our Lord. Rom. 6:9-11

RECOMPENSE

Say not thou, I will recompense evil; but wait on the LORD, and he shall save thee. Prov. 20:22

Flee out of the midst of Babylon, and deliver every man his soul; be not cut off in her iniquity; for this is the time of the LORD's vengeance; he will render unto her a recompense. Jer. 51:6

Thou hast not remembered the days of thy youth, but hast fretted me in all these things; behold, therefore I also will recompense thy way upon thine head, saith the Lord GOD. Ezek. 16:43

RECONCILE, RECONCILED, RECONCILIATION

Be ye reconciled to God. 2 Cor. 5:20

If thou bring thy gift to the altar, and there rememberest that thy brother hath ought against thee; Leave there thy gift before the altar, and go thy way; first be reconciled to thy brother, and then come and offer thy gift. Matt. 5:23-24　(3Ne. 12:23-24)

Unto the married I command, yet not I, but the Lord, Let not the wife depart from her husband: But and if she depart, let her remain unmarried, or be reconciled to her husband: and let not the husband put away his wife. 1 Cor. 7:10-11

If thy brother or sister offend thee, thou shalt take him or her between him or her and thee alone; and if he or she confess thou shalt be reconciled. D&C 42:88

Reconcile yourselves unto the will of God, and not to the will of the devil and the flesh; and remember, after ye are reconciled unto God, that it is only in and through the grace of God that ye are saved. 2 Ne. 10:24

RECORD, RECORDED

Many other signs truly did Jesus in the presence of his disciples, which are not written in this book: But these are written, that ye might believe that Jesus is the Christ, the Son of God; and that believing ye might have life through his name. John 20:30-31

Now go, write it before them in a table, and note it in a book, that it may be before the time to come for ever and ever. Isa. 30:8

REDEEM, REDEEMER, REDEMPTION

Ye should come unto Christ, who is the Holy One of Israel, and partake of his salvation, and the power of his redemp-tion. Yea, come unto him, and offer your whole souls as an offering unto him and continue in fasting and praying, and endure to the end. Omni 1:26

Have ye walked, keeping yourselves blameless before God? Could ye say, if ye were called to die at this time, within yourselves, that ye have been sufficiently humble? That your garments have been cleansed and made white through the blood of

They that trust in their wealth, and boast themselves in the multitude of their riches; None of them can by any means redeem his brother. Ps. 49:6-7

Ye know that ye were not redeemed with corruptible things, as silver and gold, from your vain conversation received by tradition from your fathers. 1 Pet. 1:18

Christ, who will come to redeem his people from their sins? Behold, are ye stripped of pride? I say unto you, if ye are not ye are not prepared to meet God. Alma 5:27-31

Marvel not that all mankind, yea, men and women, all nations, kindreds, tongues and people, must be born again. Mosiah 27:25

Preach nothing save it were repentance and faith on the Lord, who had redeemed his people. Mosiah 18:20

If ye have experienced a change of heart, and if ye have felt to sing the song of redeeming love, I would ask, can ye feel so now? Alma 5:26

He offereth himself a sacrifice for sin, to answer the ends of the law, unto all those who have a broken heart and a contrite spirit. 2 Ne. 2:6-7

REDRESS

We believe that men should appeal to the civil law for redress of all wrongs and grievances, where personal abuse is inflicted or the right of property or character infringed, where such laws exist as will protect the same; but we believe that all men are justified in defending themselves, their friends, and property, and the government, from the unlawful assaults and encroachments of all persons in times of exigency, where immediate appeal cannot be made to the laws, and relief afforded. D&C 134:11

REFINE, REFINER

Behold, I have refined thee, but not with silver; I have chosen thee in the furnace of affliction. Isa. 48:10

REFRAIN

I have preached righteousness in the great congregation: lo, I have not refrained my lips, O LORD, thou knowest. Ps. 40:9

REFUSE

Poverty and shame shall be to him that refuseth instruction: but he that regardeth reproof shall be honoured. Prov. 13:18

REGARD

How much less to him that accepteth not the persons of princes, nor regard the rich more than the poor? for they all are the work of his hands. Job 34:19

Because they regard not the works of the LORD, nor the operation of his hands, he shall destroy them, and not build them up. Ps. 28:5

REJECT

Full well ye reject the commandment of God, that ye may keep your own traditions. Mark 7:9

The wise men are ashamed, they are dismayed and taken: lo, they have rejected the word of the LORD; and what wisdom is in them? Jer. 8:9

REJOICE

Rejoice in goodness. 2 Chron. 6:41

We will glory in the Lord; yea, we will rejoice, for our joy is full; yea, we will praise our God forever. Alma 26:16

My joy is more full because of the success of my brethren. Alma 29:14

Let Israel rejoice in him that made him: let the children of Zion be joyful in their King. Let them praise his name in the dance: let them sing praises unto him with the timbrel and harp. Ps. 149:2-3

Lift up your heads, and rejoice, and put your trust in God, in that God who was the God of Abraham, and Isaac, and Jacob. Mosiah 7:19

This is the day which the LORD hath made; we will rejoice and be glad in it. Ps. 118:24

Rejoice [not] to do evil, and delight in the frowardness of the wicked. Prov. 2:14

Rejoice not when thine enemy falleth, and let not thine heart be glad when he stumbleth: Lest the LORD see it, and it displease him, and he turn away his wrath from him. Prov. 24:17-18

I perceive that there is nothing better, than that a man should rejoice in his own works. Eccl. 3:22

Rejoice, O young man in thy youth; and let thy heart cheer thee in the days of thy youth, and walk in the ways of thine heart, and in the sight of thine eyes. Eccl. 11:9

We also joy in God through our Lord Jesus Christ, by whom we have now received the atonement. Rom. 5:11

Thou shouldest not have looked on the day of thy brother in the day that he became a stranger; neither shouldest thou have rejoiced over the children of Judah in the day of their destruction; neither shouldest thou have spoken proudly in the day of distress. Obad. 1:12

Let the heavens be glad, and the earth rejoice: and let men say among the nations, the LORD reigneth. 1 Chron. 16:31

Charity suffereth long, and is kind, and envieth not, and is not puffed up, seeketh not her own, is not easily provoked, thinketh no evil, and rejoiceth not in iniquity but rejoiceth in the truth, beareth all things, believeth all things, hopeth all things, endureth all things. Moro. 7:45 (1 Cor. 13:4-7)

My soul shall be joyful in the LORD: it shall rejoice in his salvation. Ps. 35:9

RELIEF, RELIEVE

Learn to do well; seek judgment, relieve the oppressed, judge the fatherless, plead for the widow. Isa. 1:17

REMEMBER, REMEMBERANCE

Remember the sabbath day, to keep it holy. Mosiah 13:16

These things have I spoken unto you, being yet present with you. But the Comforter, which is the Holy Ghost, whom the Father will send in my name, he shall teach you all things, and bring all things to your remem-brance, whatsoever I have said unto you. John 14:25-26

Remember his holy covenant. Luke 1:72

Remember the name of the LORD our God. Ps. 20:7

Come unto the Lord, the Holy One. Remember that his paths are righteous. 2 Ne. 9:41

Remember the words of your God; pray unto him continually by day, and give thanks unto his holy name by night. 2 Ne. 9:52

Reconcile yourselves unto the will of God, and not to the will of the devil and the flesh; and remember, after ye are reconciled unto God, that it is only in and through the grace of God that ye are saved. 2 Ne. 10:24

Remember his marvelous works that he hath done; his wonders, and the judgments of his mouth. Ps. 105:5

Perhaps I might persuade them that they would remember the Lord their Redeemer. 1 Ne. 19:18

If they shall confess their iniquity, and the iniquity of their fathers, with their trespass which they trespassed against me, and that also they have walked contrary unto me; And that I also have walked contrary unto them, and have brought them into the land of their enemies; if then their uncircumcised hearts be humbled, and they then accept of the punishment of their iniquity: Then will I remember my covenant with Jacob, and also my covenant with Isaac, and also my covenant with Abraham will I remember; and I will remember the land. Lev. 26:40-42

Do they remember the travails, and the labors, and the pains of the Jews, and their diligence unto me in bringing forth salvation unto the Gentiles? 2 Ne. 29:4

They are strict to remember the Lord their God from day to day; yea, they do observe to keep his statutes, and his judgments, and his commandments continually. Alma 58:40

Remember these, O Jacob and Israel; for thou art my servant: I have formed thee; thou art my servant; O Israel, thou shalt not be forgotten of me. Isa. 44:21

Remember the former things of old: for I God, and is none else; I God, and is none like me, Declaring the end from the beginning, and from ancient times that are not yet done, saying, My counsel shall stand, and I will do all my pleasure: Calling a ravenous bird from the east, the man that executeth my counsel from a far county: yea, I have spoken , I will also bring it to pass; I have purposed , I will also do it. Isa. 46:9-11

Remember ye the law of Moses my servant, which I commanded unto him in Horeb for all Israel, with the statutes and judgments. Mal. 4:4

Remember now thy creator in the days of thy youth. Eccl. 12:1

Thou hast not remembered the days of thy youth, but hast fretted me in all these things; behold, therefore I also will recompense thy way upon thine head, saith the Lord GOD. Ezek. 16:43 Preach the word of God unto them, to stir them up in remembrance of their duty. Alma 4:19

Remember the Lord your God. 1 Ne. 17:45

If thou put the brethren in remembrance of these things, thou shalt be a good minister of Jesus Christ, nourished up in the words of faith and of good doctrine, whereunto thou hast attained. 1 Tim. 4:6

Ye are swift to do iniquity but slow to remember the Lord your God. 1 Ne. 17:45

Stir them up in remembrance of the Lord their God, and perhaps they will repent and turn unto thee. Hel. 11:4

Remember the Lord your God in the things with which he hath blessed you. Hel. 13:22

REMISSION

And he took the cup, and gave thanks, and gave it to them, saying, Drink ye all of it; For this is my blood of the new testament, which is shed for many for the remission of sins. Matt. 26:28

He commanded us to preach unto the people, and to testify that it is he which was ordained of God to be the Judge of quick and dead. To him give all the prophets witness, that through his name whosoever believeth in him shall receive remission of sins. Acts 10:43

Almost all things are by the law purged with blood; and without shedding of blood is no remission. Heb. 9:22

John did baptize in the wilderness, and preach the baptism of repentance for the remission of sins. Mark 1:4

Repent, and be baptized every one of you in the name of Jesus Christ for the remission of sins, and ye shall receive the gift of the Holy Ghost. Acts 2:38

REMOVE

Turn not to the right hand nor to the left: remove thy foot from evil. Prov. 4:27

RENDER

Render to every man according to that which is his due. Mosiah 4:13

Also unto thee, O Lord, belongeth mercy: for thou renderest to every man according to his work. Ps. 62:12

See that none render evil for evil unto any man; but ever follow that which is good, both among yourselves, and to all men. 1 Thes. 5:15

Say not, I will do so to him as he hath done to me; I will render to the man according to his work. Prov. 24:29

Render therefore unto Caesar the things which are Caesar's, and unto God the things that are God's. Matt. 22:21

Render all the thanks and praise which your whole soul has power to possess, to that God who has created you. Mosiah 2:20

RENEW

They that wait upon the Lord shall renew their strength; they shall mount up with wings as eagles; they shall run, and not be weary; and they shall walk, and not faint. Isa. 40:31

Be ye transformed by the renewing of your mind, that ye may prove what is that good, and acceptable, and perfect, will of God. Rom. 12:2

REPAIR

They came forth and did confess their sins and were baptized unto repentance, and immediately returned to the Nephites to endeavor to repair unto them the wrongs which they had done. Hel. 5:17

Gather of all Israel money to repair the house of your God from year to year. 2 Chron. 24:4-5

REPENT, REPENTANCE

Do not procrastinate the day of your repentance until the end. Alma 34:33

Preach nothing save it were repentance and faith on the Lord, who had redeemed his people. Mosiah 18:20

For, behold, the Lord your Redeemer suffered death in the flesh; wherefore he suffered the pain of all men, that all men might repent and come unto him. D&C 18:11

Whosoever repented of their sins and did confess them, them he did number among the people of the church. Mosiah 26:35

O repent ye, repent ye! Why will ye die? Turn ye, turn ye unto the Lord your God. Hel. 7:18

Let your sins trouble you, with that trouble which shall bring you down unto repentance. Alma 42:29

If ye shall come unto me, or shall desire to come unto me, and rememberest that thy brother hath aught against thee - Go thy way unto thy brother, and first be reconciled to thy brother, and then come unto me with full purpose of heart, and I will receive you. 3 Ne. 12:23-24

Believe that ye must repent of your sins and forsake them, and humble yourselves before God; and ask in sincerity of heart that he would forgive you; and now, if you believe all these things see that ye do them. Mosiah 4:10

Repent, and be baptized every one of you in the name of Jesus Christ for the remission of sins, and ye shall receive the gift of the Holy Ghost. Acts 2:38

Therefore may God grant unto you, my brethren, that ye may begin to exercise your faith unto repentance, that ye begin to call upon his holy name, that he would have mercy upon you; Yea, cry unto him for mercy; for he is mighty to save. Alma 34:17

Let us search and try our ways, and turn again to the LORD. Lam. 3:40

Make merry, and be glad: for this thy brother was dead, and is alive again; and was lost, and is found. Luke 15:32

I will declare mine iniquity; I will be sorry for my sin. Ps. 38:18

Repent, and turn yourselves from your idols. Ezek. 14:6

They should repent and turn to God, and do works meet for repentance. Acts 26:20

Let the wicked forsake his way, and the unrighteous man his thoughts: and let him return unto the LORD, and he will have mercy upon him; and to our God, for he will abundantly pardon. Isa. 55:7

The time is fulfilled, and the kingdom of God is at hand: repent ye, and believe the gospel. Mark 1:15

He commandeth all men that they must repent. 2 Ne. 9:23

REPEAT, REPITITION

When ye pray, use not vain repetitions, as the heathen, for they think that they shall be heard for their much speaking. Be not ye therefore like unto them, for your Father knoweth what things ye have need of before ye ask him. 3 Ne. 13:7-8

REPLENISH

Be fruitful, and multiply, and replenish the earth, and subdue it. Gen. 1:28

REPROACH

He that backbiteth not with his tongue, nor doeth evil to his neighbour, nor taketh up a reproach against his neighbour [shall abide in thy tabernacle]. Ps. 15:3

Fear ye not the reproach of men, neither be ye afraid of their revilings. Isa. 51:7

Render unto our neighbours sevenfold into their bosom their reproach, wherewith they have reproached thee, O Lord. Ps. 79:12

REPROOF, REPROVE

He, that being often reproved hardeneth his neck, shall suddenly be destroyed, and that without remedy. Prov. 29:1

All scripture is given by inspiration of God, and is profitable for doctrine, for reproof, for correction, for instruction in righteousness: That the man of God may be perfect, throughly furnished unto all good works. 2 Tim. 3:16-17

Correction is grievous unto him that forsaketh the way: and he that hateth reproof shall die. Prov. 15:10

He is in the way of life that keepeth instruction: but he that refuseth reproof erreth. Prov. 10:17

As an earring of gold, and an ornament of fine gold, so is a wise reprover upon an obedient ear. Prov. 25:12

RESPECT

At that day shall a man look to his Maker, and his eyes shall have respect to the Holy One of Israel. Isa. 17:7

Regardest not the person of men. Matt. 22:16

I charge thee before God, and the Lord Jesus Christ, and the elect angels, that thou observe these things without preferring one before another, doing nothing by partiality. 1 Tim. 5:21

Ye shall not esteem one flesh above another, or one man shall not think himself above another. Mosiah 23:7

We believe that every man should be honored in his station, rulers and magistrates as such, being placed for the protection of the innocent and the punishment of the guilty; and that to the laws all men show respect and deference, as without them peace and harmony would be supplanted by anarchy and terror; human laws being instituted for the express purpose of regulating our interests as individuals and nations, between man and man; and divine laws given of heaven, prescribing rules on spiritual concerns, for faith and worship, both to be answered by man to his Maker. D&C 134:6

It is not good to have respect of persons in judgment. Prov. 24:23

REST

They returned, and prepared spices and ointments; and rested the sabbath day according to the commandment. Luke 23:56

Persuade them to come unto Christ, and partake of the goodness of God, that they may enter into his rest. Jacob 1:7

Rest in the LORD, and wait patiently for Him. Ps. 37:7

Enter into the rest of God. Alma 12:37

RESTORATION, RESTORE, RESTORED

It is a light thing that thou shouldest be my servant to raise up the tribes of Jacob, and to restore the preserved of Israel: I will also give thee for a light to the Gentiles, that thou mayest be my salvation unto the end of the earth. Isa. 49:6

RESURRECT, RESURRECTION

I know that he shall rise again in the resurrection at the last day. Jesus said unto her, I am the resurrection, and the life: he that believeth in me, though he were dead, yet shall he live. John 11:24-25

There are also celestial bodies, and bodies terrestrial: but the glory of the celestial is one, and the glory of the terrestrial is another. There is one glory of the sun, and another glory of the moon, and another glory of the stars: for one star differeth from another star in glory. So also is the resurrection of the dead. 1 Cor. 15:40-42

RETAIN

Even as they did not like to retain God in their knowledge, God gave them over to a reprobate mind, to do those things which are not convenient. Rom. 1:28

RETURN

His mischief shall return upon his own head, and his violent dealing shall come down upon his own pate. Ps. 7:16

Return unto me and I will return unto you, saith the Lord of Hosts. But ye say: Wherein shall we return? Will a man rob God? Yet ye have robbed me. But ye say: Wherein have we robbed thee? In tithes and offerings. 3 Ne. 24:7-12 (Mal. 3:8)

Let the wicked forsake his way, and the unrighteous man his thoughts: and let him return unto the LORD, and he will have mercy upon him; and to our God, for he will abundantly pardon. Isa. 55:7

If ye do return unto the LORD with all your hearts, then put away the strange gods and Ashtaroth from among you, and prepare your hearts unto the LORD, and serve him only: and he will deliver you out of the hand of the Philistines. 1 Sam. 7:3

I will give them an heart to know me, that I am the LORD: and they shall be my people, and I will be their God: for they shall return unto me with their whole heart. Jer. 24:7

REVEAL, REVELATION

I neither received it of man, neither was I taught it, but by the revelation of Jesus Christ. Gal. 1:12

We believe in the gift of tongues, prophecy, revelation, visions, healing, interpretation of tongues, and so forth. A of F-7

Call unto me, and I will answer thee, and shew thee great and mighty things, which thou knowest not. Jer. 33:3

Behold, look ye unto the revelations of God; for behold, the time cometh at that day when all these things must be fulfilled. Morm. 8:33

I will pour out my spirit upon all flesh; and your sons and your daughters shall prophesy, your old men shall dream dreams, your young men shall see visions. Joel 2:28

There is a God in heaven that revealeth secrets. Dan. 2:28

The God of our Lord Jesus Christ, the Father of glory, may give unto you the spirit of wisdom and revelation in the knowledge of him: The eyes of your understanding being enlightened; that ye may know what is the hope of his calling, and what the riches of the glory of his inheritance in the saints. Eph. 1:17-18 ‖

REVENGE

The scripture says - man shall not smite, neither shall he judge; for judgment is mine, saith the Lord, and vengeance is mine also, and I will repay. Morm. 8:20

REVILE, REVILING

Wo unto them that turn aside the just for a thing of naught and revile against that which is good, and say that it is of no worth! 2 Ne. 28:16

I would exhort you to have patience, and that ye bear with all manner of afflictions; that ye do not revile against those who do cast you out because of your exceeding poverty, lest ye become sinners like unto them. Alma 34:40

REVOLT

As for our iniquities, we know them: in transgressing and lying against the LORD, and departing away from our God, speaking oppression and revolt, conceiving and uttering from the heart words of falsehood. Isa. 59:12-13

REWARD

Justify [not] the wicked for reward 2 N.e 15:23

Say ye to the daughter of Zion, Behold, thy salvation cometh; behold, his reward is with him, and his work before him. Isa. 62:11

He that receiveth you receiveth me, and he that receiveth me receiveth him that sent me. He that receiveth a prophet in the name of a prophet shall receive a prophet's reward; and he that receiveth a righteous man in the name of a righteous man shall receive a righteous man's reward. Matt. 10:40-41

The LORD rewarded me according to my righteousness; according to the cleanness of my hands hath he recompensed me. Ps. 18:20

Blessed are ye, when men shall revile you, and persecute you, and shall say all manner of evil against you falsely, for my sake. Rejoice, and be exceeding glad: for great is your reward in heaven: for so persecuted they the prophets which were before you. Matt 5:11-12

But without faith it is impossible to please him: for he that cometh to God must believe that he is, and that he is a rewarder of them that diligently seek him. Heb. 11:6

Whoso rewardeth evil for good, evil shall not depart from his house. Prov. 17:13

RICH, RICHES, RICHLY

Before ye seek for riches, seek ye for the kingdom of God. And after ye have obtained a hope in Christ ye shall obtain riches, if ye seek them; and ye will seek them for the intent to do good–to clothe the naked, and to feed the hungry, and to liberate the captive, and administer relief to the sick and afflicted. Jacob 2:18-19

A good name is rather to be chosen than great riches, and loving favour rather than silver and gold. Prov. 22:1

Can ye be puffed up up the pride of your hearts; yea, will ye still persist in the wearing of costly apparel and setting your hearts upon the vain things of the world, upon your riches? Alma 5:53

It is easier for a camel to go through the eye of a needle, than for a rich man to enter into the kingdom of God. Matt 19:24

Seek not for riches, but for wisdom. D&C 6:7

Charge them that are rich in this world, that they be not highminded, nor trust in uncertain riches, but in the living God, who giveth us richly all things to enjoy. 1 Tim. 6:17

He that oppresseth the poor to increase his riches, and he that giveth to the rich, shall surely come to want. Prov. 22:16

Be rich in good works, ready to distribute, willing to communicate. 1 Tim. 6:18

A faithful man shall abound with blessings: but he that maketh haste to be rich shall not be innocent. Prov. 28:20

He that hasteth to be rich hath an evil eye, and considereth not that poverty shall come upon him. Prov. 28:22

As the partridge sitteth on eggs, and hatcheth them not; so he that getteth riches, and not by right, shall leave them in the midst of his days, and at his end shall be a fool. Jer. 17:11

Trust not in oppression, and become not vain in robbery: if riches increase, set not your heart upon them. Ps. 62:10

Better is a little with righteousness than great revenues without right. Prov. 16:8

Labour not to be rich: cease from thin own wisdom. Prov. 23:4

They that trust in their wealth, and boast themselves in the multitude of their riches; None of them can by any means redeem his brother. Ps. 49:6-7

Be not highminded, nor trust in uncertain riches, but in the living God, who giveth us richly all things to enjoy. 1 Tim. 6:17-19

Wo unto the rich, who are rich as to the things of the world. For because they are rich they despise the poor, and they persecute the meek, and their hearts are upon their treasures; wherefore, their treasure is their god. And behold, their treasure shall perish with them also. 2 Ne. 9:30

Think of your brethren like unto yourselves, and be familiar with all and free with your substance, that they may be rich like unto you. Jacob 2:17

RIGHT, RIGHTEOUS, RIGHTEOUSNESS

He did do that which was right in the sight of God continually. Hel. 3:20

Come unto the Lord, the Holy One. Remember that his paths are righteous. 2 Ne. 9:411

Offer unto the Lord an offering in righteousness. 3 Ne. 24:3

Open ye the gates, that the righteous nation which keepeth the truth may enter in. Isa. 26:2

Ye shall do no unrighteousness in judgment: thou shalt not respect the person of the poor, nor honor the person of the mighty: but in righteousness shalt thou judge thy neighbour. Lev. 19:15

Better is a little with righteousness than great revenues without right. Prov. 16:8

Walk in the paths of righteousness. 1 Ne. 16:5

Behold, my soul abhorreth sin, and my heart delighteth in righteousness; and I will praise the holy name of my God. 2 Ne. 9:49

Know the righteousness of the LORD. Micah 6:5

The labour of the righteous tendeth to life: the fruit of the wicked to sin. Prov. 10:16

A righteous man falling down before the wicked is as a troubled fountain, and a corrupt spring. Prov. 25:26

He shall not judge after the sight of his eyes, neither reprove after the hearing of his ears, but with righteousness shall he judge the poor, and reprove with equity for the meek of the earth; and he shall smite the earth with the rod of his mouth, and with the breath of his lips shall be slay the wicked. 2 Ne. 21:3-4

He listeth to obey the evil spirit, and becometh an enemy to all righteousness. Mosiah 2:37

Ye will not suffer your children that they go hungry, or naked; neither will ye suffer that they transgress the laws of God, and fight and quarrel one with another, and serve the devil, who is the master of sin, or who is the evil spirit which hath been spoken of by our fathers, he being an enemy to all righteousness. Mosiah 4:14

The righteous considereth the cause of the poor: but the wicked regardeth not to know it. Prov. 29:7

Blessed are all they who do hunger and thirst after righteousness. 3 Ne. 12:6

Awake, my sons; put on the armor of righteousness. Shake off the chains with which ye are bound, and come forth out of obscurity, and arise from the dust. 2 Ne. 1:23

I know that the words of truth are hard against all uncleanness; but the righteous fear them not, for they love the truth and are not shaken. 2 Ne. 9:40

With my soul have I desired thee in the night; yea, with my spirit within me will I seek thee early: for when thy judgments are in the earth, the inhabitants of the world will learn righteousness. Isa. 26:9

Thou shalt do that which is right and good in the sight of the LORD: that it may be well with thee, and that thou mayest go in and possess the good land which the LORD swear unto thy fathers, To cast out all thine enemies from before thee, as the LORD hath spoken. Deut. 6:18-19

Discretion shall preserve thee, understanding shall keep thee; to deliver thee from the way of the evil man, from the man that speaketh froward things; who leave the paths of righteousness, to walk in the ways of darkness. Prov. 2:11-13

Take away the wicked from before the king, and his throne shall be established in righteousness. Prov. 25:5

When the righteous are in authority, the people rejoice: but when the wicked beareth rule, the people mourn. Prov. 29:2

Hearken unto me, ye stouthearted, that are far from righteousness. Isa. 46:12

I will greatly rejoice in the LORD, my soul shall be joyful in my God; for he hath clothed me with the garments of salvation, he hath covered me with the robe of righteousness. Isa. 61:10

Execute ye judgment and righteous-ness. Jer. 22:3-5

As the partridge sitteth on eggs, and hatcheth them not; so he that getteth riches, and not by right, shall leave them in the midst of his days, and at his end shall be a fool. Jer. 17:11

He hath done that which is lawful and right; he shall surely live. Ezek. 33:16

Delight thyself also in the LORD; and he shall give thee the desires of thine heart. Ps. 37:4

Blessed are they that keep judgment, and he that doeth righteousness at all times. Ps. 106:3

Lay not wait, O wicked man, against the dwelling of the righteous; spoil not his resting place: For a just man falleth seven times, and riseth up again: but the wicked shall fall into mischief. Prov. 24:15-16

Whoso causeth the righteous to go astray in an evil way, he shall fall himself into his own pits; but the upright shall have good things in possession. Prov. 28:10

Be not righteous over much; neither make thyself over wise: why shouldest thou destroy thyself? Eccl. 7:16

Be a greater follower of righteousness. Abr. 1:2

Teach them all things pertaining to righteous-ness. Alma 21:23

They began to be a righteous people; and they did walk in the ways of the Lord. Alma 25:14

When a righteous man turneth away from his right-eousness, and committeth iniquity, and dieth in them; for his iniquity that he hath done shall he die. Ezek. 18:26

He did that which was right in the sight of the LORD. 2 Chron. 29:2

I have set the LORD always before me: because he is at my right hand, I shall not be moved. Ps. 16:8

Let them shout for joy, and be glad, that favour my righteous cause: yea, let them say continually, Let the LORD be magnified, which hath pleasure in the prosperity of his servant. Ps. 35:27

He that walketh righteously, and speaketh uprightly; he that despiseth the gain of oppressions, that shaketh his hands from holding of bribes, that stoppeth his ears from hearing of blood, and shutteth his eyes from seeing evil; He shall dwell on high: his defence shall be the munitions of rocks: bread shall be given him; his waters shall be sure. Isa. 33:15-16

If thou warn the righteous man, that the righteous sin not, and he doth not sin, he shall surely live, because he is warned; also thou hast delivered thy soul. Ezek. 3:21

Let thy priests be clothed with righteousness. Ps. 132:9

The LORD rewarded me according to my righteousness; according to the cleanness of my hands hath he recompensed me. Ps. 18:20

Go in the strength of the Lord GOD: I will make mention of thy righteousness, even of thine only. Ps. 71:16

Treasures of wickedness profit nothing; but righteousness delivereth from death. Prov. 10:2

He that followeth after righteousness and mercy, findeth life, righteousness, and honour. Prov. 21:21

Follow after righteousness. 2 Ne. 8:1

Blessed are they which do hunger and thirst after righteousness: for they shall be filled. Matt. 5:6

RIGHTS

We believe that religion is instituted of God; and that men are amenable to him, and to him only, for the exercise of it, unless their religious opinions prompt them to infringe upon the rights and liberties of others; but we do not believe that human law has a right to interfere in prescribing rules of worship to bind the consciences of men, nor dictate forms for public or private devotion; that the civil magistrate should restrain crime, but never control conscience; should punish guilt, but never suppress the freedom of the soul. D&C 134:4

We do not believe it just to mingle religious influence with civil government, whereby one religious society is fostered and another proscribed in its spiritual privileges, and the individual rights of its members, as citizens, denied. D&C 134:9

RIOTING, RIOTOUS

Whoso keepeth the law is a wise son: but he that is a companion of riotous men shameth his father. Prov. 28:7

RISE, RISEN, ROSE

Rise up, ye women that are at ease; hear my voice, ye careless daughters; give ear unto my speech. Many days and years shall ye be troubled, ye careless women: for the vintage shall fail, the gathering shall not come. Isa. 32:9-10

ROB, ROBBERY

Trust not in oppression, and become not vain in robbery: if riches increase, set not your heart upon them. Ps. 62:10 Whoso robbeth his father or his mother, and saith, It is no transgression; the same is the companion of a destroyer. Prov. 28:24

Return unto me and I will return unto you, saith the Lord of Hosts. But ye say: Wherein shall we return? Will a man rob God? Yet ye have robbed me. But ye say: Wherein have we robbed thee? In tithes and offerings. 3 Ne. 24:7-12 (Mal. 3:8)

ROBE

I will greatly rejoice in the LORD, my soul shall be joyful in my God; for he hath clothed me with the garments of salvation, he hath covered me with the robe of righteousness. Isa. 61:10

ROD

Feed thy people with thy rod, the flock of thine heritage, which dwell solitarily in the wood. Micah 7:14

RULE, RULER

The merciful man doeth good to his own soul: but he that is cruel troubleth his own flesh. Prov. 11:17

He that hath no rule over his own spirit is like a city that is broken down and without walls. Prov. 25:28

If a man know not how to rule his own house, how shall he take care of the church of God? 1 Tim. 3:4-5

When the righteous are in authority, the people rejoice: but when the wicked beareth rule, the people mourn. Prov. 29:2

Let the peace of God rule in your hearts. Col. 3:15

He that is slow to anger is better than the mighty; and he that ruleth his spirit than he that taketh a city. Prov. 16:32

RUN

Do not run faster or labor more than you have strength and means. D&C 10:4

Seeing we also are compassed about with so great a cloud of witnesses, let us lay aside every weight, and the sin which doth so easily beset us, and let us run with patience the race that is set before us. Heb. 12:1

SABBATH

Remember the sabbath day, to keep it holy. Mosiah 13:16

Hallow the sabbath day, to do no work therein. Jer. 17:24

The seventh day is the sabbath of the LORD thy God: in it thou shalt not do any work, thou, nor thy son, nor thy daughter, thy manservant, nor thy maidservant, nor thy cattle, nor thy stranger that is within thy gates: Ex. 20:10

Thou hast despised mine holy things, and hast profaned my sabbaths. Ezek. 22:8

That thou mayest more fully keep thyself unspotted from the world, thou shalt go to the house of prayer and offer up thy sacraments upon my holy day. D&C 59:9

If thou turn away thy foot from the sabbath, from doing thy pleasure on my holy day; and call the sabbath a delight, the holy of the LORD, honorable; and shalt honor him, not doing thy own ways, nor finding thine own pleasure, nor speaking thine own words: Then shalt thou delight thyself in the LORD; and I will cause thee to ride upon the high places of the earth, and feed thee with the heritage of Jacob thy father: for the mouth of the LORD hath spoken it. Isa. 58:13-14

The sabbath was made for man, and not man for the sabbath: Therefore the Son of man is Lord also of the sabbath. Mark 2:27-28

Remember the sabbath day, to keep it holy. Six days shalt thou labour, and do all thy work: But the seventh day is the sabbath of the LORD thy God: in it thou shalt not do any work, thou, nor thy son, nor thy daughter, thy manservant, nor thy maidservant, nor thy cattle, nor thy stranger that is within thy gates: For in six days the LORD made heaven and earth, the sea, and all that in them is, and rested the seventh day: wherefore the LORD blessed the sabbath day, and hallowed it. Ex. 20:8-11

They returned, and prepared spices and ointments; and rested the sabbath day according to the commandment. Luke 23:56

Do well on the sabbath days. Matt. 12:12

Observe the Sabbath day to keep it holy. D&C 68:29

SACRAMENT

The Lord Jesus the same night in which he was betrayed took bread: And when he had given thanks, he brake it, and said, Take, eat: this is my body, which is broken for you: this do in remembrance of me. After the same manner also he took the cup, when he had supped, saying, This cup is the new testament in my blood: this do ye, as oft as ye drink it, in remembrance of me. For as often as ye eat this bread, and drink this cup, ye do shew the Lord's death till he come. 1 Cor. 11:23-26

Whosoever shall eat this bread, and drink this cup of the Lord, unworthily, shall be guilty of the body and blood of the Lord. But let a man examine himself, and so let him eat of that bread, and drink of that cup. For he that eateth and drinketh unworthily, eateth and drinketh damnation to himself, not discerning the Lord's body. 1 Cor. 11:27-29

SACRED

Trifle not with sacred things. D&C 6:12

SACRIFICE

Thou shalt offer a sacrifice unto the Lord thy God in righteousness, even that of a broken heart and a contrite spirit. D&C 59:8

Ye also, as lively stones, are built up a spiritual house, an holy priesthood, to offer up spiritual sacrifices, acceptable to God by Jesus Christ. 1 Pet. 2:5

I will offer to thee the sacrifice of thanksgiving, and will call upon the name of the Lord. Ps. 116:17

Offer sacrifices of righteousness. Deut. 33:19

When ye offer your gifts, when ye make your sons to pass through the fire, ye pollute yourselves with all your idols, even unto this day. Ezek. 20:31

If thou wilt be perfect, go and sell that thou hast, and give to the poor, and thou shalt have treasure in heaven: and come and follow me. Matt. 19:21-22

SAINTS

Beloved, when I gave all diligence to write unto you of the common salvation, it was needful for me to write unto you, and exhort you that ye should earnestly contend for the faith which was once delivered unto the saints. Jude 1:3

Ye are no more strangers and foreigners, but fellowcitizens with the saints, and of the household of God; And are built upon the foundation of the apostles and prophets, Jesus Christ himself being the chief corner stone. Eph. 2:19-20

SAKE

LORD, thou knowest: remember me, and visit me, and revenge me of my persecutors; take me not away in thy longsuffering: know that for thy sake I have suffered rebuke. Jer. 15:15

SALT

Ye are the salt of the earth: but if the salt have lost his savour, wherewith shall it be salted? it is thenceforth good for nothing, but to be cast out, and to be trodden under foot of men. Matt. 5:13

SALVATION

Believest thou in the power of Christ unto salvation? Alma 15:6

My soul shall be joyful in the LORD: it shall rejoice in his salvation. Ps. 35:9

How shall we escape, if we neglect so great salvation; which at the first began to be spoken by the Lord, and was confirmed unto us by them that heard him; God also bearing them witness, both with signs and wonders, and with divers miracles, and gifts of the Holy Ghost, according to his own will? Heb. 2:3-4

It is a light thing that thou shouldest be my servant to raise up the tribes of Jacob, and to restore the preserved of Israel: I will also give thee for a light to the Gentiles, that thou mayest be my salvation unto the end of the earth. Isa. 49:6

Work out your own salvation in fear and trembling. Philip. 2:12

God hath from the beginning chosen you to salvation through sanctification of the Spirit and belief of the truth. 2 Thes. 2:13

Believe that salvation was, and is, and is to come, in and through the atoning blood of Christ, the Lord Omnipotent. Mosiah 3:18

Ye should come unto Christ, who is the Holy One of Israel, and partake of his salvation, and the power of his redemption. Yea, come unto him, and offer your whole souls as an offering unto him and continue in fasting and praying, and endure to the end. Omni 1:26

SAME

Do we not read that God is the same yesterday, today, and forever, and in him there is no variableness neither shadow of changing? Morm. 9:9

SANCTIFICATION, SANCTIFIED, SANCTIFY

Sanctify the Lord God in your heats; and be ready always to give an answer to every man that asketh you a reason of the hope that is in you with meekness and fear: Having a good conscience; that, whereas they speak evil of you, as of evildoers, they may be ashamed that falsely accuse your good conversation in Christ. 1 Pet. 3:15-16

Sanctify yourselves therefore, and be ye holy: for I am the LORD your God. Lev. 20:7-8

When he seeth his children, the work of mine hands, in the midst of him, they shall sanctify my name, and sanctify the Holy One of Jacob, and shall fear the God of Israel. Isa. 29:23

If a man therefore purge himself from these, he shall be a vessel unto honour, sanctified, and meet for the master's use, and prepared unto every good work. 2 Tim. 2:21

SANCTUARY

We are confounded, because we have heard reproach: shame hath covered our faces: for strangers are come into the sanctuaries of the LORD's house. Jer. 51:51

Thou hast defiled thy sanctuaries by the multitude of thine iniquities, by the iniquity of thy traffick; therefore will I bring forth a fire from the midst of thee, it shall devour thee. Ezek. 28:18-19

Thus saith the Lord GOD; No stranger uncircumcised in heart, nor circumcised in flesh, shall enter into my sanctuary, of any strangers that is among the children of Israel. Ezek. 44:9

SATISFIED, SATISFY

He that tilleth his land shall be satisfied with bread: but he that followeth vain persons is void of understanding. Prov. 12:11

SAVE, SAVED

Whosoever will save his life shall lose it; but whosoever shall lose his life for my sake and the gospel's, the same shall save it. For what shall it profit a man, if he shall gain the whole world, and lose his own soul? Mark 8:36

We labor diligently to write, to persuade our children, and also our brethren, to believe in Christ, and to be reconciled to God; for we know that it is by grace that we are saved, after all we can do. 2 Ne. 25:23

Be it known unto you all, and to all the people of Israel, that by the name of Jesus Christ of Nazareth, whom ye crucified, whom God raised from the dead, even by him doth this man stand here before you whole. This is the stone which was set at nought of you builders, which is become the head of the corner. Neither is there salvation in any other: for there is none other name under heaven given among men, whereby we must be saved. Acts 4:10-12

What doth it profit, my brethren, though a man say he hath faith, and have not works? can faith save him? James. 2:14

Now, the decrees of God are unalterable; therefore, the way is prepared that whosoever will may walk therein and be saved. Alma 41:8

Look unto me, and be ye saved, all the ends of the earth: for I am God, and there is none else. Isa. 45:22

I have told you this that ye may learn wisdom, that ye may learn of me that there is no other way or means whereby man can be saved, only in and through Christ. Alma 38:9

Strengthen ye the weak hands, and confirm the feeble knees. Say to them that are of a fearful heart, Be strong, fear not: behold, your God will come with vengeance, even God with a recompense; he will come and save you. Isa. 35:3-4

Save yourselves from this untoward generation. Acts 2:40

Go ye out from among the wicked. Save yourselves. D&C 38:42

SAVIOR

I am the LORD thy God from the land of Egypt, and thou shalt know no god but me: for there is no saviour beside me. Hosea 13:4

Trust in the living God, who is the Saviour of all men, specially of those that believe. 1 Tim. 4:10

SAVOR

He rebuked Peter, saying, Get thee behind me, Satan: for thou savourest not the things that be of God, but the things that be of men. Mark 8:33

SAY, SAYINGS

Say among the heathen that the LORD reigneth. Ps. 96:10

It shall come to pass at that time, that I will search Jerusalem with candles, and punish the men that are settled on their lees: that say in their heart, The LORD will not do good, neither will he do evil. Zeph. 1:12

My son, attend to my words; incline thine ear unto my sayings. Let them not depart from thine eyes; keep them in the midst of thine heart. For they are life unto those that find them, and health to all their flesh. Prov. 4:20-22

Say ye to the daughter of Zion, Behold, thy salvation cometh; behold, his reward is with him, and his work before him. Isa. 62:11

Zion said, the LORD hath forsaken me, and my LORD hath forgotten me. Can a woman forget her sucking child, that she should not have compassion on the son of her womb? yea, they may forget, yet will I not forget thee. Isa. 49:14-15

They shall call on my name, and I will hear them: I will say, It is my people: and they shall say, The LORD is my God. Zech. 13:9

SCATTER

Woe be unto the pastors that destroy and scatter the sheep of my pasture! saith the LORD. Jer. 23:1

SCORN, SCORNER, SCORNFUL

Cast out the scorner, and contention shall go out; yea, strife and reproach shall cease. Prov. 22:10

Blessed is the man that walketh not in the counsel of the ungodly, nor standeth in the way of sinners, nor sitteth in the seat of the scornful. Ps. 1:1

If thou be wise, thou shalt be wise for thyself; but if thou scornest, thou alone shalt bear it. Prov. 9:12

SCRIPTURE

They received the word with all readiness of mind, and searched the scriptures daily, whether those things were so. Acts 17:11

All scripture is given by inspiration of God, and is profitable for doctrine, for reproof, for correction, for instruction in righteousness: That the man of God may be perfect, throughly furnished unto all good works. 2 Tim. 3:16-17

They were men of a sound understanding and they had searched the scriptures diligently, that they might know the word of God Alma 17:2

Paul, as his manner was, went in unto them, and three sabbath days reasoned with them out of the scriptures. Acts 17:2

When therefore he was risen from the dead, his disciples remembered that he had said this unto them; and they believed the scripture, and the word which Jesus had said. John 2:22

Search the scriptures; for in them ye think ye have eternal life: and they are they which testify of me. John 5:39

SEAL, SEALED, SEALING

Grieve not the holy Spirit of God, whereby ye are sealed unto the day of redemption. Eph. 4:30

SEARCH

Search the prophecies of Isaiah. Morm. 8:23

They received the word with all readiness of mind, and searched the scriptures daily, whether those things were so. Acts 17:11

Let us search and try our ways, and turn again to the Lord. Lam. 3:40

Ye should search diligently in the light of Christ that ye may know good from evil; and if ye will lay hold upon every good thing and condemn it not, ye certainly will be a child of Christ. Moro. 7:19

Search diligently, pray always, and be believing, and all things shall work together for your good. D&C 90:24

They were men of a sound understanding and they had searched the scriptures diligently, that they might know the word of God Alma 17:2

Eye hath not seen, nor ear heard, neither have entered into the heart of man, the things which God hath prepared for them that love him. But God hath reveled them unto us by his Spirit; for the Spirit searcheth all things, yea, the deep things of God. 1 Cor. 2:9-10

Search the scriptures; for in them ye think ye have eternal life: and they are they which testify of me. John 5:39

I would ask if ye have read the scriptures? If ye have, how can ye disbelieve on the Son of God. Alma 33:14

The rich man is wise in his own conceit; but the poor that hath understanding searcheth him out. Prov. 28:11

SEASON

To every thing there is a season, and a time to every purpose under heaven; A time to be born, and a time to die; a time to plant, and a time to pluck up that which is planted; A time to kill, and a time to heal; a time to break down, and a time to build up; A time to weep, and a time to laugh; a time to mourn, and a time to dance; A time to cast away stones, and a time to father stones together; a time to embrace, and a time to refrain from embracing; A time to get, and a time to lose; a time to keep, and a time to cast away; A time to rend, and a time to sew; a time to keep silence, and a time to speak; A time to love, and a time to hate; a time of war, and a time of peace. Eccl. 3:1-8

The Lord GOD hath given me the tongue of the learned, that I should know how to speak a word in season to him that is weary. Isa. 50:4

If ye walk in my statutes and keep my commandments, and do them; Then I will give you rain in due season, and the land shall yield her increase, and the trees of the field shall yield her fruit. Lev. 26:3-4

A man hath joy by the answer of his mouth: and a word spoken in due season, how good is it. Prov. 15:23

SECOND COMFORTER

If ye love me, keep my commandments. And I will pray the Father, and he shall give you another Comforter, that he may abide with you for ever; Even the Spirit of truth; whom the world cannot receive, because it seeth him not, neither knoweth him: but ye know him; for he dweleth with you, and shall be in you. John 14:16 &

SECOND COMING

We which are alive and remain shall be caught up together with them in the clouds, to meet the Lord in the air: and so shall we ever be with the Lord. 1 Thes. 4:17

Heaven and earth shall pass away, but my words shall not pass away. But of that day and hour knoweth no man, no, not the angels of heaven, by my Father only. Matt 24:36

I, the Lord God, have spoken it; but the hour and the day no man knoweth, neither the angels in heaven, nor shall they know until he comes. D&C 49:7

Let no man deceive you by any means: for that day shall not come, except there come a falling away first, and that man of sin be revealed, the son of perdition; who opposeth and exalteth himself above all that is called God, or that is worshiped; so that he as God sitteth in the temple of God, shewing himself that he is God. 2 Thes. 2:3-4

SECOND DEATH

He that overcometh shall inherit all things; and I will be his God, and he shall be my son. But the fearful, and unbelieving, and the abominable, and murderers, and whoremongers, and sorcerers, and idolaters, and all liars, shall have their part in the lake which burneth with fire and brimstone: which is the second death. Rev. 21:7

For it is impossible for those who were once enlightened, and have tasted of the heavenly gift, and were made partakers of the Holy Ghost, And have tasted the good word of God, and the powers of the world to come, If they shall fall away, to renew them again unto repentance; seeing they crucify to themselves the Son of God afresh, and put him to an open shame. Heb. 6:4

SECRET

Debate thy cause with thy neighbour; and discover not a secret to another: lest he that heareth put thee to shame, and thine infamy turn not away. Prov. 25:9-10

When thou fasteth, anoint thine head, and wash thy face; That thou appear not unto men to fast, but unto thy Father which is in secret; and thy Father, which seeth in secret, shall reward thee openly. Matt. 6:17-18

The secret which the king hath demanded cannot the wise men, the astrologers, the magicians, the soothsayers, shew unto the king; But there is a God in heaven that revealeth secrets, and maketh known to the king Nebuchadnezzar what shall be in the latter days. Dan. 1:27-28

There is a God in heaven that revealeth secrets. Dan. 2:28

When thou prayest thou shalt not do as the hypocrites, for they love to pray, standing in the synagogues and in the corners of the streets, that they may be seen of men. Verily I say unto you, they have their reward. But thou, when thou prayest, enter into thy closet, and when thou hast shut thy door, pray to thy Father who is in secret; and thy Father, who seeth in secret, shall reward thee openly. 3 Ne. 13:5-6

SEE, SEEN, SAW

I have seen God face to face, and my life is preserved. Jer. Gen. 32:24-30

O taste and see that the LORD is good: blessed is the man that trusteth in him. Ps. 34:8

All ye inhabitants of the world, and dwellers on the earth, see ye, when he lifted up an ensign on the mountains; and when he bloweth a trumpet, hear ye. Isa. 18:3

Make the heart of this people fat, and make their ears heavy, and shut their eyes; lest they see with their eyes, and hear with their ears, and understand with their heart, and convert, and be healed. Isa. 6:10

He that walketh righteously, and speaketh uprightly; he that despiseth the gain of oppressions, that shaketh his hands from holding of bribes, that stoppeth his ears from hearing of blood, and shutteth his eyes from seeing evil; He shall dwell on high: his defence shall be the munitions of rocks: bread shall be given him; his waters shall be sure. Isa. 33:15-16

[Do not] say, Let him make speed, and hasten his work, that we may see it: and let the counsel of the Holy One of Israel draw nigh and come, that we may know it! Isa. 5:19

SEDUCE

False Christs and false prophets shall rise, and shall shew signs and wonders, to seduce, if it were possible, even the elect. Mark 13:22

SEED

If ye have faith as a grain of mustard seed, ye shall say unto this mountain, Remove hence to yonder place; and it shall remove; and nothing shall be impossible unto you. Matt. 17:20

SEEK, SOUGHT

We believe in being honest, true, chaste, benevolent, virtuous, and in doing good to all men; indeed, we may say that we follow the admonition of Paul - We believe all things, we hope all things, we have endured many things, and hope to be able to endure all things. If there is anything virtuous, lovely, or of good report or praise-worthy, we seek after these things. A of F-13

Seek not to counsel the Lord, but to take counsel from his hand. Jacob 4:10

But without faith it is impossible to please him: for he that cometh to God must believe that he is, and that he is a rewarder of them that diligently seek him. Heb. 11:6

It is given unto you to judge, that ye may know good from evil; and the way to judge is as plain, that ye may know with a perfect knowledge, as the daylight is from the dark night. Moro. 7:15

Charity suffereth long, and is kind, and envieth not, and is not puffed up, seeketh not her own, is not easily provoked, thinketh no evil, and rejoiceth not in iniquity but rejoiceth in the truth, beareth all things, believeth all things, hopeth all things, endureth all things. Moro. 7:45 (1 Cor. 13:4-7)

Seek the LORD, and his strength: seek his face evermore. Ps. 105:3-4

The wicked, through the pride of his countenance, will not seek after God: God is not in all his thoughts. Ps. 10:4

Beware, lest there shall arise contentions among you, and ye list to obey the evil spirit. Mosiah 2:32

Woe unto them that seek deep to hide their counsel from the LORD and their works are in the dark, and they say, Who seeth us? and who knoweth us? Isa. 29:15

Seek ye the priesthood also. Num. 16:10

I applied mine heart to know, and to search, and to seek out wisdom, and the reason of things, and to know the wickedness of folly, even of foolishness and madness. Eccl. 7:25

Sow to yourselves in righteousness, reap in mercy; break up your fallow ground: for it is time to seek the LORD, till he come and rain righteousness upon you. Hosea 10:12

Seek ye the LORD, all ye meek of the earth, which have wrought his judgment; seek righteousness, seek meekness: it may be ye shall be hid in the day of the LORD's anger. Zeph. 2:3

Come unto me, all ye that labour and are heavy laden, and I will give you rest. Take my yoke upon you, and learn of me; for I am meek and lowly in heart: and ye shall find rest unto your souls. Matt. 11:28-29

When they shall say unto you, Seek unto them that have familiar spirits, and unto wizards that peep, and that mutter: should not a people seek unto their God? Isa. 8:19

Draw nigh to God, and he will draw nigh to you. James 4:8

Evil men understand not judgment: but they that seek the LORD understand all things. Prov. 28:5

Seek ye first the kingdom of God, and his righteousness; and all these things shall be added unto you. Matt. 6:33-34

In the day of my trouble I will call upon thee: for thou wilt answer me. Ps. 86:7

Ask, and it shall be given unto you; seek, and ye shall find; knock, and it shall be opened to you. 3 Ne. 14:7-8

Ask, and it shall be given you; seek, and ye shall find; knock, and it shall be opened unto you. Luke 11:9

Seek after wisdom. 1 Cor. 1:22

An evil and adulterous generation seeketh after a sign; and there shall no sign be given to it, but the sign of the prophet Jonas. Matt. 12:38-39

Thou shalt seek the LORD thy God, thou shalt find him, if thou seek him with all thy heart and with all thy soul. Deut. 4:29

O GOD, thou art my God; early will I seek thee: my soul thirsteth for thee. Ps. 63:1

In the day of my trouble I will call upon thee: for thou wilt answer me. Ps. 86:7

Draw near unto me and I will draw near unto you; seek me diligently and ye shall find me; ask, and ye shall receive; knock, and it shall be opened unto you. D&C 88:63

SELF CONTROL

He that hath no rule over his own spirit is like a city that is broken down and without walls. Prov. 25:28

SEPARATE

All you that are desirous to follow the voice of the good shepherd, come ye out from the wicked, and be ye separate, and touch not their unclean things. Alma 5:57

Your iniquities have separated between you and your God, and your sins have hid his face from you, that he will not hear. Isa. 59:2

Who shall separate us from the love of Christ? shall tribulation, or distress, or persecution, or famine, or nakedness, or peril, or sword? Rom. 8:35

And before him shall be gathered all nations: and he shall separate them one from another, as a shepherd divideth his sheep from the goats. Matt. 25:32

SERVANT

Whosoever will be chief among you, let him be your servant. Matt. 20:27

Masters, give unto your servants that which is just and equal; knowing that ye also have a Master in heaven. Col. 4:1

Do I now persuade men, or God? or do I seek to please men? for if I yet pleased men, I should not be the servant of Christ. Gal. 1:10

Repent ye, and seek no more to destroy my servants whom I have sent unto you to declare good tidings. Hel. 5:29

Help thy servants to say, with thy grace assisting them: Thy will be done, O Lord, and not ours. D&C 109:44

Ye that is called in the Lord, being a servant is the Lord's freeman: likewise also he that is called, being free, is Christ's servant. Ye are bought with a price; be not ye the servants of men. 1 Cor 7:22-23

As the LORD liveth, and as my lord the king liveth, surely in what place my lord the king shall be, whether in death or life, even there also will thy servant be. 2 Sam 15:21

So is the will of God, that with well doing ye may put to silence the ignorance of foolish men: As free, and not using your liberty for a cloke of maliciousness, but as the servants of God. 1 Pet. 2:15-16

Discern between the righteous and the wicked, between him that serveth God and him that serveth him not. 3 Ne. 24:18

Servants, be obedient to them that are your masters according to the flesh, with fear and trembling, in singleness of your heart, as unto Christ. Eph. 6:5

If thou wilt be a servant unto this people this day, and wilt serve them, and answer them, and speak good words to them, then they will be thy servants for ever. 1 Kgs. 12:7

Blessed be he that cometh in the name of the LORD: we have blessed you out of the house of the LORD. Ps. 118:26

Remember these, O Jacob and Israel; for thou art my servant: I have formed thee; thou art my servant; O Israel, thou shalt not be forgotten of me. Isa. 44:21

Who is among you that feareth the LORD, that obeyeth the voice of his servant, that walketh in darkness, and hath no light? let him trust in the name of the LORD, and stay upon his God. Isa. 50:10

Blessed be the God of Shadrach, Meshach, and Abed-nego, who hath sent his angel, and delivered his servants that trusted in him, and have changed the king's word, and yielded their bodies, that they might not serve nor worship any god, except their own God. Dan. 3:28

He that receiveth you receiveth me, and he that receiveth me receiveth him that sent me. He that receiveth a prophet in the name of a prophet shall receive a prophet's reward; and he that receiveth a righteous man in the name of a righteous man shall receive a righteous man's reward. Matt. 10:40-41

SERVE, SERVICE

Choose ye this day, to serve the Lord God who made you. Moses 6:33

Turn not aside from following the LORD, but serve the LORD with all your heart. 1 Sam 12:20

Ye will not suffer your children that they go hungry, or naked; neither will ye suffer that they transgress the laws of God, and fight and quarrel one with another. Mosiah 4:14

Turn to the Lord with full purpose of heart, and put your trust in him, and serve him with all diligence of mind. Mosiah 7:33

Thy God whom thou servest continually, he will deliver thee. Dan. 6:16

[Serve] the LORD thy God with joyfulness, and with gladness of heart, for the abundance of all things. Deut. 28:47

Thou shalt fear the lord thy God; Him shalt thou serve, and to Him shalt thou cleave, and swear by His name. Deut. 10:20

Be not now negligent: for the LORD hath chosen you to stand before him, to serve him, and that ye should minister unto him. 2 Chron. 29:11

Woe unto him that buildeth his house in unrighteousness, and his chambers by wrong; that useth his neighbour's service without wages, and giveth him not for his work. Jer. 22:13

Worship God, for him only shalt thou serve. Moses 1:15

By love, serve one another. Gal. 5:13

Choose ye this day, whom ye will serve. Alma 30:8

Turn to the Lord with full purpose of heart, and put your trust in him, and serve him with all diligence of mind. Mosiah 7:33

Serve the living and true God. 1 Thes. 1:9

No man can serve two masters: for either he will hate the one, and love the other; or else he will hold to the one, and despise the other. Ye cannot serve God and mammon. Matt. 6:24

If it seem evil unto you to serve the LORD, choose you this day whom ye will serve; whether the gods which your fathers served that were on the other side of the flood, or the gods of the Amorites, in whose land ye dwell: but as for me and my house, we will serve the LORD. Josh. 24:15

Ye shall serve the LORD your God, and he shall bless thy bread, and thy water; and I will take sickness away from the midst of thee. Ex. 23:25

I say unto you that if ye should serve him who has created you from the beginning, and is preserving you from day to day, by lending you breath, that ye may live and move and do according to your own will, and even supporting you from one moment to another - I say, if ye should serve him with all your whole souls yet ye would be unprofitable servants. Mosiah 2:21

Thou shalt love the Lord thy God with all thy heart, with all thy might, mind and strength; and in the name of Jesus Christ thou shalt serve him. D&C 59:5

SEVEN, SEVENTH

I saw another sign in heaven, great and marvellous, seven angels having the seven last plagues; for in them is filled up the wrath of God. Rev. 15:1

The seventh day is the sabbath of the LORD thy God: in it thou shalt not do any work, thou, nor thy son, nor thy daughter, thy manservant, nor thy maidservant, nor thy cattle, nor thy stranger that is within thy gates: Ex. 20:10

Then came Peter to him, and said, Lord, how oft shall my brother sin against me, and I forgive him? till seven times? Jesus saith unto him, I say not unto thee, Until seven times: but, until seventy times seven. Matt. 18:21-22

SEVENTY

The Lord appointed other seventy also, and sent them two by two before his face into every city and place, whither he himself would come. Luke 10:1

SHEEP

Feed my sheep. John 21:16

My sheep hear my voice, and I know them, and they follow me; And I give unto them eternal life; and they shall never perish, neither shall any man pluck them our of my hand. John 10:27

Woe be unto the pastors that destroy and scatter the sheep of my pasture! saith the LORD. Jer. 23:1

Beware of false prophets, which come to you in sheep's clothing, but inwardly they are ravening wolves. Ye shall know them by their fruits. Matt. 7:15-16

And before him shall be gathered all nations: and he shall separate them one from another, as a shepherd divideth his sheep from the goats. Matt. 25:32

What shepherd is there among you having many sheep doth not watch over them? Alma 5:59

SHEPHERD

When the chief Shepherd shall appear, ye shall receive a crown of glory that fadeth not away. 1 Pet. 5:4

All you that are desirous to follow the voice of the good shepherd, come ye out from the wicked, and be ye separate, and touch not their unclean things. Alma 5:57

SICK, SICKNESS

That ye may walk guiltless before God, I would that ye should impart of your substance to the poor, every man according to that which he hath, such as feeding the hungry, clothing the naked, visiting the sick and administering to their relief, both spiritually and temporally, according to their wants. Mosiah 4:26

SIGN

Discern the signs of the times. Matt. 16:3

Therefore shall ye lay up these my words in your heart and in your soul, and bind them for a sign upon your hand, that they may be as frontlets between your eyes. Deut. 11:18

I saw another sign in heaven, great and marvellous, seven angels having the seven last plagues; for in them is filled up the wrath of God. Rev. 15:1

[Do not] say, Let him make speed, and hasten his work, that we may see it: and let the counsel of the Holy One of Israel draw nigh and come, that we may know it! Isa. 5:19

False Christs and false prophets shall rise, and shall shew signs and wonders, to seduce, if it were possible, even the elect. Mark 13:22

Thus saith the Lord, learn not the way of the heathen, and be not dismayed at the signs of heaven; for the heathen are dismayed at them. Jer. 10:2

An evil and adulterous generation seeketh after a sign; and there shall no sign be given to it, but the sign of the prophet Jonas. Matt. 12:38-39

What am I that I should tempt God to show unto thee a sign in the thing which thou knowest to be true? Jacob 7:14

Watch therefore: for ye know not what hour your Lord doth come. Matt. 24:42

SILENCE, SILENT

But the LORD is in his holy temple: let all the earth keep silence before him. Hab. 2:20

Be silent, O all flesh, before the LORD: for he is raised up out of his holy habitation. Zech. 2:13

Let the lying lips be put to silence; which speak grievous things proudly and contemptuously against the righteous. Ps. 31:18

SILVER

He that loveth silver shall not be satisfied with silver; nor he that loveth abundance with increase: this is also vanity. Eccl. 5:10

SIMPLE, SIMPLENESS

By small and simple things are great things brought to pass; and small means in many instances doth confound the wise. Alma 37:6-7

He sent fiery flying serpents among them; and after they were bitten he prepared a way that they might be healed; and the labor which they had to perform was to look, and because of the simpleness of the way, or the easiness of it, there were many who perished. 1 Ne. 17:41

SIN

I will declare mine iniquity; I will be sorry for my sin. Ps. 38:18

Seeing we also are compassed about with so great a cloud of witnesses, let us lay aside every weight, and the sin which doth so easily beset us, and let us run with patience the race that is set before us. Heb. 12:1

Speaketh harshly against sin, according to the plainness of the truth. 2 Ne. 33:5

And above all things have fervent charity among yourselves: for charity shall cover the multitude of sins. 1 Pet 4:8

When thou shalt vow a vow unto the LORD thy God, thou shalt not slack to pay it: for the LORD thy God will surely require it of thee; and it would be sin in thee. Deut. 23:21

The Lord surely should come to redeem his people, but that he should not come to redeem them in their sins, but to redeem them from their sins. Hel. 5:10

He that persists in his own carnal nature, and goes on in the ways of sin and rebellion against God, remaineth in his fallen state and the devil hath all power over him. Mosiah 16:5

Go your ways and sin no more. D&C 6:35

Let your sins trouble you with that trouble which shall bring you down unto repentance. Alma 42:29

Knowing that Christ being raised from the dead dieth no more; death hath no more dominion over him. For in that he died, he died unto sin once: but in that he liveth, he liveth unto God. Likewise reckon ye also yourselves to be dead indeed unto sin, but alive unto God through Jesus Christ our Lord. Rom. 6:9-11

Do not endeavor to excuse yourself in the least point because of your sins, by denying the justice of God; but do you let the justice of God, and his mercy, and his long suffering have full sway in your heart, and let it bring you down to the dust in humility. Alma 42:30

Be purified and cleansed from all sin. D&C 50:28

He that covereth his sins shall not prosper: but whoso confesseth and forsaketh them shall have mercy. Prov. 28:13

Suffer not thy mouth to cause thy flesh to sin; neither say thou before the angel, that it was an error. Eccl. 5:6

Cry aloud, spare not, lift up thy voice like a trumpet, and shew my people their transgression, and the house of Jacob their sins. Isa. 58:1

If thou warn the righteous man, that the righteous sin not, and he doth not sin, he shall surely live, because he is warned; also thou hast delivered thy soul. Ezek. 3:21

Sin not. Ex. 20:20

Woe unto them that draw iniquity with cords of vanity, and sin as it were with a cart rope. Isa. 5:18

Turn from transgression. Isa. 59:20

He that sinneth against me wrongeth his own soul: all they that hate me love death. Prov. 8:36

Turn away from your sins; shake off the chains of him that would bind you fast; come unto that God who is the rock of your salvation. 2 Ne. 9:45

Behold, my soul abhorreth sin, and my heart delighteth in righteousness; and I will praise the holy name of my God. 2 Ne. 9:49

Bear thine own shame for thy sins that thou hast committed. Ezek. 16:52

SINCERE, SINCERITY

Approve things that are excellent; that ye may be sincere and without offense till the day of Christ. Philip. 1:10

As newborn babes, desire the sincere milk of the word, that ye may grow thereby. 1 Pet. 2:2

SING, SONG

Is any merry? Let him sing psalms. James 5:13

If thou art merry, praise the Lord with singing, with music, with dancing, and with a prayer of praise and thanksgiving. If thou art sorrowful, call on the Lord thy God with supplication, that your souls may be joyful. D&C 136:28-29

If ye have experienced a change of heart, and if ye have felt to sing the song of redeeming love, I would ask, can ye feel so now? Alma 5:26

Blessed be the name of our God; let us sing to his praise, yea, let us give thanks to his holy name, for he doth work righteousness forever. Alma 26:8

Sing ceaseless praises with the choirs above, unto the Father, and unto the Son, and unto the Holy Ghost, which are one God, in a state of happiness which hath no end. Morm. 7:7

Let the word of Christ dwell in you richly in all wisdom; teaching and admonishing one another in psalms and hymns and spiritual songs, singing with grace in your hearts to the Lord. Col. 3:16

Behold, God is my salvation; I will trust, and not be afraid; for the Lord JEHOVAH is my strength and my song; he also has become my salvation. 2 Ne. 22:2

The ransomed of the LORD shall return, and come to Zion with songs and everlasting joy upon their heads: they shall obtain joy and gladness, and sorrow and sighing shall flee away. Isa. 35:10

Sing praise to the name of the LORD most high. Ps. 7:17

SISTER

He stretched forth his hand toward his disciples, and said, Behold my mother and my brethren! For whosoever shall do the will of m Father which is in heaven, the same is my brother, and sister, and mother. Matt. 12:49-50

SLACK, SLAKEN

In that day it shall be said to Jerusalem, Fear thou not: and to Zion, Let not thine hands be slack. Zeph. 3:16

SLANDER

He that hideth hatred with lying lips, and he that uttereth a slander, is a fool. Prov. 10:18

SLEEP, SLEPT

Love not sleep, lest thou come to poverty. Prov. 20:13

Cease to sleep longer than is needful; retire to thy bed early, that ye may not be weary; arise early, that your bodies and your minds may be invigorated. D&C 88:124

SLOTHFUL, SLOTHFULNESS

They were slothful, and forgot to exercise their faith and diligence. Alma 37:41

Oh my son, do not let us be slothful because of the easiness of the way; for so was it with our fathers; for so was it prepared for them, that if they would look they might live; even so it is with us. The way is prepared, and if we will look we may live forever. Alma 37:46

Be not slothful, but followers of them who through faith and patience inherit the promises. Heb. 6:12

He also that is slothful in his work is brother to him that is a great waster. Prov. 18:9

SMITE, SMITTEN, SMOTE

The scripture says - man shall not smite, neither shall he judge; for judgment is mine, saith the Lord, and vengeance is mine also, and I will repay. Morm. 8:20

I gave my back to the smiters and my cheeks to them that plucked off the hair: I hid not my face from shame and spitting. For the Lord GOD will help me; therefore shall I not be confounded. Isa. 50:6-7

SOBER, SOBERNESS

Be sober. D&C 6:19

Ye will teach them to walk in the ways of truth and soberness. Mosiah 4:15

Cease drunkenness. D&C 136:24

Be sober, be vigilant; because your adversary the devil, as a roaring lion, walketh about, seeking whom he may devour: 1 Pet. 5:8

Go unto this people and declare the word, and be sober. Alma 37:47

Take upon you the name of Christ, and speak the truth in soberness. D&C 18:21

Young men likewise exhort to be sober minded. Titus 2:6

SORCERER, SORCERY

By thy sorceries were all nations deceived. Rev. 18:23

Hearken not ye to your prophets, nor to your diviners, nor to your dreamers, nor to your enchantments, nor to your sorcerers, which speak unto you, saying, Ye shall not serve the king of Babylon: For they prophesy a lie unto you. Jer. 27:9-10

SORROW, SORROWFUL

My soul shall be filled with sorrow because of this the wickedness of my brethren. Hel. 7:9

If thou art merry, praise the Lord with singing, with music, with dancing, and with a prayer of praise and thanksgiving. If thou art sorrowful, call on the Lord thy God with supplication, that your souls may be joyful. D&C 136:28-29

The love of money is the root of all evil: which while some coveted after, they have erred from the faith, and pierced themselves through with many sorrows. 1 Tim. 6:9

All these are the beginning of sorrows. Then shall they deliver you up to be afflicted, and shall kill you: and ye shall be hated of all nations for my name's sake. And then shall many be offended, and shall betray one another, and shall hate one another. Matt. 24:8-10

SOUL

Whosoever will save his life shall lose it; but whosoever shall lose his life for my sake and the gospel's, the same shall save it. For what shall it profit a man, if he shall gain the whole world, and lose his own soul? Mark 8:36

Behold, my soul abhorreth sin, and my heart delighteth in righteousness; and I will praise the holy name of my God. 2 Ne. 9:49

If thou draw out thy soul to the hungry, and satisfy the afflicted soul; then shall thy light rise in obscurity, and thy darkness be as the noonday: And the LORD shall guide thee continually. Isa. 58:10

I will greatly rejoice in the LORD, my soul shall be joyful in my God; for he hath clothed me with the garments of salvation, he hath covered me with the robe of righteousness. Isa. 61:10

Ye should come unto Christ, who is the Holy One of Israel, and partake of his salvation, and the power of his redemption. Yea, come unto him, and offer your whole souls as an offering unto him and continue in fasting and praying, and endure to the end. Omni 1:26

Thorns and snares are in the way of the froward: he that doth keep his soul shall be far from them. Prov. 22:5

Fear not them which kill the body, but are not able to kill the soul: but rather fear him which is able to destroy both soul and body in hell. Matt. 10:28

SOUND

This witness is true. Wherefore rebuke them sharply, that they may be sound in the faith. Titus 1:13

Speak thou the things which become sound doctrine: That the aged men be sober, grave, temperate, sound in faith, in charity, in patience. Titus 2:1-2

Hold fast the form of sound words, which thou hast heard of me, in faith and love which is in Christ Jesus. 2 Tim. 1:13

SOW, SOWER, SOWN

Break up your fallow ground, and sow not among thorns. Jer. 4:3

He that soweth to his flesh shall of the flesh reap corruption; but he that soweth to the Spirit shall of the Spirit reap life everlasting. Gal. 6:8

He that soweth iniquity shall reap vanity: and the rod of his anger shall fail. Prov. 22:8

He which soweth sparingly shall reap also sparingly; and he which soweth bountifully shall reap also bountifully. 2 Cor. 9:6

Another parable put he forth unto them, saying, The kingdom of heaven is like to a grain of mustard seed, which a man took, and sowed in his field. Matt. 13:31

Be not deceived; God is not mocked: for whatsoever a man soweth, that shall he also reap. Galtians 6:7

SPARE, SPARED, SPARINGLY

He which soweth sparingly shall reap also sparingly; and he which soweth bountifully shall reap also bountifully. 2 Cor. 9:6

SPEAK, SPOKEN

He that speaketh flattery to his friends, even the eyes of his children shall fail. Job 17:5

Cease from all your light speeches, from all laughter, from all your lustful desires, from all your pride and light-mindedness, and from all your wicked doings. D&C 88:121

Use boldness, but not overbearance. Alma 38:12

I know that the words of truth are hard against all uncleanness; but the righteous fear them not, for they love the truth and are not shaken. 2 Ne. 9:40

Though I speak with the tongues of men and of angels, and have not charity, I am become as sounding brass, or a tinkling cymbal. 1 Cor. 13:1

Speak not with a stiff neck. Ps. 75:5

For my soul delighteth in plainness; for after this manner doth the Lord God work among the children of men. For the Lord God giveth light unto the understanding; for he speaketh unto men according to their language, unto their understanding. 2 Ne. 31:3

These things have I spoken unto you in proverbs: but the time cometh, when I shall no more speak unto you in proverbs, but I shall shew you plainly of the Father. John 16:25

Speak concerning the doctrine of Christ. 2 Ne. 31:2

Speak in the name of God the Lord, even the Savior of the world. D&C 1:20

Let every man be swift to hear, slow to speak, slow to wrath. James 1:19

The Lord GOD hath given me the tongue of the learned, that I should know how to speak a word in season to him that is weary. Isa. 50:4

Take no thought how or what ye shall speak: for it shall be given you in that same hour what ye shall speak. For it is not ye that speak, but the Spirit of your Father which speaketh in you. Matt. 10:19-20

He that walketh righteously, and speaketh uprightly; he that despiseth the gain of oppressions, that shaketh his hands from holding of bribes, that stoppeth his ears from hearing of blood, and shutteth his eyes from seeing evil; He shall dwell on high: his defence shall be the munitions of rocks: bread shall be given him; his waters shall be sure. Isa. 33:15-16

Do violence to no man, neither accuse any falsely; and be content with your wages. Luke 3:14

Speaketh truth. Prov. 12:17

A word fitly spoken is like apples of gold in pictures of silver. Prov. 25:11

In all things shewing thyself a pattern of good works: in doctrine shewing uncorruptness, gravity, sincerity, Sound speech, that cannot be condemned; that he that is of the contrary part may be ashamed, having no evil thing to say of you. Titus 2:7-8

Let no corrupt communication proceed out of your mouth, but that which is good to the use of edifying, that it may minister grace unto the hearers. Eph. 4:29

Hear; for I will speak of excellent things; and the opening of my lips shall be right things. For my mouth shall speak truth; and wickedness is an abomination to my lips. Prov. 6:7

Let your speech be alway with grace, seasoned with salt, that ye may know how ye ought to answer every man. Col. 4:6

Say not, I am a child: for thou shalt go to all that I shall send thee, and whatsoever I command thee thou shalt speak. Be not afraid of their faces: for I am with thee to deliver thee, saith the LORD. Jer. 1:7-8

He that hath my word, let him speak my word faithfully. Jer. 23:28

Keep thy tongue from evil, and thy lips from speaking guile. Ps. 34:13

They speak vanity every one with his neighbour: with flattering lips and with a double heart. Ps. 12:2

Speak ye every man the truth to his neighbour; execute the judgment of truth and peace in your gates. Zech. 8:16

Obey, I beseech thee, the voice of the LORD, which I speak unto thee: so it shall be well unto thee, and thy soul shall live. Jer. 38:20

Let the lying lips be put to silence; which speak grievous things proudly and contemptuously against the righteous. Ps. 31:18

Speak evil of no man, to be no brawlers, but gentle, shewing all meekness unto all men. Titus 3:2

Stand in the court of the LORD'S house, and speak unto all the cities of Judah, which come to worship in the LORD's house, all the words that I command thee to speak unto them; diminish not a word. Jer. 26:2

When a man speaketh by the power of the Holy Ghost, the power of the Holy Ghost carrieth it unto the hearts of the children of men. 2 Ne. 33:1

For he that will love life, and see good days, let him refrain his tongue from evil, and his lips that they speak no guile: Let him eschew evil, and do good; let him seek peace, and ensue it. 1 Pet. 3:10-11

Speak freely to all; yea, preach, exhort, declare the truth. D&C 19:37

Speaketh harshly against sin, according to the plainness of the truth. 2 Ne. 33:5

My lips shall not speak wickedness, nor my tongue utter deceit. Job 27:4

Speak forth the words of truth and soberness. Acts 26:25

Take heed to speak that which the Lord hath put in thy mouth. Num. 23:12

SPIRIT

They that are after the flesh do mind the things of the flesh; but they that are after the Spirit the things of the Spirit. For to be carnally minded is death; but to be spiritually minded is life and peace. Rom. 8:5-6

Worship God in spirit and in truth, the true and the living God. Alma 43:10

Jesus answered, Verily, verily, I say unto thee, Except a man be born of water and of the Spirit, he cannot enter into the kingdom of God. John 3:5

The Spirit shall be given unto you by the prayer of faith; and if ye receive not the Spirit ye shall not teach. D&C 42:14

He that is slow to anger is better than the mighty; and he that ruleth his spirit than he that taketh a city. Prov. 16:32

Eye hath not seen, nor ear heard, neither have entered into the heart of man, the things which God hath prepared for them that love him. But God hath reveled them unto us by his Spirit; for the Spirit searcheth all things, yea, the deep things of God. 1 Cor. 2:9-10

He that soweth to his flesh shall of the flesh reap corruption; but he that soweth to the Spirit shall of the Spirit reap life everlasting. Gal. 6:8

The natural man receiveth not the things of the Spirit of God: for they are foolishness unto him: neither can he know them, because they are spiritually discerned. 1 Cor. 2:14

Take no thought how or what ye shall speak: for it shall be given you in that same hour what ye shall speak. For it is not ye that speak, but the Spirit of your Father which speaketh in you. Matt. 10:19-20

Be not drunk with wine, wherein is excess; but be filled with the Spirit. Eph. 5:18

If any man among you be strong in the Spirit, let him take with him him that is weak, that he may be edified in all meekness, that he may become strong also. D&C 84:106

Be directed by the Spirit. D&C 42:13

Quench not the spirit. 1 Thes. 5:19

He that hath no rule over his own spirit is like a city that is broken down and without walls. Prov. 25:28

SPIRITUAL, SPIRITUALITY, SPIRITUALLY

Be spiritually minded. Rom. 8:6

SPITE

Love your enemies, bless them that curse you, do good to them that hate you, and pray for them which despitefully use you, and persecute you. Matt. 5:44

SPOIL

Lay not wait, O wicked man, against the dwelling of the righteous; spoil not his resting place: For a just man falleth seven times, and riseth up again: but the wicked shall fall into mischief. Prov. 24:15-16

SPRANG, SPRINGING, SPRUNG

But whosoever drinketh of the water that I shall give him shall never thirst; but the water that I shall give him shall be in him a well of water springing up into everlasting life. John 4:14

STAKES

Enlarge the place of thy tent, and let them stretch forth the curtains of thine habitations; spare not, lengthen the cords, and strengthen thy stakes. Isa. 54:2-3

STAND, STAND FAST, STEADFAST

Stand fast in the faith of Christ. Alma 46:27

The grass withereth, the flower fadeth: but the word of our God shall stand for ever. Isa. 40:8

Look forward with steadfastness unto Christ. 2 Ne. 25:24

Thus saith the LORD, Stand ye in the ways, and see, and ask for the old paths, where is the good way, and walk therein, and ye shall find rest for your souls. Jer. 6:16

Stand fast in the liberty where with ye have been made free. Mosiah 23:13

I have set the LORD always before me: because he is at my right hand, I shall not be moved. Ps. 16:8

Be ye stedfast, unmoveable, always abounding in the work of the Lord, forasmuch as ye know that your labour is not in vain in the Lord. 1 Cor. 15:58

Ye must press forward with a steadfastness in Christ having a perfect brightness of hope, and a love of God and of all men. 2 Ne. 31:20

Stand fast therefore in the liberty wherewith Christ hath made us free, and be not entangled again in the yoke of bondage. Gal. 5:1

I will forgive you of your sins with this commandment - that you remain steadfast in your minds in solemnity and the spirit of prayer, in bearing testimony to all the world of those things which are communicated unto you. D&C 84:61

Stand as witnesses of God at all times and in all things, and in all places. Mosiah 18:9

STANDARD

Lift up a standard for the people. Isa. 62:10

STATURE

Jesus increased in wisdom and stature, and in favour with God and man. Luke 2:52

STATUTE

I have inclined mine heart to perform thy statutes always, even unto the end. Ps. 119:112

STEAL

Thou shalt not steal. Ex. 20:15

Lay not up for yourselves treasures upon earth, where moth and rust doth corrupt, and where thieves break through and steal: But lay up for yourselves treasures in heaven, where neither moth nor rust doth corrupt, and where thieves do not break through nor steal: For where your treasure is, there will your heart be also. Matt. 6:19-21

STEWARD, STEWARDSHIP

His lord said unto him: Well done, thou good and faithful servant: thou hast been faithful over a few things, I will make thee ruler over many things: enter thou into the joy of thy lord. Matt. 25:21

Unto whomsoever much is given, of him shall be much required: and to whom men have committed much, of him they will ask the more. Luke 12:48

STICK

Moreover, thou son of man, take thee one stick, and write upon it, For Judah, and for the children of Israel his companions: then take another stick, and write upon it For Joseph, the stick of Ephraim, and for all the house of Israel his companions: And join them one to another into one stick; and they shall become one in thine hand. Ezek. 37:16-17

STIFFNECKED, STIFFNECKEDNESS

Speak not with a stiff neck. Ps. 75:5

Be ye not stiffnecked, as your fathers were, but yield yourselves unto the Lord. 2 Chron. 30:8

O ye wicked and ye perverse generation; ye hardened and ye stiffnecked people, how long will ye suppose that the Lord will suffer you? Yea, how long will ye suffer yourselves to be led by foolish and blind guides? Yea, how long will ye choose darkness rather than light? Hel. 13:29

STIR

Stir them up in remembrance of the Lord their God, and perhaps they will repent and turn unto thee. Hel. 11:4

Behold, this is not my doctrine, to stir up the hearts of men with anger, one against another; but this is my doctrine, that such things should be done away. 3 Ne. 11:30

STONE

Have ye not read this scripture; The stone which the builders rejected is become the head of the corner? Mark 12:10

Be it known unto you all, and to all the people of Israel, that by the name of Jesus Christ of Nazareth, whom ye crucified, whom God raised from the dead, even by him doth this man stand here before you whole. This is the stone which was set at nought of you builders, which is become the head of the corner. Neither is there salvation in any other: for there is none other name under heaven given among men, whereby we must be saved. Acts 4:10-12

STORE, STOREHOUSE

Bring ye all the tithes into the storehouse, that there may be meat in mine house, and prove me now herewith, saith the LORD of hosts, if I will not open you the windows of heaven, and pour you out a blessing. Mal. 3:8-12

Bring ye all the tithes into the storehouse, that there may be meat in my house; and prove me now herewith, saith the Lord of Hosts, if I will not open you the windows of heaven, and pour you out a blessing that there shall not be room enough to receive it. And I will rebuke the devourer for your sakes, and he shall not destroy the fruits of your ground; neither shall your vine cast her fruit before the time in the fields, saith the Lord of Hosts. 3 Ne. 24:10-11

STOUT, STOUTHEARTED

I will punish the fruit of the stout heart. 2 Ne. 20:12

Hearken unto me, ye stouthearted, that are far from righteousness. Isa. 46:12

STRAIGHT, STRAIT

Strive to enter in at the strait gate: for many, I say unto you, will seek to enter in, and shall not be able. Luke 13:24

O then, my beloved brethren, repent ye, and enter in at the strait gate, and continue in the way which is narrow. Jacob 6:11

Enter ye in at the strait gate; for wide is the gate, and broad is the way, which leadeth to destruction, and many there be who go in thereat; Because strait is the gate, and narrow is the way, which leadeth unto life, and few there be that find it. 3 Ne. 14:13-14 (Matt. 7:13-14)

I will go before thee, and make the crooked places straight: I will break in pieces the gates of brass, and cut in sunder the bars of iron. Isa. 45:2

STRANGER

Ye shall have one manner of law, as well for the stranger, as for one of your own country: for I am the LORD your God. Lev. 24:22

Oppress not the widow, nor the fatherless, the stranger, nor the poor; and let none of you imagine evil against his brother in your heart. Zech. 7:10

Be not forgetful to entertain strangers: for thereby some have entertained angels unawares. Heb. 13:2

If a stranger sojourn with thee in your land, ye shall not vex him, But the stranger that dwelleth with you shall be unto you as one born among you, and thou shalt love him as thyself. Lev. 19:33-34

STRENGTH, STRENGTHEN

I know, in the strength of the Lord thou canst do all things. Alma 20:4

I can do all things through Christ which strengtheneth me. Philip. 4:13

They that wait upon the Lord shall renew their strength; they shall mount up with wings as eagles; they shall run, and not be weary; and they shall walk, and not faint. Isa. 40:31

Enlarge the place of thy tent, and let them stretch forth the curtains of thine habitations; spare not, lengthen the cords, and strengthen thy stakes. Isa. 54:2-3

Why do ye commit whoredoms and spend your strength with harlots? Mosiah 12:29

See that ye do not boast in your own wisdom, nor of your much strength. Alma 38:11

I will not boast of myself, but I will boast of my God, for in his strength I can do all things. Alma 26:12

Go in the strength of the Lord GOD: I will make mention of thy righteousness, even of thine only. Ps. 71:16

Give not thy strength to women, nor thy ways to that which destroyeth kings. Prov. 31:3

Ascribe ye strength unto God; his excellency is over Israel, and his strength is in the clouds. Ps. 68:34

Strengthen ye the weak hands, and confirm the feeble knees. Say to them that are of a fearful heart, Be strong, fear not: behold, your God will come with vengeance, even God with a recompense; he will come and save you. Isa. 35:3-4

Behold, God is my salvation; I will trust, and not be afraid; for the Lord JEHOVAH is my strength and my song; he also has become my salvation. 2 Ne. 22:2

Therefore, strengthen your brethren in all your conversation, in all your prayers, in all your exhortations, and in all your doings. D&C 108:7

STRICT

They are strict to remember the Lord their God from day to day; yea, they do observe to keep his statutes, and his judgments, and his commandments continually. Alma 58:40

STRIFE

Walk honestly, as in the day; not in rioting and drunkenness, not in chambering and wantonness, not in strife and envying. Rom. 13:13

He is proud, knowing nothing, but doting about questions and strifes of words, whereof cometh envy, strife, railings, evil surmisings, Perverse disputings of men of corrupt minds, and destitute of the truth, supposing that gain is godliness: from such withdraw thyself. 1 Tim. 6:4-5

For where envying and strife is, there is confusion and every evil work. James 3:16

Let there be no strife, I pray thee, between me and thee, and between my herdmen and thy herdmen; for we be brethren. Gen. 13:8

STRIKE

Be not thou one of them that strike hands, or of them that are sureties for debts. Prov. 22:26

STRIVE, STROVE

Go not hastily to strive, lest thou know not what to do in the end thereof, when thy neighbour hath put thee to shame. Prov. 25:8

Of these things put them in remembrance, charging them before the Lord that they strive not about words to no profit, but to the subverting of the hearers. 2 Tim. 2:14

Woe unto him that striveth with his Maker! Isa. 45:9

Strive to enter in at the strait gate: for many, I say unto you, will seek to enter in, and shall not be able. Luke 13:24

STRONG, STRONGER, STRONGEST

Be strong, all ye people of the land, saith the LORD, and work: for I am with you, saith the LORD of hosts. Hag. 2:4

Wine is a mocker, strong drink is raging: and whosoever is deceived thereby is not wise. Prov. 20:1

Let us be strong like unto Moses. 1 Ne. 4:2

STUBBORN, STUBBORNESS

For rebellion is as the sin of witchcraft, and stubbornness is as iniquity and idolatry. Because thou hast rejected the word of the LORD, he hath also rejected thee from being king. 1 Sam 15:23

STUDY

As all have not faith, seek ye diligently and teach one another words of wisdom; yea, seek ye out of the best books words of wisdom; seek learning, even by study and also by faith. D&C 88:118

Study to shew thyself approved unto God, a workman that needeth not to be ashamed, rightly dividing the word of truth. 2 Tim. 2:15

Study and learn, and become acquainted with all good books and with languages, tongues, and people. D&C 90:15

Let your time be devoted to the studying of the scriptures. D&C 26:1

The heart of the righteous studieth to answer: but the mouth of the wicked poureth out evil things. Prov. 15:28

STUMBLE, STUMBLING BLOCK

Let us not therefore judge one another any more: but judge this rather, that no man put a stumbling block or an occasion to fall in his brother's way. Rom. 14:13

SUBJECT, SUBJECTION

We believe in being subject to kings, presidents, rulers, and magistrates, in obeying, honoring, and sustaining the law. A of F-12

I keep under my body, and bring it into subjection: lest that by any means, when I have preached to others, I myself should be a castaway. 1 Cor. 9:27

SUBMIT

Likewise, ye younger, submit your-selves unto the elder. Yea, all of you be subject one to another, and be clothed with humility: for God resisteth the proud, and giveth grace to the humble. 1 Pet. 5:5

Wives, submit yourselves unto your own husbands as unto the Lord. For the husband is the head of the wife, even as Christ is the head of the church: and he is the saviour of the body. Therefore as the church is subject unto Christ, so let the wives be to their own husbands in every thing. Eph. 5:22-24

Submit cheerfully and with patience to all the will of the Lord. Mosiah 24:15

SUBSTANCE

Honour the Lord with thy substance, and with the first fruits of all thine increase. Prov. 3:9-10

Think of your brethren like unto yourselves, and be familiar with all and free with your substance, that they may be rich like unto you. Jacob 2:17

SUBTLE, SUBTLETY

O full of all subtilty and all mischief, thou child of the devil, thou enemy of all righteousness, wilt thou not cease to pervert the right ways of the Lord. Acts 13:10

SUCCESS

My joy is more full because of the success of my brethren. Alma 29:14

This book of the law shall not depart out of thy mouth; but thou shalt meditate therein day and night, that thou mayest observe to do according to all that is written therein: for then thou shalt make thy way prosperous, and then thou shalt have good success. Josh. 1:8

SUCCOR

Succor those that stand in need of your succor; ye will administer of your substance unto him that standeth in need; and ye will not suffer that the beggar putteth up his petition to you in vain, and turn him out to perish. Mosiah 4:16

SUE

If any man will sue thee at the law and take away thy coat, let him have thy cloak also. 3 Ne. 12:40 (Matt. 5:40)

SUFFER, SUFFERING

Ye will not suffer your children that they go hungry, or naked; neither will ye suffer that they transgress the laws of God, and fight and quarrel one with another, and serve the devil, who is the master of sin, or who is the evil spirit which hath been spoken of by our fathers, he being an enemy to all righteousness. Mosiah 4:14

Whosoever shall put their trust in God shall be supported in their trials, and their troubles, and their afflictions. Alma 36:3

They spit upon him, and he suffereth it, because of his loving kindness and his long-suffering towards the children of men. 1 Ne. 19:9

Charity suffereth long, and is kind, and envieth not, and is not puffed up, seeketh not her own, is not easily provoked, thinketh no evil, and rejoiceth not in iniquity but rejoiceth in the truth, beareth all things, believeth all things, hopeth all things, endureth all things. Moro. 7:45 (1 Cor. 13:4-7)

SUFFICIENT

Eat so much as is sufficient for thee, lest thou be filled therewith, and vomit it. Prov. 25:16

SUPERSTITIOUS

Paul stood in the midst of Mars' hill, and said, Ye men of Athens, I perceive that in all things ye are too superstitious. Acts 17:22

SUPPLICATION

I have come having great hopes and much desire that I should find that ye had humbled yourselves before God, and that ye had continued in the supplicating of his grace, that I should find that ye were blameless before him. Alma 7:3

If thou art merry, praise the Lord with singing, with music, with dancing, and with a prayer of praise and thanksgiving. If thou art sorrowful, call on the Lord thy God with supplication, that your souls may be joyful. D&C 136:28-29

SUPPORT

Cry unto God for all thy support; yea, let all thy doings be unto the Lord, and whithersoever thou goest let it be in the Lord; yea, let all thy thoughts be directed unto the Lord; yea, let the affections of thy heart be placed upon the Lord forever. Alma 37:36

Every man should impart to the support of the widows and their children, that they might not perish with hunger. Mosiah 21:17

SWEAR, SWORN

Swear not, neither by heaven, neither by the earth, neither by any other oath: but let your yea be yea; and your nay, nay; lest ye fall into condemnation. James 5:12

Woe unto you, ye blind guides, which say, Whosoever shall swear by the temple, it is nothing; but whosoever shall swear by the gold of the temple, he is a debtor! Ye fools and blind: for whether is greater, the gold, or the temple that sanctifieth the gold? And, Whosoever shall swear by the altar, it is nothing; but whosoever sweareth by the gift that is upon it, he is guilty. Matt. 23:16-18

The LORD hath a controversy with the inhabitants of the land, because there is no truth, nor mercy, nor knowledge of God in the land. By swearing, and lying, and killing, and stealing, and committing adultery, they break out, and blood toucheth blood. Hosea 4:1-2

SWIFT, SWIFTLY

Ye are swift to do iniquity but slow to remember the Lord your God. 1 Ne. 17:45

SWORD

Be ye afraid of the sword: for wrath bringeth the punishments of the sword, that ye may know there is a judgment. Job 19:29

TABERNACLE

LORD, who shall abide in thy tabernacle? Who shall dwell in thy holy hill? He that walketh uprightly, and worketh righteous-ness, and speaketh the truth in his heart. Ps. 15:1-2

TAKE, TAKEN, TOOK

Take upon you the name of Christ, and speak the truth in soberness. D&C 18:21

Take no thought how or what ye shall speak: for it shall be given you in that same hour what ye shall speak. For it is not ye that speak, but the Spirit of your Father which speaketh in you. Matt. 10:19-20

Take therefore no thought for the morrow, for the morrow shall take thought for the things of itself. Sufficient is the day unto the evil thereof. 3 Ne. 13:34

Friend, I do thee no wrong: didst not thou agree with me for a penny? Take that thine is, and go thy way: I will give unto this last, even as unto thee. Matt. 20:1-14

Only take heed to thyself, and keep thy soul diligently, lest thou forget the things which thine eyes have seen, and lest they depart from thine heart all the days of thy life: but teach them thy sons, and thy sons sons. Deut. 4:9

There hath no temptation taken you but such as is common to man: but God is faithful, who will not suffer you to be tempted above that ye are able; but will with the temptation also make a way to escape, that ye may be able to bear it. 1 Cor. 10:13

TALEBEARER

Thou shalt not go up and down as a tale-bearer among thy people. Lev. 19:16

TALENT

Well done thou good and faithful servant: thou hast been faithful over a few things, I will make thee ruler over many things; enter thou into the joy of thy lord. Matt. 25:21

Thou shalt not idle away thy time, neither shalt thou bury thy talent that it may not be known. D&C 60:13

TALK

When I speak with thee, I will open thy mouth, and thou shalt say unto them, Thus saith the Lord GOD; He that heareth, let him hear; and he that forbeareth, let him forbear. Ezek. 3:27

TASTE

O taste and see that the LORD is good: blessed is the man that trusteth in him. Ps. 34:8

TAX

Render therefore unto Caesar the things which are Caesar's, and unto God the things that are God's. Matt. 22:21

TEACH, TEACHABLE, TEACHER

Ye will teach them to walk in the ways of truth and soberness. Mosiah 4:15

[King Benjamin] taught them to keep the commandments of God, that they might rejoice and be filled with love towards God and all men. Mosiah 2:4

Teach the young women to be sober, to love their husbands, to love their children, To be discreet, chaste, keepers at home, good, obedient to their own husbands, that the word of God be not blasphemed. Titus 2:4-5

The servant of the Lord must not strive; but be gentle unto all men, apt to teach, patient. 2 Tim. 2:24

Teach any man the right way; for the right way is to believe in Christ and deny him not; for by denying him ye also deny the prophets and the law. 2 Ne. 25:28

Teach them to never be weary of good works. Alma 37:34

For when for the time ye ought to be teachers, ye have need that one teach you again which be the first principles of the oracles of God; and are become such as have need of milk, and not of strong meat. Heb 5:12

Believe in these words, for they are the words of Christ, and he hath given them unto me; and they teach all men that they should do good. 2 Ne. 33:10

There shall be false teachers among you, who privily shall bring in damnable heresies. 2 Pet. 2:1

They shall also teach their children to pray, and to alk uprightly before the Lord. D&C 68:28

Trust no one to be your teacher nor your minister, except he be a man of God, walking in his ways and keeping his commandments. Mosiah 23:14

None received authority to preach or to teach except it were by him from God. Mosiah 23:17

They taught the people the ways of the Lord. Jarom 1:7

Behold, if ye were holy I would speak unto you of holiness; but as yea re not holy, and ye look upon me as a teacher, it must needs be expedient that I teach you the consequences of sin. 2 Ne. 9:48

Come ye, and let us go up to the mountain of the Lord, to the house of the God of Jacob; and he will teach us of his ways, and we will work in his paths; for out of Zion shall go forth the law and the word of the Lord from Jerusalem. 2 Ne. 12:3

There shall be many which shall teach after this manner, false and vain and foolish doctrines. 2 Ne. 28:9

If ye teach the law of Moses, also teach that it is a shadow of those things which are to come. Mosiah 16:14

Teach them that redemption cometh through Christ the Lord, who is the very Eternal Father. Mosiah 16:15

I give unto you a commandment that you shall teach one another the doctrine of the kingdom. D&C 88:77

They had given themselves to much prayer, and fasting; therefore they had the spirit of prophecy, and the spirit of revelation, and when they taught, they taught with power and authority of God. Alma 17:3

Teach them all things pertaining to righteous-ness. Alma 21:23

To one is given by the Spirit of God, that he may teach the word of wisdom. Moro. 10:9

To another, that he may teach the word of knowledge by the same Spirit. Moro. 10:10

I will cast thee from off the face of the earth: this year thou shalt die, because thou hast taught rebellion against the LORD. Jer. 28:16

They were preachers of righteousness, and spake and prophesied, and called upon all men, everywhere, to repent; and faith was taught unto the children of men. Moses 6:23

Appoint among yourselves a teacher, and let not all be spokesmen at once; but let one speak at a time and let all listen unto his sayings, that when all have spoken that all may be edified of all, and that every man may have an equal privilege. D&C 88:122

And these words, which I command thee this day, shall be in thine heart: And thou shalt teach them diligently unto thy children, and shalt talk of them when thou sittest in thine house, and when thou walkest by the way and when thou liest down, and when thou risest up. And thou shalt bind them for a sign upon thine hand, and they shalt be as frontlets between thine eyes. And thou shalt write them upon the posts of thy house, and on thy gates. Deut. 6:6-9

Teach my people the difference between the holy and profane, and cause them to discern between the unclean and the clean. Ezek. 44:23

My father taught me in all the ways of God. Moses 6:41

This people draweth nigh unto me with their mouth, and honoureth me with their lips; but their heart is far from me. But in vain they do worship me, teaching for doctrines the command-ments of men. Matt. 15:8-9

I send you out to reprove the world of all their unrighteous deeds and to teach them of a judgment which is to come. D&C 84:87

Be not carried about with divers and strange doctrines. For it is a good thing that the heart be established with grace; not with meats, which have not profited them that have been occupied therein. Heb. 13:9

The Spirit shall be given unto you by the prayer of faith; and if ye receive not the Spirit ye shall not teach. D&C 42:14

[Appoint] just men to be their teachers. Mosiah 2:4

I give unto you a commandment, to teach these things freely unto your children. Moses 6:58

As all have not faith, seek ye diligently and teach one another words of wisdom; yea, seek ye out of the best books words of wisdom; seek learning, even by study and also by faith. D&C 88:118

Teach ye diligently and my grace shall attend you, that you may be instructed more perfectly in theory, in principle, in doctrine, in the law of the gospel, in all things that pertain unto the kingdom of God, that are expedient for you to understand. D&C 88:78

Thou shalt teach them ordinances and laws, and shalt shew them the way wherein they must walk, and the work that they must do. Ex. 18:20

Teach his commandments unto the children of men, that they also might enter into his rest. Alma 13:6

They should teach nothing save it were the things which he had taught, and which had been spoken by the mouth of the holy prophets. Mosiah 18:19

Yea, we believe all the words which thou hast spoken unto us; and also, we know of their surety and truth, because of the Spirit of the Lord Omnipotent, which has wrought a mighty change in us, or in our hearts, that we have no more disposition to do evil, but to do good continually. Mosiah 5:2

I am called by his Holy Spirit to teach these things unto this people, that they may be brought to a knowledge of that which is just and true. Alma 18:34

We did magnify our office unto the Lord, taking upon us the responsibility, answering the sins of the people upon our own heads if we did not teach them the word of God with all diligence. Jacob 1:19

Teach them to withstand every temptation of the devil, with their faith on the Lord Jesus Christ. Alma 37:33

TEMPERANCE, TEMPERATE

Be patient; be sober; be temperate; have patience, faith, hope and charity. D&C 6:19

I would that ye would be diligent and temperate in all things. Alma 38:10

Every man that striveth for the mastery is temperate in all things. 1 Cor. 9:25

TEMPLE

One thing have I desired of the LORD, that will I seek after; that I may dwell in the house of the LORD all the days of my life, to behold the beauty of the LORD, and to enquire in his temple. Ps. 27:4

They, continuing daily with one accord in the temple, and breaking bread from house to house, did eat their meat with gladness and singleness of heart. Acts 2:46

I will worship toward thy holy temple, and praise thy name for thy lovingkindness and for thy truth: for thou hast magnified thy word above all thy name. Ps. 138:2

Thou oughtest to behave thyself in the house of God, which is the church of the living God, the pillar and ground of the truth. 1 Tim. 3:15

What? Know ye not that your body is a temple of the Holy Ghost which is in you, which ye have of God, and ye are not your own? For ye are bought with a price: therefore glorify God in your body, and in your spirit, which are God's. 1 Cor. 6:20

But the LORD is in his holy temple: let all the earth keep silence before him. Hab. 2:20

There shall in no wise enter into [the temple] any thing that defileth, neither whatsoever worketh abomination, or maketh a lie: but they which are written in the Lamb's book of life. Rev. 21:27

TEMPT, TEMPTATION, TEMPTED

They turned back and tempted God, and limited the Holy One of Israel. Ps. 78:41

Why should I give way to temptations, that the evil one have place in my heart to destroy my peace and afflict my soul? 2 Ne. 4:27

Humble yourselves before the Lord, and call on his holy name, and watch and pray continually, that ye may not be tempted above that which ye can bear, and thus be led by the Holy Spirit, becoming humble, meek, submissive, patient full of love and all long suffering; Having faith on the Lord; having a hope that ye shall receive eternal life; having the love of God always in your heats, that ye may be lifted up at the last day and enter into his rest. Alma 13:28-29

After this manner therefore pray ye: Our Father who art in heaven, hallowed be thy name. Thy will be done on earth as it is in heaven. And forgive us our debts, as we forgive our debtors. And lead us not into temptation, but deliver us from evil. For thine is the kingdom, and the power, and the glory, forever. Amen. 3 Ne. 13:9-13 (Matt. 6:9-13)

What am I that I should tempt God to show unto thee a sign in the thing which thou knowest to be true? Jacob 7:14

Harden not your hearts, as in the provocation, in the day of temptation in the wilderness: When your fathers tempted me, proved me, and saw my works forty years. Heb. 3:8

It must needs be that the devil should tempt the children of men, or they could not be agents unto themselves; for if they never should have bitter they could not know the sweet. D&C 29:39

Endureth temptation. James 1:12-15

Thou shalt not tempt the Lord thy God. Luke 4:12

There hath no temptation taken you but such as is common to man: but God is faithful, who will not suffer you to be tempted above that ye are able; but will with the temptation also make a way to escape, that ye may be able to bear it. 1 Cor. 10:13

They tempted God in their heart by asking meat for their lust. Ps. 78:18

Teach them to withstand every temptation of the devil, with their faith on the Lord Jesus Christ. Alma 37:33

Yield to no temptation. D&C 9:13

TERRESTRIAL

There are also celestial bodies, and bodies terrestrial: but the glory of the celestial is one, and the glory of the terrestrial is another. There is one glory of the sun, and another glory of the moon, and another glory of the stars: for one star differeth from another star in glory. So also is the resurrection of the dead. 1 Cor. 15:40-42

TESTIFY, TESTIMONY

I am thy fellowservant, and of thy brethren that have the testimony of Jesus: worship God: for the testimony of Jesus is the spirit of prophecy. Rev. 19:10

Testify that a man must be obedient to the commandments of God. 1 Ne. 22:30

Ye have received all things, both things in heaven, and all things which are in the earth, as a witness that they are true. Hel. 8:24

I, Jacob spake many more things unto the people of Nephi, warning them against fornication and lasciviousness, and every kind of sin, telling them the awful consequences of them. Jacob 3:12

Confess by the power of the Holy Ghost that Jesus is the Christ. Moro. 7:44

Only take heed to thyself, and keep thy soul diligently, lest thou forget the things which thine eyes have seen, and lest they depart from thine heart all the days of thy life: but teach them thy sons, and thy sons sons. Deut. 4:9

Bind up the testimony, seal the law among my disciples. Isa. 8:16

Testify and warn the people, and it becometh every man who hath been warned to warn his neighbor. D&C 88:81

There was a man sent from God, whose name was John. The same came for a witness, to bear witness of the Light, that all men through him might believe. John 1:7

Declare the things which ye have heard, and verily believe, and know to be true. D&C 80:4

Let all the house of Israel know assuredly, that God hath made that same Jesus, whom ye have crucified, both Lord and Christ. Acts 2:36

Whosoever shall confess that Jesus is the Son of God, God dwelleth in him, and he in God. 1 Jn. 4:15

Be not thou therefore ashamed of the testimony of our Lord. 2 Tim. 1:8

Remain steadfast in your minds in solemnity and the spirit of prayer, in bearing testimony to all the world. D&C 84:61

I will speak of thy testimonies also before kings, and will not be ashamed. Ps. 119:46

Speak of the glory of thy kingdom, and talk of thy power; To make known to the sons of men his mighty acts, and the glorious majesty of his kingdom Ps. 145:11-12

Blessed are they that keep his testimonies, and that seek him with the whole heart. Ps. 119:2

THANK. THANFUL, THANKS, THANKSGIVING

I will offer to thee the sacrifice of thanksgiving, and will call upon the name of the Lord. Ps. 116:17

Offer unto God thanksgiving; and pay thy vows unto the most High: And call upon me in the day of trouble: I will deliver thee and thou shalt glorify me. Ps. 50:14-15

Now the Spirit speaketh expressly, that in the latter times some shall depart from the faith, giving heed to seducing spirits, and doctrines of devils; Speaking lies in hypocrisy; having their conscience seared with a hot iron; Forbidding to marry, and commanding to abstain from meats, which God hath created to be received with thanksgiving of them which believe and know the truth. 1 Tim. 4:1-3

They did humble themselves before the Lord, and did give thanks unto him. 1 Ne. 16:32

If thou art merry, praise the Lord with singing, with music, with dancing, and with a prayer of praise and thanksgiving. If thou art sorrowful, call on the Lord thy God with supplication, that your souls may be joyful. D&C 136:28-29

Render all the thanks and praise which your whole soul has power to possess, to that God who has created you, and has kept and preserved you, and has caused that ye should rejoice, and has granted that ye should live in peace one with another. Mosiah 2:20

Thank and praise the LORD God of Israel. 1 Chron. 16:4

Verily I say unto you my friends, fear not, let your hearts be comforted; yea, rejoice evermore, and in everything give thanks. D&C 98:1

Every creature of God is good, and nothing to be refused, if it be received with thanksgiving: For it is sanctified by the word of God and prayer. 1 Tim. 4:4-5

Let the peace of God rule in your hearts, to the which also ye are called in one body; and be ye thankful. Col. 3:15

Receive all things with thankfulness. D&C 78:19

In everything give thanks: for this is the will of God in Christ Jesus concerning you. 1 Thes. 5:18

Thou shalt thank the Lord thy God in all things. D&C 59:7

Let us come before his presence with thanksgiving and take a joyful noise unto him with psalms. Ps. 95:2

I would that ye should be humble, and be submissive and gentle; easy to be entreated; full of patience and long-suffering; being temperate in all things; being diligent in keeping the commandments of God at all times; asking for whatsoever things ye stand in need, both spiritual and temporal; always returning thanks unto God for whatsoever things ye do receive. Alma 7:23

Give thanks unto the LORD, call upon his name, make known his deeds among the people. 1 Chron. 16:8

THIEF

Do not despise a thief, if he steal to satisfy his soul when he is hungry. Prov. 6:30-31

Whoso is partner with a thief hateth his own soul. Prov. 29:24

THINGS

How is it that ye have forgotten what great things the Lord hath done for us? 1 Ne. 7:11

By small and simple things are great things brought to pass; and small means in many instances doth confound the wise. Alma 37:6

Love not the world, neither the things that are in the world. 1 Jn. 2:15

He rebuked Peter, saying, Get thee behind me, Satan: for thou savourest not the things that be of God, but the things that be of men. Mark 8:33

THINK, THOUGHT

Thou hast lied unto God; for behold, he knows all thy thoughts. Alma 12:3

Know that there is none else save God that knowest thy thoughts and the intents of thy heart. D&C 6:16

The thoughts of the wicked are an abomination to the LORD: but the words of the pure are pleasant words Prov. 15:26

Take no thought how or what ye shall speak: for it shall be given you in that same hour what ye shall speak. For it is not ye that speak, but the Spirit of your Father which speaketh in you. Matt. 10:19-20

Think of your brethren like unto yourselves, and be familiar with all and free with your substance, that they may be rich like unto you. Jacob 2:17

Charity suffereth long, and is kind, and envieth not, and is not puffed up, seeketh not her own, is not easily provoked, thinketh no evil, and rejoiceth not in iniquity but rejoiceth in the truth, beareth all things, believeth all things, hopeth all things, endureth all things. Moro. 7:45 (1 Cor. 13:4-13)

If thou hast done foolishly in lifting up thyself, or if thou has thought evil, lay thine hand upon thy mouth. Prov. 30:32

Commit thy works unto the LORD, and thy thoughts shall be established. Prov. 16:3

The wicked, through the pride of his countenance, will not seek after God: God is not in all his thoughts. Ps. 10:4

Cry unto God for all thy support; yea, let all thy doings be unto the Lord, and whithersoever thou goest let it be in the Lord; yea, let all thy thoughts be directed unto the Lord; yea, let the affections of thy heart be placed upon the Lord forever. Alma 37:36

Though we walk in the flesh, we do not war after the flesh: Casting down imaginations, and every high thing that exalteth itself against the knowledge of God, and bringing into captivity every thought to the obedience of Christ. 2 Cor. 10:3,5

Cast away your idle thoughts and your excess laughter far from you. D&C 88:69

Look unto me in every thought; doubt not, fear not. D&C 6:36

How long shall thy vain thoughts lodge within thee? Jer. 4:14

That which cometh out of the man, that defileth the man. For from within, out of the heart of men, proceed evil thoughts, adulteries, fornications, murders, thefts, covetousness, wicked-ness, deceit, lasciviousness, an evil eye, blasphemy, pride, foolish-ness: All these evil things come from within, and defile the man. Mark 7:20-23

Therefore, take ye no thought for the morrow, for what ye shall eat. Therefore, let the morrow take thought for the things of itself. D&C 84:81-84

GOD saw that the wickedness of man was great in the earth, and that every imagination of the thoughts of his heart was only evil continually. Gen. 6:5

I know that thou canst do every thing, and that no thought can be withholden from thee. Job 42:2

In the multitude of my thoughts within me thy comforts delight my soul. Ps. 94:19

THIRST

Blessed are they which do hunger and thirst after righteousness: for they shall be filled. Matt. 5:6

Blessed are all they who do hunger and thirst after righteousness. 3 Ne. 12:6

But whosoever drinketh of the water that I shall give him shall never thirst; but the water that I shall give him shall be in him a well of water springing up into everlasting life. John 4:14

THOU SHALT

Thou shalt love the LORD thy God with all thine heart, and with all thy soul, and with all thy might. Deut. 6:5

Thou shalt love thy neighbor as thyself. Matt. 22:39

Thou shalt love thy neighbor as thyself. D&C 59:6

Jesus said unto him, Thou shalt love the Lord thy God with all thy heart, and with all thy soul, and with all thy mind. This is the first and great commandment. And the second is like unto it, Thou shalt love thy neighbour as thyself. On these two command-ments, hang all the law and the prophets. Matt 22:37-40

Thou shalt love the Lord thy God with all thy heart, and with all thy soul, and with all thy mind, and with all thy strength: this is the first commandment. Mark 12:30

Thou shalt seek the LORD thy God, thou shalt find him, if thou seek him with all thy heart and with all thy soul. Deut. 4:29

Forsake all evil and cleave unto all good, that ye shall live by every word which proceedeth forth out of the mouth of God. D&C 98:11

Thou shalt love thy wife with all thy heart, and shalt cleave unto her and none else. D&C 42:22

Honour thy father and thy mother: that thy days may be long upon the land which the LORD thy God giveth thee. Ex. 20:12

Thou shalt thank the Lord thy God in all things. D&C 59:7

Thou shalt live together in love. D&C 42:45

Ye shall also forgive one another your trespasses. Mosiah 26:31

Thou shalt have no other God before me. Mosiah 12:35

Thou shalt have no other gods before me. Ex. 20:3

Wherefore, thou shalt do all that thou doest in the name of the Son, and thou shalt repent and call upon God in the name of the Son forevermore. Moses 5:8

Thou shalt worship the Lord thy God, and him only shalt thou serve. Luke 4:8

Thou shalt keep my covenant therefore, thou, and thy seed after thee in their generations. Gen. 17:9

Remember the sabbath day, to keep it holy. Six days shalt thou labour, and do all thy work: But the seventh day is the sabbath of the LORD thy God: in it thou shalt not do any work, thou, nor thy son, nor thy daughter, thy manservant, nor thy maidservant, nor thy cattle, nor thy stranger that is within thy gates: For in six days the LORD made heaven and earth, the sea, and all that in them is, and rested the seventh day: wherefore the LORD blessed the sabbath day, and hallowed it. Ex. 20:8-11

THOU SHALT NOT

Thou shalt not take the name of the LORD thy God in vain; for the LORD will not hold him guiltless that taketh his name in vain. Ex. 20:7

Thou shalt not kill. Ex. 20:13

Thou shalt not commit adultery. Ex. 20:14

Thou shalt not steal. Ex. 20:15

Thou shalt have no other gods before me. Ex. 20:3

The seventh day is the sabbath of the LORD thy God: in it thou shalt not do any work, thou, nor thy son, nor thy daughter, thy manservant, nor thy maidservant, nor thy cattle, nor thy stranger that is within thy gates: Ex. 20:10

Thou shalt not bear false witness against thy neighbour. Ex. 20:16

Thou shalt not tempt the Lord thy God. Luke 4:12

Thou shalt not lie with mankind, as with womankind: it is abomination. Lev. 18:22

Thou shat not covet thy neighbour's house, thou shalt not covet thy neighbour's wife, nor his manservant, nor his maidservant, nor his ox, nor his ass, nor anything that is thy neighbour's. Ex. 20:17

Thou shalt not defraud thy neighbour, neither rob him. Lev. 19:13

Thou shalt not lie. D&C 42:21

Thou shalt not take the name of the Lord thy God in vain. Mosiah 13:15

Thou shalt not bear false witness against thy neighbor. Mosiah 13:23

They shalt not commit whoredoms, like unto them of old, saith the Lord of Hosts. Jacob 2:31-33

Thou shalt not make unto thee any graven image, or any likeness of any thing that is in heaven above, or that is in the earth beneath, or that is in the water under the earth. Thou shalt not bow down thyself to them, nor serve them: For I the LORD thy God am a jealous God, visiting the iniquity of the fathers upon the children unto the third and fourth generation of them that hate me; And shewing mercy unto thousands of them that love me, and keep my commandments. Ex. 20:4-6

Thou shalt not avenge, nor bear any grudge against the children of thy people, but thou shalt love thy neighbour as thyself: I the LORD. Lev. 19:18

Thou shalt not hate thy brother in thine heart: thou shalt in any wise rebuke thy neighbour and not suffer sin upon him. Lev. 19:17

TIME, TIMELY

The simple believeth every word: but the prudent man looketh well to his going. Prov. 14:15

Walk in wisdom toward them that are without, redeeming the time. Col. 4:5

Write the vision, and make it plain upon tables, that he may run that readeth it. For the vision is yet for an appointed time. Haba 2:2-3

To every thing there is a season, and a time to every purpose under heaven; A time to be born, and a time to die; a time to plant, and a time to pluck up that which is planted; A time to kill, and a time to heal; a time to break down, and a time to build up; A time to weep, and a time to laugh; a time to mourn, and a time to dance; A time to cast away stones, and a time to father stones together; a time to embrace, and a time to refrain from embracing; A time to get, and a time to lose; a time to keep, and a time to cast away; A time to rend, and a time to sew; a time to keep silence, and a time to speak; A time to love, and a time to hate; a time of war, and a time of peace. Eccl. 3:1-8

Be not over much wicked, neither be thou foolish: why shouldest thou die before thy time? Eccl. 7:17

Humble yourselves therefore under the mighty hand of God, that he may exalt you in due time. 1 Pet. 5:5-6

Thou shalt not idle away thy time, neither shalt thou bury thy talent that it may not be known. D&C 60:13

Let your time be devoted to the studying of the scriptures, and to preaching. D&C 26:1

TITHE, TITHING

Bring ye all the tithes into the storehouse, that there may be meat in my house; and prove me now herewith, saith the Lord of Hosts, if I will not open you the windows of heaven, and pour you out a blessing that there shall not be room enough to receive it. And I will rebuke the devourer for your sakes, and he shall not destroy the fruits of your ground; neither shall your vine cast her fruit before the time in the fields, saith the Lord of Hosts. 3 Ne. 24:10-11

Our father Abraham paid tithes of one-tenth part of all he possessed. Alma 13:15

Honour the LORD with thy substance, and with the firstfruits of all thine increase. Prov. 3:9

The sons of Levi, who receive the office of the priesthood, have a commandment to take tithes of the people according to the law. Heb. 7:5

Bring ye all the tithes into the storehouse, that there may be meat in mine house, and prove me now herewith, saith the LORD of hosts, if I will not open you the windows of heaven, and pour you out a blessing. Mal. 3:8-12

TODAY

He is the same yesterday, today, and forever; and the way is prepared for all men from the foundation of the world. 1 Ne. 10:18

Take therefore no thought for the morrow, for the morrow shall take thought for the things of itself. Sufficient is the day unto the evil thereof. 3 Ne. 13:34

This is the day which the LORD hath made; we will rejoice and be glad in it. Ps. 118:24

TOLERANCE

For what knowest thou, O wife, whether thou shalt save thy husband? or how knowest thou, O man, whether thou shalt save thy wife? 1 Cor. 7:16

TOMORROW

Boast not thyself of tomorrow; for thou knowest not what a day may bring forth. Prov. 27:1

Take therefore no thought for the morrow, for the morrow shall take thought for the things of itself. Sufficient is the day unto the evil thereof. 3 Ne. 13:34

TONGUE, TONGUES

We believe in the gift of tongues, prophecy, revelation, visions, healing, interpretation of tongues, and so forth. A of F-7

A wholesome tongue is a tree of life: but perverseness therein is a breach in the spirit. Prov. 15:4

He that hath a froward heart findeth no good: and he that hath a perverse tongue falleth into mischief. Prov 17:20

The Lord GOD hath given me the tongue of the learned, that I should know how to speak a word in season to him that is weary. Isa. 50:4

Keep thy tongue from evil, and thy lips from speaking guile. Ps. 34:13

My tongue shall speak of thy word: for all thy commandments are righteousness. Ps. 119:172

I would that ye all spake with tongues, but rather that ye prophesied: for greater is he that prophesieth than he that speaketh with tongues, except he interpret, that the church may receive edifying. 1 Cor. 14:5

TOUCH

Depart ye, depart ye, go ye out from thence, touch not that which is unclean; go ye out of the midst of her; be ye clean that bear the vessels of the Lord. 3 Ne. 20:41

Touch not the evil gift, nor the unclean thing. Moro. 10:30

TRADITION

Full well ye reject the commandment of God, that ye may keep your own traditions. Mark 7:9

We command you, brethren, in the name of our Lord Jesus Christ, that ye withdraw yourselves from every brother that walketh disorderly, and not after the tradition which he received of us. 2 Thes. 3:6

Ye know that ye were not redeemed with corruptible things, as silver and gold, from your vain conversation received by tradition from your fathers. 1 Pet. 1:18

TRAIN

Train up a child in the way he should go: and when he is old, he will not depart from it. Prov. 22:6

TRANSFORM

Be ye transformed by the renewing of your mind, that ye may prove what is that good, and acceptable, and perfect, will of God. Rom. 12:2

TRANSGRESS, TRANSGRESSION

Turn from transgression. Isa. 59:20

Whoso robbeth his father or his mother, and saith, It is no transgression; the same is the companion of a destroyer. Prov. 28:24

Cast away from you all your transgressions, whereby ye have transgressed; and make you a new heart and a new spirit; for why will ye die, O house of Israel? Ezek. 18:31

Ye will not suffer your children that they go hungry, or naked; neither will ye suffer that they transgress the laws of God, and fight and quarrel one with another, and serve the devil, who is the master of sin, or who is the evil spirit which hath been spoken of by our fathers, he being an enemy to all righteousness. Mosiah 4:14

As for our iniquities, we know them: in transgressing and lying against the LORD, and departing away from our God, speaking oppression and revolt, conceiving and uttering from the heart words of falsehood. Isa. 59:12-13

It is no good report that I hear: ye make the LORD's people to transgress. 1 Sam. 2:24

Remember the awfulness in transgressing against that Holy God, and also the awfulness of yielding to the enticings of that cunning one. 2 Ne. 9:39

TREASURE

Wo unto the rich, who are rich as to the things of the world. For because they are rich they despise the poor, and they persecute the meek, and their hearts are upon their treasures; wherefore, their treasure is their god. And behold, their treasure shall perish with them also. 2 Ne. 9:30

Then Jesus beholding him loved him, and said unto him, One thing thou lackest: go thy way, sell whatsoever thou hast, and give to the poor, and thou shalt have treasure in heaven: and come, take up the cross, and follow me. Mark 10:21

For I will, saith the Lord, that they shall hide up their treasures unto me; and cursed be they who hide not up their treasures unto me; for none hideth up their treasures unto me save it be the righteous; and he that hideth not up his treasures unto me, cursed is he, and also the treasures, and none shall redeem it because of the curse of the land. Hel. 13:19

Incline thine ear unto wisdom, and apply thine heart to understanding. Prov. 2:2

The getting of treasures by a lying tongue is a vanity tossed to and fro of them that seek death. Prov. 21:6

Treasures of wickedness profit nothing; but righteousness delivereth from death. Prov. 10:2

Whoso treasureth up my word, shall not be deceived. JS-M 1:37

Because thou hast trusted in thy works and in thy treasure thou shalt also be taken. Jer. 48:7

Lay not up for yourselves treasures upon earth, where moth and rust doth corrupt, and where thieves break through and steal: But lay up for yourselves treasures in heaven, where neither moth nor rust doth corrupt, and where thieves do not break through nor steal: For where your treasure is, there will your heart be also. Matt. 6:19-21

If thou wilt be perfect, go and sell that thou hast, and give to the poor, and thou shalt have treasure in heaven: and come and follow me. Matt. 19:21-22

TREAT, TREATMENT

Let the husband render unto the wife due benevolence: and likewise also the wife unto the husband. 1 Cor. 7:3-5

Warn them that are unruly, comfort the feebleminded, support the weak, be patient toward all men. 1 Thes. 5:14

TRESPASS

Ye shall also forgive one another your trespasses. Mosiah 26:31

If thy brother shall trespass against thee, go and tell him his faults between thee and him alone. Matt. 18:15

TRIAL, TRIED

Show unto the world that faith is things which are hoped for and not seen; wherefore dispute not because ye see not, for ye receive no witness until after the trial of your faith. Ether 12:6

Fear none of those things which thou shalt suffer: behold, the devil shall cast some of you into prison, that ye may be tried; and ye shall have tribulation ten days: be thou faithful unto death, and I will give thee a crown of life. Rev. 2:10

TRIBULATION

Fear none of those things which thou shalt suffer: behold, the devil shall cast some of you into prison, that ye may be tried; and ye shall have tribulation ten days: be thou faithful unto death, and I will give thee a crown of life. Rev. 2:10

Blessed be God, even the Father of our Lord Jesus Christ, the Father of mercies, and the God of all comfort; Who comforteth us in all our tribulation, that we may be able to comfort them which are in any trouble, by the comfort wherewith we ourselves are comforted of God. For as the sufferings of Christ abound in us, so our consolation also aboundeth by Christ. 2 Cor. 1:3-5

TROUBLE, TROUBLED

Let your sins trouble you, with that trouble which shall bring you down unto repentance. Alma 42:29

Let not your hearts be troubled, neither let it be afraid. John 14:27

In the day of my trouble I will call upon thee: for thou wilt answer me. Ps. 86:7

TRUE, TRUTH

And now as I said concerning faith—faith is not to have a perfect knowledge of things; therefore if ye have faith ye hope for things which are not seen, which are true. Alma 32:21

He is proud, knowing nothing, but doting about questions and strifes of words, whereof cometh envy, strife, railings, evil surmisings, Perverse disputings of men of corrupt minds, and destitute of the truth, supposing that gain is godliness: from such withdraw thyself. 1 Tim. 6:4-5

The LORD is the true God, he is the living God, and an everlasting king: at his wrath the earth shall tremble, and the nations shall not be able to abide his indignation. Jer. 10:10

Worship God in spirit and in truth, the true and the living God. Alma 43:10

Ye will teach them to walk in the ways of truth and soberness. Mosiah 4:15

My soul delighteth in proving unto my people the truth of the coming of Christ. 2 Ne. 11:4

I must tell you the truth according to the plainness of the word of God. Jacob 2:11

Wo unto all those who tremble, and are angry because of the truth of God! For behold, he that is built upon the rock receiveth it with gladness; and he that is built upon a sandy foundation trembleth lest he shall fall. 2 Ne. 28:28

Declare the word of God unto the church. Alma 6:8

Ye will teach them to walk in the ways of truth and soberness. Mosiah 4:15

What added more to his joy, they were still his brethren in the Lord; yea, and they had waxed strong in the knowledge of the truth; for they were men of a sound understanding and they had searched the scriptures diligently, that they might know the word of God. Alma 17:2

The Lord said unto him: Believest thou the words which I shall speak? And he answered: Yea, Lord, I know that thou speakest the truth, for thou art a God of truth, and canst not lie. Ether 3:12

Bear record according to the truth which is in the Lamb of God. 1 Ne. 13:24

LORD, who shall abide in thy tabernacle? Who shall dwell in thy holy hill? He that walketh uprightly, and worketh righteous-ness, and speaketh the truth in his heart. Ps. 15:1-2

I have chosen the way of truth. Ps. 119:30

Speaketh truth. Prov. 12:17

Teach me thy way, O LORD; I will walk in thy truth: unite my heart to fear thy name. Ps. 86:11

Buy the truth, and sell it not; also wisdom, and instruction, and understanding. Prov. 23:23

Open ye the gates, that the righteous nation which keepeth the truth may enter in. Isa. 26:2

None calleth for justice, nor any pleadeth for truth: they trust in vanity, and speak lies; they conceive mischief, and bring forth iniquity. Isa. 59:4

Let not mercy and truth forsake thee: bind them about thy neck: write them upon the table of thine heart; So shalt thou find favour and good understanding in the sight of God and man. Prov. 3:3-4

Speak ye every man the truth to his neighbour; execute the judgment of truth and peace in your gates. Zech. 8:16

Love the truth and peace. Zech. 8:19

Take upon you the name of Christ, and speak the truth in soberness. D&C 18:21

Hear; for I will speak of excellent things; and the opening of my lips shall be right things. For my mouth shall speak truth; and wickedness is an abomination to my lips. Prov. 6:7

They are not valiant for the truth upon the earth, for they proceed from evil to evil, and they know not me, saith the LORD. Jer. 9:3

God hath from the beginning chosen you to salvation through sanctification of the Spirit and belief of the truth. 2 Thes. 2:13

Speak freely to all; yea, preach, exhort, declare the truth. D&C 19:37

Speak forth the words of truth and soberness. Acts 26:25

I know that the words of truth are hard against all uncleanness; but the righteous fear them not, for they love the truth and are not shaken. 2 Ne. 9:40

Bring many to the knowledge of the truth, yea, convince them of the error of their ways. D&C 6:11

They were men who were true at all times in whatsoever thing they were entrusted. Alma 53:20

TRUST, TRUSTWORTHINESS, TRUSTWORTHY

Be not highminded, nor trust in uncertain riches, but in the living God, who giveth us richly all things to enjoy. 1 Tim. 6:17-19

Trust not in oppression, and become not vain in robbery: if riches increase, set not your heart upon them. Ps. 62:10

Trust in him at all times; ye people, pour out your heart before him: God is a refuge for us. Ps. 62:8

Commit thy way unto the Lord; trust also in Him; and He shall bring it to pass. And he shall bring forth thy righteousness as the light, and thy judgment as the noonday. Ps. 37:5-6

O my God, I trust in thee: let me not be ashamed, let not mine enemies triumph over me. Yea, let none that wait on thee be ashamed: let them be ashamed which transgress without cause Ps. 25:2

Whosoever shall put their trust in God shall be supported in their trials, and their troubles, and their afflictions. Alma 36:3

Blessed be the God of Shadrach, Meshach, and Abed-nego, who hath sent his angel, and delivered his servants that trusted in him, and have changed the kings word, and yielded their bodies, that they might not serve nor worship any god, except their own God. Dan. 3:28

The name of the LORD is a strong tower: the righteous runneth into it, and is safe. Prov. 18:10

This is thy lot, the portion of thy measures from me, saith the LORD; because thou hast forgotten me, and trusted in falsehood. Jer. 13:25

Neither trust in the arm of flesh. D&C 1:19

He that handleth a matter wisely shall find good: and whoso trusteth in the LORD, happy is he. Prov. 16:20

Turn to the Lord with full purpose of heart, and put your trust in him, and serve him with all diligence of mind. Mosiah 7:33

I am like a green olive tree in the house of God: I trust in the mercy of God for ever and ever. Ps. 52:8

Let thy mercies come also unto me, O LORD, even thy salvation, according to thy word. So shall I have wherewith to answer him that reproacheth me: for I trust in thy word. Ps. 119:41-42

Trust in the LORD with all thine heart; and lean not unto thine own understanding. Prov. 3:5

He doth not command us that we shall subject ourselves to our enemies, but that we should put our trust in him, and he will deliver us. Alma 61:13

None calleth for justice, nor any pleadeth for truth: they trust in vanity, and speak lies; they conceive mischief, and bring forth iniquity. Isa. 59:4

Trust ye not in lying words. Jer. 7:4

Cursed be the man that trusteth in man, and maketh flesh his arm, and whose heart departeth from the LORD. Jer. 17:5

He that trusteth in his own heart is a fool: but whoso walketh wisely, he shall be delivered. Prov. 28:26

O taste and see that the LORD is good: blessed is the man that trusteth in him. Ps. 34:8

How excellent is thy lovingkindness, O God! therefore the children of men put their trust under the shadow of thy wings. Ps. 36:7

He shall not be afraid of evil tidings: his heart is fixed, trusting in the LORD. His heart is established, he shall not be afraid. Ps. 112:7-8

Thou hast trusted in thy wickedness: thou hast said, None seeth me. Thy wisdom and thy knowledge, it hath perverted thee; and thou hast said in thine heart, I am, and none else beside me. Isa. 47:10

Put your trust in that Spirit which leadeth to do good–yea, to do justly, to walk humbly, to judge righteously; and this is my Spirit. D&C 11:12

Trust in the living God, who is the Saviour of all men, specially of those that believe. 1 Tim. 4:10

Vain is the help of man. Ps. 60:11

Lift up your heads, and rejoice, and put your trust in God, in that God who was the God of Abraham, and Isaac, and Jacob. Mosiah 7:19

Trust in the LORD, and do good. Ps. 37:3

TRY

Alma thought it was expedient that they should try the virtue of the word of God. Alma 31:5

Awake and arouse your faculties, even to an experiment upon my words. Alma 32:27

Let us search and try our ways, and turn again to the Lord. Lam. 3:40

TURN

Hear what God the LORD will speak: for he will speak peace unto his people, and to his saints: but let them not turn again to folly. Ps. 85:8

God forbid that we should rebel against the LORD, and turn this day from following the LORD. Josh 22:29

Turn away from your sins; shake off the chains of him that would bind you fast; come unto that God who is the rock of your salvation. 2 Ne. 9:45

When a righteous man turneth away from his righteousness, and committeth iniquity, and dieth in them; for his iniquity that he hath done shall he die. Ezek. 18:26

Turn to the Lord with full purpose of heart, and put your trust in him, and serve him with all diligence of mind. Mosiah 7:33

Turn ye again now every one from his evil way, and from the evil of your doings, and dwell in the land that the LORD hath given unto you and to your fathers for ever and ever. Jer. 25:5

Turn not aside from following the LORD, but serve the LORD with all your heart. 1 Sam 12:20

He shall turn the heart of the fathers to the children, and the heart of the children to their fathers, lest I come and smite the earth with a curse. Mal. 4:6

I marvel that ye are so soon removed from him that called you into the grace of Christ unto another gospel. Gal. 1:6

Set thee up waymarks, make thee high heaps: set thine heart toward the highway, even the way which thou wentest: turn again. Jer. 31:21

Ye should turn from these vanities unto the living God, which made heaven, and earth, and the sea, and all things that are therein. Acts 14:15

Turn ye even to me with all your heart, and with fasting, and with weeping, and with mourning: And rend your heart, and not your garments, and turn unto the LORD your God: for he is gracious and merciful, slow to anger, and of great kindness, and repenteth him of the evil. Joel 2:12-13

Let us search and try our ways, and turn again to the Lord. Lam. 3:40

UNALTERABLE

Now, the decrees of God are unalterable; therefore, the way is prepared that whosoever will may walk therein and be saved. Alma 41:8

UNBELIEF, UNBELIEVING

He that overcometh shall inherit all things; and I will be his God, and he shall be my son. But the fearful, and unbelieving, and the abominable, and murderers, and whore-mongers, and sorcerers, and idolaters, and all liars, shall have their part in the lake which burneth with fire and brimstone: which is the second death. Rev. 21:7

UNCHANGING

Do we not read that God is the same yesterday, today, and forever, and in him there is no variableness neither shadow of changing? Morm. 9:9

UNCIRCUMCISED

Thus saith the Lord GOD; No stranger uncircumcised in heart, nor circumcised in flesh, shall enter into my sanctuary, of any strangers that is among the children of Israel. Ezek. 44:9

UNCLEAN, UNCLEANESS, UNCLEANLINESS

Cease to be unclean. D&C 88:124

Depart ye, depart ye, go ye out from thence, touch not that which is unclean; go ye out of the midst of her; be ye clean that bear the vessels of the Lord. 3 Ne. 20:41

Paul, being grieved, turned and said to the spirit, I command thee in the name of Jesus Christ to come out of her. And he came out the same hour. Acts 16:18

He set the porters at the gates of the house of the LORD, that none which was unclean in any thing should enter in. 2 Chron. 23:19

Who being past feeling have given themselves over unto lasciviousness, to work all uncleanness with greediness? Eph. 4:19

Depart ye, depart ye, go ye out from thence, touch no unclean; go ye out of the midst of her; be ye clean, that bear the vessels of the LORD. Isa. 52:11

Teach my people the difference between the holy and profane, and cause them to discern between the unclean and the clean. Ezek. 44:23

Strip yourselves of all uncleanness. Morm. 9:28

Come out from among them, and be ye separate, saith the Lord, and touch not the unclean thing; and I will receive you, And will be a Father unto you, and ye shall be my sons and daughters. 2 Cor. 6:17

I know that the words of truth are hard against all uncleanness; but the righteous fear them not, for they love the truth and are not shaken. 2 Ne. 9:40

UNDEFILED

Marriage is honourable in all, and the bed undefiled: but whoremongers and adulterers God will judge. Heb. 13:4

UNDERSTAND, UNDERSTANDING

Give me understanding, and I shall keep thy law; yea, I shall observe it with my whole heart. Ps. 119:34

What added more to his joy, they were still his brethren in the Lord; yea, and they had waxed strong in the knowledge of the truth; for they were men of a sound understanding and they had searched the scriptures diligently, that they might know the word of God. Alma 17:2

Trust in the LORD with all thine heart; and lean not unto thine own under-standing. Prov. 3:5

The light which shineth, which giveth you light, is through him who enlighteneth your eyes, which is the same light that quickeneth your understandings. D&C 88:11

But behold, the Jews were a stiffnecked people; and they despised the words of plainness, and killed the prophets, and sought for things that they could not understand. Jacob 4:14

He that received seed into the good ground is he that heareth the word, and understandeth it; which also beareth fruit, and bringeth forth, some an hundredfold, some sixty, some thirty. Matt. 13:23

Incline thine ear unto wisdom, and apply thine heart to understanding. Prov. 2:2

Be ye of an understanding heart. Prov. 8:5

Forsake the foolish, and live; and go in the way of understanding. Prov. 9:6
A man of understanding holdeth his peace. Prov. 11:12

The man that wandereth out of the way of understanding shall remain in the congregation of the dead. Prov. 21:16

Buy the truth, and sell it not; also wisdom, and instruction, and understanding. Prov. 23:23

Through wisdom is an house builded; and by understanding it is established: And by knowledge shall the chambers be filled with all precious and pleasant riches. Prov. 24:3-4

Evil men understand not judgment: but they that seek the LORD understand all things. Prov. 28:5

For precept must be upon precept, precept upon precept; line upon line, line upon line; here a little, and there a little: For with stammering lips and another tongue will he speak to this people. Isa. 28:10

From the first day that thou didst set thine heart to understand, and to chasten thyself before thy God, thy words were heard, and I am come for thy words. Dan. 10:12

I have filled him with the spirit of God, in wisdom, in understanding, and in knowledge, and in all manner of workmanship. Ex. 31:3

He sought God in the days of Zechariah, who had understanding in the visions of God: and as long as he sought the LORD, God made him to prosper. 2 Chron. 26:5

Be ye not as the horse, or as the mule, which have no understanding: whose mouth must be held in with bit and bridle, lest they come near unto thee. Ps. 32:9

They were men of a sound understanding and they had searched the scriptures diligently, that they might know the word of God Alma 17:2

For my soul delighteth in plainness; for after this manner doth the Lord God work among the children of men. For the Lord God giveth light unto the understanding; for he speaketh unto men according to their language, unto their understanding. 2 Ne. 31:3

UNGODLINESS, UNGODLY

Ye, come unto Christ, and be perfected in him, and deny yourselves of all ungodliness. Moro. 10:32

UNHOLINESS, UNHOLY

If the Lamb of God, he being holy, should have need to be baptized by water, to fulfill all righteousness, O then, how much more need have we, being unholy, to be baptized, yea, even by water! 2 Ne. 31:5

UNITE, UNITED, UNITY

Be of one mind. 2 Cor. 13:11
And he gave some, apostles; and some, prophets; and some, evangelists; and some, pastors and teachers; For the perfecting of the saints, for the work of the ministry, for the edifying of the body of Christ: Till we all come in the unity of the faith, and of the knowledge of the Son of God, unto a perfect man, unto the measure of the stature of the fulness of Christ. Eph. 4:11-13

Be likeminded one toward another according to Christ Jesus: That ye may with one mind and one mouth glorify God, even the Father of our Lord Jesus Christ. Rom. 15:5-6

How good and how pleasant it is for brethren to dwell together in unity! Ps. 133:1

Be men, and be determined in one mind and in one heart, united in all things. 2 Ne. 1:21

UNRIGHTEOUS, UNRIGTEOUSNESS

WOE unto them that decree unrighteous decrees, and that write grievousness which they have prescribed. Isa. 10:1

We have learned by sad experience that it is the nature and disposition of almost all men, as soon as they get a little authority, as they suppose, they will immediately begin to exercise unrighteous dominion. D&C 121:39

Know ye not that the unrighteous shall not inherit the kingdom of God? Be not deceived: neither fornicators, nor idolaters, nor adulterers, nor effeminate, nor abusers of themselves with mankind, Nor thieves, nor covetous, nor drunkards, nor revilers, nor extortioners, shall inherit the kingdom of God. 1 Cor. 6:9-10

God shall send them strong delusion, that they should believe a lie: That they all might be damned who believed not the truth, but had pleasure in unrighteousness. 2 Thes. 2:11-12

When we undertake to cover our sins, or to gratify our pride, our vain ambition, or to exercise control or dominion or compulsion upon the souls of the children of men, in any degree of unrighteousness, behold, the heavens withdraw themselves. D&C 121:37

UNSTEADY

A double minded man is unstable in all his ways. James 1:8

Behold how false, and also the unsteadiness of the hearts of the children of men; yea, we can see that the Lord in his great infinite goodness doth bless and prosper those who put their trust in him. Hel. 12:1

UNRULY

We command you, brethren, in the name of our Lord Jesus Christ, that ye withdraw yourselves from every brother that walketh disorderly, and not after the tradition which he received of us. 2 Thes 3:6

UNWORTHINESS, UNWORTHILY, UNWORTHY

Whosoever shall eat this bread, and drink this cup of the Lord, unworthily, shall be guilty of the body and blood of the Lord. But let a man examine himself, and so let him eat of that bread, and drink of that cup. For he that eateth and drinketh unworthily, eateth and drinketh damnation to himself, not discerning the Lord's body. 1 Cor. 11:27-29

It was necessary that the word of God should first have been spoken to you: but seeing ye put it from you, and judge yourselves unworthy of everlasting life, lo, we turn to the Gentiles. Acts 13:46

UPRIGHT, UPRIGHTLY, UPRIGHTNESS

If ye were righteous and were willing to hearken to the truth, and give heed unto it, that ye might walk uprightly before God, then ye would not murmur because of the truth, and say: Thou speakest hard things against us. 1 Ne. 16:3

He that walketh righteously, and speaketh uprightly; he that despiseth the gain of oppressions, that shaketh his hands from holding of bribes, that stoppeth his ears from hearing of blood, and shutteth his eyes from seeing evil; He shall dwell on high: his defence shall be the munitions of rocks: bread shall be given him; his waters shall be sure. Isa. 33:15-16

USE

But we know that the law is good, if a man use it lawfully. 1 Tim 1:8

UTTER, UTTERANCE

The vile person will speak villany, and his heart will work iniquity, to practise hypocrisy, and to utter error against the LORD, to make empty the soul of the hungry. Isa. 32:6

VAIN, VANITY

Thou shalt not take the name of the LORD thy God in vain; for the LORD will not hold him guiltless that taketh his name in vain. Ex. 20:7

Thou shalt not take the name of the Lord thy God in vain. Mosiah 13:15

I have not sat with vain persons, neither will I go in with dissemblers. I have hated the congregation of evil doers; and will not sit with the wicked. Ps. 26:4-5

Let no man beguile you of your reward in a voluntary humility and worshiping of angels, intruding into those things which he hath not seen, vainly puffed up by his fleshly mind. Col. 2:18

He that tilleth his land shall be satisfied with bread: but he that followeth vain persons is void of understanding. Prov. 12:11

Woe unto them that draw iniquity with cords of vanity, and sin as it were with a cart rope. Isa. 5:18

I trust that ye are not lifted up in the pride of your hearts; yea, I trust that ye have not set your hearts upon riches and the vain things of the world. Alma 7:6

How long shall thy vain thoughts lodge within thee? Jer. 4:14

Ye should turn from these vanities unto the living God, which made heaven, and earth, and the sea, and all things that are therein. Acts 14:15

O ye workers of iniquity; ye that are puffed up in the vain things of the world. Alma 5:37

He that tilleth his land shall have plenty of bread: but he that followeth after vain persons shall have poverty enough. Prov. 28:19

He that loveth silver shall not be satisfied with silver; nor he that loveth abundance with increase: this is also vanity. Eccl. 5:10

Keep yourselves from evil to take the name of the Lord in vain. D&C 136:21

When ye pray, use not vain repetitions, as the heathen, for they think that they shall be heard for their much speaking. Be not ye therefore like unto them, for your Father knoweth what things ye have need of before ye ask him. 3 Ne. 13:7-8

Can ye be puffed up up the pride of your hearts; yea, will ye still persist in the wearing of costly apparel and setting your hearts upon the vain things of the world, upon your riches? Alma 5:53

Turn away mine eyes from beholding vanity; and quicken thou me in thy way. Ps. 119:37

None calleth for justice, nor any pleadeth for truth: they trust in vanity, and speak lies; they conceive mischief, and bring forth iniquity. Isa. 59:4

They made Israel to sin, in provoking the LORD God of Israel to anger with their vanities. 1 Kgs. 16:13

Suffer not yourself to be led away by any vain or foolish thing. Alma 39:11

Seek not after riches nor the vain things of this world; for behold, you cannot carry them with you. Alma 39:14

VALIANT

They are not valiant for the truth upon the earth, for they proceed from evil to evil, and they know not me, saith the LORD. Jer. 9:3

VALUE

Why do ye not think that greater is the value of an endless happiness than that misery which never dies -- because of the praise of the world? Morm. 8:38

VENGEANCE

Declare in Zion the vengeance of the LORD our God, the vengeance of His temple. Jer. 50:28

The scripture says - man shall not smite, neither shall he judge; for judgment is mine, saith the Lord, and vengeance is mine also, and I will repay. Morm. 8:20

VESSELS

Depart ye, depart ye, go ye out from thence, touch no unclean; go ye out of the midst of her; be ye clean, that bear the vessels of the LORD. Isa. 52:11 (3Ne. 20:41, D&C 38:42)

VIGILANT

Be sober, be vigilant; because your adversary the devil, as a roaring lion, walketh about, seeking whom he may devour: 1 Pet. 5:8

A bishop then must be blameless, the husband of one wife, vigilant, sober, of good behaviour, given to hospitality, apt to teach. 1 Tim. 3:2

VINE, VINEYARD

I am the vine, yea are the branches: He that abideth in me, and I in him, the same bringeth forth much fruit: for without me ye can do nothing. John 15:5

Will they not receive the strength and nourishment from the true vine? Yea, will they not come unto the true fold of God? 1 Ne. 15:15

VIOLENT, VIOLENCE

A violent man enticeth his neighbour, and leadeth him into the way that is not good. Prov. 16:29

His mischief shall return upon his own head, and his violent dealing shall come down upon his own pate. Ps. 7:16

Do violence to no man, neither accuse any falsely; and be content with your wages. Luke 3:14

A man that doeth violence to the blood of any person shall flee to the pit. Prov. 28:17

VIRTUE, VIRTUOUS

Let every man esteem his brother as himself, and practice virtue and holiness before me. D&C 38:24

Who can find a virtuous woman? for her price is far above rubies. The heart of her husband doth safely trust in her, so that he shall have no need of spoil. She will do him good and not evil all the days of her life. Prov. 31:10-12

A virtuous woman is a crown to her husband: but she that maketh ashamed is as rottenness in his bones. Prov. 12:4

Alma thought it was expedient that they should try the virtue of the word of God. Alma 31:5

Practice virtue and holiness before me continually. D&C 46:33

VISION, VISONARY

Where there is no vision, the people perish: but he that keepeth the law, happy is he. Prov. 29:18

There shall be no more any vain vision nor flattering divination within the house of Israel. Ezek. 12:24

Behold, he hath heard my cry by day, and he hath given me knowledge by visions in the night-time. 2 Ne. 4:23

He sought God in the days of Zechariah, who had understanding in the visions of God: and as long as he sought the LORD, God made him to prosper. 2 Chron. 26:5

I will pour out my spirit upon all flesh; and your sons and your daughters shall prophesy, your old men shall dream dreams, your young men shall see visions. Joel 2:28

Write the vision, and make it plain upon tables, that he may run that readeth it. For the vision is yet for an appointed time. Haba 2:2-3

We believe in the gift of tongues, prophecy, revelation, visions, healing, interpretation of tongues, and so forth. A of F-7

When he came out, he could not speak unto them: and they perceived that he had seen a vision in the temple: for he beckoned unto them, and remained speechless. Luke 1:22

VISIT, VISITATION

Ye must visit the poor and the needy and administer to their relief. D&C 44:6

That ye may walk guiltless before God, I would that ye should impart of your substance to the poor, every man according to that which he hath, such as feeding the hungry, clothing the naked, visiting the sick and administering to their relief, both spiritually and temporally, according to their wants. Mosiah 4:26

Visit the house of each member, and exhort them to pray vocally and in secret and attend to all family duties. D&C 20:47

VOCATION

Walk worthy of the vocation wherewith ye are called. Eph. 4:1

VOICE

Hearken unto the voice of the good shepherd. Hel. 7:18

Let your preaching be the warning voice, every man to his neighbor, in mildness and in meekness. D&C 38:41

Obey, I beseech thee, the voice of the LORD, which I speak unto thee: so it shall be well unto thee, and thy soul shall live. Jer. 38:20

His head and his hairs were white like wool, as white as snow; and his eyes were as a flame of fire; And his feet like unto fine brass, as if they burned in a furnace; and his voice as the sound of many waters. Rev. 1:15

All you that are desirous to follow the voice of the good shepherd, come ye out from the wicked, and be ye separate, and touch not their unclean things. Alma 5:57

Cry aloud, spare not, lift up thy voice like a trumpet, and shew my people their transgression, and the house of Jacob their sins. Isa. 58:1

[Obey] the voice of the Lord our God, to walk in his laws, which he set before us by his servants the prophets. Dan. 9:10

We believe that all governments necessarily require civil officers and magistrates to enforce the laws of the same; and that such as will administer the law in equity and justice should be sought for and upheld by the voice of the people if a republic, or the will of the sovereign. D&C 134:3

VOMIT

If after they have escaped the pollutions of the world through the knowledge of the Lord and Savior Jesus Christ, they are again entangled therein, and overcome, the latter end is worse with them than the beginning. For it had been better for them not to have known the way of righteousness, than, after they have known it, to turn from the holy commandment delivered unto them. But it is happened unto them according to the true proverb, The dog is turned to his own vomit again; and the sow that was washed to her wallowing in the mire. 2 Pet. 2:20-22

VOW

Keep thy solemn feasts, perform thy vows. Nahum 1:15

When thou shalt vow a vow unto the LORD thy God, thou shalt not slack to pay it: for the LORD thy God will surely require it of thee; and it would be sin in thee. Deut. 23:21

That which is gone out of thy lips thou shalt keep and perform; even a freewill offering, according as thou has vowed unto the LORD thy God, which thou hast promised with thy mouth. Deut. 23:23

When thou vowest a vow unto God, defer not to pay it; for he hath no pleasure in fools: pay that which thou hast vowed. Eccl. 5:4

WAGE, WAGES

Be content with your wages. Luke 3:14

Woe unto him that buildeth his house in unrighteousness, and his chambers by wrong; that useth his neighbour's service without wages, and giveth him not for his work. Jer. 22:13

WAIT

Wait for the coming of the Messiah. 2 Ne. 6:13

They that wait upon the Lord shall renew their strength; they shall mount up with wings as eagles; they shall run, and not be weary; and they shall walk, and not faint. Isa. 40:31

Rest in the LORD, and wait patiently for Him. Ps. 37:7

Wait on the LORD: be of good courage, and he shall strengthen thine heart: wait, I say, on the LORD. Ps. 27:14

Wait on the LORD, and keep his way and he shall exalt thee to inherit the land. Ps. 37:34

Thou shalt know that I am the Lord; for they shall not be ashamed that wait for me. 1 Ne. 21:23

WALK

They began to be a righteous people; and they did walk in the ways of the Lord. Alma 25:14

If ye were righteous and were willing to hearken to the truth, and give heed unto it, that ye might walk uprightly before God, then ye would not murmur because of the truth, and say: Thou speakest hard things against us. 1 Ne. 16:3

Let us walk honestly, as in the day; not in rioting and drunkenness, not in chambering and wantonness, not in strife and envying. Rom. 13:13

Now, the decrees of God are unalterable; therefore, the way is prepared that whosoever will may walk therein and be saved. Alma 41:8

Walk in wisdom toward them that are without, redeeming the time. Col. 4:5

Ye shall walk in all the ways which the LORD your God hath commanded you, that ye may live, and that ye may prolong your days in the land which ye shall posses. Deut. 5:33

Learn of me, and listen to my words; walk in the meekness of my Spirit, and you shall have peace in me. D&C 19:23

Come ye and let us walk in the light of the Lord. 2 Ne. 12:5

Walk worthy of the Lord unto all pleasing, being fruitful in every good work, and increasing in the knowledge of God. Col. 1:10

Rejoice, O young man in thy youth; and let thy heart cheer thee in the days of thy youth, and walk in the ways of thine heart, and in the sight of thine eyes. Eccl. 11:9

O Lord, wilt thou not shut the gates of thy righteousness before me, that I may walk in the path of the low valley, that I may be strict in the plain road! 2 Ne. 4:32

Ye will teach them to walk in the ways of truth and soberness. Mosiah 4:15

Trust no one to be your teacher nor your minister, except he be a man of God, walking in his ways and keeping his commandments. Mosiah 23:14

That ye may walk guiltless before God, I would that ye should impart of your substance to the poor, every man according to that which he hath, such as feeding the hungry, clothing the naked, visiting the sick and administering to their relief, both spiritually and temporally, according to their wants. Mosiah 4:26

Walk in the name of the LORD our God for ever and ever. Micah 4:5

How quick to be lifted up in pride; yea, how quick to boast, and do all manner of that which is iniquity; and how slow are they to remember the Lord their God, and to give ear unto his counsels, yea, how slow to walk in wisdoms paths. Hel. 12:5

Walk in the meekness of my Spirit. D&C 19:23

Walk not after the flesh, but after the Spirit. Rom. 8:4

Ye were sometimes darkness, but now are ye light in the Lord: walk as children of light. Eph. 5:8

I am the Almighty God; walk before me, and be thou perfect. Gen. 17:1

Blessed is the man that walketh not in the counsel of the ungodly, nor standeth in the way of sinners, nor sitteth in the seat of the scornful. Ps. 1:1

The just man walketh in his integrity: his children are blessed after him. Prov. 20:7

Thus saith the LORD, Stand ye in the ways, and see, and ask for the old paths, where is the good way, and walk therein, and ye shall find rest for your souls. Jer. 6:16

They said, There is no hope: but we will walk after our own devises, and we will every one do the imagination of his evil heart. Jer. 18:12

Come ye, and let us walk in the light of the LORD. Isa. 2:5

Discretion shall preserve thee, understanding shall keep thee; to deliver thee from the way of the evil man, from the man that speaketh froward things; who leave the paths of righteousness, to walk in the ways of darkness. Prov. 2:11-13

There is a way which seemeth right unto a man, but the end thereof are the ways of death. Prov. 14:12

As for them whose heart walketh after the heart of their detestable things and their abominations, I will recompense their way upon their own heads, saith the Lord GOD. Ezek. 11:21

They shall also teach their children to pray, and to walk uprightly before the Lord. D&C 68:28

He that walketh righteously, and speaketh uprightly; he that despiseth the gain of oppressions, that shaketh his hands from holding of bribes, that stoppeth his ears from hearing of blood, and shutteth his eyes from seeing evil; He shall dwell on high: his defence shall be the munitions of rocks: bread shall be given him; his waters shall be sure. Isa. 33:15-16

Walk in the ways of good men, and keep the paths of the righteous. Prov. 2:20

Neither shall they walk any more after the imagination of their evil heart. Jer. 3:17

He that walketh with wise men shall be wise: but a companion of fools shall be destroyed. Prov. 13:20

My people have changed their glory for that which doth not profit. Jer. 2:8

He that saith he abideth in him ought himself also so to walk, even as he walked. 1 Jn. 2:6

Walk in the ways of the Lord. Mosiah 6:6

WANDER, WANDERER

Hide the outcasts; bewray not him that wandereth. Isa. 16:3-5

WAR

Scatter thou the people that delight in war. Ps. 68:30

WARN, WARNINGS

Warn the wicked from his wicked way. Ezek. 3:18-19

Let your preaching be the warning voice, every man to his neighbor, in mildness and in meekness. D&C 38:41

Warn them that are unruly, comfort the feebleminded, support the weak, be patient toward all men. 1 Thes. 5:14

If thou warn the righteous man, that the righteous sin not, and he doth not sin, he shall surely live, because he is warned; also thou hast delivered thy soul. Ezek. 3:21

Testify and warn the people, and it becometh every man who hath been warned to warn his neighbor. D&C 88:81

WASH, WASHINGS

There is a generation that are pure in their own eyes, an yet is not washed from their filthiness. Prov. 30:12

O Jerusalem, wash thine heart from wickedness, that thou mayest be saved. Jer. 4:14

If I then, your Lord and Master, have ashed your feet; ye also ought to wash one another's feet. For I have given you an example, that ye should do as I have done to you. John 13:14-15

WASTE

He also that is slothful in his work is brother to him that is a great waster. Prov. 18:9

Wo be unto man that sheddeth blood or that wasteth flesh and hath no need. D&C 49:21

WATCH, WATCHFUL, WATCHFULNESS

Be watchful unto prayer continually. Alma 34:39

We made our prayer unto our God, and set a watch against them day and night. Neh. 4:9

Watch therefore: for ye know not what hour your Lord doth come. Matt. 24:42

Gird up your loins and be watchful and be sober, looking forth for the coming of the Son of Man, for he cometh in an hour you think not. D&C 61:38

If ye do not watch yourselves, and your thoughts, and your words, and your deeds, and observe the commandments of God, and continue in the faith of what ye have heard concerning of our Lord, even unto the end of your lives, ye must perish. O man, remember, and perish not. Mosiah 4:30

WATER

Jesus answered, Verily, verily, I say unto thee, Except a man be born of water and of the Spirit, he cannot enter into the kingdom of God. John 3:5

WAVER, WAVERING

If any of you lack wisdom, let him ask of God, that giveth to all men liberally, and upbraideth not; and it shall be given him. But let him ask in faith, nothing wavering. For he that wavereth is like a wave of the sea driven with the wind and tossed. James 1:5-6

Let us hold fast the profession of our faith without wavering; (for he is faithful that promised). Heb. 10:23

WAY, WAYS

Prepare ye the way of the Lord, and make his paths straight. 1 Ne. 10:8

Turn away mine eyes from beholding vanity; and quicken thou me in thy way. Ps. 119:37

Now, the decrees of God are unalterable; therefore, the way is prepared that whosoever will may walk therein and be saved. Alma 41:8

A double minded man is unstable in all his ways. James 1:8

Walk in the ways of the Lord. Mosiah 6:6

Forsake the foolish, and live; and go in the way of understanding. Prov. 9:6

For my soul delighteth in plainness; for after this manner doth the Lord God work among the children of men. For the Lord God giveth light unto the understanding; for he speaketh unto men according to their language, unto their understanding. 2 Ne. 31:3

Enter ye in at the strait gate; for wide is the gate, and broad is the way, which leadeth to destruction, and many there be who go in thereat; Because strait is the gate, and narrow is the way, which leadeth unto life, and few there be that find it. 3 Ne. 14:13-14 (Matt. 7:13-14)

God hath set some in the church, first apostles, secondarily prophets, thirdly teachers, after that miracles, then gifts of healings, helps, governments, diversities of tongues. Are all apostles? are all prophets? are all teachers? are all workers of miracles? Have all the gifts of healing? do all speak with tongues? do all interpret? But covet earnestly the best gifts: and yet shew I unto you a more excellent way. 1 Cor. 12:28-31

Thou hast avouched the LORD this day to be thy God, and to walk in his ways, and to keep his statutes, and his commandments, and his judgments, and to hearken unto his voice. Deut. 26:17

Thorns and snares are in the way of the froward: he that doth keep his soul shall be far from them. Prov. 22:5

If after they have escaped the pollutions of the world through the knowledge of the Lord and Savior Jesus Christ, they are again entangled therein, and overcome, the latter end is worse with them than the beginning. For it had been better for them not to have known the way of righteousness, than, after they have known it, to turn from the holy commandment delivered unto them. But it is happened unto them according to the true proverb, The dog is turned to his own vomit again; and the sow that was washed to her wallowing in the mire. 2 Pet. 2:20-22

I suppose that ye ponder somewhat in your hearts concerning that which ye should do after ye have entered in by the way. 2 Ne. 32:1

I proclaimed a fast there, at the river of Ahava, that we might afflict ourselves before our God, to seek of him a right way for us, and for our little ones, and for all our substance. Ezra 8:21-23

Behold, great and marvelous are the works of the Lord. How unsearchable are the depths of the mysteries of him; and it is impossible that man should find out all his ways. And no man knoweth of his ways save it be revealed unto him; wherefore, brethren, despise not the revelations of God. Jacob 4:8

Envy not the oppressor, and choose none of his ways. Prov. 3:31-32

The wisdom of the prudent is to understand his way: but the folly of fools is deceit. Prov. 14:8

I will get me unto the great men, and will speak unto them; for they have known the way of the LORD, and the judgment of their God: but these have altogether broken the yoke, and burst the bonds. Jer. 5:5

Come, and let us go up to the mountain of the LORD, and to the house of the God of Jacob; and he will teach us of his ways, and we will walk in his paths; for the law shall go forth of Zion, and the word of the LORD from Jerusalem. Micah 4:2

I know that if ye are brought up in the way ye should go ye will not depart from it. 2 Ne. 4:5

Teach me thy way, O LORD; I will walk in thy truth: unite my heart to fear thy name. Ps. 86:11

Ye will teach them to walk in the ways of truth and soberness. Mosiah 4:15

Thou shalt teach them ordinances and laws, and shalt shew them the way wherein they must walk, and the work that they must do. Ex. 18:20

They taught the people the ways of the Lord. Jarom 1:7

All those who preach false doctrines, and all those who commit whoredoms, and pervert the right way of the Lord, wo, wo, wo be unto them, saith the Lord God Almighty, for they shall be thrust down to hell. 2 Ne. 28:15

Trust no one to be your teacher nor your minister, except he be a man of God, walking in his ways and keeping his commandments. Mosiah 23:14

Prepare ye the way of the Lord, make his paths straight. Luke 3:4

Train up a child in the way he should go: and when he is old, he will not depart from it. Prov. 22:6

Enter ye in at the strait gate: for wide is the gate, and broad is the way, that leadeth to destruction, and many there be which go in thereat: Because strait is the gate, and narrow is the way, which leadeth unto life, and few there be that find it. Matt. 7:13-14

O full of all subtilty and all mischief, thou child of the devil, thou enemy of all righteousness, wilt thou not cease to pervert the right ways of the Lord. Acts 13:10

Walk in the ways of good men, and keep the paths of the righteous. Prov. 2:20

He is in the way of life that keepeth instruction: but he that refuseth reproof erreth. Prov. 10:17

In all thy ways acknowledge him, and he shall direct thy paths. Prov. 3:6

Make no friendship with an angry man; and with a furious man thou shalt not go: Lest thou learn his ways, and get a snare to thy soul. Prov. 22:24-25

Give not thy strength to women, nor thy ways to that which destroyeth kings. Prov. 31:3

Hear thou, my son, and be wise, and guide thine heart in the way. Prov. 23:19

Thus saith the LORD of hosts, the God of Israel, Amend your ways and your doings, and I will cause you to dwell in this place. Jer. 7:3

Be ye not as your fathers, unto whom the former prophets have cried, saying, Thus saith the LORD of hosts; Turn ye now from your evil ways, and from your evil doings: but they did not hear, nor hearken unto me, saith the LORD. Zech. 1:4

Ye have not kept my ways, but have been partial in the law. Mal. 2:9

Let us search and try our ways, and turn again to the Lord. Lam. 3:40

Be ashamed and confounded for your own ways, O house of Israel. Ezek. 36:32

The man that wandereth out of the way of understanding shall remain in the congregation of the dead. Prov. 21:16

Come and let us go up to the mountain of the Lord, and to the house of the God of Jacob; and he will teach us of his ways, and we will walk in his paths; for the law shall go forth of Zion and the word of the Lord from Jerusalem. Micah 4:2

Whoso causeth the righteous to go astray in an evil way, he shall fall himself into his own pits; but the upright shall have good things in possession. Prov. 28:10

Prepare ye the way of the Lord, make straight in the desert a highway for our God. Isa. 40:3

Let the wicked forsake his way, and the unrighteous man his thoughts: and let him return unto the Lord, and he will have mercy upon him; and to our God, for he will abundantly pardon. Isa. 55:7

I have chosen the way of truth. Ps. 119:30

Thus saith the Lord, learn not the way of the heathen, and be not dismayed at the signs of heaven; for the heathen are dismayed at them. Jer. 10:2

Return ye now every one from his evil way, and make your ways and your doings good. Jer. 18:11

Turn ye again now every one from his evil way, and from the evil of your doings, and dwell in the land that the LORD hath given unto you and to your fathers for ever and ever. Jer. 25:5

Set thee up waymarks, make thee high heaps: set thine heart toward the highway, even the way which thou wentest: turn again. Jer. 31:21

Through thy precepts I get understanding: therefore I hate every false way. Ps. 119:104

Surely these are poor; they are foolish: for they know not the way of the LORD, nor the judgment of their God. Jer. 5:4

Thus saith the LORD, Stand ye in the ways, and see, and ask for the old paths, where is the good way, and walk therein, and ye shall find rest for your souls. Jer. 6:16

Correction is grievous unto him that forsaketh the way: and he that hateth reproof shall die. Prov. 15:10

Ponder the path of thy feet and let all thy ways be established. Prov. 4:26

Thus saith the Lord of Hosts; Consider your ways. Hag. 1:4-5

The way of life is above to the wise, that he may depart from hell beneath. Prov. 15:24

I will meditate in thy precepts, and have respect unto thy ways. Ps. 119:15

A violent man enticeth his neighbour, and leadeth him into the way that is not good. Prov. 16:29

There is a way which seemeth right unto a man, but the end thereof are the ways of death. Prov. 14:12

My father taught me in all the ways of God. Moses 6:41

It is a people that do err in their heart, and they have not known my ways. Ps. 95:10

Commit thy way unto the Lord; trust also in Him; and He shall bring it to pass. And he shall bring forth thy righteousness as the light, and thy judgment as the noonday. Ps. 37:5-6

Ye will teach them to walk in the ways of truth and soberness. Mosiah 4:15

Keep the way of the Lord. Gen. 18:19

Oh my son, do not let us be slothful because of the easiness of the way; for so was it with our fathers; for so was it prepared for them, that if they would look they might live; even so it is with us. The way is prepared, and if we will look we may live forever. Alma 37:46

Discretion shall preserve thee, understanding shall keep thee; To deliver thee from the way of the evil man, from the man that speaketh froward things; who leave the paths of righteousness, to walk in the ways of darkness. Prov. 2:11-13

Ye shall walk in all the ways which the LORD your God hath commanded you, that ye may live, and that ye may prolong your days in the land which ye shall posses. Deut. 5:33

WEAK, WEAKNESS

Acknowledge your unworthiness before God at all times. Alma 38:14

The Lord God showeth us our weakness that we may know that it is by his grace, and his great condescensions unto the children of men, that we have power to do these things. Jacob 4:7

WEALTH, WEALTHY

Let no man seek his own, but every man another's wealth. 1 Cor. 10:24

WEARINESS, WEARY

Teach them to never be weary of good works. Alma 37:34

Withdraw thy foot from thy neighbour's house; lest he be weary of thee, and so hate thee. Prov. 25:17

The Lord GOD hath given me the tongue of the learned, that I should know how to speak a word in season to him that is weary. Isa. 50:4

Ye have wearied the LORD with your words. Yet ye say, Wherein have we wearied him? When ye say, Every one that doeth evil is good in the sight of the LORD. Mal. 2:17

Be not weary in well doing. D&C 64:33

WEIGH, WEIGHT

A false balance is abomination to the LORD: but a just weight is his delight. Prov. 11:1

Seeing we also are compassed about with so great a cloud of witnesses, let us lay aside every weight, and the sin which doth so easily beset us, and let us run with patience the race that is set before us. Heb. 12:1

WHOLE

The light of the body is the eye; if, therefore, thine eye be single, thy whole body shall be full of light. 3 Ne. 13:22 (Matt. 6:22)

Wilt thou be made whole? John. 5:6

Peter said unto him, Aeneas, Jesus Christ maketh thee whole: arise, and make thy bed. And he arose immediately. Acts 9:34

WHOLESOME

A wholesome tongue is a tree of life: but perverseness therein is a breach in the spirit. Prov. 15:4

WHORE, WHOREDOM, WHOREMONGER

They shalt not commit whoredoms, like unto them of old, saith the Lord of Hosts. Jacob 2:31-33

Why do ye commit whoredoms and spend your strength with harlots? Mosiah 12:29

Do not prostitute thy daughters, to cause her to be a whore; lest the land fall into whoredom, and the land become full of wickedness. Lev. 19:29

WICKED, WICKEDNESS

Thou hast trusted in thy wickedness: thou hast said, None seeth me. Thy wisdom and thy knowledge, it hath perverted thee; and thou hast said in thine heart, I am, and none else beside me. Isa. 47:10

Justify [not] the wicked for reward 2 N.e 15:23

When the righteous are in authority, the people rejoice: but when the wicked beareth rule, the people mourn. Prov. 29:2

I know that the words of truth are hard against all uncleanness; but the righteous fear them not, for they love the truth and are not shaken. 2 Ne. 9:40

For we wrestle not against flesh and blood, but against principalities, against powers, against the rulers of the darkness of this world, against spiritual wickedness in high places. Eph. 6:12

The wicked, through the pride of his countenance, will not seek after God: God is not in all his thoughts. Ps. 10:4

The thoughts of the wicked are an abomination to the LORD: but the words of the pure are pleasant words Prov. 15:26

Cease from all your light speeches, from all laughter, from all your lustful desires, from all your pride and light-mindedness, and from all your wicked doings. D&C 88:121

The wicked shall be turned into hell, and all the nations that forget God. Ps. 9:17

Treasures of wickedness profit nothing; but righteousness delivereth from death. Prov. 10:2

Ye would be more miserable to dwell with a holy and just God, under a consciousness of your filthiness before him, than ye would to dwell with the damned souls in hell. Morm. 9:4

O Jerusalem, wash thine heart from wickedness, that thou mayest be saved. Jer. 4:14

He that justifieth the wicked, and he that condemneth the just, even they both are abomination to the LORD. Prov. 17:15

Take away the wicked from before the king, and his throne shall be established in righteousness. Prov. 25:5

A righteous man falling down before the wicked is as a troubled fountain, and a corrupt spring. Prov. 25:26

Be not over much wicked, neither be thou foolish: why shouldest thou die before thy time? Eccl. 7:17

Cease from all your light speeches, from all laughter, from all your lustful desires, from all your pride and light-mindedness, and from all your wicked doings D&C 88:121

Warn the wicked from his wicked way. Ezek. 3:18-19

Go ye out from among the wicked. Save yourselves. D&C 38:42

My soul shall be filled with sorrow because of this the wickedness of my brethren. Hel. 7:9

Wo be unto you because of your wickedness and abominations! Hel. 7:27

WIDOW

Every man should impart to the support of the widows and their children, that they might not perish with hunger. Mosiah 21:17

Oppress not the widow, nor the fatherless, the stranger, nor the poor; and let none of you imagine evil against his brother in your heart. Zech. 7:10

Pure religion and undefiled before God and the Father is this, To visit the fatherless and widows in their affliction, and to keep himself unspotted from the world. James 1:27

WIFE, WIVES

Their husbands love their wives, and their wives love their husbands; and their husbands and their wives love their children. Jacob 3:7

Whoso findeth a wife findeth a good thing, and obtaineth favour of the LORD. Prov. 18:22

A virtuous woman is a crown to her husband: but she that maketh ashamed is as rottenness in his bones. Prov. 12:4

Let the husband render unto the render unto the wife due benevolence: and likewise also the wife unto the husband. 1 Cor. 7:3-5

For there shall not any man among you have save it be one wife; and concubines ye shall have none. Jacob 2:27

A bishop then must be blameless, the husband of one wife, vigilant, sober, of good behaviour, given to hospitality, apt to teach. 1 Tim. 3:2

Thou shalt love thy wife with all thy heart, and shalt cleave unto her and none else. D&C 42:22

For this cause shall a man leave his father and mother, and cleave to his wife; And they twain shall be one flesh: so then they are no more twain, but one flesh. Mark 10:7-8

Who can find a virtuous woman? for her price is far above rubies. The heart of her husband doth safely trust in her, so that he shall have no need of spoil. She will do him good and not evil all the days of her life. Prov. 31:10-12

He that is unmarried careth for the things that belong to the Lord, how he may please the Lord: But he that is married careth for the things that are of the world, how he may please his wife. 1 Cor. 7:32-33

Therefore shall a man leave his father and his mother, and shall cleave unto his wife; and they shall be one flesh. Moses 3:24 (Gen. 2:24)

Live joyfully with the wife whom thou lovest all the days of the life of thy vanity, which he hath given thee under the sun, all the days of thy vanity: for that is thy portion in this life, and in thy labour which thou takest under the sun. Eccl. 9:9

Wives, submit yourselves unto your own husbands as unto the Lord. For the husband is the head of the wife, even as Christ is the head of the church: and he is the saviour of the body. Therefore as the church is subject unto Christ, so let the wives be to their own husbands in every thing. Eph. 5:22-24

WILL, WILLING, WILLINGLY

So is the will of God, that with well doing ye may put to silence the ignorance of foolish men: As free, and not using your liberty for a cloke of maliciousness, but as the servants of God. 1 Pet. 2:15-16

Thou shalt not ask that which is contrary to my will. Hel. 10:5

In everything give thanks: for this is the will of God in Christ Jesus concerning you. 1 Thes. 5:18

I keep under my body, and bring it into subjection: lest that by any means, when I have preached to others, I myself should be a castaway. 1 Cor. 9:27

After this manner therefore pray ye: Our Father who art in heaven, hallowed be thy name. Thy will be done on earth as it is in heaven. And forgive us our debts, as we forgive our debtors. And lead us not into temptation, but deliver us from evil. For thine is the kingdom, and the power, and the glory, forever. Amen. 3 Ne. 13:9-13 (Matt. 6:9-13)

Submit cheerfully and with patience to all the will of the Lord. Mosiah 24:15
Not every one that saith unto me, Lord, Lord, shall enter into the kingdom of heaven; but he that doeth the will of my Father who is in heaven. Many will say to me in that day: Lord, Lord, have we not prophesied in thy name, and in thy name have cast out devils, and in thy name done many wonderful works? And then will I profess unto them: I never knew you; depart from me, ye that work iniquity. Matt. 7:21-23

He stretched forth his hand toward his disciples, and said, Behold my mother and my brethren! For whosoever shall do the will of m Father which is in heaven, the same is my brother, and sister, and mother. Matt. 12:49-50

Men should be anxiously engaged in a good cause, and do many things of their own free will, and bring to pass much righteousness; For the power is in them, wherein they are agents unto themselves. And inasmuch as men do good they shall in nowise lose their reward. D&C 58:27-28

If ye be willing and obedient, ye shall eat the good of the land: But if ye refuse and rebel, ye shall be devoured with the sword. Isa. 1:19-20

Help thy servants to say, with thy grace assisting them: Thy will be done, O Lord, and not ours. D&C 109:44

Reconcile yourselves unto the will of God, and not to the will of the devil and the flesh; and remember, after ye are reconciled unto God, that it is only in and through the grace of God that ye are saved. 2 Ne. 10:24

Do after the will of your God. Ezra 7:18

Neither yield ye your members as instruments of unrighteousness unto sin: but yield yourselves unto God, as those that are alive from the dead, and your members as instruments of righteousness unto God. Rom. 6:13

WINE

Be not drunk with wine, wherein is excess; but be filled with the Spirit. Eph. 5:18

Wo unto them that rise up early in the morning, that they may follow strong drink, that continue until night, and wine inflame them. 2 Ne. 15:11-12

Wine is a mocker, strong drink is raging: and whosoever is deceived thereby is not wise. Prov. 20:1

Be not among winebibbers; among riotous eaters of flesh: for the drunkard and the glutton shall come to poverty: and drowsiness shall clothe a man with rags. Prov. 23:20-21

WISDOM, WISE, WISELY

Be wise; what can I say more. Jacob 6:12

A wise man will hear, and will increase learning; and a man of understanding shall attain unto wise counsels. Prov. 1:5

The wisdom of the prudent is to understand his way: but the folly of fools is deceit. Prov. 14:8

If any of you lack wisdom, let him ask of God, that giveth to all men liberally, and upbraideth not; and it shall be given him. But let him ask in faith, nothing wavering. For he that wavereth is like a wave of the sea driven with the wind and tossed. James 1:5-6

Let us be wise and look forward to these things, and do that which will make for the peace of this people. Mosiah 29:10

Jesus increased in wisdom and stature, and in favour with God and man. Luke 2:52

Be not righteous over much; neither make thyself over wise: why shouldest thou destroy thyself? Eccl. 7:16

The God of our Lord Jesus Christ, the Father of glory, may give unto you the spirit of wisdom and revelation in the knowledge of him: The eyes of your understanding being enlightened; that ye may know what is the hope of his calling, and what the riches of the glory of his inheritance in the saints. Eph. 1:17-18

He that handleth a matter wisely shall find good: and whoso trusteth in the LORD, happy is he. Prov. 16:20

Wherefore, honest men and wise men should be sought for diligently, and good and wise men ye should observe to uphold. D&C 98:10

I have told you this that ye may learn wisdom, that ye may learn of me that there is no other way or means whereby man can be saved, only in and through Christ. Alma 38:9

See that all these things are done in wisdom and order, for it is not requisite that a man should run faster than he has strength. Mosiah 4:27

Therefore also said the wisdom of God, I will send them prophets and apostles, and some of them they shall slay and persecute: That the blood of all the prophets, which was shed from the foundation of the world, may be required of this generation. Luke 11:49-50

See that ye do not boast in your own wisdom, nor of your much strength. Alma 38:11

Let the word of Christ dwell in you richly in all wisdom; teaching and admonishing one another in psalms and hymns and spiritual songs, singing with grace in your hearts to the Lord. Col. 3:16

Thus saith the LORD, Let not the wise man glory in his wisdom, neither let the mighty man glory in his might, let not the rich man glory in his riches: But let him that glorieth glory in this, that he understandeth and knoweth me Jer. 9:23-24

I have filled him with the spirit of God, in wisdom, in understanding, and in knowledge, and in all manner of workmanship. Ex. 31:3

Walk in wisdom toward them that are without, redeeming the time. Col. 4:5

The fear of the LORD is the beginning of knowledge: but fools despise wisdom and instruction. Prov. 1:7

Incline thine ear unto wisdom, and apply thine heart to understanding. Prov. 2:2

Keep sound wisdom and discretion: So shall they be life unto thy soul, and grace to thy neck. Prov. 3:21-22

Speak not in the ears of a fool: for he will despise the wisdom of thy words. Prov. 23:9

Buy the truth, and sell it not; also wisdom, and instruction, and understanding. Prov. 23:23

As an earring of gold, and an ornament of fine gold, so is a wise reprover upon an obedient ear. Prov. 25:12

As all have not faith, seek ye diligently and teach one another words of wisdom; yea, seek ye out of the best books words of wisdom; seek learning, even by study and also by faith. D&C 88:118

Through wisdom is an house builded; and by understanding it is established: And by knowledge shall the chambers be filled with all precious and pleasant riches. Prov. 24:3-4

I applied mine heart to know, and to search, and to seek out wisdom, and the reason of things, and to know the wickedness of folly, even of foolishness and madness. Eccl. 7:25

Be not wise in thine own eyes: fear the Lord, and depart from evil. It shall be health in thy navel, and marrow to thy bones. Prov. 3:7-8

Hear instruction, and be wise, and refuse it not. Prov. 8:33

If thou be wise, thou shalt be wise for thyself; but if thou scornest, thou alone shalt bear it. Prov. 9:12

The wise in heart will receive command-ments: but a prating fool shall fall. Prov. 10:8

He that walketh with wise men shall be wise: but a companion of fools shall be destroyed. Prov. 13:20

The way of life is above to the wise, that he may depart from hell beneath. Prov. 15:24

Bow down thine ear and hear the words of the wise, and apply thine heart unto my knowledge. Prov. 22:17

Hear thou, my son, and be wise, and guide thine heart in the way. Prov. 23:19

Woe unto them that are wise in their own eyes, and prudent in their own sight! Isa. 5:21

For wisdom is better than rubies; and all the things that may be desired are not to be compared to it. Prov. 8:11

Labour not to be rich: cease from thin own wisdom. Prov. 23:4

Teach us to number our days, that we may apply our hearts unto wisdom. Ps. 90:12

Be ye therefore wise as serpents and harmless as doves. Matt. 10:16

Seek after wisdom. 1 Cor. 1:22

Seek not for riches, but for wisdom. D&C 6:7

Canst thou be humble and meek, and conduct thyself wisely before me? D&C 19:41

I will give unto the children of men line upon line, precept upon precept, here a little and there a little; and blessed are those who hearken unto my precepts, and lend an ear unto my counsel, for they shall learn wisdom; for unto him that receiveth I will give more; and from them that shall say, We have enough, from them shall be taken away even that which they have. 2 Ne. 28:30

Learn wisdom in thy youth; yea, learn in thy youth to keep the commandments of God. Alma 37:35

WITCH, WITCHCRAFT

For rebellion is as the sin of witchcraft, and stubbornness is as iniquity and idolatry. Because thou hast rejected the word of the LORD, he hath also rejected thee from being king. 1 Sam 15:23

WITHSTAND, WITHSTOOD

Teach them to withstand every temptation of the devil, with their faith on the Lord Jesus Christ. Alma 37:33

WITNESS

How shall we escape, if we neglect so great salvation; which at the first began to be spoken by the Lord, and was confirmed unto us by them that heard him; God also bearing them witness, both with signs and wonders, and with divers miracles, and gifts of the Holy Ghost, according to his own will? Heb. 2:3-4

Seeing we also are compassed about with so great a cloud of witnesses, let us lay aside every weight, and the sin which doth so easily beset us, and let us run with patience the race that is set before us. Heb. 12:1

Show unto the world that faith is things which are hoped for and not seen; wherefore dispute not because ye see not, for ye receive no witness until after the trial of your faith. Ether 12:6

Against an elder, receive not an accusation but before two or three witnesses. 1 Tim. 5:19

What greater witness can you have than from God? D&C 6:23

Ye are my witnesses, saith the Lord, that I am God. Isa. 43:9-12

There was a man sent from God, whose name was John. The same came for a witness, to bear witness of the Light, that all men through him might believe. John 1:7

WIZARD, WIZARDRY

When they shall say unto you, Seek unto them that have familiar spirits, and unto wizards that peep, and that mutter: should not a people seek unto their God? Isa. 8:19

WOLF, WOLVES

Beware of false prophets, which come to you in sheep's clothing, but inwardly they are ravening wolves. Ye shall know them by their fruits. Matt. 7:15-16, 3 Ne. 14:15-20

WOMAN, WOMANHOOD, WOMEN

Give not thy strength to women, nor thy ways to that which destroyeth kings. Prov. 31:3

Likewise also the men, leaving the natural use of the woman, burned in their lust one toward another; men with men working that which is unseemly, and receiving in themselves that recompence of their error which was meet. Rom. 1:27

The woman shall not wear that which pertaineth unto a man, neither shall a man put on a women's garment: for all that do so are abomination unto the LORD thy God. Deut. 22:5

WONDER, WONDERS, WONDROUS

False Christs and false prophets shall rise, and shall shew signs and wonders, to seduce, if it were possible, even the elect. Mark 13:22

WONDERFUL

Not every one that saith unto me, Lord, Lord, shall enter into the kingdom of heaven; but he that doeth the will of my Father who is in heaven. Many will say to me in that day: Lord, Lord, have we not prophesied in thy name, and in thy name have cast out devils, and in thy name done many wonderful works? And then will I profess unto them: I never knew you; depart from me, ye that work iniquity. Matt. 7:21-23

For unto us a child is born, unto us a son is given; and the government shall be upon his shoulder; and his name shall be called, Wonderful, Counselor, The Mighty God, The Everlasting Father, The Prince of Peace. 2 Ne. 19:6 (Isa. 9:6)

WORD, WORDS

In the beginning was the Word, and the Word was with God, and the Word was God. John 1:1

The grass withereth, the flower fadeth: but the word of our God shall stand for ever. Isa. 40:8

Hold fast the form of sound words, which thou hast heard of me, in faith and love which is in Christ Jesus. 2 Tim. 1:13

Feed thy people with thy rod, the flock of thine heritage, which dwell solitarily in the wood. Micah 7:14

Of these things put them in remembrance, charging them before the Lord that they strive not about words to no profit, but to the subverting of the hearers. 2 Tim. 2:14

It was necessary that the word of God should first have been spoken to you: but seeing ye put it from you, and judge yourselves unworthy of everlasting life, lo, we turn to the Gentiles. Acts 13:46

Come, and let us go up to the mountain of the LORD, and to the house of the God of Jacob; and he will teach us of his ways, and we will walk in his paths; for the law shall go forth of Zion, and the word of the LORD from Jerusalem. Micah 4:2

Ye shall not add unto the word which I command you, neither shall ye diminish ought from it, that ye may keep the commandments of the LORD your God which I command you. Deut. 4:2

Who shall say that it was not a miracle that by his word the heaven and the earth should be; and by the power of his word man was created of the dust of the earth; and by the power of his word have miracles been wrought? Morm. 9:17

Stand in the court of the LORD's house, and speak unto all the cities of Judah, which come to worship in the LORD's house, all the words that I command thee to speak unto them; diminish not a word. Jer. 26:2

Give heed unto the word of the Lord; yea, I did exhort them with all the energies of my soul, and with all the faculty which I possessed, that they would give heed to the word of God and remember to keep his commandments in all things. 1 Ne. 15:25

Receive the word with joy. Alma 16:17

All ye that are pure in heart, lift up your heads and receive the pleasing word of God, and feast upon his love. Jacob 3:2

You shall live by every word that proceedeth forth from the mouth of God. D&C 84:44

Yea, all were gathered together that believed on his word, to hear him. And he did teach them, and did preach unto them repentance, and redemption, and faith on the Lord. Mosiah 18:7

Impart the word of God, one with another, without money and without price. Alma 1:20

Because ye were compelled to be humble ye were blessed, do ye not suppose that they are more blessed who truly humble themselves because of the word? Alma 32:14

Feast upon the words of Christ; for behold, the words of Christ will tell you all things what ye should do. 2 Ne. 32:3

I know that the words of truth are hard against all uncleanness; but the righteous fear them not, for they love the truth and are not shaken. 2 Ne. 9:40

They were admonished continually by the word of God. Omni 1:13

I have refrained my feet from every evil way, that I might keep thy word. Ps. 119:101

The simple believeth every word: but the prudent man looketh well to his going. Prov. 14:15

The eyes of them that see shall not be dim, and the ears of them that hear shall hearken. Isa. 32:3

As newborn babes, desire the sincere milk of the word, that ye may grow thereby. 1 Pet. 2:2

As the fire devoureth the stubble, and the flame consumeth the chaff, so their root shall be as rottenness, and their blossom shall go up as dust: because they have cast away the law of the LORD of hosts, and despised the word of the Holy One of Israel. Isa. 5:24

Let the word of Christ dwell in you richly in all wisdom; teaching and admonishing one another in psalms and hymns and spiritual songs, singing with grace in your hearts to the Lord. Col. 3:16

Many of the brethren in the Lord, waxing confident by my bonds, are much more bold to speak the word without fear. Philip. 1:14

My mother and my brethren are these which hear the word of God, and do it. Luke 8:21

As for our iniquities, we know them: in transgressing and lying against the LORD, and departing away from our God, speaking oppression and revolt,

conceiving and uttering from the heart words of falsehood. Isa. 59:12-13

The burden of the LORD shall ye mention no more: for every man's word shall be his burden; for ye have perverted the words of the living God. Jer. 23:36

Should ye not hear the words which the LORD hath cried by the former prophets, when Jerusalem was inhabited and in prosperity, and the cities thereof round about her, when men inhabited the south and the plain? Zech. 7:7

Stand in the court of the LORD'S house, and speak unto all the cities of Judah, which come to worship in the LORD's house, all the words that I command thee to speak unto them; diminish not a word. Jer. 26:2

Ye have wearied the LORD with your words. Yet ye say, Wherein have we wearied him? When ye say, Every one that doeth evil is good in the sight of the LORD, and he delighteth in them. Mal. 2:17

Hear ye the word of the LORD, O house of Jacob, and all the families of the house of Israel. Jer. 2:4

Stand in the gate of the LORD's house, and proclaim there this word, and say, Hear the word of the LORD. Jer. 7:2

The wise men are ashamed, they are dismayed and taken: lo, they have rejected the word of the LORD; and what wisdom is in them? Jer. 8:9

He that hath my word, let him speak my word faithfully. Jer. 23:28

Stand in the court of the LORD's house, and speak unto all the cities of Judah, which come to worship in the LORD's house, all the words that I command thee to speak unto them; diminish not a word. Jer. 26:2

A word fitly spoken is like apples of gold in pictures of silver. Prov. 25:11

The terrible one is brought to nought, and the scorner is consummed, and all that watch for iniquity are cut off: That make a man an offender for a word, and lay a snare for him that reproveth in the gate, and turn aside the just thing for a thing of nought. Isa. 29:20-21

Who is this that darkeneth counsel by words without knowledge? Job 38:2

Give ear, O my people, to my law: incline your ears to the words of my mouth. Ps. 78:1

My tongue shall speak of thy word: for all thy commandments are righteousness. Ps. 119:172

The preacher sought to find out acceptable words: and that which was written was upright, even words of truth. Eccl. 12:10-11

Seest thou a man that is hasty in his words? there is more hope of a fool than of him. Prov. 29:20

Because ye despise this word, and trust in oppression or perverseness, and stay thereon: Therefore this iniquity shall be to you as a breach ready to fall, swelling out in a high wall, whose breaking cometh suddenly at an instant. Isa. 30:12-13

My soul fainteth for thy salvation: but I hope in thy word. Ps. 119:81

Be ye doers of the word, and not hearers only, deceiving your own selves. For if any be a hearer of the word, and not a doer, he is like unto a man beholding his natural face in a glass: For he beholdeth himself, and goeth his way, and straightway forgetteth what manner of man he was. James 1:22-24

The thoughts of the wicked are an abomination to the LORD: but the words of the pure are pleasant words Prov. 15:26

My son, attend to my words; incline thine ear unto my sayings. Let them not depart from thine eyes; keep them in the midst of thine heart. For they are life unto those that find them, and health to all their flesh. Prov. 4:20-22

Man shall not live by bread alone, but by every word that proceedeth out of the mouth of God. Matt. 4:4

He humbled thee, and suffered thee to hunger, and fed thee with manna, which thou knewest not, neither did thy fathers know; that he might make thee know that man doth not live by bread only, but by every word that proceedeth out of the mouth of the LORD doth man live. Deut. 8:3

A man hath joy by the answer of his mouth: and a word spoken in due season, how good is it. Prov. 15:23

I cannot go beyond the word of the LORD my God, to do less or more. Num. 22:18

Let thy mercies come also unto me, O LORD, even thy salvation, according to thy word. So shall I have wherewith to answer him that reproacheth me: for I trust in thy word. Ps. 119:41-42

Therefore shall ye lay up these my words in your heart and in your soul, and bind them for a sign upon your hand, that they may be as frontlets between your eyes. Deut. 11:18

Hear the word, and receive it, and bring forth fruit. Mark 4:20

They received the word with all readiness of mind, and searched the scriptures daily, whether those things were so. Acts 17:11

We ought to give the more earnest heed to the things which we have heard, lest at any time we should let them slip. Heb. 2:1

Understand the words of the law. Neh. 8:13

He was obedient unto the word of the Lord. 1 Ne. 2:3

They have come up hither to hear the pleasing word of God, yea, the word which healeth the wounded soul. Jacob 2:8

Remember the words of your God; pray unto him continually by day, and give thanks unto his holy name by night. 2 Ne. 9:52

WORK, WORKS

Teach them to never be weary of good works. Alma 37:34

What doth it profit, my brethren, though a man say he hath faith, and have not works? can faith save him? James. 2:14

I must work the works of him that sent me, while it is day: the night cometh, when no man can work. John. 9:4

Remember the sabbath day, to keep it holy. Six days shalt thou labour, and do all thy work: But the seventh day is the sabbath of the LORD thy God: in it thou shalt not do any work, thou, nor thy son, nor thy daughter, thy manservant, nor thy maidservant, nor thy cattle, nor thy stranger that is within thy gates: For in six days the LORD made heaven and earth, the sea, and all that in them is, and rested the seventh day: wherefore the LORD blessed the sabbath day, and hallowed it. Ex. 20:8-11

Cursed be he that doeth the the work of the LORD deceitfully. Jer. 48:10

Say not, I will do so to him as he hath done to me; I will render to the man according to his work. Prov. 24:29

Because they regard not the works of the LORD, nor the operation of his hands, he shall destroy them, and not build them up. Ps. 28:5

Remember his marvelous works that he hath done; his wonders, and the judgments of his mouth. Ps. 105:5

If a man therefore purge himself from these, he shall be a vessel unto honour, sanctified, and meet for the master's use, and prepared unto every good work. 2 Tim. 2:21

In all things shewing thyself a pattern of good works: in doctrine shewing uncorruptness, gravity, sincerity, Sound speech, that cannot be condemned; that he that is of the contrary part may be ashamed, having no evil thing to say of you. Titus 2:7-8

All scripture is given by inspiration of God, and is profitable for doctrine, for reproof, for correction, for instruction in righteousness: That the man of God may be perfect, throughly furnished unto all good works. 2 Tim. 3:16-17

I perceive that there is nothing better, than that a man should rejoice in his own works. Eccl. 3:22

Because thou hast trusted in thy works and in thy treasure thou shalt also be taken. Jer. 48:7

Woe unto him that buildeth his house in unrighteousness, and his chambers by wrong; that useth his neighbour's service without wages, and giveth him not for his work. Jer. 22:13

Be strong, all ye people of the land, saith the LORD, and work: for I am with you, saith the LORD of hosts. Hag. 2:4

They regard not the work of the LORD, neither consider the operation of his hands. Isa. 5:12

For as the body without the spirit is dead, so faith without works is dead also. James 2:26

Be ye stedfast, unmoveable, always abounding in the work of the Lord, forasmuch as ye know that your labour is not in vain in the Lord. 1 Cor. 15:58

By the sweat of thy face shalt thou eat bread, until thou shalt return unto the ground. Moses 4:25

Stand still and consider the wondrous works of God. Job 37:14

Commit thy works unto the LORD, and thy thoughts shall be established. Prov. 16:3

Also unto thee, O Lord, belongeth mercy: for thou renderest to every man according to his work. Ps. 62:12

Their land also is full of idols; they worship the work of their own hands, that which their own fingers have made own fingers have made. Isa. 2:8

For even when we were with you, this we commanded you, that if any would not work, neither should he eat. 2 Thes. 3:10

Work the works of God. John 6:28

Yea, come unto me and bring forth works of righteousness. Alma 5:35

WORLD, WORLDLINESS, WORLDLY

O ye workers of iniquity; ye that are puffed up in the vain things of the world. Alma 5:37

Know that an idol is nothing in the world, and that there is none other God but one. 1 Cor. 8:4

Love not the world, neither the things that are in the world. 1 Jn. 2:15

WORSHIP

We claim the privilege of worshiping Almighty God according to the dictates of our own conscience, and allow all men the same privilege, let them worship how, where, or what they may. A of F-11

Believe in Christ and worship the Father in his name, with pure hearts and clean hands, and look not forward any more for another Messiah. 2 Ne. 25:16

I trust that you do not worship idols, but that ye do worship the true and the living God. Alma 7:6

Their land also is full of idols; they worship the work of their own hands, that which their own fingers have made own fingers have made. Isa. 2:8

Let them labor with their own hands that there be no idolatry nor wickedness practised. D&C 52:39

I will worship toward thy holy temple, and praise thy name for thy lovingkindness and for thy truth: for thou hast magnified thy word above all thy name. Ps. 138:2

Blessed be the God of Shadrach, Meshach, and Abed-nego, who hath sent his angel, and delivered his servants that trusted in him, and have changed the king's word, and yielded their bodies, that they might not serve nor worship any god, except their own God. Dan. 3:28

Come, let us worship and bow down: let us kneel before the LORD our maker. Ps. 95:6

Thy graven images also will I cut off, and thy standing images out of the midst of thee; and thou shalt no more worship the work of thine hands. Micah 5:13

Give unto the LORD the glory due unto his name; worship the LORD in the beauty of holiness. Ps. 29:2

Worship God in spirit and in truth, the true and the living God. Alma 43:10

Worship God, for him only shalt thou serve. Moses 1:15

Worship the Lord thy God, and honor thy father and thy mother, that thy days may be long in the land. 1 Ne. 17:55
Thou shalt worship the Lord thy God, and him only shalt thou serve. Luke 4:8

WORTH

I have laboured in vain, I have spent my strength for nought, and in vain: yet surely my judgment is with the LORD, and my work with my God. Isa. 49:4

Woe unto you, scribes and Pharisees, hypocrites! for ye pay tithe of mint and anise and cummin, and have omitted the weightier matters of the law, judgment, mercy, and faith: these ought ye to have done, and not to leave the other undone. Matt. 23:23

Wo unto them that turn aside the just for a thing of naught and revile against that which is good, and say that it is of no worth! 2 Ne. 28:16

What profit hath he that hath laboured for the wind? Eccl. 5:16-20

WORTHINESS, WORTHY

See that ye do all things in worthiness. Morm. 9:29

Acknowledge your unworthiness before God at all times. Alma 38:14

Whosoever shall eat this bread, and drink this cup of the Lord, unworthily, shall be guilty of the body and blood of the Lord. But let a man examine himself, and so let him eat of that bread, and drink of that cup. For he that eateth and drinketh unworthily, eateth and drinketh damnation to himself, not discerning the Lord's body. 1 Cor. 11:27-29

Walk worthy of the Lord unto all pleasing, being fruitful in every good work, and increasing in the knowledge of God. Col. 1:10

WRATH

Let every man be swift to hear, slow to speak, slow to wrath. James 1:19

A SOFT answer turneth away wrath: but grievous words stir up anger. Prov. 15:1

Surely the churning of milk bringeth forth butter, and the wringing of the nose bringeth forth blood: so the forcing of wrath bringeth forth strife. Prov. 30:33

Cease from anger, and forsake wrath: fret not thyself in any wise to do evil. Ps. 37:8

He that is slow to wrath is of great understanding: but he that is hasty of spirit exalteth folly. Prov. 14:29

A stone is heavy, and the sand weighty; but a fool's wrath is heavier than them both. Prov. 27:3

Wrath killeth the foolish man, and envy slayeth the silly one. Job 5:2

WRESTLE, WRESTLED, WRESTLING

Jacob was left alone; and there wrestled a man with him until the breaking of the day. Gen. 32:24

For we wrestle not against flesh and blood, but against principalities, against powers, against the rulers of the dark-ness of this world, against spiritual wickedness in high places. Eph. 6:12

WRITE, WRITTEN

Now go, write it before them in a table, and note it in a book, that it may be before the time to come for ever and ever. Isa. 30:8

The preacher sought to find out acceptable words: and that which was written was upright, even words of truth. Eccl. 12:10-11

If any man shall take away from the words of the book of this prophecy, God shall take away his part out of the book of life, and out of the holy city, and from the things which are written in this book Rev. 22:19

Write the vision, and make it plain upon tables, that he may run that readeth it. For the vision is yet for an appointed time. Haba 2:2-3

Let not mercy and truth forsake thee: bind them about thy neck: write them upon the table of thine heart; So shalt thou find favour and good understanding in the sight of God and man. Prov. 3:3-4

YEAR

Proclaim the acceptable year of the Lord, and the day of vengeance of our God; to comfort all that mourn. Isa. 61:2

YESTERDAY

He is the same yesterday, today, and forever; and the way is prepared for all men from the foundation of the world. 1 Ne. 10:18 (Heb. 13:8)

YIELD

Yield to no temptation. D&C 9:13

Yield to the persuasions of men no more. D&C 5:21

Be ye not stiffnecked, as your fathers were, but yield yourselves unto the Lord. 2 Chron. 30:8

Neither yield ye your members as instruments of unrighteousness unto sin: but yield yourselves unto God, as those that are alive from the dead, and your members as instruments of righteousness unto God. Rom. 6:13

YOKE

Be ye not unequally yoked together with unbelievers: for what fellowship hath righteousness with unrighteousness? and what communion hath light with darkness. 2 Cor. 6:14

Come unto me, all ye that labour and are heavy laden, and I will give you rest. Take my yoke upon you, and learn of me; for I am meek and lowly in heart: and ye shall find rest unto your souls. For my yoke is easy, and my burden is light. Matt. 11:28-30

YOUNG

Likewise, ye younger, submit yourselves unto the elder. Yea, all of you be subject one to another, and be clothed with humility: for God resisteth the proud, and giveth grace to the humble. 1 Pet. 5:5

Rebuke not an elder, but intreat him as a father; and the younger men as brethren; The elder women as mothers; the younger as sisters, with all purity. 1 Tim. 5 1-2

YOUTH

Remember now thy creator in the days of thy youth. Eccl. 12:1

Learn wisdom in thy youth; yea, learn in thy youth to keep the commandments of God. Alma 37:35

Thou hast not remembered the days of thy youth, but hast fretted me in all these things; behold, therefore I also will recompense thy way upon thine head, saith the Lord GOD. Ezek. 16:43

Rejoice, O young man in thy youth; and let thy heart cheer thee in the days of thy youth, and walk in the ways of thine heart, and in the sight of thine eyes. Eccl. 11:9

ZION

Let us declare in Zion the work of the LORD our God. Jer. 51:10

Wherefore also it is contained in the scripture, Behold, I lay in Sion a chief corner stone, elect, precious: and he that believeth on him shall not be confounded. 1 Pet. 2:6

Come, and let us go up to the mountain of the LORD, and to the house of the God of Jacob; and he will teach us of his ways, and we will walk in his paths; for the law shall go forth of Zion, and the word of the LORD from Jerusalem. Micah 4:2

Let them all be confounded and turned back that hate Zion. Ps. 129:5

It shall even be as when an hungry man dreameth, and, behold, he eateth; but he awaketh, and his soul is empty: or as when a thirsty man dreameth, and, behold, he drinketh; but he awaketh, and, behold, he is faint, and his soul hath appetite: so shall the multitude of all the nations be, that fight against mount Zion. Isa. 29:8

They shall ask the way to Zion with their faces thitherward, , Come, and let us join ourselves to the LORD in a perpetual covenant that shall not be forgotten. Jer. 50:5

How beautiful upon the mountains are the feet of him that bringeth good tidings, that publisheth peace; that bringeth good tidings of good, that publisheth salvation; that saith unto Zion, Thy God reigneth! Isa. 52:7

Say ye to the daughter of Zion, Behold, thy salvation cometh; behold, his reward is with him, and his work before him. Isa. 62:11

Arise ye, and let us go up to Zion unto the LORD our God. Jer. 31:6

Declare in Zion the vengeance of the LORD our God, the vengeance of His temple. Jer. 50:28

Ye are come unto mount Sion, and unto the city of the living God, the heavenly Jerusalem, and to an innumerable company of angels. Heb. 12:22

Blow ye the trumpet in Zion, and sound an alarm in my holy mountain: let all the inhabitants of the land tremble: for the day of the Lord cometh, for nigh at hand. Joel 2:1

If ye know these things,
happy are ye if ye do them.

John 13:17

ON COMMON GROUND

TOPICAL INDEX

Topical Index

Topical Index

Topical Index

Topical Index

Topical Index

Topical Index

Topical Index

Topical Index

Topical Index

Topical Index

Topical Index

About the Author

Vincent DiGirolamo is the author and publisher of *On Common Ground: Bridging the Mormon-Evangelical Divide* and the *Principles with Promise* series. He has been previously published in the *Church News*, the *New Era* and the *Ensign* magazines. Originally from Bay Shore, New York, Mr. DiGirolamo is married to Dana Lynn Nielsen of Bountiful, Utah. They have eleven children between them and reside in Raleigh, North Carolina.

Mr. DiGirolamo became a member of The Church of Jesus Christ of Latter-day Saints while attending the U.S. Naval Academy in 1976 and has been actively cataloging principles for more than 25 years. He is currently President of Applied Science International supporting homeland defense initiatives and multiple fields of scientific research. At church, he continues to serve in various teaching callings and has learned that God teaches us all in similar ways; precept upon precept; line upon line; here a little, and there a little. Isaiah 28:10

ISBN: 978-0-9786815-3-1

5 1 9 9 5

9 780978 681531

www.ingramcontent.com/pod-product-compliance
Lightning Source LLC
Chambersburg PA
CBHW051939090426
42741CB00008B/1207